TOURISM AND CITIZENSHIP

More than 60 years since the 1948 Universal Declaration of Human Rights first enshrined the right to freedom of movement in an international charter of human rights, the issue of mobility and the right to tourism itself have become increasingly significant areas of scholarly interest and political debate. However, despite the fact that cross-border travel implies certain citizenship rights as well as the material capacity to travel, the manifold intersections between tourism and citizenship have not received the attention they deserve in the literature.

This book endeavours to fill this gap by being the first to fully examine the role of tourism in wider society through a critically informed sociological reflection on the unfolding relationships between international tourism and distinct renderings of citizenship, with particular emphasis on the ideological and political alignments between the freedom of movement and the right to travel. The text weaves its analysis of citizenship and travel in the context of addressing large-scale societal transformations engendered by globalization, neoliberalism and the geopolitical realignments between states, as well as comprehending the internal reconfiguring of the relationship between citizens and states themselves. By doing so, it focuses on key themes including: tourism and social citizenship rights; race, culture and minority rights; states, markets and the freedom of movement; tourism, peace and geopolitics; consumerism and class; and ethical tourism, global citizenship and cosmopolitanism. The book concludes that the advancement of genuinely democratic and just forms of tourism must be commensurate with demands for distributive justice and a democratic politics of mobility encompassing all of humanity.

This timely and significant reflection on the sociology and politics of international tourism through the lens of citizenship is a must read for students and scholars in both tourism studies and the social sciences.

The royalties received from this book will be donated to the International Porter Protection Group.

Raoul V. Bianchi is Principal Lecturer in International Tourism at the University of East London. He has published widely on the political economy of international tourism and has a particular interest in exploring the intersections between politics, the economy and civil society, within a variety of tourism contexts. He has conducted research on tourism development, sustainable tourism, World Heritage and urban cultural heritage, primarily in the Mediterranean and the Canary Islands.

Marcus L. Stephenson is an Associate Professor of Tourism Management at Middlesex University Dubai (United Arab Emirates). He has published extensively on the sociology of tourism, especially in relation to aspects of race, ethnicity, nationality, culture and religion. Marcus has also conducted tourism-based research in the Caribbean, Middle East, Tanzania and the UK. He is currently researching socialist models of tourism development in a range of destination contexts.

Contemporary Geographies of Leisure, Tourism and Mobility

Series Editor:C. Michael Hall, Professor at the Department of Management, College of Business and Economics, University of Canterbury, Christchurch, New Zealand

The aim of this series is to explore and communicate the intersections and relationships between leisure, tourism and human mobility within the social sciences.

It will incorporate both traditional and new perspectives on leisure and tourism from contemporary geography, e.g. notions of identity, representation and culture, while also providing for perspectives from cognate areas such as anthropology, cultural studies, gastronomy and food studies, marketing, policy studies and political economy, regional and urban planning, and sociology, within the development of an integrated field of leisure and tourism studies.

Also, increasingly, tourism and leisure are regarded as steps in a continuum of human mobility. Inclusion of mobility in the series offers the prospect to examine the relationship between tourism and migration, the sojourner, educational travel, and second home and retirement travel phenomena.

The series comprises two strands:

Contemporary Geographies of Leisure, Tourism and Mobility aims to address the needs of students and academics, and the titles will be published in hardback and paperback. Titles include:

1. **The Moralisation of Tourism**
   Sun, sand....and saving the world?
   Jim Butcher

2. **The Ethics of Tourism Development**
   Mick Smith and Rosaleen Duffy

3. **Tourism in the Caribbean**
   Trends, development, prospects
   Edited by David Timothy Duval

4. **Qualitative Research in Tourism**
   Ontologies, epistemologies and methodologies
   Edited by Jenny Phillimore and Lisa Goodson

5. **The Media and the Tourist Imagination**
   Converging cultures
   Edited by David Crouch, Rhona Jackson and Felix Thompson

Routledge Studies in Contemporary Geographies of Leisure, Tourism and Mobility is a forum for innovative new research intended for research students and academics, and the titles will be available in hardback only. Titles include:

Forthcoming:

Trust, Tourism Development and Planning
Edited by Robin Nunkoo and Stephen Smith

Travel, Tourism and Green Growth
Edited by Min Jiang, Terry DeLacy and Geoffrey Lipman

Research Volunteer Tourism
Angela M. Benson

Volunteer Tourism and Development
Jim Butcher and Peter Smith

Social Memory and Heritage Tourism
Edited by David L. Butler, Perry Carter, Stephen P. Hanna, Arnold Modlin and Amy E. Potter

The Business of Sustainable Tourism
Edited by Michael Hughes, David Weaver and Christof Pforr

Tourism and Development in Sub-Sahara Africa
Marina Novelli

Work and Organisation in Tourism and Tourism Industries
Edited by David Jordhus- Lier and Anders Underthun

Scientific and Research Tourism
Edited by Susan L. Slocum, Carol Kline and Andrew Holden

TOURISM AND CITIZENSHIP

Rights, freedoms and responsibilities in the global order

Raoul V. Bianchi and
Marcus L. Stephenson

Routledge
Taylor & Francis Group

LONDON AND NEW YORK

First published 2014
by Routledge
2 Park Square, Milton Park, Abingdon, Oxon OX14 4RN

and by Routledge
711 Third Avenue, New York, NY 10017

Routledge is an imprint of the Taylor & Francis Group, an informa business

British Library Cataloguing in Publication data
A catalogue record for this book is available from the British Library

Library of Congress Cataloguing in Publication data
Bianchi, Raoul V.
Tourism and citizenship : rights, freedom and responsibilities in the
global order / Raoul V. Bianchi and Marcus L. Stephenson.
pages cm. – (Contemporary geographies of leisure, tourism and mobility)
Includes bibliographical references and index.
1. Tourism – Political aspects. 2. Social mobility. 3. Citizenship. 4. Human rights. I. Title.
G155.A1B53 2013
338.4'791–dc23
2013025916

ISBN: 978-0-415-70739-8 (hbk)
ISBN: 978-0-415-70738-1 (pbk)
ISBN: 978-1-315-88682-4 (ebk)

Typeset in Bembo
by Out of House Publishing

Printed and bound in Great Britain by
TJ International Ltd, Padstow, Cornwall

For Alia, Golnoosh, Eva and Craig

CONTENTS

ILLUSTRATIONS

Plates

Tables

ACKNOWLEDGEMENTS

We are indebted to many people who in different ways have helped us to develop and clarify the ideas and arguments that eventually came together to form this book. For their steadfast support, intellectual guidance and friendship during the years of writing we would like to thank Kevin Hannam, David Harrison, Andrew Holden, Howard Hughes, Jonathan Karkut, Julie Scott and Tom Selwyn. Linda Richter and Christine Chin also provided valuable critiques of some of the earlier ideas that since found their way into some of the chapters, at the International Studies Association annual conferences in Honolulu in 2005 and New York City in 2009 respectively. Thanks are also due to Rami Kassis and Frans de Man for helping to clarify certain aspects of the book on which they are noted experts. Writing such a book, particularly during times of personal difficulty and the wider professional struggles taking place within higher education, has involved a great deal of stamina and perseverance. For their friendship, support and con-tribution to the intellectual climate in which we have worked, we are grateful for the support of many friends and colleagues. In particular, we would like to thank Ala Al-Hamarneh, Nazia Ali, Raed Awamleh, Lulu Baddar, John Chandler, Anya Diekmann, Yaz Djebbour, Alun Epps, Brett Freeman, Meg Hart, Michael Hitchcock, I-Ling Kuo, Diana Luck, Scott McCabe, Cody Morris Paris, Melanie Smith, John Sparrowhawk and Rafal Tomaszewski. The sentiments expressed in this book also recognize the steadfast work of Lara Marsh, friend, campaigner and global justice activist who sadly passed away in 2012.

The completion of this book ultimately is down to the patience and under-standing of our respective partners, children and families, who have tolerated the late nights, mood swings, cancelled social engagements and general anti-social behaviour that inevitably accompany an endeavour of such magnitude!

INTRODUCTION

Tourism and citizenship – points of departure

> Democracies should be judged not only by how they treat their members but by how they treat their strangers.
>
> *(Benhabib 1998: 108)*

During the spring and summer of 2008, neo-fascist vigilante squads orchestrated a series of violent attacks on Roma gypsies in several Italian cities, including Naples, many of whom were in fact native Italians, urging their expulsion from Italy, aided and abetted by members of local organized crime syndicates or *camorristi* (Kington 2008). Subsequently, the Italian interior minister at the time embarked on a scheme to fingerprint tens of thousands of Roma, a move which bore dark echoes of Italy's fascist past and cast a dark shadow over Europe's own increasingly miserable record with regard to the treatment of the Roma and other 'ethnic minority' peoples (see Sigona and Trehan 2009). At around the same time, two Italian-born Roma girls, who had been selling trinkets to sunbathers on a popular beach in Naples, drowned after briefly entering the water to cool down. Apparently, the two girls lay on the beach for three hours until an ambulance finally arrived. During that time the holidaymakers continued to sunbathe nearby and play ball games seemingly indifferent to the macabre scene before them (Popham 2008).

Local accounts differ regarding the apparent indifference of those who were on the beach at the time, with some claiming to have tried to rescue the drowning girls. Nonetheless, a heated debate erupted in the local media condemning such apparent callousness towards their death (Zagaria 2008). From one perspective, this incident serves as a timely reminder that tourism may reflect a stubborn demand for enjoyment and the right to participate in travel and recreation, particularly in a world that is often oblivious to the lack of mobility freedoms and citizenship rights faced by those without the 'right credentials for travel' (Kaur and Hutnyk 1999: 3). From another perspective, however, the holidaymakers in this tragic incident were largely local Neapolitans, frequenting beaches running adjacent to the many overcrowded working-class quarters in one of Italy's poorest cities. This tragic event thus serves as a stark illustration of the differential mobility empowerments of 'holidaymakers' and other mobile 'denizens' with impoverished mobility rights.

Mobility, and in particular the freedom of movement and travel, arouses a multitude of representations and is expressed through a variety of ever-changing discourses. Indeed, Creswell (2010: 19) comments that 'Mobility has been figured as adventure, as tedium, as education, as freedom, as modern, as threatening'. The contrasting experiences of mobility among immigrants and migrant workers, asylum seekers and refugees, compared to that of politicians, diplomats, journalists, celebrities, business people and international tourists are indicative of the many tensions and contradictions that mark the freedom of movement and the right to travel. More than 65 years since the Universal Declaration of Human Rights (UNDHR) (United Nations 1948) first enshrined the right to freedom of movement in an international charter of human rights, the attitudes of different states towards the principle and practice of the right to travel remain highly ambiguous and politically charged. The right and ability of humans to travel freely and without hindrance across international borders has in many ways become one of the defining ideological and material concerns of the twenty-first century, albeit one that is far from being universally acknowledged and institutionalized.

The fundamental right to the freedom of movement and travel is encoded into the very DNA of Western industrialized societies. However, the idea that we are living in an increasingly mobile world, and that international travel has become more 'democratic', is contradicted by the growing panoply of controls and techniques to regulate, constrain or impede altogether the cross-border movements of people deemed to lack the right credentials for travel. The movement of tourists across international borders has historically enjoyed a much higher standing in the eyes of most governments than does the movement of labour, immigrants and refugees, and, at times, 'ethnic minority' citizens of the advanced capitalist states of the West. Nevertheless, that is not to dismiss the role of tourism as a social need and perhaps a universal right as some have argued (McCabe 2009). Rather, it serves as a necessary reminder of the manner in which inequalities of mobility unfold at different levels in the contemporary global order, and in so doing transform and constitute new forms of citizenship.

In a lucid analysis of travel writing, Pratt (2008) draws attention to the similarities and contrasts between the movement of settlers to the 'new world' during earlier periods of European colonialism and the more recent settlement of ex-colonial diasporas in the metropole at the end of the twentieth century. She notes: 'Enlightenment travellers came home laden with curiosities and specimens, the contemporary global workforce returns in the other direction with suitcases of clothing, car parts, boxed appliances, oversized bundles with wares that will be sold to pay for the trip' (Pratt 2008: 241). She goes on to discuss how we are encouraged to view such movements as flows, suggesting that they will eventually find a 'natural equilibrium', one that is determined for the most part by the demands of capital for endless supplies of cheap labour. There is clearly a vast ocean of inequality and injustice that separates the mobility of workers flowing on the reverse tide of modernity towards the metropole in search of a better life, and the mobility rights and privileges of the contemporary tourists and other members of the so-called 'kinetic elite' (Hannam *et al.* 2006: 6). In addition, participation in different forms of international travel itself is also highly uneven and often discriminatory. This book seeks to expose the falsity of promises held out by neoliberal globalization and the universal embrace of liberal democracy that was hailed by certain conservative commentators in the aftermath of the Cold War (see Fukuyama 1989), namely that international travel represents a quintessential expression of a more democratic, mobile and inclusive world order of consumer citizens. Equally, it challenges the libertarian view that promotes tourism as a benign modernizing force associated almost exclusively with freedom, innocence and fun. It is the nexus of relationships between the freedom of movement, the right to travel (and indeed, to the right to tourism itself) and discourses of citizenship, that merits further attention if we are to fully comprehend the profound transformations associated with tourism and travel in contemporary societies.

Globalization and the 'democratization' of international tourism?

Since the days of privileged elite travel in the late nineteenth century and the early part of the twentieth century, participation in international travel has become a major aspiration for the consuming classes and a marker of status. This was despite the fact that Thomas Cook had originally harnessed travel to progressive ideals in bringing mobility to the masses (see Brendon 1991). Indeed, Cook's early tours had been inspired by his devotion to the ideals of 'temperance' and 'universal brotherhood', but were later eclipsed by a more business-focused mindset when his son, John Mason Cook, later took charge of the firm. This change was also underpinned by the integration of Cook's endeavours into the full scope of British imperial expansion (Turner and Ash 1975: 56–59). By the 1930s, the economic gains of Fordist manufacturing techniques, which cheapened the price of consumer commodities, together with US monopolization of 90 per cent of the world's oil production, paved the way for the rise of an 'automobile consumer class' in the United States, fuelling the expansion of a new culture of mobility (Urry 2013: 43). In the aftermath of the Second World War, the advent of the jet engine and rising disposable incomes ensured the consolidation of uneven patterns of 'north–south' mobility that have more or less endured to the present day.

In a series of influential reports published by some of the world's leading international organizations (e.g. UNCTAD 1973), international mass tourism quickly became identified as one of the principal means through which newly independent 'developing' countries could kick-start the process of modernization (Wood 1979). Further to the belief that tourism could stimulate economic development, organizations such as the newly formed World Tourism Organization (WTO) in 1974, extolled the ability of tourism to 'contribute to the establishment of a new international economic order', thus eliminating the income gap between rich and poor states (WTO 1980: 1). This view reflected the ideological sentiments espoused by the Non-Aligned Movement founded in Bandung in 1955, which were further supported by the UN Conference on Trade and Development (UNCTAD), established in 1964 (Matthews 1978). Until the publication of a series of more cautionary studies commissioned by the World Bank and UNESCO (e.g. De Kadt 1979; Noronha 1979), the overall economic benefits of tourism to 'developing' or 'less developed' countries were often considerably exaggerated, at the expense of recognizing the deleterious social and environmental consequences (Hills and Lundgren 1977: 255).

Elsewhere, in the Communist bloc countries between 1945 and 1989, the freedom of movement and the right to travel were strictly regulated and curtailed by the Communist state apparatus. Despite the draconian restrictions that existed on the freedom of movement of both foreign tourists and their own citizens in former Communist bloc states, tourism activities did of course exist. This travel was predominantly organized by state enterprises, trade unions and youth organizations with a view to cultivating the ideal socialist citizen. Travel was more accessible in some states rather than others, for example, in Hungary and Yugoslavia, where state controls were less stringent and living standards for manual workers were slightly higher (Allcock and Przeclawski 1990: 5). Domestically, travel was nevertheless primarily geared towards fostering socialist solidarity (or rather, ensuring consent) and the reproduction of the labour force. Foreign travel was primarily restricted to the visiting of other Communist states (e.g. Vietnam and Cuba) for the purposes of engendering international solidarity among citizens of the Communist bloc states (Horáková 2010). Members of the *nomenklatura* and state diplomatic elites, on the other hand, were able to enjoy privileged access to hard currencies and international travel, as well as being in a position to expropriate domestic tourism assets (e.g. holiday villas and private resorts) in prime tourist locations along the Black Sea and elsewhere.

Participation in travel and tourism became increasingly widespread over the course of the twentieth century, and tourism itself has come to be seen as a vital social need and a right. This implies more than the right to merely consume other places and cultures, but rather, illuminates the potential for the redefinition of citizenship rights within the context of mobile and globalizing societies. The collapse of Communist rule and subsequent democratization and market reforms in the Soviet Union and across Eastern Europe marked a major turning point in the scope and embrace of the freedom of movement, as members of former Communist bloc states (re)claimed their status as citizens in newly sovereign states. It also symbolized a new era of capitalist globalization as well as the integration of millions of potential new consumers and tourists into the global marketplace (Munar 2007: 348).

Nevertheless, as the forthcoming discussion will indicate, it is pertinent to remain circumspect of the claim that 'mobility remains a relative privilege but one that is becoming more widespread' (Franklin and Crang 2001: 11). As an exception to the apparent trend towards greater mobility freedoms worldwide, the state of Cuba still places heavy restrictions on outbound travel, in spite of the recent scrapping of exit visas for Cubans wishing to travel abroad, while the United States continues to regulate and limit travel by US citizens to the island. Despite the lifting of some restrictions on travel and money transfers between Cuba and the United States since the election of President Obama in 2008, and the formal request from the American Society of Travel Agents that its government remove all sanctions (Chen 2009), the greater part of the US economic embargo and travel ban remains in place (Shear 2009).

In the aftermath of the Cold War, international tourism arrivals grew by an impressive 55 per cent, rising from 435 million in 1990 to 674 million in 2000 (UNWTO 2012), until the attacks on New York City in September 2001 brought this rapid rate of expansion to a stuttering, albeit temporary, halt. By the early 1990s, international tourism had established itself as one of the most dynamic and sought after industries worldwide, not just for many 'developing' countries still struggling to find a secure foothold in the globalizing economy, but increasingly also for the newly democratic states of Eastern Europe as well as the emerging BRIC economies of Brazil, Russia, India and China. Such has been the scale of their vertiginous growth that some estimates suggest that by 2050, 60 per cent of world economic output will originate from what are also known as the MBRIIC economies (Mexico, Brazil, Russia, India, Indonesia and China), further fuelling demand for outbound travel (Yeoman 2012: 17).

In 2011 international tourism generated US$1.2 trillion in annual export earnings worldwide, and comprised around 30 per cent of the world's exports of commercial services and over 6 per cent of overall exports of goods and services (UNWTO 2012: 3). However, the starkest transformation in terms of the relative balance of power in global tourism has been the shifting momentum towards Asia as well as the Americas, both in terms of the relative distribution of arrivals and receipts, as well as outbound traffic. As a consequence of double-digit economic growth, rapid urbanization and rising disposable incomes, the market share of international tourism arrivals in emerging economies as a whole increased from 30 per cent in 1980 to 47 per cent in 2011 (UNWTO 2012: 2). At the same time, it is necessary to remind ourselves that the vast majority of tourist movements are domestic, not least in the emerging economies (Gladstone 2005).

Given the relatively uninterrupted growth and expansion of international tourism arrivals since the Second World War, followed more recently by the rapid growth of outbound tourism from a few key emerging economies, it is often assumed that international tourism has become increasingly democratized, or, at the very least, that participation in international travel is becoming more widespread. International tourism arrivals increased from 277 million in 1980 to 528 million in 1995, and in 2012 exceeded 1 billion arrivals for the first time (UNWTO 2013: 1). This trend is anticipated to continue unabated with international arrivals to experience an average annual growth of 3.3 per cent from 2010 to 2030 and total arrivals anticipated to reach 1.8 billion (UNWTO 2012: 2). Nevertheless, a word of caution is warranted. Much of this increase has been due to greater flows of intra-regional 'south–south' travel (see Ghimire 2001). Moreover, the international nature of intra-European travel is enhanced purely by the fact that there are many national borders in an area roughly equivalent to the size of the United States, leading to what Arremberi (2009: 371) calls 'the exaggerated importance of Europe in the UNWTO database'. In addition, given that international arrivals include multiple trips and travel by business people, diplomats and many other non-tourist mobilities, international tourism remains a privilege for a minority of the world's population, albeit one that, based on current projections, will continue to expand. If current levels of inequality continue to rise, not least in the much acclaimed BRICs, the trend towards divergent experiences and patterns of mobility looks only set to continue (see Halimi 2013).[1]

Growth in international travel, particularly for the working classes in industrialized states, improved dramatically throughout the 1960s and into the early 1970s. Rising disposable incomes and declining transportation costs enabled many to travel overseas for the first time (Gladstone 2005: 56). Thereafter, the oil crisis and ensuing global recession depressed real wages in high-income countries from around the mid-1970s until the mid-1990s (see Brenner 2003: 25). Nevertheless, the aspiration for overseas travel had already begun to take a firm hold among ordinary working people, while business and other 'alternative' forms of tourism had begun to develop, thus counteracting the reduced rate of growth in international arrivals (Gladstone 2005: 59). The effects of the global recession on international travel demand were also offset by the cheapening of travel brought about by the increased corporate concentration of independent airlines and package holiday companies in the generating markets, such as in the UK where the Mediterranean package holiday was pioneered (Lyth 2009).

Despite a slowdown in international tourism arrivals in the early 1980s, the cost of international travel, particularly to a range of new destinations in the 'developing' countries, was held down, partly as a result of the currency devaluations imposed on low-income developing countries as part of the 'structural adjustment programmes' led by the International Monetary Fund (IMF) (Gladstone 2005: 59). In the major generating countries, the strengthening of currencies in the major markets together with the expansion of cheap credit, heralded by the launch of the *Access* credit card in 1972, continued to spur the growth of outbound travel. In the UK, for instance, the strength of sterling was associated with the tightening of monetary policy by Margaret Thatcher's Conservative government. This put further pressure on the UK's manufacturing base and thus increased industrial unemployment (Glyn 2007: 53). It was during this period that convulsive social changes, such as those associated with advancement of youth sub-cultures, feminism and consumerism, contributed to the growing aspirations for increasingly diverse forms of international travel. Overseas travel, once the privilege of the upper-income groups, started to become the norm for a wider spectrum of social groups and to be seen as a right for the millions who had begun to experience the pleasures of international tourism during the boom period of 1960 to the mid-1970s (Lyth 2009).

Hence, the expectation of an annual holiday in the sun began to outweigh the thriftiness of earlier generations and the fear of getting into debt. However, outbound international travel from the core markets in Europe and North America stalled once again, mainly because of the economic slowdown at the end of the 1980s and recession of the early 1990s. More recently, the 2007–2008 financial crash and ensuing recession, which have had a severe impact on European economies, have resulted in increased domestic and intra-regional travel (Euromonitor International 2011). Although the European market continues to generate just over half of international tourist arrivals worldwide, the fastest growth in outbound international travel is in the Asia-Pacific region, which in 2011 accounted for 22 per cent of outbound tourists. This was closely followed by other emerging economies operating outside of the traditional capitalist heartlands, in places such as Eastern Europe, Southern Africa, South America and the Middle East (UNWTO 2012: 12).

It remains uncertain whether these patterns of altered and accelerated growth in tourism do in fact signal a more fundamental structural reconfiguration in the coordinates of global travel. Indeed, Arremberi (2009) wisely counsels against the tendency to exaggerate the global significance of tourism. Not only are domestic flows of travel far greater than international tourism,[2] the majority of international tourism flows are structured around three central regions – Europe and the Mediterranean, North America and the Caribbean, and Northeast and Southeast Asia – which draw predominantly on their immediate hinterlands for tourists. This is particularly significant in the case of Europe, which in 2011 accounted for 51 per cent of global travel (UNWTO 2012: 4).

However, it is not the intention in this book to map fluctuations in the flows of outbound travel on to changing economic fortunes of different regions around the world. Rather, it is to interrogate the assumption that international travel has become more 'democratized' in the light of recent global transformations and the increasingly complex and unequal cross-border movements of people. Specifically, it is to think through the implications of these changes for the relationship between tourism and citizenship. While the growth in aggregate international tourism arrivals certainly suggests that tourism is becoming more widespread, that is not to say it is becoming more democratic. Moreover, it should not be assumed that participation in travel and tourism implies the diffusion of existing, Western notions of citizenship throughout the globe. Not only is the uneven distribution of potential travel opportunities within and across states significant, the lack of participation in holiday-taking remains constant throughout Europe and stands at around 40 per cent of the population (Minnaert *et al.* 2011: 20). The rapid expansion of 'low-cost carriers' (LCCs) since the early 1990s improved access to intra-regional travel within Europe, as well as in other continents as seen in the launch of Fastjet in Africa (Topham 2012).[3] However, the evidence suggests that low-cost air travel within the European Union (EU) has benefited middle-class travellers more than it has the less well off. It also has been utilized significantly by those with the financial resources to purchase second homes (Gillett 2004).

If it is the case that economic globalization and market integration are key factors in the cheapening of travel commodities, then cheaper global travel also comes at a price. The period of neoliberal globalization from the early 1980s until just prior to the onset of the 2007–2008 financial crisis was characterized by highly uneven patterns of economic development and significant growth in income inequalities (Pollin 2005: 132–136). Nevertheless, considerable reductions in global poverty have been witnessed over the past decade. This is partly due to above average economic growth rates in Brazil, China, India and parts of sub-Saharan Africa, spurred on by price increases in key export commodities, as well as pockets of rapid industrial development (particularly in China). Yet world income distribution remains stubbornly unequal, continuing to rise in some cases (UNDP 2013: 25–26). More recently, as a result of the 2007–2008 financial crisis and ensuing recession, the United States, the UK, and parts of the Eurozone have experienced increased levels of unemployment and a growth in poverty (see Lapavitsas *et al.* 2012; OECD 2011). In addition, world unemployment reached 197.3 million in 2012, an increase of 4.2 million over the previous year (ILO 2013: 16).

Despite a significant reduction in the numbers living in absolute or extreme poverty (those living on less than US$1.25 a day), the Chinese 'economic miracle' has developed on the back of the stark differences in standards of living between rural and urban areas and growing wage inequalities (Park *et al.* 2003). Although India too has been heralded by leading travel industry representatives 'as one of the world's largest out-bound travel nations and most exciting inbound destinations' (eTurboNews 2011), in 2009 just under 42 per cent of its 1.2 billion citizens were living in extreme poverty (UNDP 2011: 144). Thus, the impoverished peasantry and the lower echelons of the urban workforce, in poor and emerging economies alike, are increasingly left behind by the minority of citizens who can count themselves among the prosperous 'new middle classes'. Overall, despite significant declines in the numbers of people living in extreme poverty over the past decade or so, the International Labour Organization (ILO) estimates that in 2011 around 58.4 per cent of the developing world's workforce was still classified as 'poor' (living on less than US$2 a day) and 'near poor' (living on between US$2 and US$4 a day) (ILO 2013: 40). Even in developed states, the international travel industry has responded to the fallout from the global financial crisis by placing greater emphasis on 'all-inclusive' resorts in order to reduce the price of holidays sold to austerity-hit Europeans (see Tourism Concern 2012). Paradoxically, the past few years have witnessed the expansion of 'luxury travel' services and resorts for those whose wealth has been unaffected by, or indeed who have prospered from, the current economic recession and austerity policies (see Euromonitor International 2012). Ironically, these trends have even prompted the traditional flag-bearers for neoliberalism, such as the IMF, to reprimand the world's leading industrialized economies for failing to do enough to halt rising inequalities due to the dampening effect on consumption and economic growth (Halimi 2013: 2)!

Notwithstanding the continued effects of the 2007–2008 global financial crisis, standards of living and disposable incomes for the 'new middle classes' in emerging economies continue to rise, fuelling growth in consumption. The *2013 Human Development Report*, produced by the United Nations Development Programme

(UNDP), indicates that a significant global rebalancing of economic wealth and power is taking place. The report notes that the share of the global middle class living in the global South increased from 26 per cent to 58 per cent between 1990 and 2008. By 2030, it is projected that more than 80 per cent of the world's middle classes will reside in the global South, representing around 70 per cent of 'total consumption expenditure' (UNDP 2013: 14). Furthermore, it is expected that by 2020 the aggregate production of Canada, France, Germany, Italy, the United Kingdom and the United States will be exceeded by the collective economic output of Brazil, China and India alone (Al Tamimi 2013). In addition to the rising economic strength of the BRIC countries, there has also been a significant rise of new consumer classes in the next wave of strategically important emergent economies, including Argentina, Indonesia, Mexico, South Africa, South Korea and Turkey (Elliot 2012). Indonesia, a member of the 20 largest global economies (G20), is anticipated to become the world's seventh largest economy by 2030. It has a sizeable middle-class population predicted to expand to around 90 million people (Oberman *et al.* 2012). Due to a lack of good quality domestic healthcare provision Indonesia is also rapidly becoming one of the world's leading generators of 'medical tourists', significant numbers of whom are travelling to countries elsewhere in the region, such as Malaysia, in order to purchase private health services (see Ormond 2011a, 2011b).

The embrace of new consumer freedoms in the developing world is likely to continue to fuel the demand for international travel, reinforcing the momentum behind the shifting tectonics of global travel towards Asia and South America. However, this in itself does not constitute the democratization of travel as such but represents an extension of capitalist class privilege to a minority of upper-middle-class and super-rich consumers in emerging economies and developing countries (see Mark 2012). Moreover, the right to travel and the freedom of movement can be experienced very differently according to one's class, gender, ethnicity, sexuality, religion and nationality, while the right to paid holidays is by no means universally acknowledged. Overall, despite the much proclaimed opening up of former Communist states to capitalist economic globalization and the growth of the so-called 'middle class' in emergent economies, wealth distribution is considerably uneven and in some cases has worsened over the past decade (Ortíz and Cummins 2011).

During the 1990s, convulsive market reforms, mass privatizations and unemployment, combined with the imposition of hard currency and visa requirements, significantly compromised the possibilities for foreign travel for much of the population in the new democracies of Eastern Europe, and in particular Russia (Hall and Brown 2012: 121–122). Today, however, Russia is hailed as the world's sixth largest source market for outbound tourism with 43 million Russians travelling abroad in 2011. Russia has achieved this largely due to the rapid economic growth brought about by a boom in energy exports, a doubling of real disposable income and falling levels of unemployment (Dimireva 2012), in conjunction with the relaxation of visa controls in many destinations (Tourism Review 2012). In the process of becoming citizens of new democratic states, as well as consumers of capitalist commodities, both the new middle classes and a considerable number of workers in the new East European democracies have staked their claim to become international tourists and mobile citizens, alongside the expanding middle classes of other emerging economies.

As succinctly demonstrated by Gladstone (2005: 132–139), growing demand for international travel and the considerable expansion of domestic formal tourism in countries such as India have been fuelled by rising disposable incomes and increased purchasing power among a narrow socio-economic spectrum. Such demand has of course bypassed the growing ranks of the impoverished farmers and urban slum dwellers in the mega-cities of the 'developing' world whose numbers are estimated at around a third of the world's urban population (see Davis 2004: 13). Therefore, we should remain sceptical towards simple correlations between the aggregate growth in international tourism arrivals and the democratization of travel, notwithstanding the rapid expansion of outbound travel among a small albeit growing proportion of upper-income groups in emerging economies. Nonetheless, the question then remains, what do these changing patterns and forms of global travel imply for the multiplex and emergent relationship between tourism, the right to travel, and the making and remaking of citizenship?

Thinking through the tourism and citizenship interface

In one of the few sustained reflections on the relationship between tourism and citizenship, Rojek (1998) highlights three specific interconnections between the mobilities associated with tourism and questions of citizenship. First, the sheer volume of cross-border travel and the pervasiveness of tourism, together with diverse forms of cross-border mobility worldwide, have contributed to the cultural diversification and transnationalization of societies in such a way as to render state–citizen relations increasingly problematic on a number of fronts. Second, the manifold social, cultural and environmental consequences attributed to tourism raise a number of concerns regarding the relative balance of power between the rights of tourists to pass freely into particular territories to consume a range of tangible and intangible resources, and the development rights of the individuals and communities who encounter and serve tourists locally. Third, and perhaps the most potent interface between tourism and citizenship, is signalled by Rojek's remark that 'we don't think of tourism as a citizenship right until our freedom to travel is threatened' (1998: 291) This points to a series of tensions – material and ideological – underlying the seemingly peaceful spread of the universal right to travel worldwide, that will be considered in this book..

The upsurge in terrorist attacks on tourists from the early to mid-1990s onwards signalled a series of violent attacks on the freedom of movement and right to travel. Accordingly, the question of the degree to which the world should be 'made safe' for tourists and 'open to' the business of tourism is one which goes to the heart of the many tensions and paradoxes that permeate political responses to international tourism and its implications for citizenship. The seemingly impossible compromise between the freedom of movement and right to travel on the one hand, and the security of tourists to travel to certain territories in relative safety on the other, implies a further series of difficult and politically sensitive questions regarding the duties of states to ensure the well-being of their own citizens vis-à-vis those of tourists. Regardless of the motives of those who seek to harm tourists, such attacks raise serious concerns regarding the responsibility of states to intervene in tackling the underlying social conditions of deprivation in destinations, whether or not these are in any way linked to violence against tourists. The spate of terrorist attacks against tourists in the late 1990s and early 2000s in a range of destinations in the Middle East, Africa and Asia thus serves as a stark reminder of the closely intertwined nature of international tourism and geopolitics, and the manner in which 'our' right to travel freely may be violently abrogated or indeed contested and restrained through some other means. However, understanding the political rationale, source and foundation for such rights is complex, especially when competing notions of justice and freedom collide in the context of international travel. As Higgins-Desbiolles (2007: 324) explains: 'the act of enjoying this right to travel is an ideological act which is predicated on a system of inequity and therefore may invite another ideological act, terrorism, as a response'.

These issues go to the heart of the tensions and contradictions surrounding debates concerning the rights and freedoms encompassed within the diverse and intersecting worlds of tourism and tourist-related mobility. Specifically, there are profound concerns regarding differential access to what Torpey (2000) describes as the 'means of movement', and what such asymmetries of mobility imply for the kind of citizenship rights that are revealed within and shaped by participation in tourism. Crossing (or interacting across) borders can involve a set of fluid and multi-scalar transnational social relationships rooted in structural inequalities of power and wealth. What then are the implications for the kind of 'social contract' that underlies what was once commonly referred to as the 'host–guest' relationship?

Participation in international tourism is increasingly becoming one among many benchmarks of a 'civilized life' and seen as a marker of citizenship. Although the work of Rojek (1998), Urry (1995, 2000) and Coles (2008a, 2008b) provides a springboard for further reflection on the relationship between tourism and citizenship, this book aims to significantly advance our understanding of the emergent and differentiated relationships between tourism and citizenship. Accordingly, the work presents a theoretically engaged, sociological reflection on the various discourses and practices of the freedom of movement and the right to travel (and to be a tourist). In this regard, the book considers how evolving historical definitions and practices of citizenship have shaped international travel. In turn, it evaluates the varying ways in which participation in international tourism acts a means by which existing models of citizenship are being transformed and redefined. These transformations are shaped by a range of factors: neoliberal globalization; the marketization of advanced capitalist societies; the shifting balance of global economic and political power; the large-scale international movements of people, culture and finance;

the reconfiguration of states; and the emergence of new collective forms of social mobilization and decision-making. Consequently, citizenship does not merely refer to a set of static rights and duties organized and enforced within a national politico-legal framework. It can also be defined as: 'that set of practices (juridical, political, economic and cultural) which define a person as a competent member of society, and which as a consequence shape the flow of resources to persons and social groups' (Turner 1994a: 2).

In addition to questions of changing individual and group relations to the state, citizenship constitutes a lens through which to explore issues concerning the utilization and control of productive or 'common pool' resources, and the social relations existing between different actors and institutions. Isin and Wood (1999: 4) identify citizenship with the struggle of individuals and social groups with common interests, who seek to formulate and claim new rights or to reinforce existing ones in the face of the challenges presented by contemporary globalization. Such struggles are borne out through the rise of 'global civil society' (Falk 1994: 138) and the growing involvement of new social movements in struggles in which the politics of cultural recognition intersect with material issues of wealth and power (Morris-Suzuki 2000: 75). Transnational NGO (non-governmental organization) campaigns often combine with minority struggles for recognition, human rights and social justice throughout many different tourism settings, helping to formulate, define and apply new ideas and practices of citizenship. These struggles often occur within localized settings involving resource conflicts. They can be concerned, for instance, with the custodianship of cultural amenities or particular environments in as much as they take place at a transnational scale.

Swain (2009) sees cosmopolitan ideals expressed in the United Nations World Heritage and Geo-Parks programmes as well as attempts by the United Nations World Tourism Organization (UNWTO) to construct a global framework for the advancement of ethical and sustainable tourism (e.g. WTO 1999). However, in spite of its ostensibly internationalist credentials, the UN continues to be governed according to the principles of national self-determination, which have consistently 'hampered the development of a common will and the application of common principles of law and human rights across the world' (Gamble 2009: 158). In addition, in the absence of a clearly defined balance of reciprocal rights and duties to regulate the interface between tourists and less well-off destination communities, let alone an appropriate and legitimate institutional authority through which such a balance could be governed, it is left to the numerous civil society movements and NGOs to step into this vacuum. In many ways, civil society increasingly acts as the vehicle through which grievances are expressed. In some cases, it can also act as an interlocutor between the various competing interests and actors in the contested spaces and meeting grounds of tourism.

There can be little doubt that these examples represent substantive changes in the meanings and practices associated with modern citizenship, and which may in turn indicate a shift towards a more open, progressive and cosmopolitan world. Although globalization and the rescaling of states has paved the way for cultural rights claims and transnational activism, this has taken place alongside the unparalleled growth and expansion of corporate power and inequalities, eroding hard-won politically guaranteed citizenship rights usually associated with social citizenship and development rights. Neoliberal globalization and the concomitant marketization of the public sphere have increasingly cultivated and reinforced the role of citizens as consumers, thus supplanting the more traditional modernist notion of citizens as workers and members of a democratically managed political community, anchored in the nation-state.

Given that consumption has become increasingly central to social life and the shaping of individual identities (Bell and Valentine 1997), postmodern cultural critics have also increasingly advocated notions of 'empowered consumerism'. This takes the notion of the sovereign consumer even further and implies an increasingly marketized conception of citizenship no longer anchored exclusively in the state (see Streeck 2012). Such notions of consumer citizenship arguably lie at the heart of the expanding world of international tourism and the putative rights of consumers to enjoy the benefits of travel, as set out in Articles 7 and 8 of the *Global Code of Ethics for Tourism* (WTO 1999). Consumer citizenship arguably implies the fallacy that consumers are somehow more sophisticated and emboldened to make free choices and to travel unhindered by the material determinations of class, ethnicity, religion, gender and sexuality. However, as this book will demonstrate, the rights associated with tourism consumption run the risk of concealing the class dynamics of power and discriminatory politics that underscore the dynamics of neoliberal globalization and which inhibit access to a more just and equal participation in travel and tourism.

One of the principal issues to be analyzed in this book concerns the fact that international tourism has not merely become a marker of citizenship, as noted by Urry (1995: 165), but is also regarded as an inalienable human right extending across international borders. Given that international tourism presupposes the power and ability to move around the world with a minimum of hindrances, one central question concerns an understanding of what kind of rights and duties should be attached to international tourism and 'being a tourist'? Furthermore, it is not clear at which level in the global order such rights and duties should be institutionalized, or indeed, by whom? The relative balance between rights and duties in a world of globalizing travel and differentiated mobility is an ideologically complex and as yet undefined terrain of politico-legal practice. Indeed, international tourism is organized and managed by a multi-layered spectrum of institutions and actors that transcend the borders of the state. With the exception of the provisions providing for the freedom of movement established in the 1948 UNDHR, and the statement of principles contained in the WTO's *Global Code of Ethics*, international tourism and the right to travel and consume other cultures as a tourist are not subject to any clearly demarcated set of mutually agreed rights and responsibilities. Travel as a fundamental human right is nevertheless a notion that has gained political currency over the past two decades in tandem with the globalization of free market capitalism and tourism. As a major component of the diverse and proliferating avenues of cross-border mobility, tourism presupposes the power and ability to move around the world with minimum hindrance. However, as the book will argue, although the freedom of movement is indeed a fundamental human right that is enshrined in the UNDHR, albeit within restricted parameters, it is increasingly elided with the right to travel and indeed the right to tourism itself.

The debate over the right to travel in general, and the right to tourism in particular, not only presupposes the capacity of individuals to consume an ever-widening array of tourist products and services, it also serves to nourish a discourse of privatized leisure mobility and tourism consumption that lies at the very core of the new political economy of consumer citizenship. Additionally, the right to travel and to partake in tourism is often defended on the grounds that it serves an economically useful, at times altruistic role in contributing to development in low-income countries, as well as a democratic right and marker of citizenship in a globalized and increasingly mobile world. The question of balancing the rights of tourists (to travel/consume) with the rights of destination communities (to a clean environment and to determine their own development) have also framed discussions around the ethics of all-inclusive resorts (Tourism Concern 2012) and reactions to the much-maligned Balearic eco-tax in Spain (see Palmer and Riera 2003). When this tax was first proposed, a number of tourists voiced concerns that they had already paid directly through the cost of their holiday and (in some cases) indirectly through EU financial transfers to Spain! Therefore, the contention was that tourists should not be forced to pay an additional tax on top of this, despite the fact that it was to be specifically targeted at projects devoted to environmental and heritage conservation (Bungay 1999a). The trope of the 'overtaxed' tourist is a familiar one. It is one that also surfaced in the United States during the late 1960s in the context of opposition to President Johnson's attempt to tax travel by American citizens overseas in an attempt to stem the outflow of US dollars (Endy 2004: 194).

Although the state remains the principal regulator of mobility through its control over borders, passports and visa regimes, the expansion and diversification of international cross-border mobility and tourism over the three decades has helped to transform the relationship between the citizen and the nation-state. In so far as tourism is concerned, the emergence of an increasingly networked, transnational and polycentric global order challenges scholars of mobility and tourism to think seriously about the ways in which the diverse patterns and flows of global tourism become implicated in new conceptions and practices of citizenship.

International tourism and the paradoxes of mobility

In a world of hyper-mobile capital, instantaneous communications and accelerated patterns of global mobility, international tourism encapsulates the contradictory forces of mobility and freedom on the one hand and immobility and disenfranchisement on the other. Conrad's (2012) exposition concerning life and survival at the Dandora waste-disposal site in Nairobi (Kenya) powerfully depicts the crude distinctions between these mobile and immobile worlds. His narrative begins with a description of the dump truck routinely waiting in line at Nairobi's Jomo Kenyatta International Airport together with 'airport taxis full of deep-pocketed safari goers, business travellers and missionaries' (2012: 8). The truck's purpose at the airport is to transport food waste and other refuse gathered from the day's flights to Dandora Municipal Dump Site. He observes:

> Once the scraps have entered Dandora, they hardly make it out of the truck before dozens of men fight over the haul. Baked by the heat of the Kenyan sun and reeking of spoilt milk, the congealed food waste is thrown into the mouths or placed in strewn Kenya Airway bags for later … The Dandora waste-disposal site is a symbol of Nairobi's inequality – an eyesore for the privileged and toxic lifeline for the deprived.
>
> *(Conrad 2012: 8)*

This book exposes a series of paradoxes and tensions that are shaped by and revealed within the unfolding global realignments of mobility, wealth and power that shape international tourism. While powerful states have sought to reconfigure the world economy according to the logics of neoliberal market capitalism, at least until China and the other BRIC states became serious economic actors on the global stage, and the end of the Cold War briefly heralded a more mobile and cosmopolitan world, borders have hardened and barriers to mobility have proliferated. Many states appear determined to place a range of obstacles on the free mobility of persons, at least in comparison to that of capital. One of the many contradictions apparent within the neoliberal world order is that the state must above all else seek to uphold the untrammelled mobility of capital and, one might add, the movement of international tourists, while restricting the comparable mobility of labour, refugees and other migrants.

In the aftermath of the 'war on terror', unleashed by the United States and her allies in response to the terrorist attacks on the World Trade Center in New York City on 11 September 2001 (henceforth 9/11), leading Western governments became increasingly concerned with the maintenance of security and concomitant hardening of border regimes. At the same time, however, these states have also attempted to uphold the freedoms deemed necessary for the smooth functioning of the capitalist world economy. They have also become resolute in the extension of the powers of surveillance at a period when the nation-state is increasingly being challenged and reordered by an explosion of 'diverse interacting systems of mobility' (Hannam *et al.* 2006: 2). Such eagerness to reassert the power of the sovereign territorial nation-state through the discourses and practices of 'national security', has occurred in tandem with targeted restrictions on the cross-border mobility of immigrants and other mobile persons deemed 'undesirable' or 'suspicious'.

The expansion of digital surveillance and development of biometric technologies throughout the global nodes of travel and ports-of-entry has been considerable over the past decade or so. These include the introduction and increased use of identification cards, web-based surveillance and biometrics, including fingerprint-ing, vein pattern recognition, retinal scanning, iris and facial recognition, and gait recognition systems (Lyon 2004). Among many increasingly common instruments of surveillance has been the deployment of rigorous forms of passenger profiling that help to identify and ultimately prevent 'risky' travellers from moving across international borders (Salter 2004). Such technologies, introduced ostensibly to prevent terrorism and enhance the security of travel, while justifiable in terms of protecting innocent human beings from harm, have nevertheless reinforced dif-ferentiated flows and patterns of mobility in which those with privileged mobility entitlements are able to move more freely through airports and a cross borders with a minimum of hindrance. At the same time, they act to restrict and possibly impede the mobility of less privileged travellers, notably 'illegal' immigrants, asy-lum seekers and refugees, and those who merely 'look' and/or 'act' suspicious, thus excluding them from the basic rights of freedom of movement. Although the 9/11 attacks seriously aggravated the difficulties experienced by individuals of Asian and Middle Eastern descent passing to and from their own countries of domicile, the racialized and constrained movements of ethnic minority citizens are long-standing societal problems. Furthermore, these concerns relate to still unresolved tensions between national citizenship and multicultural rights which are borne out through the experience of travel (Stephenson 2006; Stephenson and Ali 2010).

As was so vividly demonstrated by the euphoric scenes that accompanied the fall of the Berlin Wall on 7 November 1989, the struggle for democracy and pol-itical rights in the Soviet Union and Eastern bloc countries was partly premised upon demands for the freedom of movement and the right to travel, both intern-ally as well as across international borders. However, in ways that perhaps could not be foreseen at the time, the actions of East European citizens struggling to break free from the iron chains of Soviet Communism also foretold the emergence of neoliberal discourses of mobility centred on the norms and values of free market capitalism and the right to consume. This leads us to a further paradox concern-ing the problematic intersection between the democratization of travel and the belief that participation in tourism is akin to a form of citizenship and a human right. While on the one hand, a loose network of transnational advocacy NGOs and other grass-roots organizations have sought to address the damaging effects of tourism on destination environments and cultures, on the other, advocates of the untrammelled right to travel have forcefully claimed that any attempt to limit or to 'morally regulate' tourism in the name of conservation and/or the protection of local cultures, whether by governments or NGOs, represents an attack on such fundamental rights as the freedom to travel. Furthermore, it is argued that such constraints potentially represent an unfair hindrance on the ability of low-income states to stimulate economic development through tourism (see Butcher 2003).

While we would take issue with such a staunchly libertarian stance, this book is nevertheless concerned with upholding the ideal that *all* people regardless of class, ethnicity, gender, sexuality, religion and nationality should be able to enjoy and consume the pleasures associated with leisure and travel. However, alongside this, we will argue that a truly democratic and just tourism must be commensurate with both the right to travel as well as the demands for distributive justice and economic democracy within destination societies themselves. This takes us beyond the kind of fallacious division set up by Butcher (2003), which distinguishes between those who seek to restrict and curtail the right to travel against those for whom only mobility without ethical constraint can be justified, towards a vision of tourism that is genuinely democratic, just and egalitarian.

Tourism, citizenship and the determinants of (im)mobility

Given that the right and the ability to travel are unequally distributed among the world's population, where only a small minority is currently able to enjoy the freedom to travel for pleasure, the perception and defence of not just the right to travel but tourism itself, as a facet of citizenship, have serious social and political repercussions for disenfranchised citizens and minority populations. In examining tourist mobilities through the lens of citizenship, this book aims to construct a sociologically nuanced analysis of the differentiated patterns of mobility and the implications for the manner in which both existing and emergent constructions of citizenship are imagined, reconfigured and institutionalized.

While the economic and material inequalities both within and across states are fundamental determinants of the asymmetrical flows of people and tourists around the world, the forces shaping uneven patterns of mobility do not rest on the edifice of economics alone. Beyond material constraints, unequal access to travel is shaped by the ideologically motivated actions of states and wider discursive practices through which certain forms of mobility are selectively authorized and/or legitimated, or not as the case may be, in accordance with certain ethnic, religious, gendered and/or sexualized identities. Therefore, the right to travel presupposes the freedom to move and cross international borders free from arbitrary political constraints. The right to tourism, however, extends this to imply access to a certain disposable income and an individual's right to consume a variety of different tourism experiences, which may involve the commodification of peoples, cultures and places. It is thus a right premised upon the role of the citizen as a consumer. If one is to envisage international travel as a genuinely universal right, it cannot be left to the market alone nor defined in terms of the untrammelled right to travel and consume different places and cultures. Rather, the universal right to travel should secure the rights of people to travel and enjoy the benefits of tourism without fear of prejudice, racism or social discrimination of any kind, in a manner that is premised upon the rights of development and social justice for destination communities (see Higgins-Desbiolles 2007).

Given then, that international tourism is increasingly perceived as a marker of citizenship and a right within an increasingly globalized world, the principal focus of this book is to think through the myriad interconnections between international tourism and citizenship, particularly in the light of differentiated patterns and uneven flows of mobility. It was not so long ago that mobility was regarded as a threat and indeed still is, in the case of those defined as 'strangers' or 'outsiders'. However, in the late twentieth and early twenty-first centuries certain forms of privileged mobility and international tourism are increasingly viewed as exemplary manifestations of cosmopolitanism and a facet of a new, emergent conception of global citizenship. Our aim is that the considered reflections put forward in this book should provoke theoretically rich debates surrounding the manifold connections and dissonances between tourism and citizenships, and concerning the rights and freedoms encompassed within different modes of international travel and tourism.

Going forward

This book is about the diverse and uneven movements of people across international frontiers as tourists, and the implications that this seemingly prosaic and innocent act brings to bear on one of the most complex and contested notions of contemporary political and sociological thinking: citizenship. In this book, we develop a theoretically engaged analysis of the manifold relationships between the freedom of movement, the right to travel and differentiated notions of citizenship. The principal thrust of the argument is motivated by the fact that the sociology of tourism has for the most part ignored the significance of citizenship in both shaping participation in travel and international tourism, as well as the forms of citizenship that are expressed and indeed extended through the very act of travel and consumption of tourism experiences themselves.

With regard to the theoretical perspective adopted in this book, we argue that the discussion of tourism's manifold intersections with existing and emergent forms of citizenship cannot be left to the realms of cultural and discourse analysis alone. Rather, it must consider the politically guaranteed rights of national citizenship, in conjunction with the complex and unfolding architecture of international relations and diplomacy that facilitates and hinders cross-border mobility. While the analysis *does* acknowledge the unique role of tourism to shape social identities and engender new forms of association between travellers, and perhaps also in a minority of cases, tourists and host communities, the book argues that any understanding of tourism and citizenship must also be considered in the context of the shifting tectonics of globalizing capitalism and the geopolitical entanglements between states that are making and remaking the volatile landscapes of global travel.

Chapter 1 presents a broad overview of the principal concepts and theoretical perspectives that have historically framed diverse approaches to the understanding of citizenship. This forms the basis of our analysis of the diverse avenues through which existing ideas and practices of citizenship are implicated in (and are being reshaped by) international tourism. It begins by setting out the major ideas and debates informing our understanding of citizenship. It then examines the relationship between social welfare ideals espoused within the scope of early capitalist industrialization, the rise of the nation-state, and the democratization and historical expansion of travel in Western Europe. The chapter identifies ways in which different states through policies aimed at widening participation in leisure and travel signalled the dawn of tourism as a facet of modern citizenship. Such objectives were manifest in various experimentations of social tourism provision by different states and attempts to foster the social rights of its citizens. The discussion, however, illustrates that ideological influences and political manipulation by particular states can influence the nature and intent of public-sector support for tourism mobility. Nonetheless, the conception of modern citizenship, characterized by the state's encouragement of tourism participation as a social right, has been increasingly challenged by the expansion of the holiday as a commodity and the social differentiation of travel experiences.

Chapter 2 takes as its point of departure the changes brought about by capitalist globalization and the rise of market liberalism within European/Western societies, which have increasingly challenged the foundations of citizenship and its historic association with the sovereign territorial nation-state. The reconfiguration of states and their relationship to capital has resulted in both the emergence of 'new' elite transnational classes with minimal allegiance to the state, in tandem with the cosmopolitanization of societies brought about by large-scale and diverse forms of migration and cross-border patterns of movement (permanent and temporary). These convulsive transformations are expanding and reshaping existing conceptions of citizenship that are manifest in the unfolding dynamics and patterns of global tourism. This chapter examines these and other changes, especially the role of travel and tourist activities in creating a context within which new conceptions of citizenship are emerging, particularly in relation to ideas of global, cosmopolitan and multicultural citizenships.

Chapter 3 recognizes ways in which mobility privileges have been discursively represented and materially enabled from the colonial to the post-colonial era. It considers the diverse and contradictory interpretations of freedom underpinning international travel. It does so by interrogating further the various articulations between tourism and the ideas informing our understanding of the freedom of movement and the right to travel. It argues that an unresolved tension lies at the heart of neoliberal discourses shaping the globalization of tourism that ignores the distinction between the freedom of movement and right to travel, and the right to tourism or to be a tourist. Accordingly institutionalized discourses of tourism promote a vision of a seamless global order in which tourism brings prosperity, peace and cultural exchange to all those who participate in it. Accordingly, this chapter explores the transformation of international tourism from its association with earlier post-war ideals linked to modernization and the economic progress of developing nations, to a marketized commodity shaped by discourses of market individualism and the unfettered right to travel. It thus draws attention to the alignment between tourism and market-based renderings of citizens as consumers, which, however, belie the extent to which the rights and freedoms to travel are unevenly distributed within and across states.

Chapter 4 builds on the analysis of the freedom of movement and right to travel developed in Chapter 3. It scrutinizes the interplay between the shifting alignments of state power and capital, and the implications for the freedom of movement and right to travel. In doing so, the chapter examines the political and ideological forces at work that privilege the mobility of some while inhibiting the movement of others, focusing in particular on the role of diverse passport and visa regimes. The emerging contradictions between security and commerce and how these define the global landscapes of travel in the twenty-first century are also dealt with in this chapter. Special attention focuses on the critical role of the international airport in governing and stratifying the mobility of tourists and those without the 'right' or 'legitimate' credentials for travel. This chapter also indicates how questions of race and ethnicity shape the mobility of groups whose credentials to travel are often deemed suspect or insufficient. The argument asserts that notions of 'bona fide' tourists conceal a range of congealed discourses concerning who has the legitimate right to travel and to access the benefits of mobile citizenship. Finally, this chapter examines contradictory discourses and practices that underscore the EU's commitment to advancing freedom of movement and right to travel within its ever-hardening external frontiers. It scrutinizes the implications of this in terms of how travel and tourism determine those who are and who are not perceived to be legitimate members of the EU thus giving rise to distinctive hierarchies of citizenship within the EU as well as between EU citizens and non-members alike.

Chapter 5 examines the relationship between tourism and citizenship through the prism of geopolitics and the discourses of peace, security and risk. It examines the concept of 'tourism as peace' and how state-orchestrated policies of tourism as facilitators of peace have increasingly given way to new discourses of risk and (in) security which are shaping the parameters of global tourism. It then considers the manner in which the securitization of global tourism has arisen in the context of transnational terrorism and the targeting of tourists, and the particular implications this has for our understandings of tourism as a form of cosmopolitan global citizenship, as well as on the development rights of destination communities. It will argue that the geopolitical realignments that have emerged since the end of the Cold War, in tandem with recent events related to transnational terrorism, call into question a number of (neo)liberal assumptions that underlie the rights of mobility and freedom to travel. In this regard, the book rejects the crude instrumentalism of most other studies of tourism and terrorism, which tend to ask merely how the world can be 'made safe for tourism' rather than interrogate the underlying political, economic and ideological forces that are shaping the emerging landscapes of global tourism.

In the next chapter, Chapter 6, we critically inspect discourses of cosmopolitanism and global citizenship and how these reveal themselves in the context of 'ethical' and 'responsible' forms of travel. The consumption of such forms of travel is widely believed to carry the potential for progressive change aligned with cosmopolitan political ideals. It thus interrogates a number of debates that assume that participation in culturally and environmentally respectful forms of travel reflects the rise of a new 'active citizen' personified by the concerned tourist. Accordingly, it considers the idea that participation in ethical forms of tourist consumption constitutes a means through which tourists are able to exercise a global civic responsibility and moral commitment towards the people, places and cultures they visit. Further to this, consideration is given to the manifold ways in which the discourses and practices of ethical tourism have aligned themselves with a variety of new social movements, bringing together civil society from the local to the transnational scale, dedicated to bringing about more just, sustainable and participatory forms of tourism. In the process of doing so, these new forms of travel and civil society advocacy contest and reshape the meaning of citizenship, constituting new forms of solidarity and transnational bonds that are not reducible to consumption or enacted primarily through the mechanism of market exchange. Finally, it considers whether the embrace of tourism as a means of re-balancing the unequal relations of power between mobile and immobile peoples, based on the ideals of justice and reconciliation, genuinely heralds the potential for tourism to contribute to the nurturing of civic and participatory forms of citizenship.

This book offers a timely and original contribution to the thinking on the sociology and politics of international tourism through the lens of citizenship. In the final chapter, in addition to drawing together and synthesizing the spectrum of tourism/citizenship relations mapped in the book, we indicate a number of potential avenues for future theoretical engagement and research concerning the manifold ways in which tourism is implicated in the transformation and reshaping of the ideas and practices of contemporary citizenship. This book presents the reader with a provocative analysis of the diverse and unequal intersections between mobility, tourism and citizenship in order to challenge the normative preoccupation with order and crisis management, in which tourism is seen as a neutral and apolitical sphere of human activity. It is also highly sceptical of culturalist and discursive analyses of tourism, which have a tendency to underplay the manner in which structures of global capitalism and power mediate and shape patterns of international travel and the potential scope for a citizenship of mobility. We believe that a focus on citizenship enables us to place tourism firmly in the centre of current debates in sociology, politics and international relations. This should also therefore encourage an assessment that transcends the tendency towards isolationist thinking in tourism, and heeds the various calls to reconnect it with a more comprehensive evaluation of the wider politics of human mobility.

Notes

1   From 2003 to 2008 Indian billionaires increased their share of the nation's wealth from 1.8 per cent to 22 per cent (Halimi 2013: 2).
2   In 2005 there were 1.2 billion recorded domestic trips in China, and in 2004, 1.4 billion domestic trips were recorded in the United States (Arremberi 2009: 368).
3   Evidence published by the news agency Reuters indicates that 52 per cent of seat capacity in Asia is operated by low-cost carriers (Daga 2013).

1

TRAVELLING THROUGH CITIZENSHIP

From social rights to the consumer society

> To allow a man [*sic*] to travel is to allow him to do something that one has no
> right to deny: it is a social injustice.
>
> *(Peuchet, 1790, cited in Torpey 2000: 25)*

This chapter presents a broad overview of the principal concepts and theoretical perspectives that have historically framed interpretations of citizenship. It evaluates diverse
avenues through which existing ideas and practices of citizenship are implicated in
(and are being reshaped by) international tourism. It begins by setting out the major
ideas and debates informing our understanding of citizenship, indicating how a range
of social and economic processes originating within and beyond the state have transformed existing models of citizenship. In order to elucidate various ways in which
citizenship shapes and determines people's mobility, the chapter examines the social
welfare ideals underpinning the provision of leisure opportunities and the historical
expansion of travel. It then draws attention to the ways in which tourism access and
participation issues shed light on a social rights agenda by forming a framework with
which to comprehend tourism's relationship with the discourse of social citizenship.
The discussion identifies ways in which various state initiatives, especially those associated with the development and establishment of 'social tourism', signalled the dawn
of leisure and recreational travel as facets of modern citizenship. Nonetheless, this
chapter also demonstrates how the endeavours of states and supra-national entities to
pursue a 'tourism for all' agenda are challenged by both the growth of commoditized
forms of tourism and the growing complexity of global society.

The borders of citizenship: theories, concepts and debates

Given the profound socioeconomic transformations associated with globalization,
especially increased migration, cross-border mobility and transnational affiliations

between individuals, issues of citizenship and belonging are of significant concern for analysts and policy-makers alike. As the diverse movements of people with different cultural values 'threaten' the stability and identity of the nation-state, the very notion of *who* is a citizen has become increasingly prominent in policy circles and the broader public domain (see Riddell and Whitehead 2011; Tesfahuney 1998). It is no longer possible, therefore, to theorize exclusively about citizenship in relation to national identity and the nation-state alone. Subsequently, a fundamental question arises: How can we identify a suitably robust definition of citizenship in the age of globalization, mobility and transnationalism?

Tellingly perhaps, Turner (1994b: vii) reminds us that 'citizenship may not be a universal concept' in so far as it arose from a 'particular conjuncture of cultural and structural conditions which may be peculiar to the West'. Citizenship theorists trace the origins of modern citizenship to classical antiquity and ancient Greece. The Athenian notion of citizenship possessed no conception of democracy, which was defined by membership of the city-state. This affiliation excluded such groups as slaves and resident foreign merchants, or 'metics', from political and social representation. Significantly, 'citizens' formed a 'leisure class', which was 'exempt from gainful labour' (Sabine and Thorson 1973: 20–21). Therefore, deeply engrained attributes of social superiority and innate privilege characterized the classical principle of citizenship. For centuries afterwards, the notion of citizenship had very little, if any, connection to notions of nationhood. Rights and duties were largely the preserve of the inhabitants of medieval European towns (Weber 1958). This is markedly different from modern conceptions of citizenship associated with the evolution of the nation-state and industrial capitalism.

Modern citizenship rights, as manifest in Western capitalist democracies, are rooted in the membership of a sovereign territorial nation-state. This affiliation entitles the 'citizen' to a specific set of rights in return for a series of duties and obligations enshrined in law and/or a written constitution (e.g. payment of taxes, national insurance and social security contributions, compulsory schooling and consent to the rule of law). In the modern era, citizenship manifests the Western philosophical principles of democracy, welfare, human rights, economic development and the market economy. However, citizenship not only embodies a set of formal legal entitlements or simply, rights, guaranteed by the state and supra-state entities like such as the EU, it also encompasses a set of practices embedded in the cultural, symbolic and economic processes of the society. Isin and Wood (1999) contend that citizenship is both a status and a process continuously contested and redefined over time, and in the context of changing social, historical and political circumstances. Notions of citizenship are also often anchored in particular narratives of national or regional identity. These draw upon a variety of contested ethnic, cultural, linguistic and religious symbolisms, commonly serving to demarcate the axes along which states and regions mobilize their citizens against the 'Other' (see Handler 1988; Smith and Mar-Molinero 1996). It is also a principal means through which a variety of states and revolutionary regimes seek legitimacy to rule over ethnically, nationally and/or ideologically defined populations and territories (see Anderson 1991).

Although citizenship is 'one of the central organizing features of Western political discourse' (Hindness 1994: 19), unified notions of citizenship are problematic as they are increasingly difficult to maintain in plural societies and globalized states. Turner (1994b) highlights the influence of different national cultures and political traditions on diverse formulations of citizenship. Accordingly, it is possible to distinguish between two distinctive ideals of modern citizenship: first, where citizenship is rooted in a tradition of revolutionary struggle (as in the cases of America and France, for instance); second, where citizenship has evolved from an evolutionary, 'top-down' tradition of government (as in the case of Great Britain, for instance). During the French Revolution, for instance, the notion of the *citoyen* (derived from the Old French word for 'capital city' – *cité*) was wedded to the republican values of liberty, equality and fraternity, and centred on the bourgeois republican nation-state. Equally, these values became associated with the rights of the citizen *against* the state itself (Castles and Miller 2000: 36).

Activities and actions taking place in the nascent public realm rather than the private domain have thus helped to define notions of citizenship. Here, 'citizens could act as political agents and secure new social rights' (Turner 1997: 15). In contrast, given popular suspicion towards centralized political authority in North America, the US Constitution of 1787 reinforced a liberal–individualist definition of the citizen. This conception related to the foundation of democracy and the maximization of individual liberty, built upon the 'free development of mercantile capitalism' at the heart of which lay an enterprising (white male) citizen and property holder (Zinn 2003: 73). From the Enlightenment onwards, the evolution of Western capitalist societies was marked by two overlapping yet distinctive traditions of citizenship: (1) classical liberalism, in which citizenship is defined in relation to market society and the institution of private property; (2) modern democracy and republicanism, in which civic and political rights are the foundations of citizenship (Delanty 2000: 13). This dualism is one that is highly significant for a critical examination of the relationships between tourism and citizenship, and one that will be explored in later chapters. It lies at the heart of contrasting interpretations of the rights and freedoms implied and enacted through tourism, while signalling the existence of two, if not more, variants of citizenship (libertarian and civic) that are revealed through participation in different kinds of travel.

Modern ideas of citizenship are perhaps most commonly associated with the work of British sociologist T. H. Marshall (1992, 1963, 1964). His conception of citizenship is based largely on observations of the British post-war experience and revolves around three central pillars: civil, political and social rights. Civil rights comprise those rights deemed crucial for the complete expression of individual freedom, especially freedom of thought, speech and religion, and indeed property rights. These rights, brought about by the rise of a new capitalist bourgeoisie, came to be institutionalized in English common law, that is, 'habeas corpus' and the jury system during the seventeenth and eighteenth centuries (Isin and Turner 2007: 7–8). This element of citizenship also includes the right to enter valid contracts and the right to justice. Political citizenship evolved throughout the nineteenth and early twentieth centuries through sanctions of parliament and the extension of the franchise, thus granting the populace (initially on a limited basis) the right to participate in the exercise of such forms of political power as the right to vote or the right of access to public office. Finally, social citizenship is strongly associated with the emergence of the organized labour movement and working-class struggles over pay and the establishment of the post-war welfare state, as well as the right to access public spaces, leisure opportunities and the right to work. Marshall (1992: 8) defined social rights as: 'the right to a modicum of economic welfare and security to the right to share to the full in the social heritage and to live the life of a civilised being according to the standards prevailing in the society'.

Social rights incorporate the right of access to social institutions and to live a civilized social life, but at the same time include the right to receive financial support by the state where access becomes restricted by socio-economic circumstances that are beyond the control of the individual. Turner (2009: 70) emphasizes that the real issue here concerns the extent to which these rights can be considered as legitimate entitlements rather than simply 'claims'. Moreover, any such legitimacy rests with the prevailing politico-ideological stance of the state, together with the available economic resources to encourage such access and continued participation. However, individuals may only be eligible for social rights if they are prepared to adhere to particular social obligations or responsibilities: legal, social, environmental or otherwise. One may have the right to free primary and secondary education in the UK, for instance, but be duty-bound to attend an educational institution on a daily basis. Similarly, one may have the right to enter a UK national park for recreational purposes but have a legal responsibility to respect these public amenities, that is, not to pollute or alter that environment.

Marshall (1992) frames citizenship rights in the light of socio-economic and class inequalities that pervade advanced capitalist states. He views citizenship essentially as a buffer to the inequalities produced by capitalism, channelled through the state via redistributive social and economic policies. The state is thus the legitimate and sole sponsor of formal citizenship rights. According to Marshall (1992:18): 'Citizenship is a status bestowed on those who are "full" members of a community. All who possess the status are equal with respect to the rights and duties with which the status is endowed.' This view conceives the state as the benevolent protector of a passive citizenry. It thus ignores the way in which modern citizenship has evolved, most notably through the bargaining processes and political struggles involved in attaining such citizenship rights (Tilly 1999). In this regard, Marxist analysts stress the deficit of liberal democracies when it comes to the genuine aspirations of citizenship, highlighting the class conflict that is endemic to capitalist societies (Mann 1987; Smith 2002). Specifically, Marxist thinking takes issue with the manner in which liberal democracies emphasize the advancement of political freedoms at the expense of economic rights and democracy in the workplace. Workers may be 'free' to sell their labour in return for a wage but such freedoms come at the price of capitalists' appropriation of surpluses produced by workers, subordinating them to the demands of the market. Equally, however, liberal perspectives contend that Communism, particularly the state socialist regimes of the Soviet bloc, failed to uphold individual liberties in the face of unaccountable and authoritarian state power (see Berlin 2002; Fukuyama 1989).

Marx was critical of the formal political equality advanced by liberal democracies, emphasizing that human emancipation cannot be fully achieved in the context of prevailing material inequalities inherent in capitalist societies (Smith 2002). Radical perspectives thus, on the whole, contend that the capitalist system 'privileges the rights of citizenship and representation to corporate capital and large investors' (Gill 1998: 23). Others of a less Marxist persuasion claim that citizenship represents a status bestowed on the ruling classes or 'dominant economic class', and the 'political' and 'military rulers' (Mann 1987: 340). Nevertheless, Marx was critical of the notions of rights that were ingrained within the French and American revolutionary treatises of the late eighteenth century, which he believed espoused a notion of the citizen as an egoistic individual whose freedom is largely expressed in terms of their relation to property: 'the right of man [sic] to property is the right to enjoy his possessions and dispose of the same arbitrarily, without regard for other men, independently from society, the right of selfishness' (Marx 1977: 53).

However, liberal democratic societies, principally the United States, have historically been adept at transcending the politics of class struggle, largely by absorbing the demands of the labouring classes into a framework of civil and political rights (and to a lesser extent social rights) (Mann 1987). The demands by workers for greater equality, and to benefit from the fruits of their labour across industrialized societies, have nevertheless served to illustrate the limitations of liberal democratic models of citizenship in terms of their ability to advance genuine equality among all citizens. Although, as defenders of the liberal perspective on citizenship may argue, the promotion of a rights agenda, strongly enforced within liberal democracies, may in fact work to inhibit profit-making and act as a brake on capital accumulation. This point notwithstanding, enforcing the right to strike and protest, advancing an equal opportunities agenda for ethnic minorities and women, and imposing penalties for racial discrimination are nevertheless largely pursued within the parameters of profitability set by the capitalist political economy.

The evolution of citizenship rights within liberal capitalist democracies also manifests the struggle of the working class to expand the realm of leisure participation and access to travel opportunities. The combination of liberal and socialist ideas in different historic-political contexts reveals the ideologically diverse nature of this endeavour. Since the earliest days of industrial society, social values associated with free time, leisure and travel embodied intrinsic benefits for its participants. Over time, these values have become key indicators of a civilized society. As Clarke and Critcher's (1985: 61) seminal analysis of capitalism and leisure in Britain illustrates, by the second half of the nineteenth century industrialization and the concomitant growth of myriad forms of municipal and private entrepreneurship were driving the democratization of leisure, manifest in the growth of music halls, seaside resorts and cultural institutions (e.g. museums). Nevertheless, the expansion of leisure and holidaymaking was driven rather more by a paternalistic 'middle-class morality' and the goals of capitalist productivity, and rather less by the values and aspirations of the emerging working classes. Yet, what began as a 'moral crusade', as illustrated by the game of football whose public school origins were soon eviscerated once it was established as a professional sport in 1888, soon gave way to the commercial imperative to provide mass entertainment for the working classes (Clarke and Critcher 1985: 62).

Throughout the nineteenth century, a series of laws were enacted designed to suppress and eliminate the customary pleasures and leisure activities of the working classes. For instance, the Enclosure Act of 1793, by virtue of facilitating the privatization of land, began to reduce the amount of space that could be devoted to social activities for the masses. Later, the 1834 Poor Law Act placed restrictions on the mobility of working people, especially such groups as the balladeers and entertainers who were defined as 'vagabonds' and risked being returned to their parishes of origin by the authorities (Clarke and Critcher 1985: 56). In Britain, the institutionalization of routinized leisure and paid holidays served as a counterpoint to the heavy toil of industrial labour. It was the squalor of the Victorian industrial towns and the subsequent 'concern' of the ruling class for the health and well-being of its workers that precipitated the large-scale construction of a leisure-based infrastructure for the benefit of the masses, under the influence of what became known as the 'rational recreation' movement. Notwithstanding genuine aspirations for a healthier and more contented populace, the overwhelming motivation for the development of leisure and growing levels of working-class forms of travel was to quell working-class dissent and simultaneously improve productivity. By the late nineteenth century, however, leisure and holiday travel had become increasingly commodified and incorporated into the expanding sphere of capitalist production itself, providing a platform for the democratization of leisure and holidaymaking, albeit through the mechanism of private enterprise.

The development of social tourism, or rather, socialized forms of tourism, was to become prevalent in both social democratic states and state socialist societies in Eastern Europe. While socialized forms of leisure and travel reflected the needs of capitalist profitability in the 'West', in the Soviet Union and other socialist states social tourism became a crucial plank of communist ideology and a means of forging a new socialist citizen. Across Europe and to a lesser extent North America, a plethora of voluntary, faith and workers' organizations began to lobby and provide for enhanced leisure and holiday opportunities for the working classes and socially disadvantaged members of society. However, given the distinctive politico-ideological contexts in which they were conceived, while the principle of the right to travel underlies most Western social tourism programmes, in contrast, collective forms of social tourism in Eastern Europe were developed in tandem with severe constraints on the freedom of movement (Diekmann and McCabe 2011: 419).

Social reform and the ability to travel: social citizenship practices

Przeclawski (1988: 11) claims that tourism has the potential to enable humanity to 'reach the true value of modern man [sic]'. The perception of tourism as a valued ideal and social right arguably has its origins in the pioneering endeavours of such individuals as Thomas Cook. The increase in the productive labour of the working classes and state intervention granting time off from work were crucial to this new conception of tourism. In the UK, the passing of the Factory Acts commencing in 1802 and the Bank Holiday Act of 1871 marked a series of reforms designed to limit working hours and enhance participation in the leisure and the social life of the community. However, it was not until paid annual holidays became enshrined within a framework of law (e.g. UK Holidays with Pay Act in 1938) that the material foundations of tourism as a social right were clearly established (Haulot 1981). In the United States officially sanctioned holidays were only to be established after the New Deal was launched by Roosevelt in 1932 (Inglis 2000: 50). Notable distinctions in statutory leisure time and variations in cultural attitudes towards work and recreation continue to exist between North America and Western Europe, as indeed they do elsewhere.

The frontier spirit of the early pioneers established clear foundations for widening access to travel in North America, augmented by the work of transport entrepreneurs such as J. C. Fargo, whose annoyance at not being able to transport cash easily from one place to another, particularly overseas, eventually led to the creation of the traveller's cheque in 1891. This development was complemented by the establishment and expansion of one of the world's leading travel financial conglomerates, American Express, which pioneered effective ways to ensure that currency, securities and goods were efficiently mobile (Goldstone 2001). Widening access to travel and its commercialization in the nineteenth century did not, however, pass without human tragedy. In the US, for instance, competition in the steamboat industry was relentless, leading to the number of accidents and passenger deaths becoming a national concern by the early 1850s. Steamboats often touted aggressively to attain more passengers, and often operated with excess numbers as they raced one another to arrive earlier than scheduled at their given destinations. Even after the passing of the Steamboat Act of 30 May 1852, which led to the mandate of a federal maritime inspection and the formalization of captain licences, serious accidents continued to occur. Two months following this legislation, 80 passengers on the *Henry Clay* died on the Hudson River due to its engine overheating after racing a rival steamboat (White 2011).

In Britain, a combination of Victorian paternalism and the struggle for shorter working hours and improved working conditions in the factories eventually influenced the extension of rights concerning the advancement of routinized leisure and the ability of the working classes to travel for pleasure. In the midst of the transformation from a static to a mobile state, Thomas Cook famously brought mobility to the masses at a time when tourism was considered to be a 'social menace and then as a bad joke' (Brendon 1991: 1). His initial motives were fundamentally religious ones, rooted in a desire to improve people's minds, bodies and spirits through the development of temperance excursions. Cook was also motivated by a genuine desire to emancipate workers from the drudgery of factory labour, utilizing tourism to help promote 'universal brotherhood' (1991: 31). Although he was no revolutionary, his organized mass excursion to a working men's meeting in Paris in 1861 was one notable event that reflected his altruistic approach to tourism (Turner and Ash 1975: 53). He also enabled women to travel without their husbands, which prompted Brendon to comment that Cook made 'a significant contribution to female emancipation' (1991: 52). In reply to criticisms of the 'vulgarity' of 'his' tourists from the upper echelons of society, Cook is said to have remarked that the tours were simply 'agencies for the advancement of human progress' (Boorstin 1963: 96).

By the 1870s, a more business-focused mindset began to eclipse the philanthropic endeavour of Thomas Cook's earlier work, especially when the firm came under the control of his son, John Mason Cook. Subsequently, there was a progressive realization that tourism could be a highly profitable enterprise and that corporate prestige could result from being associated with the full scope and scale of the British imperial enterprise. By the late nineteenth century, Thomas Cook & Son had become one of the world's leading tour companies with a monopoly on numerous transport agencies, including Egyptian passenger steamers on the Nile (Turner and Ash 1975). The only other competitive threat to the company's power and influence in the emerging enterprise of international travel was the growth of American Express across the Atlantic, whose influence was to extend into Europe through the advent of traveller's cheques (see Goldstone 2001). While Cook extended the possibility of affordable travel to the working and middle classes of northern Europe, it was the combined influence of the emergent labour movement and the expansion of state welfare provision in the twentieth century, that later signalled the genuine impulse towards the democratization of travel for the working classes.

According to Rifkin (2000: 149), Cook 'probably deserves to be regarded as the father also of cultural production and the first practitioner of experiential capitalism'. The logic behind this association relates to the fact that Cook traded in the commodification of experiences and cultural encounters, adopted a 'supplier–user' model of travel planning, and applied the law of mass standardization to the packaging of tourism – half a century before Henry Ford's mass production of cars. Cook not only pioneered the development of excursions and package tourism, he was also instrumental in disseminating ideas and knowledge about travel. He established travel magazines, most notably the *Excursionist*, published shortly after the 1851 Great Exhibition, which by 1892 had an international circulation of 120,000. Its distribution list included America, Austria, Australia, France, Germany and India (Steward 2005). Cook's business also issued guidebooks and from 1875 sold on average 10,000 copies yearly. These guidebooks enhanced an existing market of travel handbooks and guides already established by Karl Baedeker, a German publisher which produced guidebooks for various countries including Canada, Egypt and India (Mackenzie 2005).

Recreational tourism was still, however, very much a minority pursuit in the mid-nineteenth century. Widening participation was borne out of the struggle between the working classes and the rulers of Victorian Britain to defend certain forms of working-class leisure, as well as to expand forms of leisure within the cultural, social and legal constraints prescribed by the state. As a direct consequence of the working-class struggle for paid holidays and for an end to exploitative working conditions and a decent wage, the right to a paid holiday was to become closely intertwined with struggles over access to Britain's enclosed, privately owned countryside. In the Lake District, for instance, local councils attempted to preserve footpaths and extend public access to lake shorelines, sometimes resulting in prolonged court cases with landowners. Councils also became active in environmental protection and the reduction of risk associated with lake-based recreation (O'Neil 2005). In 1932, the right of citizens to access a network of public footpaths (sometimes referred to as the 'right to roam'), even where they traversed privately owned land, was given a significant boost by the organized mass trespass on Kinder Scout in the Derbyshire Peak District (England). This event was organized by the British Workers' Sports Federation in 1932 and subsequently led to the passage of the National Parks and Access to the Countryside Act in 1949, which required every council in England and Wales to map all rights-of-way in their jurisdiction (Solnit 2002: 166).

Concern among governing bodies over the 'right of access' to public spaces was also echoed in other industrialized societies during a similar period. Ford's (2009) historical analysis of beach culture and entertainment in Sydney (Australia), for instance, observed that in the early twentieth century the Department of Land in Sydney came to the realization that beaches should be freely utilized by the public and not subjected to entrepreneurial takeover by amusement companies. The public had a noteworthy role in drawing attention to concerns over restricted access to public space, placing pressure on the authorities to take action. Elsewhere, in central and northern Europe, the access of ordinary citizens to the countryside received a significant boost through the growth of voluntary associations, rambling clubs and youth groups. In Germany, for instance, there were youth organizations such as *Jugendbewegung* and *Wandervögel* ('migratory birds') whose central intentions were to enable people to escape the cities of Berlin and Hamburg in order to spend time in the countryside. These and similar organizations in Europe sought to improve access to the countryside for working people and were often inspired by radical or progressive political ideas. In Austria, for example, the slogan of the anti-monarchist *Naturfreunde* ('Friends of Nature') was 'berg frei' or free mountains (Solnit 2002: 156). Naturfreunde International has since become a transnational movement partly concerned with ensuring that nature is accessible to the wider community.

Many of these movements presage the emergence of discourses of 'tourism as peace', to be discussed in greater detail in Chapter 5. Indeed the first youth hostel to be established in France in 1930 was named the Home of Peace (Caire 2011: 83). Also, the German schoolteacher Richard Schirrmann had an influential role in promoting travel as a natural facilitator in achieving friendship, harmony and social accord. During the early part of the twentieth century he would take his students on visits to the German countryside, and at the same time exhorted them to cultivate a curiosity and appreciation for strangers, particularly people from other cultures and different linguistic backgrounds. Schirrmann was the founder of the first youth hostel in Altenia Castle, Germany, in 1912. The hostelling phenomenon spread throughout

Europe and then later America. However, the US was initially reluctant to encourage youth hostel development due to its perceived association with Nazism and the German state. Nonetheless, the International Youth Hostel Federation in its convention emphasizes that hostelling exists to encourage 'young people', particularly those with 'limited means' to travel widely for educational purposes (Moisă 2008: 162). Just prior to and after the Second World War, important changes in the scale and modus operandi of socialized leisure and tourism began to take place as a more mobile, culturally diverse and prosperous era began to dawn across Europe. Increasingly, the wider provision of opportunities for leisure, travel and holidays moved from a loose network of voluntary and faith-based organizations to part of the expanding structures of state welfare across much of Western Europe. In the Eastern bloc states, however, the ideological imperatives of Communism continued to determine the nature, structure and purpose of social tourism.

Travel is 'good for you': commodifying the social benefits of leisure and pleasure

The assumption that travel is fundamentally 'good for you' has become deeply embedded in the value systems of advanced capitalist societies. In the book, *The Importance of Being Lazy*, Gini (2003) indicates that the substance of 'doing nothing' or engaging in non-work activities and vacations was a response to growing US economic prowess after the Second World War, together with the view that Americans should have the right to enjoy the fruits of their labour. Ironically, though, this implies that economically, 'unproductive' groups (e.g. the homeless, temporary workers, the unemployed and single-parent households) do not have a moral or social entitlement to travel.

As a consequence of the rebalancing of work and free time in industrial capitalist societies, leisure and tourism are now commonly perceived to provide a range of social benefits (see Hall and Brown 2012). Social analysts thus been keen to stress that non-participation in tourism is an indicator of social exclusion and relative deprivation (Hughes 1991; Roberts 2004; Stephenson and Hughes 1995). A number of empirical studies have sought to examine these concerns, indicating the social worth associated with taking a holiday (see McCabe 2009; Smith and Hughes 1999; Stephenson 2002). For example, McCabe's (2009: 675) study provides reasons for taking a holiday among low-income families in the UK, such as the desire to lead a 'normal life', which suggests that travel is not only perceived as a social need but a benchmark of civilized life, that is, to be a full citizen. Smith and Hughes' (1999) study of economically and socially disadvantaged families with young children in the county of Yorkshire (UK) concludes that holidays provide opportunities for families to strengthen their social relationships. With regard to ethnic minorities in particular, Stephenson (2002) demonstrates the social importance of UK citizens of Caribbean descent holidaying in their ancestral homelands, with the effect of encouraging individuals to re-establish kinship and cultural associations across territorial states.

A range of 'appropriate', social forms of tourism can thus help to generate positive human outcomes for both tourists and the inhabitants of destinations. In certain respects, tourism can embody liberated experiences and transformative lifestyles, distinct from the mundane norms of everyday life. It has been suggested by certain writers that the social need to engage in tourism activities somehow relates to a need to transcend feelings of alienation that result from living in 'socially dislocated' societies (MacCannell 1999). Tourism has been described in anthropological terms as a 'ritualistic inversion' through which the 'profane' experience of work is suspended, albeit temporarily, when passing into the 'sacred' arena of tourism (Graburn 1989). Nonetheless, tourism participation can also often embody a self-centred dimension, helping to enhance one's ego (Dann 1977) and elevating one's social status (Crompton 1979); one of several unresolved tensions within contemporary forms of tourism. Appropriately, Urry (1990: 5) notes:

> To be a tourist is one of the characteristics of the 'modern' experience. Not to 'go away' is like not possessing a car or a nice house. It is a marker of status in modern societies and is also thought to be necessary to health ... If people do not travel, they lose status: travel is a marker of status. It is a crucial element of modern life to feel that travel and holidays are necessary. 'I need a holiday' is the surest reflection of a modern discourse based on the idea that people's physical and mental health will be restored if only they can 'get away' from time to time.

The evolution of industrial capitalist societies and the framework of citizenship rights associated with the emergence of the modern nation-state, reflects forms of leisure and tourism that are thought to have the potential to advance health and well-being. The therapeutic benefits of travel were associated with the flourishing of spa towns across Europe throughout the eighteenth century and the subsequent growth of English seaside resorts, which emerged in tandem with industrialization and railway expansion (Inglis 2000). Therapeutic forms of tourism were also integral to the development of tourism in islands such as Madeira and the Canary Islands, whose milder climes attracted north European sufferers of respiratory illnesses from the mid-eighteenth century onwards (González Lemus 1999). Nonetheless, spa tourism, like other forms of health tourism, was largely the preserve of the elite leisure class. In the UK, for example, certain spa resorts (e.g. Bath and Tunbridge Wells) were closely associated with members of the Royal Family and thus perceived to be rather exclusive and fashionable (Ward 1998).

One social commentator refers to a condition known as 'Vacation Deficit Disorder', where long working hours and general holiday deprivation equates to stress, heart strain and burnout, and generally unhealthy lifestyles (Robinson 2003). To this end, new versions of travel emphasizing intrinsic health benefits and spiritual and mental well-being have proliferated in recent years (Smith 2003a). These recuperative forms of travel invoke the welfare ideals associated with an earlier epoch of socialized travel and harnesses them to the development of luxury tourism products in upmarket resorts. Well-being and remedial programmes will no doubt continue to be one of the prime components of the future marketing strategies of luxury tour operators and hotel companies. The spa tourism market, for instance, is looking towards new innovative developments, notably in the field of thalassotherapy. The multinational hotel giant, Accor, is developing the Thalassa brand name and running its Thalassa Sea & Spa products in conjunction with its Sofitel hotel brand (Oakley 2012). Another such innovation is reflected in the trend towards halal spas in Indonesia, which are becoming increasingly popular, offering unique Islamic-friendly services (e.g. headscarf styling) and utilizing a range of 'halal-friendly' cosmetics, which are free from pork derivatives (Woo 2011). This movement mirrors a larger global development towards the expansion of the Islamic hospitality industry and the growing affluence of tourists from emerging economies (see Stephenson in press (2014a)).

A further sign of the growing cross-fertilization of travel and well-being can be witnessed in the proliferation of international medical travel (see Ormond 2013). Although there are obvious difficulties in terms of quantifying the phenomenon of medical tourism, largely because no universal definition of what constitutes a medical tourist actually exists, some broad estimates do indicate that it is an increasingly popular trend with significant market potential. It is estimated that over 4.3 million medical tourists visited Asian countries in 2010, producing total revenue in excess of US\$6.7 billion (KPMG 2011: 11). India, Singapore and Thailand are three of the most popular Asian destinations for medical tourism developments, where the cost of medical procedures is far less than in many developed capitalist economies. In 2011, the medical charge for a heart bypass in India, for instance, was around US\$10,000, while in the US it stood at around US\$113,000. Heart valve replacement in Thailand was around US\$9,500, while in the US it was US\$150,000. Other emerging economy countries provide cheaper healthcare options. Knee replacement in Mexico, for instance, is around US\$14,650 compared to US\$48,000 in the US (Lunt *et al.* 2011: 12). Lower prices for medical assistance mean that individuals and families are able to go to the medical tourism destination as part of a wider, all-inclusive holiday.

On a political level, however, it could be read that the movement of medical tourists from advanced capitalist states to 'developing' countries (or emerging economies) in search of cheaper medical options is partly a consequence of the failings of the tourist-generating state to provide affordable healthcare. Therefore, in one sense, medical tourism could be seen to serve the purpose of exposing the deficiencies of industrialized states in upholding the social rights of (and obligations to) its citizens in the provision of a socially sustainable and economically accessible healthcare system. For example, it was estimated by the Commonwealth Fund study that around 44 per cent (81 million) of US adults were either underinsured or uninsured in 2010, compared to 75 million in 2007 (Science Daily 2011). Also, the 2011 Commonwealth Fund Health Insurance Tracking Survey of US Adults estimated that over one-quarter (26 per cent) of all Americans of working age experienced a gap in health insurance cover (Medical News Today 2012). On the other hand, some US companies that do offer medical insurance are starting to organize medical tourism treatment through offshore arrangements and partnerships with hospitals and clinics in such countries as India, Mexico, Singapore and Thailand (United States–Mexico Chamber of Commerce 2011).

Certain types of medical tourism (e.g. 'euthanasia tourism', 'fertility and reproductive tourism' and 'transplant tourism') raise significant ethical concerns as well as indicate the capacities of the market and capital to commoditize (and corporatize) the human body through the tourism industry. Transplant tourism, for instance, concerns those tourists who have a material advantage over the body parts of those who are at a material disadvantage, that is, the less well off. According to Scheper-Hughes (2004: 36) in her ethnographic study of organ trafficking: 'Transplant tourism has become a vital asset to the medical economies of rapidly privatizing hospitals and clinics in poorer countries struggling to stay afloat.' One impoverished community in the port area of Baseco in Manila, known locally as 'No-Kidney Island' (Isla Walang Bato), has a notorious record for individuals selling their own kidneys. Almost a decade ago, an estimated 3,000 individuals out of a community of 50,000 had sold one of their kidneys (Aguilar and Siruno 2004). The Philippine Health Secretary expressed a desire to lift restrictions prohibiting the donation of kidneys by Filipinos to foreigners, suggesting that a US$3,000 gratitude package could be provided to donors. However, such government support may run the risk of reinvigorating the organ donor market (Wilson 2010). The notion that individuals should be able to construct their own healthcare plans and seek out treatment on the basis of their income, as implied in the notion of 'medical citizenship', reflects a debased neoliberal notion of rights, and further reinforces the material inequalities that lie at the heart of this particular form of cross-border travel (see Scheper-Hughes 2004). As a consequence of the material inequalities that are expressed through travel, tourist-generating (organ-recipient) societies are able to determine and shape the lives and livelihoods of those residing in tourist-receiving (organ-donor) nations.

Smith (2012) develops a critique of the neoliberal approach to medical forms of tourism in the context of developing countries. Her argument asserts that medical tourism advances a division between a highly developed private sector accommodating foreigners and rich nationals, and an under-resourced and quality-deficient health sector for the mass (local) population. A number of other studies have examined the phenomenon of medical tourism (Alsharif *et al.* 2010; Leng 2010; Leng and Whittaker 2010). Leng (2010) notes, for instance, that in Malaysia and Singapore the public sector encourages the expansion of the private medical tourism industry, suggesting that healthcare equity and public healthcare provision are not being prioritized. These two states, for instance, are proactive in the promotion and marketing activities of medical tourism. In the case of Malaysia, the government provides tax incentives for medical tourism developments, leading to a growing gap between public- and private-sector health service provision. Indeed, medical tourism throws up a range of complex issues that shed light on the reconfiguration of citizenship in twenty-first-century societies. Although medical tourism can be seen as a disturbing manifestation of the extension of commodification into the realms of healthcare, illustrating in turn, the neoliberal scaling-back of universal health provision in many European societies, a more nuanced reading suggests that links between international travel and the consumption of healthcare are far more complex. Indeed, Ormond's (2011b) analysis of medical tourism in emerging economies such as Malaysia demonstrates how it has been mobilized in the context of domestic healthcare reform, that is, privatization, as well as being harnessed to Malaysia's drive towards becoming a technologically advanced, consumer-driven economy.

Other issues concerning the relationship between medical tourism and citizenship relate to the problem of possible medical malpractice in the destination country, as well as ongoing health difficulties that may arise following treatment and repatriation to the home country. Accordingly, the main questions concern the issue of who is responsible (or liable) to ensure that the medical tourist is fully compensated and/or eligible for further treatment. Such situations are legally complex because of the range of parties involved: the citizen's own state, the destination state, the medical tourist, the private medical centre/hospital and the medical-tourist intermediary (see Cohen 2010).

Earlier notions of leisure and travel as social rights and as citizenship benefits to be enjoyed by all members of society regardless of income, class or race have thus increasingly been eroded by the ascendancy of neoliberalism and 'market fundamentalism'. While the state had previously seen its support for the provision of leisure and holidaymaking as part of its duty to protect underprivileged citizens from the vagaries of the market, neoliberal policy-making has significantly reduced this role. Indeed, as services and cultural industries increasingly began to supplant manufacturing and agriculture within advanced capitalist economies, capital's search for new avenues of profitability have fuelled the commodification of leisure and 'free time' and the shift towards more market-oriented tourism provision. Leisure and travel opportunities supported by the state in many ways underpin a Marshallian conception of citizenship in which the state viewed leisure and tourism as expressions of welfare and social rights. However, the retreat of the state from this role, under the disciplinary tutelage of neoliberal politics, has seen tourism become one of the world's leading economic activities left primarily to the market. This advancement is most welcomed by the libertarian position, which emphasizes the importance of 'depoliticizing citizenship' in order 'to convert the public realm into an ersatz version of the market' (Miller 1995: 443).

Social tourism and 'tourism for all': all but a dream?

As discussed previously, by the 1930s many European governments had begun to conceive and provide legislative frameworks for leisure and travel in terms of social rights for the benefit of all, regardless of income or class background. Not only had legislation institutionalized the entitlement to a holiday, such as the 1938 Holidays with Pay Act in Britain, the capacity of the working classes to benefit from their new-found rights was also later enhanced by the opportunities for cheap travel afforded by the nationalized state-run railways. The notion of 'social tourism', borne out of international recognition of the basic human right to rest, leisure, reasonable working hours and paid holidays, was duly expressed in the Universal Declaration of Human Rights (United Nations 1948). In broad terms, social tourism can be defined as the provision of subsidized holidays for those social groups on low and modest incomes, or who would otherwise be unable to afford to participate in a holiday. In addition the Montreal Declaration recognizes that

> making tourist leisure accessible to all – including families, youth and the elderly – necessarily means being involved in the struggle against inequality and the exclusion of the culturally different, those of limited means or abilities, or those who live in developing countries.
>
> *(International Bureau of Social Tourism 1996: 2)*

The definition and organizational basis of social tourism varies considerably both within and across those states where such programmes exist (Minnaert *et al.* 2011). These differences also relate to aspects of cultural specificity and the political economy in shaping distinctive welfare state structures (and thus holiday entitlements) and variations in patterns of holiday consumption. One significant contrast identified by Richards (1998: 158) is between the corporatist social welfare regimes of Western Europe, with a well-engrained culture of subsidized leisure and travel, with the exception of the UK, and the liberal time-constrained societies of Japan and North America.

Historically, social tourism has been organized and financed by a range of public authorities, commercial companies, charitable organizations, trade unions and inter-governmental agencies, and this support has usually varied in relation to the ideological and political circumstances of each individual state. At an international level, the International Bureau of Social Tourism was founded in Brussels in 1963 to campaign for the establishment of paid holidays as a universal right and encourage states to make provisions for all citizens to enjoy the benefits of leisure and tourism. Measures also include the 'inalienable right held by every citizen' to appreciate culture, art, nature and the common heritage of mankind (Haulot 1981: 211). In this regard, the remit of social tourism dovetails to an extent with the work of the United Nation's premier cultural organization, UNESCO (the United Nations Educational, Scientific and Cultural Organization), in the arena of cultural and natural heritage. UNESCO of course seeks to encourage 'the identification, protection and preservation of cultural and natural heritage around the world considered to be of outstanding value to humanity' (UNESCO n.d. *World Heritage*). Echoing the UN Charter, World Heritage sites are endorsed as the property of all human beings irrespective of the territory on which they are located. They are mobilized as instruments of inter-cultural understanding and economic development, and are often regarded as vital repositories of cosmopolitanism. As World Heritage speaks to the citizens of the world, it seeks to transcend the ethnic, religious and national moorings of cultural heritage.

The advanced capitalist states of Western mainland Europe arguably have a stronger tradition of social tourism provision than in the UK. France, for instance, historically benefited from the provision of social tourism, which developed from the early twentieth century through the combined efforts of youth groups, trade unions and faith-based societies. The scope of social tourism provision was further expanded once it became firmly integrated within the structures of the French state in 1936 by the Popular Front government, which created a sub-secretary for the organization of leisure and sports and also implemented paid holidays (Caire 2011: 83). Nevertheless, it was not until after the war that significant numbers of French workers would benefit from social tourism policies due to the prohibitive cost of train travel and lack of car ownership. Such was the support for the principles of social tourism in post-war France that attempts by the French government to expand luxury foreign tourism (from the US) within France were met by strong resistance from communist trade unions that believed that exclusive forms of tourism would undermine popular working-class tourism (Endy 2004: 67–70). Caire (2011), however, points out that social tourism in France was motivated by the desire to integrate different social groups as opposed to simply enabling the poorest and most underprivileged members of French society to engage in leisure and travel.

Trade unions have occupied a central role in the organization and provision of social tourism in some states, primarily through the reinvestment of their members' subscriptions in various initiatives. In Switzerland, for instance, the Swiss Travel Fund (REKA), operating since 1939, is based on a travel endowment jointly established by the tourism industry, trade unions, employers and co-operatives. REKA has been responsible for building its own holiday centres offering heavily discounted and free holidays to specific groups identified as special-need categories, especially single mothers and their children (Teuscher 1983). In contrast, in the UK, the paucity of social tourism schemes, mainly supported by charities and inner-city left-wing local authorities, reflects an altogether more liberal tradition of citizenship in which the rights of the individual to enjoy freedom from state intervention have historically held sway. The approach to social tourism adopted in France, however, was more collectivized and developed through state promotion, until market-driven reforms and the liberalization of welfare-state regimes precipitated the movement towards privatized forms of travel provision (Richards 1998). As Endy (2004) illustrates, during the early post-war period, while the US was extolling the virtues of free trade and tourism to France, the French left and Communist-backed trade unions were increasingly critical of the desire by some members of the French government to devote scarce resources to attract wealthy foreign tourists to France. Rather, they lobbied for state subsidies to enable French workers to go on vacation. Traditionally, French government had been more concerned with bolstering social and labour policies in the context of post-war reconstruction, paying only scant attention to supporting overseas tourism promotion and providing minimum financial assistance to its hotel industry (Endy 2004).

Nazi Germany too had a clear vision to produce affordable holidays for the masses at home and abroad. The Nazis embraced leisure and tourism to cultivate the 'perfect citizen'. This mirrored similar trends towards the development of social tourism in other parts of Europe at the time, albeit one that was devoted to the explicit ideological aims of the Third Reich. At the centre of this vision lay the KdF-Seebad Rügen project and the planned beach resort complex of Prora, developed on the island of Rügen in the Baltic Sea between 1936 and 1939 (Löfgren 2002: 241–243). This vast seaside complex was designed to accommodate up to 20,000 tourists at a time. However, due to the outbreak of the Second World War, the project was never fully completed. Holidays to the seaside complex at Prora were to be run through the organization 'Strength through Joy' (*Kraft durch Freude* or KdF). The KdF programme was established in 1933 with a mandate to provide accessible and purposeful leisure for workers. The organization was involved in providing affordable leisure such as sport activities, cruise ship holidays, concerts, libraries, day trips and holidays. By 1934, an estimated 2.3 million people had taken KdF holidays, rising to 10.3 million in 1938 (Mason 1993: 160). Löfgren (2002: 244) describes the project at Prora as 'modern mass tourism taken to its extreme'. According to Baranowski (2004: 2), 'Strength through Joy testified to the Nazi regime's desire to convince its racially "valuable" citizens that it enhanced their well being'. In addition, it functioned more specifically as a means of rebuilding the German psyche and reinvigorating the German nation in preparation for war.

KdF was an organization devoted to delivering the ideological objectives of the Third Reich. It was a 'tool for controlling leisure and creating a classless *Volksgemeinshcaft* of hobbyists, tourists, and pleasure-seekers' (Löfgren 2002: 241). The KdF was motivated by a desire to provide 'ordinary' German citizens with affordable access to leisure and travel, which would thereby enhance their productivity at work. It was also a key instrument of the Nazis' racialized ideology and functioned as a vital means of strengthening the identification of the workforce with the German nation and race (Baranowski 2004). The Third Reich apparently also had a wider international strategy for the development of seaside resorts. Blackpool, despite being the centre for the production of the Wellington bomber, escaped bombardment by the Luftwaffe due to its strategic importance as a place of leisure and recreation. Historic documents have been unearthed in Germany suggesting that there was an intention for this resort to be utilized as a base and recreational centre for German troops and civilians after the anticipated invasion of Britain in the early 1940s (Tran 2009).

Germany was not alone in developing social forms of tourism determined by overt ideological agendas. From the mid-1920s, the Italian Fascist party worked closely with *Opera Nazionale Dopolavoro* (National Recreation Club) to provide workers with constructive leisure time. This organization was closely associated with the Fascist party from the mid-1920s. Like KdF, the organization's main motive concerned the rationalization of leisure use and higher labour productivity. Although there was nothing overtly 'fascist' about the structure and function of *Dopolavoro*, it was nonetheless a social instrument of the Fascist state (De Grazia 1981). With the collapse of the two major Fascist states, the post-war period witnessed the expansion of Communist rule throughout Eastern Europe where the approach to social tourism was underpinned by the need to reinforce ideological discipline and loyalty to the state and party (Allcock and Przeclawski 1990). In these states the social tourism agenda was also significantly more directed towards domestic tourism development rather than the encouragement of Western tourism or, indeed, outbound travel, which was severely limited. The political rationale behind this approach concerned the view that by restricting Western tourists the populations of Communist states would be protected from two threats: first, the corruptive forms of tourism associated with bourgeois values and capitalist consumption; second, subservience to the corporate interests of foreign capital.

In the Soviet Union, the regulation of inbound travel was monopolized by the state-controlled *Intourist* agency, as foreign travellers were deemed potentially dangerous, representing a threat to the values of the socialist system. While foreign inbound tourism provided much-needed foreign currency, domestic tourism was part of a socialist educational agenda to foster communist ideals of solidarity and social unity among the workers. In the former Yugoslavia, attempts were made to create a common sense of Yugoslav citizenship based on a shared commitment to socialist ideals that would transcend inter-ethnic differences (Allcock 1995: 106). The slogan *bratstvo i jedinstvo* (brotherhood and unity) was manifest in the construction of a highway by Tito linking Croatia and Serbia, two of the nations that had been brought together under the Yugoslav Federation (Ignatieff 1995). In fact, the development of social tourism in a range of Eastern European countries became an important ethos of state development. Production enterprises, workers' organizations and the state worked towards the provision of social tourism largely based on domestic leisure travel (Kaspar 1981). However, the problem for such Eastern European countries as Bulgaria, which was one of the most internationalized destinations of all Eastern bloc states, was the extent to which the international tourism sector conflicted with the imperatives of centralized planning and the state's ideological commitment to national social tourism policies. This concern indicates a dilemma, witnessed elsewhere (e.g. post-war France), between ensuring that traditional state-subsidized forms of tourism have been adequately resourced and that the budgets for international tourism development are sufficiently financed to attract much-needed foreign exchange (Pearlman 1981). The disintegration of the Eastern bloc and subsequent marketization of the economy subsequently led to the destruction of many social tourism policies and programmes, exacerbated by the collapse of centralized planning and tourism provision in Eastern Europe (Richards 1992).

That is not to say that post-Communist states have not learnt from the benefits of proactive public-sector involvement. From 1 January 2013, around 400,000 residents of Tallinn (Estonia) were eligible for free transportation on buses, trams and trolleybuses. This initiative, subsidized by Tallinn City Government, illustrates how the public sector can aim to ensure 'equal opportunities to all social strata' (Davis 2013) in the mobility of its local residents. Although this is an intriguing illustration of how mobility can be embedded within a citizenship agenda and ways in which social tourism initiatives can have progressive socio-economic outcomes, it also indicates that social tourism directives can also be developed to constructively influence the natural environment. In this case, the anticipated decrease in car usage in urban areas through use of public transport equates to significant reductions in carbon dioxide emissions.

There are certain parts of the world where social forms of tourism continue to be moulded by an overt government ideology and state-led principles, particularly in those few states representing bastions of anti-capitalist values and socialist ideals. Venezuela, for instance, has made significant steps towards a public-sector-controlled tourism industry as part of its overall socialist-inspired economic development strategy. The government established the national tourist agency, Venetur, which not only organizes tourism packages but also operates a chain of nationalized hotels. In addition, the Hilton Hotel in Caracas was taken over by the state in 2005, followed by the acquisition of the Hilton on Margarita Island in 2009 (Steinmetz 2009a). According to former President Chávez: 'We're socialising tourism, rather than elite tourism, we're promoting popular [accessible to the majority] tourism, social tourism' (Villarreal 2012). The development of social forms of tourism only started to evolve towards the end of Chávez's second period of office, as reflected in the establishment of the Ministry of People's Power for Tourism (which has responsibility for Venetur), so its effectiveness in encouraging equitable forms of tourism participation for Venezuelan citizens has yet to stand the test of time. Nonetheless, this strategic imperative could very well change track in the post-Chávez era.

More recently, the notion of subsidized holidays has been promoted within the European Union as part of a wider initiative to promote tourism as a means of forging closer integration between the peoples and economies of the 28 member states. One such programme is the EU Calypso Programme, the stated purpose of which is to enable 'underprivileged citizens across Europe' to travel as well as 'to create a sense of European identity' (CEC 2010a).[1] The underlying principles of the programme speak both to the desire by the EU to promote universal access to travel, as well as an attempt to forge new ideas of transnational citizenship at a supra-national level: 'Every European citizen should have the right to travel. And what better way to build a sense of European citizenship than through cultural exchange?' (CEC 2010a). The EU Commissioner for Enterprise and Industry supported these sentiments, indicating that the EU should be able to advance the rights of the disabled, pensioners and young families with financial difficulties to claim subsidies to travel, by contributing up to nearly one-third of the cost of the holiday (Tourism Review 2010). There is considerable variation in policies for social tourism standards of accessibility across EU member states. However, as Ambrose (2012) notes, the foundation of a new strategic 'road map' for accessible tourism, particularly for the disabled communities, has been recognized by the European Network for Accessible Tourism. This directive purports to support greater transnational coherence across the EU. It includes the prioritization of accessible tourism as the principal responsibility of public-sector tourism providers, valued contributions from the industry and business, the development of a training curriculum at EU level for tourism workers and key personnel, and the effective advancement of employment opportunities in the tourism sector for disabled people.

In southern Europe, whose populations have not experienced overseas travel to the extent of Northern Europeans, governments have traditionally provided a greater degree of support for the collective consumption of leisure and travel. In Spain, the election of the moderate socialist government in 1982 signalled a new era of democracy and rights for ordinary people in a country previously ruled by a right-wing dictatorship between 1939 and 1975. Among the many gains implemented were the *Programa de Vacaciones para Mayores y para Mantenimiento del Empleo en las Zonas Turísticas* (Holiday Programme for Elderly Citizens and Employment in Tourism Destinations), approved in 1985 and run by IMSERSO within the Spanish Ministry of Health, Social Security and Equality (IMSERSO 2013). Although the survival of the programme has been under severe pressure since the onset of the 2007–2008 financial crisis, as the name of the programme itself suggests, its purpose is to provide subsidized holidays for retired Spaniards and boost off-season employment in tourism destination areas (see Salas 2011). This initiative demonstrates the social democratic ideals that underpinned earlier practices of socialized travel and citizenship in certain West European contexts, bringing together the rights to leisure and travel on the one hand, and the right to employment on the other.

Despite social tourism initiatives being challenged by the advancement of neoliberal economics and the marketization of social domains, the notion that tourism is of fundamental benefit to society and human well-being (among other desirable social outcomes) is enshrined in a series of international conventions and declarations on tourism: the Holidays with Pay Convention (ILO 1970); the Manila Declaration on World Tourism (WTO 1980); and the Montreal Declaration (International Bureau of Social Tourism 1996). The right to travel, which partly manifests the social value of tourism, is also evoked in the Universal Declaration of Human Rights (United Nations 1948), while the UNWTO continues to promote the principles of a social tourism agenda in Article 7 of the *Global Code of Ethics* (see WTO 1999). The Manila Declaration, however, expresses a progressive outlook concerning the notion of tourism as an extension of social policy and 'essential to the life of nations'. It proclaims the obligation of all societies to extend the capacity of all its citizens to participate in tourism:

> The right to access to holidays and to freedom of travel and tourism, a natural consequence of the right to work, is recognised as an aspect of the fulfilment of the human being by the Universal Declaration of Human Rights as well as the legislation of many States. It entails for society the duty of providing for its citizens the best practical, effective and non-discriminatory access to this type of activity.
>
> *(WTO 1980)*

The Manila Declaration was partly a response to the suspension of World Bank loans for tourism development in 1979, prompted by growing recognition of tourism's negative repercussions on social, cultural and environmental systems in less developed countries (Honey 2008: 10–11). Moreover, it presaged a shift towards more 'responsible' forms of tourism in the context of globalization and the emergence of a flexible, post-industrial capitalism (see Harvey 1989). Furthermore, in recognition of the global inequalities fostered by the capitalist world economy, the Manila Declaration explicitly underlined the potential of tourism as an instrument of equity:

> World tourism can contribute to the establishment of a new international economic order that will help to eliminate the widening economic gap between developed and developing countries and ensure the steady acceleration of economic and social development and progress, in particular of developing countries.
>
> *(WTO 1980)*

The Manila Declaration thus reflected a period of optimism among the newly independent states of the 'Third World', notably among members of the 'Non-Aligned Movement', regarding the possibilities for economic autonomy and political independence. In a direct challenge to the iniquitous international trading order that emerged since the demise of direct colonial rule, the UN General Assembly called for the establishment of a New International Economic Order (NIEO) in 1974 (Thomas 1987: 65–66). Alongside the Charter of Economic Rights and Duties of States, promoted by the United Nations Conference on Trade and Development, 'Third World' states endorsed the NIEO as a means of rebalancing the international economy in their favour. The United Nations and a myriad other international financial and development agencies envisaged tourism development as a vehicle for the economic development of 'developing states'. Tourism development was both a cause and consequence of the very inequalities that seemingly trapped these states into an unequal international trading order, which has arguably intensified in the context of neoliberal globalization (Reid 2003). However, some 'Third World' states were highly cautious of developing international tourism as a key export sector. The Arusha Declaration on Socialism and Self Reliance in 1967, for instance, perceived tourism as a tool of imperialism, which should be subordinated by the Tanzanian government in favour of developing its peasant agriculture and industrial base (Shivji 1973).

In a policy environment that is deeply influenced by the logics and values of neoliberalism, the provision of subsidized or low-cost leisure and travel more often than not is viewed as a market distortion and a potential threat to capitalist profitability. Moreover, as noted by Bauman (1998), socialized leisure and travel does not lubricate the wheels of post-industrial consumer society, nor contribute to the prosperity of an economy geared to services, and indeed tourism. Nevertheless, Diekmann *et al.* (2011) demonstrate how in some instances social tourism initiatives may directly compete with commercial tourism suppliers while in other cases they may provide a boost to occupancy levels during periods of weak demand. The focus of social tourism programmes, even in societies where collective provision of social tourism remains strong, has nevertheless shifted towards a greater emphasis on voluntarism, charity and market-based provision. In the UK, where corporatist social welfare regimes were never as entrenched as in Scandinavia and parts of Western Europe, the emphasis remains on the targeted provision of access to leisure and travel opportunities for low-income families (Diekmann *et al.* 2011: 37). The *1989 Tourism for All* report, published by the former English Tourist Board, acknowledged that given that around 40 per cent of the population did not take a holiday for four or more nights away from the home environment in a given year, there was an urgent need to prioritize strategies to increase participation for disadvantaged groups (English Tourist Board 1989). However, the proposed initiatives largely focused on the disabled communities and less on the unemployed, single-parent families, low-income families and racialized ethnic groups (Stephenson and Hughes 1995).

In the UK, one of the earliest attempts to explore the link between travel and social welfare focused on understanding the relationship between disadvantaged home situations and the propensity to travel (Haukeland 1990). In the late 1990s, the Department for Culture, Media and Sport petitioned for wider access to holidays and tourism activities as part of its overall tourism strategy (Ramrayka 2005). Shortly thereafter, in 2003, the UK Department for Work and Pensions acknowledged that being unable to travel in one given year is a crucial measurement of child poverty and an indicator of social exclusion. Despite such empathetic attitudes from formal representatives of the state, UK governments have repeatedly failed to be proactive in providing for disadvantaged groups. In fact, on occasion, the state actually sought to terminate policies concerning holiday provision for the under-privileged. In the early 1990s, the former Home Secretary for the Conservative Party, Michael Howard, attempted to curtail trips abroad for children in care. This position contrasted sharply to the social care paradigm that prevailed at that time, which perceived the holiday as a holistic mechanism in the provision of remedial treatment and therapeutic intervention. Howard's actions were mirrored in the media and public outcry towards 'holidays for hooligans', and also reflected popular derision towards young delinquents, especially in the wake of the notorious murder of the two-year-old James Bulger, by two 10-year-old boys in the Bootle district of Liverpool (UK) in February 1993 (McCrystal 1994).

The socio-economic changes brought about by the restructuring of European capitalism and the concomitant decline of manual labour in post-industrial societies, who represented the core market for social tourism in the early post-war period, have contributed significantly to the shift towards greater commercialized provision of leisure and tourism since the 1980s (Williams and Balaz 2001). Indeed, Higgins-Desbiolles (2006a) argues that the 'marketization of tourism' under neo-liberal capitalism has eclipsed the social dimension of travel, with its potential to foster cultural exchange and human well-being. In addition, somewhat ironically, the increasingly integrated commercial tourism sectors have often been able to provide holiday packages at lower cost than subsidized social tourism initiatives (Diekmann *et al.* 2011)! The scale of the challenges faced by the development of socialized modes of tourism is profound. The Belgium Federation of Hotel,

Restaurant and Café Proprietors, for instance, mounted high-level legal action in 1997 against the European Commission. In an illustration of the increasing prevalence of market values in neoliberal societies, the employers' federation argued that the Commission's provision of grants to social tourism organizations in Wallonia (Belgium) constituted unfair competition (Ryan 2002: 20). Nonetheless, the fact that socialized forms of tourism have been undermined should come as no surprise. The capitalistic pursuit of profit and individual self-interest has increasingly become sacrosanct in an age of commodified travel and mobility, during which neoliberal economics has sought to hollow out what remains of the social democratic state.

Conclusion

This chapter has sought to draw attention to the manner in which the right to leisure and travel was initially forged within the context of capitalist industrialization and the struggle for social citizenship rights in the advanced capitalist states of Western Europe. In addition to the expansion of commercial provision via the expansion of the railways as well as the rise of commercial yet philanthropically minded travel businesses, the move towards eight-hour working days and paid holidays contributed greatly towards the advancement of mass leisure activities and participation in holidaymaking in various European countries during the interwar period. Drawing on a number of illustrations and recent studies, it has been shown how the expansion of travel opportunities for the working classes and other disadvantaged groups was closely tied to social policy and social tourism programmes, particularly in Europe. While the provision of social tourism in Europe has been historically developed by a range of charitable, religious and state-run organizations, it was largely framed by a collective ethos, closely associated with the labour movement and the expansion of the welfare state, and in some cases, extremist nationalist ideologies.

This chapter also introduced a number of different perspectives on modern citizenship. Most notably, it discussed the Marshallian framework of citizenship underpinning the liberal model of citizenship in which citizenship rights amount to a balance of rights and duties organized within the framework of the sovereign territorial nation-state. The advancement of social rights thus constituted the foundations of citizens' entitlement to welfare support within a broader framework of state intervention designed to bring about social equity and contribute to the well-being of society as a whole. Such was the basis of a civilized society where capitalist inequalities would be constrained and, to some extent, mitigated, through state intervention. Although of course such ideas and practices were limited for the most part to Western Europe, and, under a different guise, the Communist Eastern bloc states.

In this chapter, it was also noted how Marshall's work, which was developed in the context of post-war welfare Britain from where he drew most of his observations, fails to take into account the diverse traditions and conceptions of citizenship arising out of different trajectories of capitalist development and the diverse coor-dinates of ideology and cultural values. Nor did Marshall foresee the challenge to the national citizenship model that came from the combined forces of globalization, economic restructuring and the pluralization of cultures and identities, which will be dealt with in the following chapter. Government provision for socialized forms of travel, particularly in Europe, has subsequently given way to more marketized forms of tourism, thus challenging the potential link between tourism and wider social goals. Despite the avowed benefits of progressive modes of social tourism, neoliberal globalization and the expansion of free market capitalism have trans-formed international tourism into a globalizing force of significant magnitude, potentially undermining the social citizenship rights associated with tourism, with negative implications for the universal right of access to travel for all.

Notes

1   The Calypso Programme identifies four such groups: underprivileged young adults aged between 18 and 30; families facing financial or other pressures; people with disabilities; and over-65s and pensioners who cannot afford travel or are daunted by the challenges of organizing a journey (CEC 2010a).

2

BEYOND THE BORDER

Travel mobilities and the foundations of global citizenship

> A man who leaves home to mend himself and others, is a philosopher; but he
> who goes from country to country, guided by the blind impulse of curiosity,
> is only a vagabond.
>
> *(Goldsmith 1819: 24)*

As discussed in the previous chapter, the modern liberal conception of citizenship
has increasingly come under scrutiny, challenged by forces associated with globalization and the political reconfiguration of states. Citizenship thus no longer implies
merely a balance of rights and duties contained within the scope of the nation-state.
Rather it has been expanded (both conceptually and politically) to embrace manifold
new conceptions and practices that are no longer exclusively tied to membership
of the nation-state. International travel is one among several forces that has shaped
new meanings of citizenship emerging from within the realignments between the
nation-state, globalized capitalism and large-scale movements of people. This chapter will consider the transformation of citizenship from one that was significantly
anchored within the confines of the sovereign territorial nation-state, towards a
much more fluid and multilayered set of ideas informed and constituted within a
variety of post-national discourses of cosmopolitanism, cultural rights and multicultural citizenship. Accordingly, it is crucial to acknowledge how international tourism
has mobilized and expressed diverse ideas and practices of citizenship.

The changing alignments of individuals, citizens and states

The ties binding citizenship, nationality and the state together in a relatively stable contract have been steadily eroded by numerous developments: the globalization of economics and politics; the transnationalization of civil societies; and the

pluralization of cultures. As argued in the previous chapter, in the 1980s and into the 1990s the welfare dimensions of social citizenship, including provisions for socialized leisure and travel, were progressively undermined and transformed by an emergent neoliberal agenda. The rise of individualized 'rights-based' discourses, predisposed to the progressive marketization of the public sphere, eclipsed citizenship discourses associated with the defence of the public realm and collective well-being. These processes served to accentuate the shortcomings of the modern conceptions of citizenship elaborated by Marshall, further facilitating the expansion and diversification of new discourses and practices of citizenship. A substantive critique of Marshall's description of the liberal model of citizenship lies in its failure to give due attention to the duties associated with the entitlements of citizenship (Delanty 2000: 19). Marshall thus treats the citizen as a passive recipient of rights, someone who looks to the state for protection from the cold winds of the market rather than being an active participant in society. More recently, explicitly normative conceptions of citizenship emerged in response to the many changes brought about by globalization and the pluralization of European societies, largely a result of immigration and the struggle for recognition by women and other minority groups (ethnic and sexual minorities). Civic republicanism, for instance, advances the notion that the civic bonds between citizens should be developed and nurtured, and that each citizen should be actively involved and engage with the political and civil affairs of the community. Such principles and practices of citizenship supplant liberal conceptions of national citizenship revolving around a benevolent state and passive citizenry. This view is associated with a particular variant of the communitarian paradigm of citizenship (Delanty 2000: 30), indicating the fundamental importance of active citizenship. This form of citizenship evolves as a direct consequence of the expanding realm of civil society, particularly as a result of the proactive role of the voluntary sector (Turner 2001), rather than under the auspices of the state or the market. It is through public action and participation rather than the rights and obligations of private individuals that citizenship is rendered valid.

One must be careful, however, not to exaggerate the decline of social participation and civic bonds under neoliberal capitalism. For Sennett (2006: 46), the organizational transformations brought about by 'new' capitalism have been characterized by a 'thickening' of social networks as a means of survival in the more fluid and networked environment of globalized capitalism. The increased prevalence of voluntary work and membership of charities in the so-called 'third sector' exemplifies such changes. There, organizations have become increasingly salient in the realm of development, public policy and tourism in the late twentieth century, where organizations such as the National Trust, Earthwatch, Raleigh International and Voluntary Service Oversees have been significantly proactive. Furthermore, Putnam (2000) emphasizes that in liberal democratic societies, voluntary associations can have a purposeful role in enabling individuals to be active and creative citizens by providing a platform for widening civic participation.

While not wishing to exaggerate the decline of the nation and national identity, one of the most marked transformations to emerge in the context of globalization and the reconfiguration of relations between citizens, states and markets has been the loosening of personal attachment to the state (Isin and Wood 1999: 7). This has stimulated a number of debates around various interrelated permutations of citizenship: 'post-national' models of citizenship (Soysal 1994, 1997), 'cosmopolitanism' (Brennan 1997, 2001) 'transnational' identities (Gustafson 2008) and related notions of 'global' (Falk 1994) or 'world' citizenship (Heater 2002). Various institutions working across state boundaries have promoted, either directly or indirectly, more broad-reaching forms of citizenship. The European Union, for instance, tentatively promotes a post-national model of citizenship, which seeks to transcend the ethnic, religious and cultural identities existing in each member state. This model represents a challenge to the very basis of national sovereignty and promotes forms of citizenship associated with European modernity and a common European identity. Although, as Tambini (2001: 201) reminds us, EU citizenship is not granted by a state, it is still the case that one has to be formally recognized as a citizen of an EU member state in order to benefit fully from EU citizenship rights. This is a key factor mediating the freedom of movement of peoples within the spatial context of the EU, as will be discussed further in Chapter 4.

A number of lessons for comprehending the relationship between tourism and citizenship can be drawn from the above, as tourism becomes an increasingly major facet of global mobility, reconfiguring the balance of rights and duties between the citizen and the state. In a useful summary of the changing alignments between individuals, citizens and states, Oommen (1997: 37) notes that citizenship:

> has become a diffuse phenomenon invested with new social meanings and endowing people with the capacity to be involved in social actions. This change in the meaning of citizenship has been characterized by *(a)* an increase in the subjectivity and freedom of individuals in mass societies, and *(b)* the incapacity of states to satisfy the increasing instrumental needs and aspirations of their citizens. These two factors in combination have prompted a series of social actions by the active citizens. And the production of the social meaning of citizenship tends to take place independent of national identity.

Global capitalism, privileged mobilities and rootless cosmopolitanism

The rise of a 'class of global nomads' or 'citizens of nowhere' (Foroohar 2006: 54) within global society exemplifies the emergence of transnational notions of citizenship, which delink citizenship from its national moorings. In the context of the rapid globalization of capital and markets, this grouping is akin to a 'denationalized global elite' whose members often lack a 'global sense of civic responsibility' (Falk 1994: 135). An increasingly homogenized global business and political elite has evolved, described as 'Rootless, unburdened by the baggage of locality or the complications of history' and who 'exist in every nation but feel attached to none' (Kingsnorth 2003: 22). Paradoxically, the 'citizens of nowhere' are still 'citizens of somewhere'. They have passports (single or multiple) and are historically rooted to a home nationality determined by birthright and origin, however tenuous such links may be in practice. Such forms of citizenship legitimacy as well as economic advantage can help determine their ability to travel and cross national borders in a relatively trouble-free manner.

Conversely, there are populations residing within national boundaries that are immobile and/or stateless. Millions of people continue to be denied formal citizenship status and full political rights, let alone have access to equal rights of work and the ability to participate in the consumer society. The *2011 Global Trends Report*, produced by the UN High Commissioner for Refugees (UNHCR 2012), estimated that although there were around 12 million stateless persons worldwide, only around a quarter of them could be accounted for as only 64 governments have actually provided data on this phenomenon. While regional conflicts and civil wars are largely responsible for the displacement of populations, the collapse of the Soviet Union in 1991 made hundreds of thousands of Soviet citizens stateless. Following the break-up of the Soviet Union, the newly democratic state of Lithuania, for instance, refused nationality to around 600,000 'ethnic' Russians. Elsewhere, an estimated 2.6 million stateless people out of a total population of 3.4 million were living in Nepal until the government began to issue proof of nationality in 2007 (Rekacewicz 2008: 9). UNHCR (2012) also reported that by the end of 2011 there were around 15.42 million refugees worldwide, 26.4 million internally displaced persons and 895,000 in the process of seeking asylum. The report acknowledges that the refugee crisis is worse than it was a decade previously and the likelihood of individuals continuing with refugee status may last for up to five years.

Whereas the privileged classes during earlier periods in the history of the modern nation-state were 'symbolized by stability', the transnational strata of elite cosmopolitans are 'marked by movement' (Foroohar 2006: 54). The peripatetic lifestyle of these new elite cosmopolitans is based on the unprecedented wealth that has been increasingly amassed by a small proportion of the world's population. Although disparities between social groups have always existed, what marks the recent growth in wealth inequalities is the manner in which they thrive on a 'newly acquired independence from territorially confined units of political and cultural power' (Bauman 1998: 3), having little attachment or obligation to the values of any particular state and its citizens. Prideaux (2004) describes these privileged mobile subjects as 'duty free citizens', whose capacity for constant travel is accompanied by a diminishing sense of social or civic responsibility to either their country of residence or places they visit. Such trends are reinforced by data suggesting that few if any of the UK's 'non-domiciled' billionaires pay much tax on their incomes. For example, in 2006, 54 billionaires paid just £14.7 million on combined fortunes of £126 billion (Winnett and Watt 2006). The world's super-rich devote an army of specialist tax advisors, lawyers and offshore tax havens to help them avoid taxation, and by implication shy away from any sense of engagement in the civic life of the nation other than through the preferred method of voluntary or charitable donations. In the UK alone, it is estimated that corporate tax avoidance costs the exchequer between £3.7 and £13 billion (Tax Reporting Team 2009).

According to the *2012 World Wealth Report*, 11 million individuals worldwide possess a total net worth equal to US$42 trillion. According to the Bloomberg Billionaires Index, the aggregate net worth of the 100 wealthiest individuals in the world for 2012 was US$1.9 trillion (Bloomberg 2013). What is all the more remarkable about such concentrations of wealth among a minority of the world's population is the fact that the fastest rate of growth has occurred outside the traditional centres of capitalist development, in Asia-Pacific, the Middle East and such countries as Brazil. Nonetheless, North America still accounts for the largest concentration of wealth overall (Capgemini and RBC Wealth Management 2012). Notably, the rapid rise of disposable incomes among the 'new middle classes' in emergent economies is reflected in rising demand for luxury goods and travel.[1] Indeed Jacques (2012: 2) estimates that by 2025 the so-called 'developing world' will account for two-thirds of global GDP. It is estimated that in 2012 the 'Chinese super-rich' spent around a third of their time travelling. France is considered to be the most popular luxury destination for Chinese tourists, while Sanya, a beach destination on Hainan Island, is their preferred domestic destination (Hotel, Travel and Hospitality News 2013).

The increased popularity of luxury travel has nevertheless occurred alongside worsening global income disparities between the rich and poor worldwide. Using various global income distribution data, Ortíz and Cummins (2011) demonstrate the severity of global inequalities. In 2007, the wealthiest 20 per cent of the world's population controlled between 70 and 83 per cent of global income while the poorest 20 per cent accounted for a mere 1 or 2 per cent of income. The growing accumulation of wealth in East Asia has fuelled the expansion of the hyper-luxury travel market and the construction of exclusive 'bijou' resorts, often designed by celebrity architects and managed by international hotel firms, including the Singapore-based Banyan Tree Group and Alila Hotels and Resorts (see Luxury Travel Advisor 2012). A further significant trend in the hotel industry concerns the way in which established luxury brands, particularly fashion labels and companies, are starting to develop significant interest in the hotel industry within selective high-profile destination regions, leading to the emergence of new branded hotels with names like the Armani Hotel Dubai, Bulgari Hotel London and Palazzo Versace Gold Coast.

Luxury travel products and experiences have been rapidly expanding because of what has been referred to as 'massclusive' appeal: royal-class airport lounges, luxury-class air terminals, all-business-class flights, private charters, long-range aircraft (e.g. Boeing Dreamliner and Airbus 380) and 'grand' boutique hotels. Commenting on the growing phenomenon of luxury tourists, the co-founder of the International Luxury Travel Market, Serge Dive, states: 'You can call them the "Jetrosexual generation" – where flying will involve casinos, night clubs, bars and spas.' The US Federal Aviation Authority has predicted a 300 per cent increase in private jet journeys from 2007 to 2017 (Luxury Travel News 2007: 70). These developments extend the stratification of passengers from the existing classifications of first, business and economy class to an even more pronounced hierarchy of elite travellers, based on their personal wealth and the exclusivity of products consumed. Frequent flyer programmes and loyalty cards are among many such schemes through which a particular set of rights are bestowed on travellers who are then able to consume preferential treatment not available to others (Coles 2008a: 64). Consequently, the hyper-mobility of tourists and travellers is fundamentally characterized by advanced and sophisticated patterns of service and product delivery, fostered by the interests of advanced capitalism, and brought about by market-led innovation in the tourism industry.

The advancement of elite forms of consumption reflects new patterns of trans-national class stratification. This is manifest in the growth of outbound travellers from such countries as China and Russia who increasingly seek out the cultural capital of Western products. With their newly acquired wealth they have been quick to buy up 'old-world' prestige, whether in the form of French vintage wines or iconographic luxury hotels on the French Riviera, once the favoured destination of Queen Victoria and Winston Churchill as well as writers, artists, celebrities and the idle rich. Examples include the exclusive Hôtel du Cap-Eden-Roc in Antibes, which is owned by Roman Abramovich, the proprietor of Chelsea Football Club (UK), and the Grand-Hôtel du Cap Ferrat, which is part of a vast network of companies owned by the London-based Russian-American billionaire industrialist, Leonard Blavatnik (Harding 2007). Blavatnik's business dealings are accompanied by lavish endowments to the arts and education, evidenced by his £75 million donation to Oxford University to build the Blavatnik School of Government (University of Oxford 2012). This would suggest a revival or indeed a continuation of the kind of elite philanthropy associated with the wealthy citizens of yesteryear, thus challenging Bauman's (1998) view of today's transnational elite classes as having little attachment to anything but the accumulation of vast fortunes. Equally, in the post-9/11 period, Hollywood celebrities have been 'snapping up' remote islands in various locations around the world (Boyes and Carr 2010: 4). Members of royal families have also sought to expand their estates and diversify their exotic holidays through island ownership. For instance, it is reported that the Emir of Qatar paid €8.5 million for six islands in the Ionian Sea (Smith 2013). Prior to the 2008 financial crisis, there was a frenzy of luxury real estate development and hotel construction, particularly in destinations seeking to attract and specialize in 'high-end' tourism markets.

The Gulf metropolis of Dubai has held its status as 'the crème de la crème of luxury and revenue per tourist' (Yeoman 2008: 140), although the recessionary downturn is creating a need to redefine its current market position and luxury orientation (Stephenson *et al.* 2010). Nevertheless, Dubai's development ethos is based on a popular desire to be 'bigger', 'better' and 'brasher' than the rest of the world, with a fundamental intention to build a financial and tourist centre to rival those of the West. Dubai is persistently associated with various high-profile luminaries of the Western world. Images of Andre Agassi and Roger Federer playing tennis on Burj Al Arab's helicopter pad, and Tiger Woods teeing off from the same location, illustrate the symbolic capital of luxury locations and buildings in representing destinations that appeal to high-income leisure tourists. Oprah Winfrey, Robert

De Niro, Janet Jackson, Michael Jordan and Kylie Minogue, as well as high-profile Michelin star chefs, flew into Dubai to be involved in the ceremonial opening of the Atlantis Hotel Resort on the artificially constructed island of Palm Jumeirah in November 2008. Other celebrity associations exist in Dubai. In the culinary industry, for instance, UK celebrity chefs have established their restaurant brands in Dubai: Gary Rhodes's 'Mezzanine', Gordon Ramsey's 'Verre' and Jamie Oliver's 'Jamie's Italian'. In the sport industry, the Dubai-based football club, Al Wasl, secured the management services of Diego Maradona from 2011 to 2012. In the film industry, Tom Cruise performed stunts on the exterior of Burj Khalifa for the movie, 'Mission Impossible: Ghost Protocol', which was released in December 2011 (Stephenson in press (2013b)). The project to construct the World, consisting of over three hundred small real estate islands in the Gulf five kilometres from Dubai's coastline, was another mega-initiative that was developed to correspond with the opulent (though currently changing) image of Dubai, especially as a playground for the rich and famous. This fits well with Dubai's self-styled role as the apotheosis of luxury consumer production and consumption (Stephenson and Ali-Knight 2010).

Notwithstanding the fact that some of today's 'high-net-worth individuals' engage in philanthropic causes and provide considerable funds to set up charitable foundations, most famously the Bill & Melinda Gates Foundation, it is difficult to speak of 'rootless cosmopolitanism' as a nascent form of civic or active citizenship. Members of the world's privileged and increasingly mobile elite classes appear to exhibit little in the way of a cohesive set of ideals, except perhaps for mutual forms of antipathy to punitive tax regimes. Beyond the philanthropy of a few high-profile members of the world's super-rich, such as for example the George Soros Foundation, there is a limited desire to challenge the forces producing social polarization and rising inequalities. The emerging schisms between national citizenship and globalization that are manifest in the mobility of elite capitalist classes and footloose global executives, were clearly made apparent in the demands for repatriation by British expatriate oil executives caught up in the civil war in Libya during 2011, at the expense of British taxpayers. Miles (2011: 21) suggests that such citizens are if anything 'global corporate citizens', where their 'allegiance to Britain appears to encompass all rights and no duties'. However, even the philanthropy of the world's mega-rich does not preclude them from lavish expenditure on property and luxury tourism facilities. One such example is the Royal Phuket Marina built by the Hong Kong-based business tycoon, Gulu Lalvani, shortly after the devastating 2004 *tsunami*. This complex targets expatriate property investors and Chinese tourists, who currently represent the largest group of arrivals to Phuket (iRealty Times 2012). The 'marina' comprises upmarket shopping facilities, restaurants and hotels, as well as luxury villas with their own private moorings and expensive yachts. Yet these developments are out of keeping with Phuket's marine and coastal ecology (Royal Phuket Marina 2012). The *tsunami* itself paved the way for such luxury projects by enabling developers and speculators to appropriate coastal lands previously inhabited by residents whose homes had been destroyed and who in many cases did not have title to their lands (see Tourism Concern 2005).

It is the elite cosmopolitan classes, or what Sklair (2001) refers to as the 'transnational capitalist class', who are in a strong position to genuinely enjoy the fruits of transnational or global citizenship, a concept to which we will return later. This positioning stands in contrast to those excluded from the cosmopolitan spaces enjoyed by the capitalist classes and the new professional-managerial classes, especially those who seek the relative familiarity and sanctuary of their own particularistic-based identities and localized allegiances: ethnic, national or social. Ong (1999) for example, refers to the emergence of 'flexible citizenship', a form of transnational citizenship that is forged in the context of the cross-border networks of kinship, capital and entrepreneurship that have proliferated under recent experiences of political upheaval and global market integration in East Asia. Ong's analysis demonstrates how Chinese business elites mobilize economic, political and social power to acquire multiple citizenships and passports, especially to exploit opportunities for investment, work and residence. She thus frames flexible citizenship in relation to: 'the strategies and the goals of managers, technocrats and mobile professionals who seek for ways to simultaneously circumvent the different regimes of the nation states and take advantage of them' (Ong 1999: 112).

Although citizenships are fluid and adaptable to both the mobility of capitalism and changing political circumstances, the predominance of 'cultural regimes' and patriarchal structures in Chinese societies predisposes men to be the officiators and practitioners of mobility. Women are often assigned immobile roles and territorialized responsibilities associated with caring for families and overseeing home life (Ong 1999: 20). That is not to say that the process of travelling and working across transnational places and spaces is consistently a male-dominated task. In fact, Pratt and Yeoh (2003: 159) claim that scholarly work on transnationalism has traditionally been 'gender-blind', formulating an assumption that work-related travel has consistently elevated men as 'entrepreneurs', 'career builders', 'adventurers' and 'breadwinners'. This perspective typecasts women as being firmly associated with domesticity and immobility. In contrast, some enquiries have started to recognize ways in which women have contributed at various levels to the transnational workforce (see Yeoh and Willis 2005; Yeoh et al. 2000). As research on labour practices in the global cruise ship industry also indicates, women, mainly those from low-income states, occupy nearly one-fifth of positions at sea in what amounts to a 'globalized multi-cultural workforce' (Chin 2008: 2).

Notwithstanding other readings of 'everyday cosmopolitanism' (Vertovec and Cohen 2002: 5), which refer to the manner in which linguistic and cultural diversities permeate all layers of society, Calhoun (2002) emphasizes that cosmopolitanism can be viewed as an ideological cover for the furtherance of class privilege. He draws attention to the growth of 'consumerist cosmopolitanism' that has mirrored the increased cosmopolitanism of capital itself (Calhoun 2002: 105), where states or companies market a mix of cultures and ethnicities in an attempt to project an image of openness, tolerance and diversity, which is nonetheless grounded in the cold logic of capitalist profit-making. Elsewhere, Calhoun (2008: 432) refers to the case of the rebranding of British Airways, which developed a more global, altruistic, cosmopolitan and multicultural appeal, but was still grounded in a sense of Britishness. He also notes the process of national branding campaigns, where countries and aspiring nation-states utilize such events as the Olympics as a way of elevating a strong sense of nationhood, most visibly expressed in the case of the 1992 Barcelona Olympic Games (see Hargreaves 2000). This observation illustrates how cosmopolitanism can be instrumentally utilized by states to appear 'worldly', while simultaneously reinforcing their unitary sensibilities and desire for global recognition.

Despite the evident transformations brought about by globalization and increased cross-border mobilities, an adequate conceptualization of post-national citizenship or transnational public good has yet to be clearly defined let alone institutionalized. In this regard, Isin and Turner (2007: 13–14) argue that it would be premature to talk of 'global citizenship' in the absence of a genuinely sovereign global state able to impose and uphold its will. Although the status of citizenship remains governed and regulated by the state, they delineate the parameters of a 'cosmopolitan citizenship' in so far as citizens are implicated in actions, rights and responsibilities that extend beyond the borders of any single state:

> The underlying rights of a cosmopolis are what we might call 'rights of mobility' and 'rights to transaction'. Many modern rights claims are implicitly or explicitly about crossing or intersecting through borders or creating new settlements – right of migrant labour, rights to hold a passport, rights to enter a country, rights of asylum, rights of refugees and other rights to residence, rights to marry outside one's own state, the right to buy property, goods and services or invest across other states.
>
> *(Isin and Turner 2007: 14–15)*

Notwithstanding the state's continued monopoly on the ability to grant, administer and enforce national citizenship rights, the proliferation of cross-border affiliations, transactions and mobilities serves to expand existing conceptions of citizenship. According to Isin and Turner (2007), not only is the state being reshaped by the increasingly diverse cross-border movement of people, the citizens of particular states are themselves implicated in a global web of practices and responsibilities through the state's involvement in a variety of multilateral legal and other accords. These multilateral arrangements may for example involve the environment (Kyoto Protocol), wildlife (CITES[2]) and culture (UNESCO World Heritage), each of which has clear ramifications for understanding tourism and its relationship to emergent notions of global and/or cosmopolitan citizenship. Crucially, there is a notable disjuncture between the 'rights of mobility', monopolized by certain societies and groups of people, vis-à-vis the rights of relatively 'immobile' populations, whether 'non-tourists' or disenfranchised members of 'host' societies. There are notable difficulties encountered in seeking to formulate and balance the reciprocal rights and duties of tourists with those of locals across different national and cultural boundaries. These complexities should be at the very heart of any informed debate surrounding the rights and duties of socially responsible forms of travel.

Given the complexity of cosmopolitanism and associated notions of global citizenship, attempts to delineate specific meanings associated with these constructs are fraught with difficulties. Moreover, global citizenship cannot be interpreted merely in terms of the presence of a privileged group of 'globally mobile people', nor can it be anchored in a linear historical worldview that places Western ideals of universality at its centre (Vertovec and Cohen 2002: 8). Rather, as we shall see, ideas of cosmopolitanism are informed by a range of philosophical ideas and political discourses, grounded in far more diverse social experiences and multiplex affiliations than implied in the image of the globetrotting, bourgeois 'bricoleur'. The question then becomes: 'What is the place of tourism and associated transnational flows of cultures, images and capital within an emergent cosmopolitan politics?' From this, it may then be possible to deduce the implications that then transpire for dealing with existing models and understandings of citizenship.

Tourism and rooted cosmopolitanism

Diverse conceptions and practices of citizenship challenge the state's monopoly over the provision and enforcement of the rights and duties of its citizens. These have evolved to fill the 'citizenship gap' and to some extent compensate for the inadequacy of existing models of national citizenship. These new applications of citizenship acknowledge the need to construct a transnational regime of [human] rights that is able to accommodate and advance the rights of citizenship beyond the state, regardless of one's national citizenship status (see Faist 2009). This then takes us further into the realm of 'global' and 'cosmopolitan' conceptions of citizenship in which different actors are brought together by a common set of interests, shifting the parameter of reciprocal rights and duties beyond the confines of the nation-state.

In his extensive discussion of 'cosmopolitical democracy', Archibugi (2000) points to two specific areas that have grown in global significance – environmentalism and human rights – which have a number of significant implications for the evolving relationship between tourism and citizenship. These notions will be examined in subsequent chapters in relation to ethical and responsible forms of travel and the socio-political contestation of tourism. Archibugi's notion of cosmopolitical democracy proposes the global extension of democracy in response to the increasing number of transnational issues that go beyond the scope of the state, especially in terms of the capacity of any one state to effectively regulate and manage a range of issues (e.g. environmental pollution, migration and financial markets) that transcend national borders. He suggests that cosmopolitan political authority is a response to the democratic deficit that exists in the current global system of territorially sovereign states and is consistent with attempts to seek an appropriate and fair balance of rights and responsibilities in the global order. Principally, this is to address problems of a transnational nature – that is, 'where a democratic state contains no representatives of the communities that suffer the – direct or indirect – consequences of the policies it employs' (Archibugi 2000: 145). Although Archibugi uses the example of French nuclear testing in the Pacific, the consequences of which were experienced by Pacific islanders (Lichfield 2006), there are clear implications here for how the relative balance of rights and responsibilities should be distributed between mobile consumers, that is, tourists, and destination communities.

However, there is nothing new in exporting 'negative externalities' to poor countries (e.g. pollution and toxic waste), where regulations are often lax or absent altogether. International travel and tourism thus involves the remaking of other societies for the purposes of pleasure and consumption, especially for the bene-fit of citizens from tourist-generating states. In the course of doing so, tourism invokes its economic contribution to the 'host' society while at the same time often transferring a number of environmental and economic risks to the local popu-lation. Notwithstanding the capacity of local planning frameworks to engineer 'sustainable' forms of tourism development, although these often prove inadequate and are easily circumvented by developers and large corporations (see Bianchi 2004a; Blanchar 2012), the mobility of tourists provides a whole new set of ethical and political challenges to host societies. These challenges relate to the nature of a mutually binding social contract underlining the interactions between putatively mobile (tourist) and immobile (local) subjects. The capacity to be mobile implies the ability to ignore the ethical consequences of our actions and perhaps even evade legal sanctions, given the complexity of transnational justice. Both the com-plex transnational organizational structure of tourism multinationals and policies of trade liberalization have made it harder for local governments to enforce certain environmental regulations. In some cases, it has also hampered attempts to pros-ecute firms where there is evidence of environmental degradation and the violation of national laws, particularly if deemed to be an 'unnecessary' barrier to trade (see Hochuli and Plüss 2005).

Without wishing to overplay the dichotomy of disempowered host and empow-ered tourist, it nonetheless serves as a means of thinking about the balance of rights and responsibilities, that is, citizenship rights that permeate international tourism and the associated flows of cross-border mobility. In the absence of any trans-national regulatory authority, or indeed sufficient political or public interest in the rescaling of states' powers at a global level, the rights of tourists and concomi-tant rights of consumption may be prioritized at the expense of the development rights of host populations. These latter rights would relate to host entitlements to economic and cultural ownership and/or custodianship of the immediate envir-onment, and political participation and representation in the decisions relating to the nature, scope and scale of tourism development in a given society. This could extend to collective struggle and the right to contest tourism, as well as the advo-cacy of community-based rights associated with access to such resources as clean water, public lands and beaches, and other so-called 'common pool resources' (see Briassoulis 2002).

In the case of Uluru Kata-Tjuta (formerly known as 'Ayers Rock') in Australia, long-standing concerns exist among the local Anungu people over tourists climbing this sacred site. Such an activity denotes deep-rooted inequalities between Aboriginal and 'White' Australia, as well as the closely related battle between demands for citizenship (i.e. land rights and cultural rights) and the right of tourism to use and exploit this space for commercial gain. In opposition to the proposed ban to climb the rock, inspired by respect for Aboriginal cultural rights, the Liberal Party environment spokesman, Greg Hunt, made the following comment, which invokes the right of all Australians to climb Uluru: 'Big Brother is coming to Uluru to slam the gate closed on an Australian tourism icon, the climb. I support allowing people to make up their own minds about whether to make the climb' (Batty 2009).

As it currently exists, the architecture and territorial scope of transnational democracy, which might underpin nascent forms of global citizenship, is weak. Global or supra-national political and civic institutions often lack full legitimacy (e.g. the EU, UN) and are thinly spread across a complex network of often competing inter-governmental entities, multilateral frameworks, international accords (e.g. UNESCO World Heritage Convention, Kyoto Protocol) and non-government organizations with diverse memberships and distinct ideological objectives. Although embodying certain ideals of transnational democracy and civic responsibility, these multilateral arrangements and international accords are determined in the main by structures of authority, governance and citizenship rooted in the nation-state. However, as the state becomes increasingly challenged and intersected by the disciplinary forces of mobile capital as well as the political and legal authority of supra-national institutions, it begs the question that if the national 'public sphere' is the location of citizenship how then can this be reconstituted transnationally? In the absence of any clearly defined institutions of transnational democracy, it is through the actions of social movements, civil society and global advocacy NGOs that such public spaces of citizenship are being forged (see Tarrow 2005). Through numerous forms of local and transnational activism, social movements and other grass-roots activists have increasingly challenged exploitative forms of tourism development and the depletion of resources associated with the 'privileged' access of foreign tourists and tourism development to particular resources and environments. Yet, such forms of citizenship are limited and have proven to be weak bulwarks against the predatory forces of mobile capital and authoritarian state power, albeit with notable exceptions, some of which will be considered in Chapter 6.

Various writers have asserted the importance of such forms of citizenship as 'world citizenship' (Heater 2002) or 'global citizenship' (Falk 1994) to understand and contextualize the influence of transnational perspectives on citizenship discourse. Heater (2002) emphasizes that the embedded nature of world citizenship would need to be legitimized by the state for any significant impact or effect to take place. He accepts the interchangeable nature and use of the concepts of both 'world citizenship' and 'cosmopolitan citizenship', though he prefers to utilize the former given that the Greek word origin of 'cosmopolitan', *kosmopolitēs*, not only denotes 'world citizen', but also due to the fact that the various interpretations and lived experiences of 'cosmopolitanism' are rather ambiguous and divergent. Nonetheless, he acknowledges that there are different meanings associated with those privileged minorities who popularly represent 'world citizens'. He notes:

> The minority who are world citizens in the fullest sense that is currently possible may be referred to as 'a world citizen elite', or 'world citizen pilgrims', or 'pioneer' or 'vanguard world citizens'. These images do not in fact convey the same meanings. The elite are the favoured, the wealthy financiers, business people, senior administrators and academics, for instance, who enjoy the privileges of a cosmopolitan lifestyle. The pilgrims … are journeying to an imagined new global 'land' where higher ethical principles may be found. And the vanguard … are those making progress in constructing a cosmopolis but in advance and on behalf of all those who in due course of time will follow.
>
> *(Heater 2002: 6)*

One might mistakably view cosmopolitanism as inextricably linked to, or derived from, the condition of mobility. Indeed, it is often uncritically assumed that tourists themselves are increasingly discerning, sophisticated and cosmopolitan, where there is a heightened desire in the postmodern era of consumption for individuals to attain new experiences and explore (and sample) new cultures and societies. These individuals have been labelled as 'post-(mass) tourists' (Feifer 1985), referring to those who travel with an aura of self-confidence and the intention of experiencing environments beyond those experienced by the tourist masses. This type of tourist arguably epitomizes life within a post-industrial 'risk society' (Beck 1992), where the endeavour to indulge in chance encounters and new experiences is an important social objective. These experiences can manifest expressions of broadmindedness and a desire to adopt a cosmopolitan outlook.

In her study of backpackers and independent travellers, Germann Molz (2006: 5) indicates that the 'round-the-world traveller' could perhaps symbolize the 'cosmopolitan figure' as 'a mobile, detached flâneur who delights in encounters with difference, displays a willingness to take risks and a stance of openness to other cultures'. She suggests that one important cosmopolitan attribute relates to the perceptive abilities of travellers to understand where to 'consume the right commodities, places, or cultures in the right way' (2006: 9). Germann Molz also draws on Beck's (1992) view of the risk society, emphasizing how the element of risk involved in travelling to other cultures often captivates round-the-world travellers. She acknowledges that white and middle-class individuals are the ones who often have access to privileged cosmopolitanism. These examples of cosmopolitanism, however, draw on the historical positioning of the term 'cosmopolitan', popularly envisaged as a 'well-travelled polyglot' who exudes an air of superiority towards the 'putative provincial' (Appiah 2006: xiii–xviii).

Nonetheless, prevailing forms of nationalism represent a challenge to cosmopolitan experiences and affinities. This can be seen by the way in which patriotic espousal of national identity may become closely intertwined with nationalist discourses of heritage and cultural tourism (Park and Stephenson 2007). Such forms of tourism work towards manufacturing a sense of history and a sense of belonging to a nation at a time of significant social change and global transformation. For example, Park's (2009, 2010) ethnographic work emphasizes how visits to the UNESCO World Heritage Site of Changdeok Palace in Seoul (South Korea) can enable South Koreans to encounter the distinctive attributes of Korean nationhood. Park acknowledges that Changdeok Palace is an essential constituent of the history of the Korean nation, which exists on an emotional, spiritual and cultural level – irrespective of the geopolitical divisions between the North and South. It represents a timeless symbol of nationhood, standing in stark contrast to Seoul's international profile as a global city integrated into globalized networks of capital and cosmopolitan forms of consumption.

The development of tourism and its insertion into different societies have nevertheless played a significant part in the reordering of social relations and affiliations across borders. The realignment of people, organizations, communities and corporations along transnational social and geographic axes extends the notion of citizenship across states, evident through the creation of new cross-border affiliations and cosmopolitan identities. Notwithstanding this claim, however, there is indeed a dilemma, what Rumford (2007: 329) terms a 'cosmopolitan paradox'. Rather than opening up territories to increased mobility and cosmopolitan forms of affiliation, states and entities such as the EU appear intent on closing them down. Accordingly, 'borders are diffused throughout society, differentiated, and networked', which thereby 'increases the chance that they are experienced differently by different groups, some of who encounter them as anything but cosmopolitan' (2007: 329).

From its earliest days international travel has given rise to 'new types of citizenship' (Rojek 1998: 303). From the Grand Tour in the eighteenth century to the cosmopolitan bohemian enclaves of leisure in the Mediterranean from the early twentieth century, and more recently, the extensive communities of secondary home dwellers and retirees that have emerged in selective destinations around the world, tourism has brought about new forms of association and collective self-identification among peripatetic and other mobile communities (see Bianchi 2000). O'Reilly (2000: 140), for instance, who has studied the British expatriate communities on the Costa del Sol, describes their situation as: 'living betwixt and between two cultures and two worlds, partly by choice and partly by circumstance, but ultimately maximising their advantage in an inherently marginal situation'.

The presence of expatriate communities along with tourism development has had a remarkable cultural impact on the cosmopolitan ambiance of destinations. Walton's (2005) historical analysis of tourism and expatriate communities in Mallorca from the 1920s to the 1950s, notably El Terreno, indicates how this seaside suburb of Palma, similar to other villages on the island, including the artists' 'colony' of Deia (Waldren 1996), had already developed into a cosmopolitan district prior to the onset of large-scale tourism development after the Second World War. In time, the massive development of tourism in southern Europe from the 1960s onwards converted the Mediterranean littoral and archipelagos into densely cosmopolitan spaces of production and consumption where tourists, retirees, migrant workers, entrepreneurs, criminals and other clandestine subjects from many parts of the world live, work and play (see Bianchi 2000).

Nevertheless, tourism and travel provide a context where 'supra-territorial affiliations' and 'transplanetary connections' (Scholte 2005: 60–64) can be formulated and fostered between people living in very different circumstances. Among those communities dispersed across continents by the rupture of colonialism, both their identities and those of subsequent generations have become increasingly hyphenated and marked by cosmopolitanism, leading to what Joseph (1999: 70) refers to as 'nomadic citizenship'. In this regard, post-colonial citizens were thrust into struggles over legal, economic and cultural rights in their new countries of residence, as well as giving rise to globally networked flows and diasporic relations linked to the phenomenon of 'diasporic tourism' (Coles and Timothy 2004). Stephenson's (2002) ethnographic work, for instance, illustrates ways in which diasporic tourism in the form of 'ethnic reunion' encourages members of the UK Caribbean community, especially the first generation, to travel as often as financially possible beyond the immediate territory of the British state to visit specific ancestral islands in the Caribbean. This practice enables members of culturally displaced communities to renew their personal associations and socio-cultural affinities with their homelands, as well as to reaffirm their kinship and friendship networks. The realities and practices of migrant groupings productively illustrate more robust forms of transnational citizenship, especially if dual or multiple identities are developed and maintained. However, while the rendering of citizenship may be reshaped and expanded by plural forms of identification, it is still formally determined by national citizenship laws.

Dual citizenship increasingly reflects cross-border associations (e.g. through marriages), and it is often in the interests of origin states to ensure that their overseas nationals retain their sense of belonging to the country in which they were born, especially for reasons associated with the economic benefits of remittances and the VFR (visiting of friends and relatives) market. For example, under the 'Balikbayan' programme in the 1970s and 1980s, Filipinos living abroad were subsidized by the Filipino government to return home – both in order to bring foreign currency back into the country but also to assuage fears among foreign states regarding the Marcos dictatorship (Richter 2000: 59). In 2011, remittance flows to the Philippines stood at around US$23 billion, the fourth largest remittance beneficiary in the world (Ratha and Silwal 2012). The mobilization of minority ethnic groups and their financial, socio-political and ideological involvement in national homeland projects illustrates how supra-territorial identities and affiliations have challenged concepts of citizenship grounded in the nation-state. Werbner's (2002) research on a women's organization in Manchester's Pakistani community provides ample illustrations of how the group philanthropically supported Pakistani communities oversees, which then developed into actively assisting social and political causes in Bosnia and Kashmir. This illustration closely parallels the global, humanitarian response to the Indian Ocean *tsunami* on 26 December 2004, which also involved organizations such as SurfAid International, a body previously established by a physician and surfer from New Zealand who was troubled by the poverty and disease that he encountered on a surfing trip to Sumatra. There are indeed a number of alternative types of tourism that have been developed ostensibly for 'benevolent' purposes, including pro-poor tourism and volun-tourism. Athletic volun-tourism, for instance, has its origins in individuals participating in international races and marathons for charity, and includes a range of other such activities as walking, wheelchair racing and cycling. Volunteer athletes utilize this activity as a way of raising money and contributing to charities (India Times 2011). Although certain writers are critical with regard to the capacity of tourists 'doing good' through their travels (see Butcher 2003), these examples do draw attention to ways in which the citizens of various states, including international tourists, can constructively engage with social and humanitarian projects in societies other than their own. The implications of altruistic-based tourism for understanding and shaping nascent ideas of (global) citizenship will be considered further in Chapter 6.

Supra-territorial affinities can also be maintained through religious and spiritual acts of solidarity, and are exemplified in the popularity of various sacred and secular forms of international pilgrimage. Indeed, traditional religious sites, including the Church of the Nativity (West Bank, Palestine), Golden Temple (India), Kerbala (Iraq), Lourdes (France), Mecca (Saudi Arabia) and Maya Devi Temple (Nepal), as well as secular commemorative sites (e.g. Vietnam's 'demilitarized' zone, Gallipoli Battlefields (Turkey) and, most recently, Ground Zero in New York City stand as pertinent illustrations of the diverse scope of pilgrimage and other meaningful, transnational affiliations (Plate 2.1). Such affiliations can partly be determined by the popularity of international forms of spiritual veneration and public commemoration, encouraging meaningful expressions of solidarity and transnational allegiances that cut across geographic, political and cultural boundaries.

In contrast to the notions of 'rootless cosmopolitism' discussed earlier, the above illustrations concerning religion, ethnicity and humanitarianism point to the existence of rather more concentrated forms of transnational affiliation, and indeed the notion of a 'rooted cosmopolitanism' (Beck 2003). This form of cosmopolitanism delineates tourism's role in providing individuals and groups with opportunities to establish, renew or maintain deep and meaningful associations with a value system or a society that exists beyond the home locality. Therefore, tourism can be associated with the promotion of a set of rights engrained in transnational issues and concerns. The types of tourists who are genuinely interested in the lives of other cultures and societies are those sociologically classified as the 'experimental' and 'existential tourists' (Cohen 1979). The 'experimental mode' of tourism characterizes those tourists who have become alienated or disenchanted with everyday life and thus wish to embark on a 'renewed quest for meaning' (1979: 186), typified by the search for authentic experiences and encounters with other communities. The 'existential mode' of tourism, however, concerns those tourists who become

PLATE 2.1 The remnants of *The Sphere* recovered from the rubble of the World Trade Center in New York City after 9/11. This large metallic sculpture once stood in the plaza between the World Trade Center towers and has become a major draw for tourists who visit the site of Ground Zero in lower Manhattan. The statue was relocated to Battery Park after the attacks and was dedicated as a memorial to the victims of 9/11. Photo: R. Bianchi, February 2009.

'deeply committed to a new "spiritual" centre' (1979: 190), and in doing so succumb 'completely to the culture or society based on an orientation to that centre' (1979: 190).

Nevertheless, D'Andrea (2006: 104) instructively reminds us that migrants, tourists and expatriates should not necessarily be perceived as inherently cosmopolitan subjects, as their experiences are not necessarily reflective of an 'interest or competence in participating or translating differences'. Although the growing importance of cosmopolitanism has attracted substantial academic discussion, we arguably need to uphold a more cautionary stance to the uncritical acceptance that individuals are becoming more cosmopolitan or indeed globally benevolent as a result of lifestyle changes associated with a putative shift towards a more globalized consciousness, and to the uncritical observation that ethnic nationalism is waning in popular significance. As Beck (2003: 27) informatively notes:

> The fundamental fact that the experiential space of the individual no longer coincides with that of the nation may give the impression that we are all going to become cosmopolitans. However, cosmopolitanization does not

automatically produce cosmopolitan sentiments. It can just as naturally give rise to the opposite, to the rebirth of ethnic nationalism, the rise of the Ugly Citizen. This has happened at the same time as cultural horizons are expanding and sensitivity to different lifestyles is growing; neither of these things necessarily increases the feeling of cosmopolitan responsibility.

However, globalization has resulted in the changing context of citizenship in which one of the most significant transformations has been the erosion of the traditional basis of social citizenship, whose origins lay in the class structure of industrial societies located within the sovereign territorial nation-state. As a consequence a new 'regime of rights' has emerged, underpinned by the shift from statism to polycentric modes of governance and driven by a common focus on global concerns that transcend the ability of any one state to deal with them (Turner 2001: 203–204). Indeed, the adopted slogan of a variety of 'anti-globalization' movements, 'Another World Is Possible' (Patomaki and Teivainen 2004), invokes notions of transnational solidarity and social justice among geographically dispersed civil society organizations, non-government organizations and disempowered indigenous groups, with the intention of constructing more just and egalitarian social orders.

Resistance to the ecological damage associated with the globalization of free market capitalism and concern for the survival of the planet under threat from climate change, have triggered manifold forms of civil society mobilization beyond the nation-state in what can be seen as a nascent form of 'environmental citizenship' (Turner 2001: 204–206). Steward (1991:74) summarizes the basis for such forms of citizenship as an embodiment of 'a new sense of the universal political subject beyond the context of the traditional nation state, and a refreshed awareness of equality in terms of our dependence on nature'. The right to a clean environment and the responsibility of human beings towards nature and wider society have a direct bearing on the relationship between tourism and a variety of civil society struggles within destination environments. These issues will be explored in further detail in Chapter 6.

Nonetheless, the notion of a 'global civil society' has its challenges, certainly in terms of how it should be achieved. One perspective, for instance, points towards cosmopolitan constitutionalism involving the development of a world governmental apparatus (Falk 1993, 1994). Another perspective, however, indicates the necessary movement towards global democracy, involving a closely coordinated network of democratic bodies (Archibugi and Held 1995; Held 1995). Indeed, Immanuel Kant, writing in the late 1700s, had already tried to visualize how an international civil society could be built through international law, with the intention of moving towards the creation of a 'cosmopolitanism constitution' across states and continents. For Kant, this would be reflected in the existence and propagation of a 'universal community', as well as a movement towards bringing about 'perpetual peace' and respecting 'universal hospitality', particularly 'the right of the stranger not to be treated with hostility when he arrives on someone else's territory' (Kant 1970: 105, quoted in Delanty 2000: 55–57).

Cosmopolitan interests have nevertheless been historically enmeshed within various imperialist projects, while the contemporary appeal of cosmopolitanism often downplays the reorganization of state power around the needs of capitalist profit-making. Brennan (2001: 84) argues that rather than being too deeply concerned at this stage with citizenship discourses that revolve around the pursuit of world governance or global democracy, cosmopolitan politics should progressively pursue transnational forms of solidarity together with the protection of labour rights and the rights of minorities, *within* the existing framework of the nation-state. Yet, globalization and large-scale migrations together with the increasingly fragmented ethno-cultural landscapes resulting from these, not only call into question national formations of citizenship but also render problematic the construction of transnational solidarities. In the midst of such ethno-cultural realignments tourism has become a pivotal context in which multicultural rights and plural identities have been represented, negotiated and ratified (or rebuffed), with manifold implications for existing understandings of citizenship and its relationship to nationhood and the state.

Tourism and cultural rights: multicultural and diasporic forms of citizenship

As we have argued, citizenship rights are historically grounded within the framework of the sovereign territorial nation-state, reaching their zenith in the social democratic and liberal capitalist states of Europe and North America in the post-Second World War era. However, for minority groups living under the jurisdiction of such states, whether in the West or elsewhere, these rights are manifestly absent or routinely ignored by governments (e.g. Turkish guest workers in Germany). In instances where the state grants full rights, discriminatory practices may impede individuals and groups from experiencing any benefits bestowed by such rights (see Ehrkamp and Leitner 2003). While liberal democratic states have become increasingly 'answerable' to the global market they have also become simultaneously enmeshed within supra-national frameworks of governance through which different minority groups and immigrant communities have sought to exercise demands for a variety of rights (e.g. linguistic rights) and the pursuit of justice. Such demands may involve tolerance of distinctive ethno-religious practices and anti-discriminatory practices in the workplace. Often the pursuit of cultural recognition and social justice go hand in hand but can be seriously undermined when race and ethnicity act as decisive instruments of discrimination and exclusion within the workplace and political sphere, and indeed, the social and cultural life of the nation (Gilroy 1987). These discriminatory practices can also have an impact on people's physical movement from one socio-cultural space to another, regardless of their social standing and formal status as a citizen.

As indicated previously, Marshall (1992) understood citizenship as not only involving full participation in the national body politic, but something amounting

to a set of rights equally shared among all members of society. If such full participation could be achieved then social justice would prevail. From this, it would be
logical to deduce that non-participation or asymmetrical participation in a 'shared
way of life', and inequitable access to the valued activities of the established society,
equate directly to the denial of social citizenship rights. The implication of this perspective of citizenship is that social boundaries between 'citizens' and 'non-citizens'
are established on the basis of ethnically derived parameters of social inclusion and
exclusion. Indeed, Marshall (1964: 92) emphasized that citizenship entails 'a direct sense of community membership based on loyalty to a civilization which is a
common possession'. Given that tourism is often institutionally defined and widely
perceived as a valued activity and a social need, then restrictive access to certain
tourism products and limited tourism mobilities cast a shadow of doubt on the
ability of all those residing within a state's boundaries as legitimate nationals to be
able to access full citizenship rights.

The inability to participate in travel on equal terms thus raises questions concerning the shared allocation of social resources and equitable forms of participation. Limited participation in travel may derive from socio-economic factors,
including poverty and inequality, and factors based on race, gender and sexuality, as
well as prescribed religious roles and beliefs may of course imply different cultural
attitudes to race, women and sexuality. As citizenship traditionally implies social solidarity and reciprocal relations between people who ostensibly share similar values
and perhaps even cultural identities, those who do not necessarily fall within this
interpretation may have their own particularistic demands for recognition subject
to scrutiny or even denied. There is a clearly developed argument, for instance, that
contemporary tourism mobility is determined and prescribed by gender and gendered relations (Simmons 2004; Wilson and Little 2008; Wolff 1993). Enloe (1989:
21) comments: 'In many societies being feminine has been defined as sticking close
to home. Masculinity, by contrast, has been the passport for travel.' A particular concern relates to what Valentine (1989) terms the 'geography of women's fear', where
places and destinations, urban or rural, are perceived to be dangerous for women
travellers or where access to certain social spaces is restricted for the preserve of
men alone (see Little et al. 2005; Scratton and Watson 1998).

Nonetheless, although Marshall did not approach cultural citizenship as a necessary constituent of citizenship, his model of citizenship invokes issues of cultural
access and participation on the basis that such 'social practices' as education would
encourage individuals to adopt a 'national system of values' (Turner 1994c: 159).
These culturally oriented practices would partly confer a common citizenship status on individuals organized within a framework of national development. In fact,
this reasoning was certainly evident in the UK in the post-Second World War era
of mass migration, especially in terms of policies and practices towards immigrant
populations, which emphasized the importance of cultural integration and assimilation. The standardization of cultural practices based on a dominant homogenous
culture was also inherent in the development of many mass forms of enclave tourism from the late 1960s. These enclaves of hedonism mushroomed across the world

beyond the centres of industrialized wealth, from Acapulco to Mallorca, reflecting the cultural and social elements of tourists' home cultures and societies rather more than those of the societies in which they were situated (Turner and Ash 1975). In fact, tourism can arguably confirm and reinforce one's (national) identity. In her ethnographic study of British holidaymakers in Mallorca, Andrews (2002) critically explores ways in which tourism behaviour in Magaluf ritually re-enacts a sense of Britishness, though admittedly influenced by the dominating elements of hetero-sexuality and whiteness. Familiar food, drink, language and social behaviour are all too evident at the destination, along with an abundance of recognizable British names for pubs, cafes and shops, adding to the destination's signification of British habits, values and eccentricities.

Specific types of tourism and tourism destinations located within multi-ethnic states often reflect one-dimensional ethnic orientations and/or dominant racial dispositions, thereby challenging any serious attempt to visualize certain types of tourism mobility as an exemplar of multicultural citizenship. English countryside heritage and rural recreation, for instance, are inherently associated with the cultural aspirations of English and/or British society and culture. This arguably reinforces nationalistic sentiments, casting a shadow of doubt on the ability of ethnic minor-ity citizens to enjoy and appreciate rural tourism activities (Stephenson 2004, 2007; Stephenson and Hughes 2005). Stephenson (2007: 172, 175, 176) notes:

> Popular representations of the English countryside pertinently illustrate how national life is presented and constructed, where countryside ideals and pas-toral myths reinforce Anglo-centric notions of identity and tradition ... The 'countryside milieu', constructed through authentic notions of 'Englishness', powerfully signifies national values and customs ... The national project, manifested in the cultural attributes of rural life and romanticised perception of the countryside, is synonymously reinforced through conceptions of rural areas as 'safe havens' for white communities.

In his book, *England: An Elegy*, Roger Scruton (2000) highlights the importance of preserving the countryside because English virtues and conventions are embodied within rural tradition. Consequently, the countryside should be protected and 'stran-gers must remain strangers, lest they pollute you with their intimacy' (2000: 50). His observations are concerned with the English entitlement to privacy, where the land represents an English person's right of possession and social contentment. In this regard, Neal (2002: 444–445) draws attention to the racial implications of pre-senting the countryside as a symbol of national identity, stating: 'In contemporary Britain the deployment of rurality as a symbol of national identity is at odds with its "multi-ethnic" composition because nostalgic notions of rurality re-inscribe and treasure hyper-whitened and thereby exclusive versions of Englishness.'

Since the 1980s, there has been concerted criticism that the heritage indus-try manipulates and presents heritage in a partial manner, often concerned with promoting nationalist agendas and elevating specific types of cultural and ethnic representation (Horne 1984; Lowenthal 1998). In his observations of various forms of European heritage, Horne indicates that national monuments and museums in various European cities represent Europe's power, imagination and imperial conquest. Stephenson's (1994) observations of the heritage industry in Manchester (UK) in the 1990s serve to illustrate some of these concerns. He notes that museums and heritage centres do not substantially acknowledge and recognize the significant socio-physical presence of such ethnic minorities as the African and Caribbean communities in the city. He also argues that Manchester's tourism product is based on a view of heritage that excludes important historical events and circumstances. Examples include the role of the African Caribbean diaspora in contributing to the economic wealth of the city through the transatlantic slave trade, and the proactive role of Manchester's Abolition Movement and its well-documented conflicts with the city's slave traders. The denial or deliberate constriction of particular forms of ethnic heritage can also be a consequence of state ideologies and the reconstruction of the nation-state in transition states. In post-Soviet Kyrgyzstan, for instance, despite a rich mix of ethnic diversity, tour operators have favoured the promotion of ethnic Kyrgyz culture and heritage at the expense of other ethnic groupings (Palmer 2007). Elsewhere, museums in Greece have a tendency to place emphasis on classical and Byzantine history, rather than providing a comprehensive heritage representation of the Ottoman period and Muslim historical trajectories (Taylor 2012).

The experiences of minority groups travelling within and across states are fraught with discriminatory responses, whether in the form of colour racism, xenophobia or, more recently, 'Islamophobia' (Stephenson 2006; Stephenson and Ali 2010). Indeed, diversity and difference are often seen as a threat to national social cohesion, challenging notions of citizenship that are firmly associated with unitary paradigms of nationhood. However, it is also important to treat the oft-repeated claim that globalization fuels the increasing ethnic and cultural diversity of nation-states with a degree of caution. While no doubt true in certain contexts, most organized political communities throughout history have been, to some degree, multi-ethnic. Rather, as Kymlicka (1995: 2) points out, the past three decades or so have witnessed the progressive decline of modernist narratives proclaiming the ethnic and cultural homogeneity of the nation-state. In this regard, Marshall's work fails to fully account for the economic forces brought to bear on erstwhile social, political and civil definitions of citizenship, as well as the manner in which the universal entitlements of citizenship are striated by divisions of race, ethnicity, gender, sexuality and cultural difference.

Notwithstanding the complexity of framing and organizing conceptions of 'minority rights' – ethnic and other 'minority' categories often become entangled within expedient political constructions for the purposes of mobilizing resources from the state – multicultural forms of citizenship do recognize a range of basic rights. These include the rights of individuals to cultural and linguistic representation, as well as associated rights of representation in the face of their historic neglect or suppression by the nation-state. The discourses associated with Spanish regional nationalisms are particularly illustrative in this respect. In the second half of the nineteenth century, peripheral nationalisms began to challenge the centralist Spanish state. Most notably this was driven by the regional intelligentsias from the Basque Country and Catalonia, and to a lesser extent Galicia and the Canary Islands (see Conversi 2000). Accordingly, regional elites set about to mine the past for markers of ethno-cultural distinctiveness, utilizing resources in the fields of archaeology, ethnology and folklore history. This provided a catalyst for affirming the existence of alternative 'sub-state' nations in conjunction with channelling a range of grievances and demands for regional autonomy. This culminated in the estabishment of Spain's peculiar matrix of autonomous communities in the 1980s, which in many ways revived the country's brief encounter with regional autonomy in the 1930s until it was brutally halted by the rise of Franco in 1936 (Smith and Mar-Molinero 1996). Fundamentally, however, the question concerns the extent to which the state is prepared to recognize, endorse and support 'minority' heritage and the cultural rights of minority groupings. Pakulski (1997: 77) indicates the importance of considering the scope and worth of cultural rights for minority groups:

> The cultural rights – which are more in the form of negotiated claims than institutionalised legal entitlements – include rights to unhindered and dignified representation, as well as to the maintenance and propagation of distinct cultural identities and lifestyles ... The claims for cultural citizenship involve not only tolerance of diverse identities but also – and increasingly – claims to dignifying representation, normative accommodation, and active cultivation of these identities and their symbolic correlates.

Pakulski (1997) also asserts that the implementation of cultural rights would broaden, intensify and foster progressive forms of social and political citizenship, as well as importing into citizenship discourse issues concerning the democratization of culture and the politics of recognition. Accordingly, claims for cultural citizenship can work in tandem with demands for a series of interrelated rights: 'the right to symbolic presence and visibility (vs marginalization); the right to dignifying representation (vs stigmatization); and the right to propagation of identity and maintenance of lifestyles (vs assimilation)' (Pakulski 1997: 80). Therefore, in this context citizenship entails not only people's right to access national cultural resources and participate in the common culture of the nation, but also their right to cultural recognition, expression and ownership. Therefore, cultural citizenship involves respect for diversity and otherness, as well as the rights of minorities to have ethnic rights or what Kymlicka terms 'polyethnic rights', thereby enabling individuals to 'express their cultural particularity and pride' (1995: 153). These types of rights would depend upon the cultural and religious needs (and obligations) of specific groups.

The touristic mobilities of minority groups potentially illustrate a number of diverse facets of ethnic and cultural rights: the rights of Muslims to have access to prayer rooms (including footbaths for ablution) in major places of transit (e.g. bus depots, train stations and international airports); the rights of members of the orthodox Jewish community not to sit near women on flights and not to be presented with dishes that combine both meat and dairy products; the rights of Sikhs not to wear helmets while travelling on motorbikes; the rights of Muslim women to wear the niqab while travelling in public places; and the rights of ethnic minorities to be able to freely celebrate their own religious and culturally specific holidays. Such rights also extend to the realm of policy in order to enable employers to allow ethnic and religious minorities time off work for participating in specific festivals (e.g. Ramadan for Muslim minorities, Nowruz for Iranian minorities and Diwali for Hindu minorities). The right of Muslim employees to work to a different set of timings during Ramadan would be an important entitlement, especially in terms of respecting the religious needs and obligations of individuals and considering the physical welfare of individuals during long periods of fasting.

Although many such rights do in fact exist, notwithstanding they may not be defended in practice, visualizing a society that submits fully to the ethnic and cultural rights and needs of minorities is difficult to conceive, unless of course those minorities happen to represent the indigenous population of the state and whose interests align almost completely with those of the state. Full recognition is certainly unimaginable in places where the state seeks to either suppress, or for reasons related to its constitutional make-up is unwilling to sanction, the cultural obligations and duties of individuals and religious groupings. In the United States, for example, a secular state since its inception (unlike France), it is legally possible to revoke a taxi driver's licence for 30 days if the driver refuses to take passengers on religious grounds. This penalty was imposed on Somali Muslim drivers who refused to pick up passengers from Minneapolis-St Paul International Airport if they were visibly carrying alcohol, despite the fact that drivers believed that their rights to religious freedom should be upheld (MPR News 2008). In France, due to the passage of recent laws allegedly to reinforce the republican values at the heart of its constitution, women wearing the full veil in public may be fined €150 or ordered to attend citizenship classes (King 2013). Similar forms of punishment now exist in Belgium and the Netherlands, which have legislated against the same type of behaviour, reaffirming a prevailing trend in Europe for states to ensure that the secularization of public space (and indeed tourism space) is not only preserved but also policed. The fact that it is now illegal for Muslims to conduct prayers in the streets and public space in Paris is another illustration of this trend (Bland 2011), where the freedom of movement is constrained by powers that do not value (or invest in) the ethnic and cultural diversity of its populace.

Consequently, the right to openly practise religion in the public realm and express one's ethnic and cultural identity outside of the home environment would be conducive to the construction and employment of a multicultural model of citizenship. For some states, however, the admission of ethnic or polycentric rights may be perceived as a threat to the freedoms of the ethnic majority, where any such rights could be seen to be questioning the state's loyalty to its citizens and their own sense of belonging to the nation-state. However, the extent to which these rights can ever reach full fruition is indeed questionable. In this regard, Joppke (2004) observes that many multicultural policies in Australia, Britain and the Netherlands are being renounced. He notes that limited popular appeal for multiculturalism is a significant factor affecting policy approaches in Australia. Also, multicultural directives in Britain and the Netherlands are somewhat undermined by the social and economic disenfranchisement and the continued self-segregation of minority ethnic groups. A significant criticism of multiculturalism, however, concerns the view that it may facilitate the suppression of women within those particular migrant communities whose rights and liberties are often restricted as a result of culturally-sanctioned norms and ascribed status roles (see Deveaux 2003; Song 2005). Thus the key argument indicates that the discourse of multiculturalism potentially depoliticizes culture and mystifies the realities of sexism and racism. Nevertheless, Joppke (2004) acknowledges that there is a new sense of state assertiveness in aiming to ensure that its secular interests and identity do not come under threat from dissenting groups. In fact, citizenship training and tests, such as the Life in the UK Test, introduced in 2005, are certainly one mechanism by which the state attempts to ensure some kind of allegiance to the state and its defining values.

Universal and modern definitions of citizenship increasingly intersect with claims for 'group-differentiated rights', as centred on the ethno-religious practices and requisites of immigrant and other minorities, where these cultural elements form a 'context of choice' (Kymlicka 1995). For Kymlicka (1989, 1995, 2001), the state should ensure that group rights are incorporated into the legal and political frameworks required to prevent minority groups from being rendered invisible and/or socially marginalized and excluded. His liberal conception of group rights is nevertheless challenged by Isin and Wood (1999: 58–60) on two fronts. First, it is predominantly based on the experience of the French-speaking minority in Canada, which while not equal in power to the Anglo-Saxon majority is nonetheless relatively well-represented throughout institutions of power at both state and federal level. Second, such liberal interpretations of group rights rest with the institutionalization of cultural diversity as opposed to any meaningful challenge to material inequalities of wealth and power, either in the workplace or society at large (e.g. land rights).

Tourism's affirmative association with multicultural models of citizenship depends very much on the state's attitude towards ethnicity and cultural recognition, and how this is contextualized in tourism policy and planning. Nevertheless, certain states have attempted to develop multicultural approaches to tourism development in order to constructively represent cultural and ethnic diversity in ways that challenge cultural stereotyping. Although this does not necessarily extend to yielding to the promotion of polyethnicity or the special rights of minorities but to simply recognize the rights of cultural representation. The problem, however, with notions of multiculturalism and multicultural citizenship, as they are currently conceived and incorporated into liberal models of citizenship, lies in their tendency to reduce minority ethnic and cultural groups to homogenous entities within the unitary confines of the state. These notions also assume that minorities are necessarily 'subordinate' to other 'majority' groups howsoever these may be defined. As highlighted in Isin and Wood's (1999) critique, not only does this ignore how struggles for representation may intersect with material struggles for subsistence and economic rights of minority groups and marginalized communities, it also fails to consider cultural scenarios where ethno-cultural group rights extend beyond the borders of a particular state. Accordingly, it has been observed by Beck (2006: 66) that 'multiculturalism rapturously celebrates the social accommodation of diversity, but it lacks a sense of cosmopolitan realism'.

Minority cultural rights and the politics of multiculturalism are increasingly important political issues that are being played out within the context of globalization, large-scale migrations and the rescaling of the nation-state. The attempt to incorporate group rights into liberal democratic polities presents a considerable challenge to national models of citizenship, particularly where group demands and interests transcend the physical and cultural boundaries of the nation-state. While multicultural citizenship may be accommodated within the confines of the nation-state, insufficient attention is given to understanding the transnational affinities of particular groups. For instance, close transnational ties between ethnic minority groups residing in the industrialized states and their ancestral homelands, may in fact challenge any significant desire to become multicultural citizens, that is, citizens of the 'host' state, albeit with different cultural values and needs. Elsewhere, however, indigenous challenges to national policies of assimilation in post-colonial Latin American states have precipitated recognition of the pluri-ethnic and multicultural character of the states, as in the case of Mexico (Carruthers 1996).

Given the increasing influence of globalization and the extensive flows of tourists, migrants, workers and refugees worldwide, and the diverse ways in which the coupling of nationhood and citizenship are being challenged from above and below, it is pertinent to acknowledge flexible forms of citizenship in relation to sociological constructions of 'nomadic citizenship' (Joseph 1999) and 'diasporic citizenship' (Laguerre 1998). Indeed, the work of Appadurai (1995) concerning the conceptual significance of 'trans-locality' is particularly germane in the sense that migrant diasporic groups create and recreate strong social associations with more than one state or nation. These ties constitute expressions of a political, religious and/or socio-cultural affinity to another place or culture that exists beyond the lived reality of their everyday lives, which may in turn be mobilized and enacted through the structures and processes of travel and tourism.

Conclusion

This chapter has argued that tourism both bears the imprint of existing models of citizenship, as well as acting as a vector through which new and more flexible notions of citizenship associated with globalization, transnational flows of people and new alignments of political praxis within civil society are being actively constituted and contested. This chapter has sought to foreshadow the various ways in which 'mobile citizenship' is developing as an emerging framework with which to understand tourism's relationship with citizenship – beyond the traditional confines of the nation-state. Bauman's (1998: 2) claim, that 'being local in a globalised world is a sign of social deprivation and degradation', has ramifications for understanding ways in which the globalization of tourism is both a powerful symbol and consequence of the expansive nature of mobility and freedom. On the other hand, however, his claim also serves to highlight the degree to which immobility and disenfranchisement are profoundly shaped by the forces of globalizing capitalism.

International tourism reflects new currencies of value for those with both the economic capacity and political freedom to travel and consume the wealth of destinations and 'products' on offer in today's globalizing world. Nonetheless, tourism has less social worth for those who are unable to travel and move freely across international borders, that is, the 'non-tourists'. Participation in different forms of international travel implies the ability to move with ease across different boundaries and the right to enter foreign territories to consume a range of cultural and recreational experiences, or participate in numerous other modes of travel, whether for the purpose of business, scientific, religious or diplomatic reasons. Although it is the right to the freedom of movement not tourism as such that is protected under international law, tourism is often promoted as a universal good and invoked as a human right in its own right, a point that will be taken up again in later chapters. While political asylum is often (though often begrudgingly) accepted by states in the exercise of their duties under international law, labour migration is treated with more caution and suspicion. In addition, this chapter has explored the relationship of global mobility to notions of cosmopolitan citizenship whereby a privileged minority of the world's citizens have staked their claim to a form of mobile citizenship by virtue of their superior wealth and ease of movement across international borders. Equally, however, the discussion has noted the existence of rooted forms of cosmopolitanism, discernible in diasporic identities and transnational affiliations amongst geographically-dispersed citizens.

As the latter part of the chapter has demonstrated, the meaning of cosmopolitanism can no longer be taken to imply a privileged, globally mobile elite. Contemporary ideas of cosmopolitanism and global citizenship are informed by a range of philosophical ideas and political discourses, which are grounded in the experiences of migrants and the multiple transnational allegiances that result from these, as well as the struggles by non–elite groups within and across states, to formulate and activate a range of rights that embrace tourism as means of advancing their claims for recognition and (cultural) citizenship rights. We must therefore consider the place of tourism within an emergent cosmopolitan politics that embraces progressive notions of cosmopolitanism and global citizenship rooted neither in the state nor subordinate to the demands of global capital. The following chapter will explore these and other related issues in further depth, in particular the ideological and political framing of the right to the freedom of movement and right to travel, and its implications for the alignments of tourism and citizenship.

Notes

1 Growth in real-terms disposable income in Russia in 2011 was estimated at above 4 per cent (Gould 2011).
2 Convention on International Trade in Endangered Species.

3

TOURISM, MOBILITY ENTITLEMENTS AND THE CONDITION OF FREEDOM

As travel, changing locations, and leaving home become central experiences for more and more people in modernity, the difference between the ways we travel, the reasons for our movements, and the terms of our participation in this dynamic must be historically and politically accounted for.

(Kaplan 1996: 102)

This chapter conceptualizes the diverse and contradictory interpretations of freedom that have helped to frame and reinforce the right to travel and be a tourist. It considers how ideas of freedom shaped early aspirations and forms of travel under colonialism, paving the way for the emergence of a taken-for-granted culture of mobility in Western industrialized societies prior to and after the Second World War. As living standards and the capacity for overseas travel began to increase in the post-war liberal capitalist order, international tourism soon became a symbol of individual autonomy and freedom, as well as a beacon of economic modernization for 'developing' countries desperate to move up the ladder of development in the aftermath of colonialism. This chapter explores the transformation of international tourism from its association with post-war ideals, notably modernization and the economic progress of developing nations, to its association with discourses of market individualism and the unfettered right to travel. The discussion draws attention to the alignment between tourism and market-based renderings of citizens as consumers, and questions the degree to which the rights and freedoms to travel can ever be distributed in an inclusive and equitable manner within and across states given the strength and pervasiveness of neoliberal ideological thinking.

Travel – the perfect freedom

In many ways, tourism represents a quintessential expression of humanity's 'natural' desire for freedom, exploration and discovery. In the age of mass mobility, globalization and neoliberalism, international tourism evokes notions of freedom and democracy as well as a range of more self-oriented interests: individual choice, social status, hedonism and self-actualization. During the height of the Cold War, the slogan adopted by the United States Travel and Tourism Administration was 'travel, the perfect freedom' (Richter 2000: 6). However, the freedoms associated with one's mobility and movement are politically ambiguous and unequally distributed. As Smith and Duffy (2003: 2) note, 'the freedoms we associate with "progress", including "free time" and the freedom to travel, are part and parcel of a society that is ever more ordered and regulated'. Whether it represents a medium of escape from society or workplace, or an ideological expression of political freedom, tourism still evokes myriad interpretations and constructions of freedom. Often, there is a strong libertarian streak running through tourism discourses. This is demonstrated by Butcher (2003) whose reflection on tourism, freedom and ethics deplores any attempt by non-governmental organizations and other arbiters of morality to promote a 'New Moral Tourism'. He thus forcefully argues against the imposition of ethical standards on tourism and the moral regulation of our freedom to travel, stating: 'Tourism need only be about enjoyment, and requires no other justification. As for moralising about tourist behaviour, how these people choose to enjoy themselves is a matter for them' (Butcher 2003: 12).

Except for the presentation of a valid passport and/or visa to the agents of border security, it is likely that few tourists think about the origins and substance of the freedoms enabling them to travel across international borders with little hindrance. Although these freedoms are far from being universally entrenched, a taken-for-granted culture of tourism mobility has embedded itself in advanced capitalist societies, and increasingly among the better-off inhabitants of emerging economies. Such ideas reach their apex among the citizens of North America and other advanced capitalist societies, for whom travel 'is a primary activity of existence and not a sign of distinct progress' (Urry 2013: 61). Ironically, however, according to the US State Department, in 2012 there were only 113.4 million US passports in circulation, approximately one-third of the total population (US Department of State 2013a). Nonetheless, such is the pervasive nature of discourses proclaiming our right to travel and visit wherever we choose that, with the exception of a few tightly controlled states and regions, international tourism is no longer perceived to be a privilege but one among many rights to which all citizens are entitled in a globalizing world of mobile consumers. The following statement from the UNWTO, warning governments not to tamper with the freedom to travel despite the global pandemic of swine flu in the summer of 2009, makes this stance very clear: 'The Committee reaffirmed its view that the respect of human rights, of non-discrimination and of freedom of movement are fundamental values inherent to tourism and are pre-requisites for any successful tourism activity' (UNWTO 2009).

The extent to which the right to travel is regarded as sacrosanct by citizens of advanced capitalist states is often brought to the fore in the context of a 'mobility crisis'. The sense of entitlement to foreign travel in the West was manifest in the response to the closure of European airspace in 2010 due to the Icelandic volcanic eruptions, as well as the disruption to cross-Channel Eurostar trains due to heavy snowfall in December 2009. The gravity of the public response was sardonically summarized by the *Observer* columnist David Mitchell: 'stranded holidaymakers are spoken to, and behave, like victims of an atrocity' (2009: 32). The sense of entitlement to the freedom of mobility was further illustrated by complaints over the disruption to the usual 'fast-track' treatment accorded to first, and business-class passengers at London's Heathrow airport, which resulted from the national strike by public-sector workers in the UK in June 2011 (which included UK Border Agency staff) (Evening Standard 2011). Further to the freedom of mobility upon which international travel depends, tourism gives expression to a sense of personal freedom or liberation (i.e. from traditional and cultural expectations) and the cultivation of one's sense of self. According to Przeclawski (1988: 6): 'Tourism constitutes one of the ways of realizing the desire for freedom, and the possibility to make a choice, so important for the subjectiveness of contemporary man [*sic*].' Although Przeclawski was writing prior to the end of the Cold War these discourses became even more pronounced during the era of neoliberal globalization and increased cross-border mobility. Urry (1995: 165) notes that in the West the 'right to travel has become a marker of citizenship'. Such rights bring with them claims to consume a variety of cultures and environments, including those sites and attractions deemed to be of global significance, notably, UNESCO World Heritage Sites (Urry 2000: 174).

Privileged freedoms: from colonial to post-colonial travel

The rise of the nation-state in the nineteenth century provided the conditions for capitalist industrialization and the exploitation of the labour and resources of colonized societies, including strategic energy reserves. Colonialism and the ensuing integration of non-European societies into the mainstream of modernity provided a springboard for the development of tourism in a number of colonies and associated enclaves of privileged luxury, from Mexico and the Caribbean to North and East Africa and the South Pacific. Subsequently, as the post-war architecture of 'neo-colonial' enclave tourism began to take shape, a number of writers argued that tourism was tantamount to a form of imperialism or neo-colonialism (e.g. Britton 1982; Kent 1977; Turner and Ash 1975). While it may no longer be valid to speak of a rigid 'north–south' divide in the globalizing political economy of international tourism, certain contemporary forms of travel do nevertheless evoke an element of colonial nostalgia that is reminiscent of Edward Said's (1978) celebrated analysis of Orientalism. Even the names of certain upmarket travel companies, such as *Coromandel* and *Voyages Jules Verne*, evoke the 'simplicity' and 'luxury' of colonial times, when travel was unencumbered by notions of rights, ethics and responsibilities.

International tourism also manifests 'civilizing' discourses that emphasize the need for social advancement and economic progress. Such discourses involving 'tourism as an instrument for development' (De Kadt 1979), 'tourism as peace' (D'Amore 1988), 'sustainable tourism' (Mowforth and Munt 2009) and even 'ethical' or 'responsible tourism' (see Chapter 6), serve in different ways to render 'peripheral' (non-Western) societies approachable for travellers to experience 'exotic' foreign locales while simultaneously extending the offer of well-meaning assistance. Increasingly also, wealthy tourists are encouraged to indulge in the opulence of upmarket eco-lodges for the purposes of achieving altruistic aims (Observer 2006). By doing so they are able to generate benefits for conservation efforts and impoverished local communities, averting any guilt associated with such indulgences. That is not to say there is anything inherently wrong with these initiatives. Rather, it points to an increasing trend within twenty-first-century political landscapes, as well as within certain 'ethical travel' niches, whereby solutions to complex problems of poverty, inequality and a lack of development can be solved by exhorting wealthy tourists to consume even more luxury, while doing little to alter the fundamental values and organizing logic of neoliberal capitalism. Chapter 6 will explore in more detail the contradictions embedded within these tourism development scenarios.

Pratt's (2008) analysis of the writings of Victorian explorers draws parallels between the dehumanizing arrogance with which they consumed and ultimately appropriated the landscape unfolding before them, and certain contemporary Western travelogues in which the post-colonial 'Third World' landscape exists without history, and one might add, agency. Pratt's analysis thus asserts that the traveller, traditionally male, has relative autonomy and visual command over the landscape. Appropriately, Minh-ha (1994: 22) claims: 'For cultures whose expansion and dominance were intimately dependent upon the colonial enterprise, travelling as part of a system of foreign investment by metropolitan powers has largely been a form of culture-collecting aimed at world hegemony.'

In the very act of 'opening up' 'new' territories travel served to immobilize other peoples, who were depicted as 'timeless' while being simultaneously disconnected from the injustices of the colonial enterprise (Pratt 2008: 213).[1] Clifford (1992: 106–107) observes how 'bourgeois travellers' during the Victorian period enjoyed the status of 'proper travellers', unlike their servants and guides ('non-white persons') whose achievements often went unrecorded. In the popular Western imagination, the 'imperialistic' endeavours of those such as Christopher Columbus, James Cook and Marco Polo dominate historical accounts of pioneering and adventurous forms of travel, ignoring the contribution of travellers from both earlier 'pre-modern' times as well as the travel experiences of the wealthier or privileged subjects of colonized societies themselves. Moreover, well before these infamous travellers undertook their respective voyages, Herodotus had already documented the numerous festivals to which Egyptians would travel several times a year (Cassen 1994: 31). Nor can the practice of modern leisure travel be traced exclusively to the rise of European modernity and the 'Grand Tour', which took place from the period of the Renaissance onwards (Turner and Ash 1975: 29–50). For instance, the travel expeditions of such non-European explorers as Zhou Dagan and the Islamic traveller-scholar Ibn Battutah have largely gone unacknowledged in the wider canon of Western literature and travel writings. Moroccan-born Battutah spent 30 years (1325–1354) of his life travelling throughout the Muslim world and other non-Muslim countries, visiting such a variety of places as Mecca, Persia, Mesopotamia, Asia Minor, Bokhara, India, China, Sumatra, southern Spain and North Africa (Dunn 2004). The writings of Arab, Chinese and Indian explorers and scholars serve to illustrate ways in which other societies and customs function from a non-Eurocentric world-view (Khair *et al.* 2005). Latin American writers and travellers, for instance, were keen on interpreting the fraught and difficult relationships between peripheral and European modernities (Pratt 2008).

For centuries, the ritual obligations of travel and hospitality have been associated with pilgrimages to the Holy Land and a multiplicity of other sites worldwide that are part of the sacred geography of religious travel. As Inayatullah (1995: 411) notes, 'Muslims had to travel' in order to make the annual pilgrimage to Mecca, a practice still held sacred among Muslim populations around the world. Referring to Ibn Battutah, Inayatullah goes on to state that 'the accumulation of wisdom or *ilm*, was the essence of Islam' and was intrinsically linked to 'the spiritual journey of the Self' (1995: 412). However, such travel was not restricted to Muslim holy sites. The principal motivation behind Battutah's travels was to 'discover differences' (1995: 412), presaging certain aspects of the Grand Tour some four hundred or so years later. Another type of journey historically grounded in the Islamic world is the 'Ziyara', which is associated with visiting auspicious places and sites of religiosity (e.g. shrines and mosques), and travelling to places to meet religious scholars or to participate in religious events and festivals (Haq and Wong 2010).

A great deal of travel during colonial times nevertheless presupposed the enterprise of conquest and the worldwide expansion of trade and commerce from the early sixteenth century onwards. This enabled individuals with the financial means and appropriate social status to take part in the privileges of travel, especially to experience the pleasures of foreign cultures in ways that would profoundly shape the intellectual and cultural life of modern European societies for centuries to come. The colonial period would also mark the birth of travel as an engine of social, economic and cultural change. During the seventeenth and eighteenth centuries, notions of cosmopolitanism came to be very much associated with and defined by the foreign travels of aristocratic men who would travel abroad in order to acquire the necessary knowledge and cultural capital expected of the ruling elite. Their 'superior' social status determined their desire and ability to attain the rich trappings of 'cosmopolitanism', which was also of course marked by an intrinsic sense of entitlement. The lives of male voyagers, scholars, missionaries and adventurers feature disproportionately in historical accounts of travel. A marked sense of the racial superiority of the white European traveller was highly prevalent in the Western imagination and popular culture, firmly depicted in Daniel Defoe's (1972) novel, *Robinson Crusoe*, originally published in 1719. His story of a shipwrecked Crusoe subduing the hostile environment through a rational and enlightened mind, and a natural ability to civilize the noble savage, perhaps typifies the racial and patriarchal conception of Western voyages and adventures in conquering other territories and societies. Indeed, Clifford notes that travel metaphors were often constructed on the basis that women were not historically perceived to be earnest travellers: "'Good travel" (heroic, educational, scientific, adventurous, ennobling) is something men (should) do. Women are impeded from serious travel' (1992: 105). Leed perceives the history of travel as a 'spermatic journey', which has been classically constructed through 'myths of traveling gods, heroes, and patriarchs' (1991: 114). He also states:

> The erotics of arrival are predicated on certain realities in the history of travel: the sessility of women; the mobility of men; the uncertainty and contingency of the relations formed between them in arrival … In the conditions of settlement and civility, travel is 'genderdized' and becomes a 'gendering' activity, underlining a difference between men and women. Historically, men have traveled and women have not, or have traveled only under the aegis of men, an arrangement that has defined the sexual relations in arrivals as the absorption of the stranger – often young, often male – within a nativizing female ground.
>
> *(Leed 1991: 113)*

However, women do of course travel and have travelled for centuries. One notable traveller was Celia Fiennes (2009), an upper-class English woman who undertook a series of excursions in England and Scotland from 1685 to 1703. She travelled by horseback and wrote about various sites, scenes, places and experiences. Fiennes presented first-hand accounts of social and domestic life in the late seventeenth century, drawing attention to the production and manufacturing activities of each locale that she visited, such as tin mining in Cornwall, pottery production in Staffordshire and cheese making in Cheshire. Her travel narratives reflect a sense of national pride, with the implication that foreign sites (glorified by the Grand Tour) were often overrated, where there was much to learn from domestic travel. Fiennes is the first recorded woman to visit every county in England, journeying at a time when travel was arduous and not without risk. The predatory activities of the notorious 'highwaymen' of the seventeenth and eighteenth centuries (see Billett 1997) produced some sense of trepidation for the independent traveller, especially for those who travelled without a protective entourage. Yet despite her accomplishment and gallantry, Fiennes, the granddaughter of William Fiennes, 1st Viscount Saye and Sele, recorded the lives and lifestyles of the less affluent populations in the north of England and Scotland in ways that castigated these impoverished communities for their indolence. In her journey into Scotland, for instance, she writes:

it seems there are very few towns except Edenburough Abberdeen and Kerk which can give better treatment to strangers, therefore for the most part persons that travel there go from one Noblemans house to another; those houses are all kind of Castles and they live great, tho' in so nasty a way, as all things are even in those houses, one has little stomach to eate or use any thing as I have been told by some that has travell'd there; and I am sure I met with a sample of it enough to discourage my progress farther in Scotland; I attribute it wholly to their sloth for I see they sitt and do little – I think there were one or two at last did take spinning in hand at a lazy way; thence I tooke my fish to carry it to a place for the English to dress it ...

(Fiennes 2009: 38)

Byron was reported to have said that 'to travel is to become a man [sic] of the world' (cited in Boorstin 1963: 91). Samuel Johnson apparently stated that 'a man [sic] who has not been to Italy, is always conscious of an inferiority, from his not having seen what is expected that a man should see' (Löfgren 2002: 157). By the late eighteenth and early nineteenth century the Grand Tour's aristocratic travellers were joined by the middle classes, who were to 'man' the outposts of Britain's colonial empire and spend their rising incomes on touristic adventures. Many of them became considerably knowledgeable and attached to the customs and societies of which they were sent to rule. Such figures as Richard Burton and most notably Warren Hastings, the first Governor-General of colonized Bengal, epitomized notions of nineteenth-century 'elitist cosmopolitanism', whereby their unquestionable fascination with other cultures, religions and customs, and indeed fluency in many languages (Hastings spoke Persian and Urdu), did not appear to contradict their inbuilt assumptions of racial superiority (Appiah 2006: 1–8).

Women's limited ability to benefit from the kind of freedom of movement that men enjoyed can be understood by reference to the 'flâneur'. This concept signifies the capacity of the opportune and almost fearless male urbanite to stroll and observe the proliferation of public places of leisure and pleasure in the nineteenth century. Wilson (1995) exposes the masculine nature of this construct:

It is this flâneur, the flâneur as a man of pleasure, as a man who takes visual possession of the city, who has emerged in postmodern feminised discourse as the embodiment of the 'male gaze'. He represents men's visual and voyeuristic mastery over women. According to this view, the flâneur's freedom to wander at will through the city is essentially a masculine freedom. Thus the very idea of the flâneur reveals it to be a masculine concept.

(cited in Wearing and Wearing 1996: 233)

Nonetheless, renowned women travellers in the Victorian era periodically surfaced to contest male space and emphasize the rights of women to experience the trials and tribulations (and pleasures!) of travel, as epitomized by Mary Kingsley and Mary Hall's expeditions in various parts of Africa and Gertrude Bell's journeys in the Middle East (see Birkett 1991). The testimonies of women travellers suggest that the history of travel and tourism was not always fully constrained by gender. Although gendered constraints have not been fully overcome, equally, we should not underestimate ways in which race and class remain crucial determinants of people's ability and right to travel. In Hall's (1907) account of her travel experiences in Africa and Egypt, for instance, there are references to comfortable hotels, luxurious trains and obedient porters. Birkett's (1991: 125) evaluation of Victorian women travellers indicates that racial authority often surpasses gender as an all-defining attribute in the host and guest relationship:

> As women travelers frequently pointed to the continuities and similarities with earlier European male travelers, the supremacy of distinctions of race above those of sex allowed them to take little account of their one obvious difference from these forebears – the fact that they were female.

As the cost of maritime travel fell with the advent of steam ships in the mid-nineteenth century, recreational travel received a significant boost alongside the expansion and intensification of colonial trade, incorporating, for example, the 'Mediterranean Atlantic' (i.e. Canary Islands and Madeira) into the orbit of European modernity (Wolf 1982: 293). Colonialism not only provided a vector through which new ideas of cosmopolitanism were forged and transmitted, it also provided the launching pad for the growth of an informal network of urban quarters and enclaves populated by transient and permanent communities of foreigners. By the early twentieth century, particularly during the interwar period, bohemians, artists and members of the European intelligentsia were attracted to a growing number of foreign-dominated enclaves, thus giving rise to 'new types of citizenship' (Rojek 1998: 303). Alongside the foreign residents and seasonal visitors, certain privileged members of the local elite were integrated into the cosmopolitan spaces of leisure and emancipated living, which germinated in these colonial outposts. However, the terms and standards put in place by the governing colonial powers often mediated and restricted their level of involvement.

One of the most well-known of these cosmopolitan spaces was the Moroccan city of Tangiers, designated as an 'international zone' between 1912 and 1956 and jointly administered by the colonial powers of Britain, France and Spain. Among the noted artistic figures who visited Tangiers at that time were the American author Paul Bowles and the 'beat poets' William Burroughs, Allen Ginsburg and Jack Kerouac, for whom the freedom to cross geographical, cultural and moral boundaries was intrinsic to their writings. The presence of these literary and artistic 'hipsters' in such far-flung colonies illustrates the archetypal adventurous traveller seeking to escape the shackles of stifling materialism and bourgeois conformity, which was characteristic of a later phase of international travel promoted by the new generation of travel guides from the late 1950s (Endy 2004: 136). As Rojek (1998) points out, these spaces offered levels of anonymity and licence for the kinds of emancipated lifestyles often associated with activities that would have attracted moral censorship in participants' home environments. Colonial powers often permitted licentious behaviour, though the privileges were available to all but a few members of the local elite. This resulted in acerbic condemnation from members of the 'Third World' intelligentsia. Franz Fanon, for instance, was critical of 'Third World' countries for subordinating themselves to the leisured desires of the metropole, claiming:

> The national bourgeoisie will be greatly helped on its way towards decadence by the Western bourgeoisies, who come to it as tourists avid for the exotic, for big game hunting and for casinos. The national bourgeoisie organises centres of rest and relaxation and pleasure resorts to meet the needs of the Western bourgeoisie.
>
> *(Fanon 1968: 153)*

Following decolonization in the post-war period, tourism became enmeshed within the process of 'Third World' nation-building and the emergent 'developmental system' (Curtis 2003). This reflected the strategy of the major powers to export Western-inspired models of development to low-income states. Tourism was thus also a conduit through which newly independent states in the 'Third World' sought to forge new models of citizenship out of the ashes of the colonial state. However, from the 1970s and early 1980s there was a rapid realization that tourism was not a panacea for independence or autonomous development, reflecting continued levels of dependency and, according to a number of critics, (neo-)colonial patterns of trade (Turner and Ash 1975). Nonetheless, it was not only academic critiques that were responsible for this realization but indeed wilful political leaders of progressive 'Third World' states that made these concerns abundantly clear. The leader of Grenada's People's Revolutionary Government (1979–83), Maurice Bishop, believed that because tourism was predominantly foreign-controlled and -owned, 'it brought with it a number of distinct socio-cultural and environmental hazards such as the race question and undesirable social and economic patterns' (Bishop 1983: 71).

The relationship between freedom and mobility rights was given practical scope via the uneven development of different forms of travel throughout the twentieth century. For the 'drifter-tourists' of the 1960s (E. Cohen 1972, 1973), for instance, the desire to be free from the constraints of bourgeois family life and career expectations, and the empty materialism of (Western) industrial capitalist society, acted as a strong impetus to embark on the infamous 'hippy trail'. In contrast to hobos and tramps (see Allsop 1967), this new 'class' of drifter-tourists normally comprised college-educated individuals from comfortable middle-class backgrounds (E. Cohen 1972: 176). Their rejection of conventional modes of travel and existence reflected the emergence of a counter-culture that had begun to take shape in the heart of a number of Western capitalist societies.

Ironically, it was the political freedoms and rising prosperity within such societies that underpinned the growing sense of entitlement among these discontented youth travellers in as much as it also enabled the growth of international travel among a new generation of working- and middle-class tourists alike. Although many early travellers, on the 'hippy trail' were adamant that they were on a spiritual journey (McGrath 2000: 10), it was precisely the changes brought about by post-war economic development and the rising prosperity of the middle classes in Western capitalist democracies that fuelled individualized aspirations to travel overseas. Significant improvements in transport technologies, principally aviation, were also facilitating factors. However, as Urry (2013) observes, none of this would have been possible without secure access to plentiful supplies of cheap oil, which for the past century has literally powered the development and globalization of carbon-fuelled economies, notably in the US and Europe. The benefits of such carbon-fuelled economics disproportionately accrued to the citizens of the US and Europe, including of course the possibility for living mobile lives and participating in overseas travel.

Although the 'hippy trail' and other offbeat forms of 'drifter-tourism' provided a convenient outlet for expressing a self-centred discontent with the prevailing norms of bourgeois capitalist society, especially among sections of Western youth, such travel was premised upon deep inequalities and highly unequal flows of mobility prevalent at the time. While international travel has to some extent become more widespread, such contradictions continue to be echoed through a range of contemporary forms of tourism: from 'neo-hippy' hedonistic forms of tourism in Goa to upmarket wellness tourism, and even certain forms of 'ethical travel' and volunteer tourism. That is not to say that such tourists move in the same circles as the globally mobile elites discussed in Chapter 2. Nevertheless, their mobilities manifest many of the contradictory meanings and interpretations of freedom that circulate throughout various arenas of tourism consumption. As identified by Higgins-Desbiolles (2006a) and as will be discussed in further detail in Chapter 6, although certain contemporary forms of niche travel are underpinned by a global and/or cosmopolitan outlook they are also marked by a series of unresolved tensions. On the one hand, travel may be seen as a social force and marker of global citizenship, while on the other, it has become an increasingly marketized commodity, the consumption of which is, moreover, premised upon having the 'right credentials' for travel.

Mobility entitlements, travel and citizenship

The transformations in the organization and structure of the international tourism industries over the past two decades, brought about by globalization, neoliberal capitalism and technological change, have rendered just about anywhere on the planet accessible to travel and tourists. Accordingly, international travel has become an altogether more corporate, institutionalized and pervasive activity, encompassed within the worldwide reach of multinational corporations and profit-driven enterprises. Such is the pervasiveness of mobility that Holzapfel (2010: 14) argues that a 'distance-intensive lifestyle', based on the 'constant availability and spatial accessibility of people and products', has become taken for granted among the inhabitants of advanced capitalist societies. Frequent flyer programmes and hotel loyalty schemes epitomize privileged access to lifestyles of permanent and seam-less mobility, available to a minority of globally mobile people and reflecting sub-tle forms of differentiated mobility. Many airline loyalty schemes now enable the fast-track passage of their members through customs and immigration. While these schemes are theoretically open to all travellers based on the ability to pay, such as the 'Registered Traveler' programme in the Unites States, additional security clearance may be granted by the state, which then enables participants to access high-speed lanes in addition to those used by frequent flyers (Coles 2008a: 66). Increasingly then, asymmetrical flows of cross-border mobility do not just express differences in wealth and income, but rather go to the heart of contemporary questions regarding the meaning of citizenship in a networked, mobile and globalized society.

Despite the apparent democratization of travel heralded by the continued growth and worldwide expansion of international tourist arrivals, particularly in the emer-ging economies of the global South, international travel continues to unfold in a differentiated and unequal manner. As indicated in the introductory chapter, global tourism encapsulates the contradictory forces of mobility and freedom on the one hand and immobility and disenfranchisement on the other. For Bauman (1998: 2), 'being local in a globalised world is a sign of social deprivation and degradation'. The tourist is often accorded a heightened social status, exemplified and reinforced through the various promotional discourses that continue to circulate through-out a variety of tourism contexts: from upmarket niche operators to mass-market resort providers. While tourism may not be as strongly marked by the stain of (neo)colonialism that was still prevalent in certain 'Third World' destinations in the 1960s and 1970s, although evidence of inferior working conditions in the tourism industries still abounds (see Beddoe 2004; ILO 2010: 14–18), a strong sense that the whims and desires of tourists must continuously be catered for still remains preva-lent. Some tourists can engage in role-reversal experiences and liberated encoun-ters during their holidays, which are not always available in everyday life. Graburn (1989: 28) informatively notes: 'Because the tourist journey lies in the nonordinary sphere of existence, the goal is symbolically sacred and morally on a higher plane than the regards of the ordinary workaday world.'

Therefore, to be a tourist represents an ability to access a range of mobility privileges that are beyond the reach of many in host societies within impoverished parts of the world, as well as a large proportion of the unemployed and deprived members of the population in developed capitalist economies. This point reinforces the claim that those who cannot afford to partake in tourism, or for whatever rea-son have their mobility freedoms curtailed, are prevented from actively enjoying the manifold benefits that tourism brings, in particular the citizenship 'rights' that accrue by virtue of being mobile.

Indeed, such is the potency of mobility as a symbol of privileged status and citi-zenship rights, that in some cases, the travel entitlements of privileged members of society, particularly public servants and politicians, may become the subject of media scrutiny or, indeed, the target of public opprobrium. Recently, the practice of accepting free holidays or accommodation from high-ranking politicians and wealthy citizens in other states by a number of senior European politicians has drawn widespread condemnation. Keen to be seen as responsive to citizens' concerns at a time of economic recession, governments responded to this apparent holiday 'gravy train' by addressing the manner in which politicians and government representatives took foreign trips. In early 2011, former President Nicolas Sarkozy publicly announced that ministers should ensure that all future overseas trips are fully authorized. This was a direct reaction to confessions by the then Prime Minister, who had accepted a New Year Nile holiday from the ousted Egyptian President, as well as the former Foreign Minister, who had travelled in a private plane financed by a Tunisian businessman. President Sarkozy also declared that holidays should be 'compatible with France's foreign policy', and that 'only by being above reproach will people holding high office strengthen their citizens' trust in the state institutions' (Telegraph 2011). The fact that these trips had taken place immediately prior to and during the 2011 'Arab Spring' uprisings makes this issue even more compelling, particularly at a time when the 'West' is supposedly keen to demonstrate the value of working towards principles of democracy, political transparency and accountability. The response of the French premier thus illustrates the potent symbolic value of travel as a marker of privilege and citizenship. Even for the powerful, the 'right' to accept free travel and holidays as a form of diplomatic exchange can quickly be curtailed when the political integrity of the state itself is at stake.

Besides constituting a mere marker of status and privilege, if tourism is to be perceived as a social necessity or benchmark of a 'civilized' life then the unfolding relationship between tourism and the differentiated axes of mobility has a number of implications for both existing and emergent understandings of citizenship. This is all the more significant in the light of the globalization of free markets and discourses of 'consumer citizenship', where rights are regarded by the apostles of neoliberalism and capitalist globalization as synonymous with the freedom to make personal consumer choices in the marketplace. Therefore, exclusion from the global marketplace of tourist consumption unequivocally implies a denial of twenty-first-century citizenship rights.

MacCannell (1999: 159) indicates that the social pressure and need to travel in order to escape daily boredom and routine implies a common perception that those who are unable to travel, or whose freedoms to travel are curtailed, are somehow *inferior* to those who travel on a more regular basis. Subsequently, in the context of neoliberalism and globalized capitalism, where mobilities are a pervasive element of market societies and help sustain the wheels of a globalized economy, immobility has increasingly become a sign of social exclusion and deprivation, as discussed in Chapter 1. Bauman (1998: 96) suggests that the 'vagabond', a term he uses to describe the impoverished majority whose mobility is either coerced or not experienced at all, is a 'flawed consumer' who contributes nothing to 'the prosperity of an economy turned into a tourist industry'. He thus draws attention to the conceptual distinction between 'tourists' and 'vagabonds', where the former refers to those who are able to travel at will to wherever they choose, and the latter to those forced to travel for reasons of economic necessity and/or fear of political persecution. While the 'tourist pays for their freedom to disregard native concerns and feelings' (Bauman 1993: 241), the *sans-papiers* and those fleeing persecution and economic hardship are actually 'trapped in the imperative of mobility' (Lyon 2008a: 44). The contrast between the ease of mobility of international tourists and the immobility of poor residents and clandestine migrants adjacent to tourism resorts, whether for political or economic reasons, can often be quite stark (see Smith 2007).

The distinctive symbolic and economic value attached to diverse modes of mobility is palpably illustrated by the negative perceptions and media treatment of 'gypsies', 'asylum seekers' and 'economic migrants' in the UK, and in other parts of Europe, whose mobilities are seen as inferior to that of tourists, among others. Media-fuelled xenophobia and public disdain against the 'flood' of immigrants and asylum seekers exacerbate the sense of differentiation between 'legitimate' and 'illegitimate' forms of mobility and travel. This is exemplified by the reactions of the UK tabloid press towards the (existing and perceived) movements of 'gypsies' (see Fagge 2004), outbreaks of violence towards the Roma in Italy (Popham 2007) and Romanian immigrants in Northern Ireland (Henry and Smythe 2009). Further typecasting has surfaced through acerbic constructions of migrants as 'citizenship tourists' or 'welfare tourists', travelling and moving to countries with advanced welfare systems in order to parasitically claim 'free' benefits of all descriptions, including public health services (Breen *et al.* 2006; Fagge 2004; Shipman 2013). Although tourists and impoverished migrants often find themselves moving through or indeed sharing the same destinations, they naturally experience quite different worlds of mobility and hospitality. Whether in the case of migrants attempting to cross the narrow straits between Turkey and the Greek Island of Samos (Smith 2007), or the rough-sleeping migrants on the beaches and public squares of the Canary Islands (La Provincia 2009), the unequal distribution of mobility rights is severe.

Paradoxically, in the light of the above, 'Third World' communities are often simultaneously romanticized and pitied by tourists seeking out 'authentic' and 'exotic' experiences, as so brilliantly captured in the film *Cannibal Tours*, which depicts a group of upmarket tourists on a voyage to see 'primitive' Papua New Guinean communities along the Sepik River (O'Rourke 1988). Such encounters constitute a form of tourism commonly known as 'ethnic tourism' (see Harron and Weiler 1992), a popular activity for those who wish to become familiar with the lifestyles of others and appreciate other ethnicities because of their perceived pristine nature, spirituality and cultural depth. The irony, however, relates to the way in which people from 'less developed' countries are converted into devalued subjects once they are seen as a threat and/or seek to enter 'developed' societies. Similar, and in some cases, harsher attitudes prevail when migrants seek to cross the border into neighbouring states in the global South, as demonstrated by the persecution of migrant workers from Bangladesh and Burma in Thailand (Rahman 2009).

A further illustration of the chasm that exists between the world of the tourist and non-tourist concerns the politicized and ideological constructions of Mexicans seeking entry to the United States. Here, the popular conception is one of hordes of poor migrants or 'wetbacks', as they are derogatively known, seeking access to the employment opportunities and riches of the US at the expense of hard-working (usually blue-collar) US citizens, whose livelihoods are threatened by such movements. The populist image of the Mexican migrant or stowaway overrides any notion of the Mexican tourist or consumer, despite the fact that cross-border shopping by Mexicans in the US is a valuable source of revenue. Perceptions of Mexicans as tourists, however, are in effect invisible and rendered problematic throughout countless media and cinematic portrayals as illegal migrant workers, if not criminals. However, Murià and Chávez (2011) recognize that, although Mexican workers are often subject to state surveillance, Mexican consumption rather than production (i.e. employment) is actually encouraged and facilitated. Market research companies and major retail outlets in San Diego often track affluent Tijuana residents, encouraging them to shop across the border through the production of sales information, coupons and discount offers. The authors suggest that US law consequently regulates the mobility of the residents of Tijuana by formulating a 'binary distinction between consumers and workers', which exposes the economic disparities between the 'rich and poor in the city' (Murià and Chávez 2011: 370).

The justification for the special treatment of international tourists is thus commonly based on the somewhat dubious economic assumption that, while tourism always provides much-needed wealth and employment to a host country, immigration almost always acts as a drain on economic resources and indeed a threat to 'native' cultural values. Despite such popular (mis)conceptions, there is evidence to suggest that migration can be of significant benefit to both the recipient countries as well as the sender countries. Mathers and Landau (2007) show how migrant labour has been a crucial ingredient in South Africa's economic success in both the formal and informal sectors, not to mention the shoppers and traders who make up a substantial proportion of cross-border tourist traffic. Migration can also have cumulative benefits to home societies, as evidenced by the substantial flow of global migrant remittances worldwide. In 2011, World Bank figures calculated the value of global remittances at around US$501 billion, an increase of 12.1 per cent from 2010. This amount represents nearly half the total value of the annual export income generated by international tourism, including passenger transportation, which in 2011 was US$1.2 trillion (UNWTO 2012: 2). Somewhat paradoxically, given their oft-hailed status as emerging powerhouse economies, of those countries reliant upon remittances for significant export revenues, India was the largest beneficiary at US$64 billion, followed by China (US$62 billion) and then Mexico (US$24 billion) (Ratha and Silwal 2012).

The boundaries between 'tourist' and 'migrant' are also in constant flux. While temporary migrants may at times engage in touristic activities, people may also use their status as tourists to gain entry into a country and remain there beyond the time allowed by the authorities. In cases where the opportunistic utilization of 'tourist visas' does take place, it relates to people's need to seek employment and decent wages relative to their home countries. It has been estimated that from

2003 to 2005 more than 70,000 of the 800,000 pilgrims who were issued with a Hajj or Umrah visa by Saudi Arabia's Hajj Ministry (9 per cent of all pilgrims) failed to return home after their visa was complete. The issue of illegal immigration apparently prompted the country authorities to introduce new rules to discourage married men under the age of 40 obtaining an Umrah visa. This specifically applies to men originating from nine countries: Bangladesh, Chad, Egypt, Ethiopia, India, Nigeria, Pakistan, the Sudan and Yemen (Gearon 2006). Missing tourists have also become a concern for those states that try to ensure that their hospitality does not get taken for granted, and whose policies concerning immigration are justified in terms of protecting the economic welfare of the nation. In 2010, for instance, Chinese and Korean authorities were concerned that over 30 Chinese cruise ship tourists had gone missing on the South Korean island of Jeju during a routine day tour (Yingying 2010). Controversially, tourism can be perceived as a platform to create opportunities for impoverished or persecuted individuals to access other countries, mobilizing illegal migrants to seek the economic means to survive and support their families and communities. In reality, however, the utilization of tourism as a ticket for survival is often thwarted by the power of the state to clearly define which individuals constitute 'tourists' and 'non-tourists' as well as 'citizens' and 'non-citizens'. Therefore, the 'non-tourists' or rather the 'deportation class' (Salter 2008a: xi) are seemingly the vagabonds of society, together with refugees, migrant workers, 'illegal' immigrants, asylum seekers and dissidents. Bauman further claims: 'As a rule, vagabonds can't and don't stay in a place as long as they want, they stay in a place only as long as they are wanted' (2003: 209). This can be contrasted to his interpretation of the 'tourist's world' where 'the strange is tame, domesticated and no longer frightens' (Bauman 1996: 29). There are parallels here with MacCannell's (1992) notion of the 'empty meeting ground' in which 'tourists' and 'vagabonds' pass each other within the same space, interacting perhaps but rarely upsetting the underlying power structures which facilitate and structure that unequal encounter.

The stark contrast between the 'mobility rich' and 'mobility poor' was illustrated in the aftermath of Hurricane Katrina, which devastated the US city of New Orleans in August 2005, leaving over one thousand dead and hundreds of thousands more homeless (Creswell 2006: 259). In contrast to the injustices experienced by residents of the hardest hit Lower Ninth Ward, one of New Orleans's poorest areas, tourists were quickly and carefully escorted to safety by the US military, and immediate arrangements were made to ensure their return to their home destinations. However, hundreds of thousands of mainly working-class African American residents were without access to private transportation (an estimated quarter of the population) and thus unable to evacuate. In an ironic twist of historically conditioned fate, New Orleans's most famous tourist assets, including the French Quarter and the Garden District, and its most patrician neighbourhoods such as Audubon Park, survived due to being built on higher ground than the poorer surrounding districts (Davis 2005). The experience of local resident Abdulrahman Zeitoun, who was arrested by the National Guard and incarcerated in a maximum-security prison for nearly a month, further illustrates the racism that fuels the attitudes and actions of the authorities when faced with the mobility of 'non-natives' or those deemed 'suspicious'. Zeitoun's apparent wrongdoing was that he rescued numerous people trapped in their homes using an old canoe. Although as Eggers (2010) recounts, it is Zeitoun's Syrian origins that were in fact the cause for 'concern' for the authorities, hence why he was accused of 'terrorist' activity.

In the aftermath of the storm, the term 'refugee' was used by broadcasters to refer to residents fleeing the stricken city and seeking refuge at the city airport and the Superdome, implying that they were somehow acting in a 'un-American' way. Accordingly, conservative pundits all but attributed the inability of many of the poor and black residents to leave the city with haste as a testament to their stubbornness rather than the ineptitude of the authorities (Scheper-Hughes 2005). This alleged stubbornness also linked to iniquitous claims, noted by Somers (2008), that such residents were generally socially apathetic and highly dependent on the government. In Spike Lee's gripping depiction of the aftermath of Katrina in the acclaimed documentary *When the Levees Broke* (2006), one resident suggests that it was as if 'the storm had blown our citizenship away'. However, as the residents had already endured many years of economic and social marginalization from mainstream American society and the wider political community, their status as citizens was already contestable (Somers 2008).

The tendency to privilege certain forms of mobility over others has to some extent also been reflected in the tendency to prioritize international tourism over domestic tourism, notwithstanding the fact that the latter far outnumbers the former (Gladstone 2005: 14). In certain popular mass tourism destinations, for example, the Canary Islands, distinctions between international and domestic travel are often physically reinforced through the enclosure of coastal areas for the purposes of developing upscale resorts for foreign tourists, thereby denying access to the shoreline to ('non-paying') domestic inhabitants and eviscerating any memory of its previous non-commodified usage (Sabaté Bel 2001). Elsewhere, Sheller (2009: 199) describes how neoliberal policies are reshaping Caribbean urbanism and coastal development 'as part of larger transnational processes of urban restructuring'. In recent years, Caribbean states have gone about liberalizing once publicly owned infrastructures (including the beachfront) and paving the way for a new generation of fortified, private tourism enclaves, in addition to the 'traditional' 'all-inclusive' resort that has traditionally occupied a predominant place in Caribbean tourism since the 1980s. More significantly, Sheller (2009: 194) points to how new, multi-scalar geographies of development and mobility linked to neoliberal policies work to free up flows of real estate investment and tourists, while simultaneously limiting 'the mobility rights afforded to local citizens and to migrant noncitizens'.

Clearly not all tourists embody the kind of one-dimensional structural power implied in neo-Marxist accounts of tourism (e.g. Britton 1991), nor are all hosts 'powerless' (Cheong and Miller 2000). The axes of power along which the diverse interactions between visitors and residents take place are more complex and multifaceted than is suggested by Bauman's tourist/vagabond dichotomy. It does

not, for instance, capture the range of placements between the tourist and vagabond, the latter referring to those with tenuous rights of mobility, such as the 'illegal'
immigrant, asylum seeker, refugee, dissident or exile, each of which are loaded with
myriad political connotations according to their socio-political contexts. Given the
plethora of diverse mobilities traversing the globe, to reduce the different modalities of movement to a single category or binary opposition between two mutually exclusive categories is thus clearly inadequate. There are various categories
and permutations existing beyond the metaphorical 'vagabond' and the 'tourist'.
Moreover, different degrees of cross-border international mobility are not based
simply on straightforward financial determinants and/or relative consumer power,
but are further mediated by determinants of ethnicity, race, religion, sexuality and
gender, which serve to restrict the freedom of movement of those who inhabit the
'margins' of the global economy.

Tourism, mobility rights and market freedoms

The freedom of movement and right to travel that enable international travel and
tourism to flourish conceal a number of tensions and paradoxes that are not always
explicit. The most significant of all is the tension between the right to the freedom of movement as set out in the UNDHR and the right to travel interpreted
as the right to tourism. This is the interpretation clearly expressed in Article 8 of
the WTO's (1999) *Code of Ethics*. Accordingly, the right to tourism implies not
only the politically guaranteed rights of the freedom of movement and the right to
travel, but it signifies the right to enter and consume other places and cultural sites
'without being subject to excessive formalities or discrimination'. These unresolved
tensions between the socially progressive and individualistic aspects of tourism can
be traced to the birth of modern industrial tourism itself; specifically, to the contrast
between the commercialized philanthropy of Thomas Cook and the more hard-
nosed business mindset of his son, J. M. Cook. Furthermore, although the right to
a holiday has been institutionalized and given practical scope through paid holidays
and socialized leisure programmes throughout most advanced capitalist societies,
the right to travel is one that is far from being universally acknowledged, not least
due to worldwide variations in statutory leisure time (see Hall 2005: 87).

Although tourism continues to embody the residue of earlier 'welfarist' ideals to
classical liberal notions of peace and cultural exchange, it has increasingly become
shaped by discourses of market individualism and the unfettered right to travel
(Higgins-Desbiolles 2006a). In a lucid summary of the contradictory values that are
inherent in contemporary tourist practices, MacCannell (1999: 193) remarks that,
'the term "touristic" names the line dividing the exchange of human notice, on
the one side, and commercial exchange on the other. "Touristic" is the place where
these two kinds of exchange meet.' Related to this, the economies of those states
that were protected from liberal capitalism have increasingly opened up through
accelerated globalization and economic integration. Whereas social tourism is

organized around various modes of state, civil society and trade union-based support, embodying an egalitarian approach to travel, the notion of tourism as a human right presupposes both the democratization of travel and the universal ability to travel, thus implying a shift towards a more individualist rights-based conception of tourism. This approach to tourism is clearly epitomized in the observations made by the travel columnist Simon Jenkins (2009), who, following the travel chaos brought about by the unusually heavy snowfalls in the UK during December 2009, argued that 'of all the human activities that bring out the selfish in mankind, nothing compares with travel'.

Such is the strength of the sense of entitlement to travel within advanced capitalist, highly marketized societies that to question the right to travel is tantamount to questioning our fundamental rights as human beings. Furthermore, Western governments may very well acknowledge that to enable their citizenry to participate fully in the rights of tourism, not only involves the legal scaffolding upholding the right to a paid holiday and rights to mobility, but also the material capacity to engage in travel. Hence, the provisions of numerous social tourism programmes for the less affluent became a defining feature of many social democratic governments, as both a means of incorporating less privileged citizens into the consumption of travel as well as to sustain the accumulation of capital itself. Nevertheless, however much the struggle for paid holidays may have embodied the rightful aspirations of working peoples in advanced capitalist societies for time off work, increasingly, the presumption that a holiday is both a necessity and a right encompasses a rather more hard-nosed set of individualistic values and market-oriented notions of citizenship, in which:

> One is *entitled* to travel since it is an essential part of one's life. Cultures become so mobile that contemporary citizens (not just Americans!) are thought to possess the rights to pass over and into other places and other cultures.
>
> *(Urry 2002: 157, original emphasis)*

In many ways, the association of tourism with the relatively unencumbered right to consume peoples, places and their cultures, embodies a 'negative' conception of freedom in which freedom, or rather 'liberty', is defined as 'the area within which a man [*sic*] can act unobstructed by others' (Berlin 2002: 169). Tourists are thus exhorted to choose between a variety of products, places and environments for their holidays, while the institutional apparatuses of the international tourism industries seek to ensure that their choices and the related expansion of tourism are as free from regulatory constraint as possible. This libertarian position ignores the manner in which such freedoms are governed by the prevailing distribution of material resources and the geostrategic intentions of states that constrain and enable the ability to travel. Further, as Higgins-Desbiolles (2007: 318–319) notes, this position also glosses over the continuing disparities between the advancement of the rights to travel and to tourism on the one hand and the 'rights to development' on the other. These latter rights are established and clarified in the 1986

UN Declaration on the Right to Development (United Nations 1986). The right to tourism and all that it implies in terms of being able to enjoy the comforts and pleasures that one can consume while on holiday often overrides the rights to development, as demanded by less mobile subjects. These demands, for instance, may concern claims by fishermen to maintain unhindered access to beaches and appeals by informal enterprises to ply their trade on beaches coveted by or turned over to large-scale hotel and tourism developments (see Hochuli and Plüss 2005: 11–13; Hodal 2013). Therefore, it follows that:

> If *liberty* means freedom to choose what and when to consume, the market can deliver that for most citizens of developed countries, in profusion. Here, the main conundrum, even in these most favourable of circumstances, is the compatibility of economic and political agendas, of free markets with democracy – which is not always so evident as the protagonists of neo-liberalism assert.
>
> *(Deakin 2001: 202, original emphasis)*

The degree to which tourism is seen as an inalienable right and one that is beyond critical scrutiny is vividly depicted in the response from the Chair of the Kathmandu Research Centre to the beating by Nepalese Maoists of a Swiss tourist who refused to pay the 'tourist fee' often demanded by the rebels. Comparing tourists to 'Gods ... whom we never beat or insult', Dr Pradhanang went on to argue that 'beating a tourist is the same as killing oneself and suicide to the national economy and tourism development' (Steinmetz 2007). Dr Pradhanang further suggested that foreign tourists beaten in Nepal, which one has to bear in mind is not a common occurrence at all, should be granted free medical care – a right not enjoyed by the majority of the Nepalese. More recently, in the heart of the European Union, the Greek government offered to compensate tourists stranded in Greece during national protests over the recent economic austerity measures imposed on Greek citizens by the EU and other financial institutions (Smith 2010). These illustrations demonstrate the various ways in which different states prioritize the needs and mobility rights of tourists, further distancing tourists from any notion of 'risk-taking' and shifting the burden of responsibility for 'protecting' tourists onto the inhabitants of the destinations themselves. Such tensions, between the right to travel and to be a tourist versus the development rights of less privileged citizens of host communities, are ones that will be explored in further detail in Chapter 6, particularly in the light of attempts by civil society groups to contest specific forms of tourism development and boycott travel to particular places in the name of universal human rights.

The emphasis on expanding the realm of individual freedoms is also of course one of the preconditions for the workings of capitalist free markets and a defining trope of neoliberal marketized societies. Indeed, according to the liberal political tradition, the right to buy and own property and the right to buy and sell labour are accorded equal status to that of other individual rights. Furthermore, the right to travel whenever and wherever we please is often deemed superior to the right of workers in the travel and transport industries to withdraw their labour in protest over wages and working conditions. Hence, citizens of advanced capitalist states are increasingly exhorted to see themselves as consumers, particularly during times of buoyant employment, as opposed to citizens whose principal orientation is towards the defence of civil and political rights and freedoms in the public realm (see Urry 2000: 184–185). Hence, citizens of neoliberal societies are less tolerant of restrictions on their freedoms to consume and to travel, whether as a consequence of the imposition of higher taxes (such as the controversial UK Air Passenger Duty[2]) or industrial action, than they are of the restrictions imposed on the movement of migrants and asylum seekers, particularly in the UK (see Lowles 2011).

In 2010, the response of British Airways management and media commentators to a strike by BA cabin crew offered an instructive insight into society's high regard for the right to travel. Disproportionate attention concerned the strike's inconvenience to millions of people's travel plans, as well as its long-term impact on the airline's brand image, rather than on the rights of workers to express discontent at management practices and working conditions (BBC 2010a). Although the right to withdraw one's labour and the related right to freedom of association are fundamental human rights enshrined in UK and international law, this point barely received an airing in the midst of the shrill of attacks on 'recalcitrant' unions and 'cosseted' airline workers (Ewing 2010). Furthermore, in a particularly spiteful attack on the mobility rights and travel privileges of BA cabin crew, the BA Chief Executive withdrew the travel perks of striking cabin crew as a means of exerting pressure on the union to withdraw its action. Thus, not only did BA management seek to deny cabin crew their lawful right to strike by seeking a court injunction, it also sought to remove their rights to 'privileged' travel freedoms as airline employees in response to the lawful withdrawal of labour as a means of protest.

This conflict exposes a number of the tensions between contrasting notions of freedom and rights as they apply to consumers on the one hand and workers on the other. Globalization and deeper and wider EU integration has facilitated (with notable exceptions) increased movements of labour, while exposing scheduled carriers (many of which were once heavily protected state airlines, such as BA) to the full force of market competition, thus bringing downward pressure to bear on airline wages (Whitelegg 2003). However, at the same time, BA cabin crew were accused of being a privileged group of airline workers in so far as they were earning double that of cabin crew working for rivals Virgin Atlantic and other low-wage carriers, at the time of writing. The implication, therefore, is that the actions of striking BA cabin crew would inflate the costs of travel for BA customers while remaining silent on the irony that profit margins must remain untouched or, better still, increased (Milmo 2010: 4). In this regard, one must concur with Wright (2009: 105) that citizenship in neoliberal, marketized societies has become little more than a 'licence' to sell one's labour and, of course, to consume. Conversely, Whitelegg (2003: 245) argues that the increasingly cosmopolitan character of cabin crew and pilots, who often live in countries other than the airlines' operational base, has brought about new forms of transnational solidarity, thus explaining the continued militancy and resilience of certain airline unions.

Individual freedom and the right to travel have in many ways come to be seen as coterminous with freedom of the market. Moreover, the latter is also regarded as a necessary precondition of the former. Any attempt to challenge or indeed abolish market freedoms is thus regarded as tantamount to a violation of human freedom (see Callinicos 2003: 115). In this regard, global tourism can be seen as the apotheosis of a (neo)liberal 'cosmopolitan' global order based on a seamless harmony between the free movement of people (with the exception of labour or 'economic migrants'), goods and capital. 'Freedom of travel' has quite literally become synonymous with the 'freedom of trade' (O' Byrne 2001: 409). The constant expansion of the realms of consumption via the relentless development of new tourist products, niche tourist segments and destinations of distinction, epitomizes the hallmark of capitalist development and indeed globalization that was foretold by Marx and Engels (1985 [1888]: 83), both writing over a century and a half ago!

> The need of a constantly expanding market for its products chases the bourgeoisie over the whole surface of the globe. It must nestle everywhere, settle everywhere, establish connections everywhere. The bourgeoisie has through its exploitation of the world market given a cosmopolitan character to production and consumption in every country.

Over the past two decades the continued growth of international tourist arrivals, which recovered remarkably quickly from the 2007–2008 financial crash (see UNWTO 2011), and the concomitant expansion of globalized tourism businesses, have been increasingly shaped and organized by the institutionalization of a neoliberal 'market fundamentalism' and associated discourses of (consumer) freedom and open borders for tourists. Such discourses underwrite a sense of entitlement to travel when, wherever and however one wishes, reinforced by the various proclamations put out by the UN World Tourism Organization and the World Travel and Tourism Council. In fact, both institutions enthusiastically promote three pillars of neoliberal tourism: (1) the opening of new markets; (2) the deregulation of corporate enterprise; and (3) the inalienable right to travel. According to the WTO (1999):

> the world tourism industry as a whole has much to gain by operating in an environment that favours the market economy, private enterprise and free trade … responsible and sustainable tourism is by no means incompatible with the growing liberalization of the conditions governing trade in services.

The elision of market freedoms and the rights of the individual are in many ways cornerstones of the US Constitution, particularly since 1886 when a Supreme Court ruling extended to corporations the same constitutional rights that had been put in place to uphold individual freedoms (Kingsnorth 2004: 285). As a consequence, the first amendment guarantee of free speech has been interpreted to enable unlimited spending on political campaign advertising by corporate donors (Freedland 2012). This echoes the increasingly blurred distinction between the right to travel and the right to tourism. As the preamble of the WTO's (1999) *Global Code of Ethics* illustrates, 'the right of all persons to use their free time for leisure pursuits and travel' is accorded equal importance with promotion of 'the market economy, private enterprise and free trade'. Across the varied landscapes of global travel promoted by the marketized tourism industries, the social and economic distinctions between tourists, consumers and citizens are therefore increasingly difficult to discern, especially as the right to travel and to tourism is subsumed within the totality of capitalist social relations and the right to profit.

Tourists, citizens and consumers

The alignment of personal liberty and market freedoms received a significant boost after the collapse of the Communist Eastern bloc regimes in 1989. The struggle for democracy in Eastern Europe and the subsequent fall of the Berlin Wall in 1989 symbolized the triumph of 'civil society' over totalitarianism (Urry 2000: 162). Former Communist states, particularly Russia, witnessed brutal economic restructuring by the International Monetary Fund while at the same time the apostles of neoliberalism claimed that societies have reached the 'end of history', that is, the universalization of free market capitalism and the worldwide embrace of Western liberal democracy (Fukuyama 1989). While struggles for rights of citizenship were simultaneously fused into demands for rights to consume, the integration of these societies into the expanding dynamics of neoliberal capitalism also signalled the opening up of new frontiers for travel as well as capital. In the course of these events, 'citizens openly declared their right to be tourists' (Munar 2007: 347) as a plethora of new places, cultures and 'products' then entered the global tourist 'market' for consumption (Plate 3.1). Ironically then, the freedoms that were ushered in on the ruins of Soviet Communism, and which heralded the birth of new democratic citizenship rights in these countries, resulted in a crisis of the very idea of citizenship itself, as it became increasingly subsumed by the market. Equally, in the capitalist heartlands, the transformations associated with neoliberalism and capitalist globalization, in particular the hollowing out of the social–democratic state, have meant that state-based definitions have begun to give way to a new, market-led definition of the citizen: 'Citizenship is becoming conflated with consumerism – truly the revenge of the market against the state in the form of an aggressive non-liberalism armed with the new ideological construction of freedom in the form of buying power' (Silverman 1992: 151).

A free market conception of citizenship also underpins the construction and expansion of the European Union. However, this sometimes brings it into conflict with other areas designed to strengthen European citizenship, including the

PLATE 3.1   A section of the Berlin Wall's infamous 'East Side Gallery'. Threatened by demolition, the 'gallery' became a symbol of the fall of the wall and a memorial to human freedom, and is now a major tourist draw. Photo: C. Morris Paris, June 2007.

goal of enabling the freedom of movement of all European citizens, and other social imperatives, such as the desire to expand social tourism (see Diekmann and McCabe 2011: 421–422). Historically, the EU has sought to reconcile the protection of social citizenship rights while removing barriers to the mobility of capital, as signalled by the terms of the 1993 Maastricht Treaty or Treaty on European Union (which included the Social Chapter) and, more recently, the 2009 Lisbon Treaty. As Shore (2000: 84) demonstrates, the EU increasingly appeals to its citizens as consumers to the extent that consumption, for example, through tourism and experiencing Europe's cultural heritage, is conceived as a defining principle and an act of European citizenship.

The discourse of tourism as freedom to travel and consume, and freedom from regulation, embodies a neoliberal ideal in which the 'citizen' has thus become increasingly synchronized with the 'consumer':

> The life of a consumer, the consuming life, is not about acquiring and possessing. It is not even about getting rid of what was been [*sic*] acquired the day before yesterday and proudly paraded a day later. It is instead, first and foremost, about *being on the move*.
>
> (Bauman 2007: 98, original emphasis)

Twenty-first-century travel experiences are not only commodities distributed through the mechanisms of market exchange, they are also vehicles of individual self-expression, freedom and autonomy. In this regard, postmodern 'critical turn' theorists such as Ateljevic (2000: 381) envisage the 'cultural practice of tourism as an arena wherein individuals create their identities based on power and knowledge'. There is no doubt that the compelling sense of liberation from traditional social norms and traditional 'real' communities, signified by such 'communities of consumption', further induced the transition from the 'allocation economy' of Fordist capitalism to the customized consumption of a flexible post-Fordist capitalism (Streeck 2012: 36).

The ability to abandon oneself to a constant vortex of conspicuous consumption, ostensibly 'surfing' from one identity to another, only serves to grant privileged access to such social identities to those with the economic means to do so. Through varying niche forms of travel, affluent tourists are able to 'cleanse themselves' of their frustrations and seek solace from their 'alienation' in the *ashrams* and upmarket yoga retreats of places such as India. Accordingly, they are able to enjoy the benefits of unhindered international travel in ways that are unimaginable to most of the residents of poor countries in the global south and, increasingly, many of those in the recession-stricken countries of the rich north. From the travels of Goethe and Byron in Italy to the semi-ethnographic adventures of T. E. Lawrence in Arabia, the act of seeking peace or spiritual renewal among the world's poor is nothing new. However, what was once the endeavour of a few maverick aristocrats or, later, a spontaneous expression of the hippy movement,[3] is now a multi-billion dollar industry (Global Spa Summit 2010). Here too, Bauman (2007: 100, original emphasis) offers a characteristically poignant insight:

> The consumerist culture is marked by a constant pressure to be *someone else*. Consumer markets focus on the prompt devaluation of their past offers, to clear a site in public demand for new ones to fill. They breed dissatisfaction with the products used by consumers to satisfy their needs – and they also cultivate constant disaffection with the acquired identity and set the needs by which such an identity is defined. Changing identity, discarding the past and seeking new beginnings, struggling to be born again – these are promoted by that culture as a *duty* disguised as a privilege.

Such views echo a kind of 'market populism' in which consumption becomes a substitute for, or more precisely, a vehicle of progressive politics and individual empowerment. This apparent 'postmodern' radicalism does not challenge the hegemony of the market but rather it is enacted through the marketplace and myriad individual acts of consumption, thus equating 'the will of the people with the deeds of the market' (Frank 2001: 287). There are parallels here with the spirit of 'ethical' tourism consumption and the belief that the market, left to its own devices, can achieve progressive outcomes in the shape of poverty alleviation and sustainability, notions which will be explored in greater detail in Chapter 6. While the rise of so-called 'ethical' and 'responsible' tourisms would appear to offer evidence of value systems that run counter to the neoliberal emphasis on market freedoms and the primacy of individual rights, they often prevail within a regime of rights that places significant emphasis on voluntarism and the empowered individual.

Conclusion

Notwithstanding the economic gains attributed to tourism, the citizens of the global South for the most part did not benefit from the massive expansion in global travel during the first decades of post-war economic development. This is particularly the case where the ability to become tourists themselves is concerned. Despite the proclaimed rise of the emerging economies, the majority of the world's inhabitants are still no closer to joining the ranks of the 'tourist citizenship class'. Moreover, a combination of deep recession and public austerity, and growing inequalities in conjunction with a series of environmentally related impacts linked primarily to global climate change, threatens to further curb or somehow derail the exponential growth and worldwide expansion of international travel to which many in the West have become accustomed over the past 60 years or so. Thus, while the global landscape of travel has become more populated as consumers in emerging economies continue to join the ranks of the one billion international arrivals, international tourism continues to expand in an uneven and differentiated manner, including some and excluding others.

This chapter concludes its examination of the relationship between tourism and ideas of freedom, by emphasizing how the discourses of freedom and rights underpinning the neoliberal logics of globalizing tourism serve to elide the distinction between the right to the freedom of movement and travel on the one hand and the right to travel and to be a tourist on the other. Accordingly, this chapter explored the transformation of international tourism, from its association with privileged freedoms and mobility privileges, and examined how these evolved and were produced in both the colonial and post-colonial era and into the present epoch. However, it was not until the early post-war period that the question of right to travel and to take a holiday became increasingly intertwined with the kinds of rights underpinning the freedom of movement, economic development and modernization.

One of the central observations of this chapter, therefore, is that international tourism has increasingly come to be regarded as a universal right rather than a privilege, as well as a marketized commodity shaped by discourses of market individualism and the unfettered right to travel. Accordingly, it has drawn attention to the alignment between tourism and market-based renderings of citizens as consumers. It also remains sceptical of the claim that international tourism has become increasingly democratized and is founded upon an equitable distribution of the right and freedom to travel. The ascendance of neoliberal globalization has reinforced the seamless connection between discourses framing the right to travel and the freedom of movement, and those associated with the expansion of an increasingly marketized tourism and the right to be a tourist. The next chapter will continue to reflect on the nature of such rights as are encompassed within international tourism, with particular emphasis on the role of states in enabling and constraining the movement of tourists, and the implications for citizenship.

Notes

1 Dube's (1999: 38) account of the travels of white missionaries in central India drew attention to the civilizing and hegemonic agendas of Anglo-European societies, in which there was a significant movement to 'civilize the heathen'.
2 The Airline Passenger Duty is an excise duty and environmental levy on aircraft emissions that is charged to outbound travellers from the UK. It was originally brought in by the UK government in 1994 but was amended in 2008 to incorporate four bands based on the distance between London and the eventual destination. It has been strongly criticized by the aviation industry and travellers alike (Fearis 2007). It has also been challenged by Caribbean island destinations, which argue that the tax discriminates against them by charging passengers less for travelling to the West Coast of the United States than it does to the less distant Caribbean region (Travel Mail Reporter 2013).
3 Ironically, MacCannell (1999: 171) referred to hippies as the 'shock troops of mass tourism'.

4

LICENSED TO TRAVEL

State power, freedom of movement and the right to travel

[F]reedom of movement has never achieved the status of a universally recognised human right.

(Adler 1985: 337)

As the previous chapters have indicated, the expansion of international travel over the past century and a half has been closely associated with the advancement of a range of citizenship rights framed within the context of the nation-state. These rights, for the most part, have been brought about by the rise of state-managed capitalism and the advent of the welfare state in the industrialized democracies of the West. This chapter draws closer attention to the ways in which the freedom of movement and right to travel have come to be regarded as inalienable human rights and cornerstones of Western ideals of citizenship. It will also demonstrate that contrary to the pervasive discourses of freedom and individual rights attributed to neoliberalism and contemporary global capitalism, states remain fundamentally ambivalent towards different modalities of movement. In this light, it considers the political and ideological forces at work that privilege the mobility of some while inhibiting the movement of others.

Particular attention will focus on the role of diverse passport and visa regimes in differentiating the freedom of movement and rights to travel, and the implications for the varying experiences and practices of contemporary citizenship. The chapter also considers the implications of various bilateral and multilateral frameworks governing the freedom of movement and right to travel, notably that of the European Union, for the mobility rights and freedoms enjoyed by tourists and other mobile peoples. A key concern in this chapter is to emphasize the extent to which existing citizenship rights, centred mainly on national affiliations, afford differential access to states and mobility into and within the EU. In doing so it also considers how questions of nationality, race and ethnicity shape and determine the mobility of those people whose 'credentials' to travel are often deemed 'risky', 'suspect' or 'illegitimate'.

Diplomatic and ideological barriers to the freedom of movement and the right to travel

The dawn of a new era of mass mobility and leisure consumption after the Second World War saw the right to travel expressed with ideological vigour. The assumption that 'we' should have the 'right' to travel everywhere and anywhere without restriction was poignantly expressed by the former British Foreign Secretary Ernest Bevin. He remarked that the principal aim of his foreign policy was to 'grapple with the whole problem of passports and visas' so that he could 'go down to Victoria Station … get a railway ticket, and go where the hell I liked without a passport or anything else' (cited in Pinder 2001: 102). His remark reveals quite clearly how the association of travel with citizenship extends beyond social citizenship rights into the realm of natural or inalienable human rights, principally, the right to the freedom of movement.

State support for the freedom of movement and the right to travel varies considerably and has evolved in the context of distinct historical and political conditions. The origins of the freedom of movement as a universal human right can be traced back to the ideological ferment surrounding the French Revolution, and in particular, the rise of the modern nation-state. As Torpey's (2000) forensic examination of the origins of the passport in the United States and Western Europe illustrates, the emergence of the French republican state and establishment of the National Assembly in the final decade of the eighteenth century, signalled the advent of the modern citizen and the proclamation of equality for all (French) citizens. Accordingly, the freedom to move, to remain and to leave was one of the first natural and civil rights granted by the new French Constitution in 1791 (Torpey 2000: 29). However, as Torpey also notes, the defence of the freedom of movement and abolition of passport controls for French citizens, a key mechanism of control during the *ancien régime*, was countered by a series of deliberations in the National Assembly concerning the status of the 'foreigner', for whom certain restrictions on their mobility should apply and indeed were imposed. Such an ambivalent stance towards the mobility of 'foreigners' vis-à-vis 'national citizens' is one that continues to fuel tensions surrounding the politics of borders, passports and visas. Nevertheless, several members of the Constituent Assembly felt that by eliminating obstacles to the freedom of movement, 'they were making a major contribution to the cause of human freedom' (Torpey 2000: 29). Increasingly stable inter-state relations after the Congress of Vienna in 1815 meant that support for the freedom of movement in Europe gained further impetus into the nineteenth century. By the end of the nineteenth century the rise of economic liberalism and the demand for labour in the industrial capitalist economies in Western Europe and North America heralded the dawn of a 'period of extraordinary freedom of movement' (Torpey 2000: 56).

In Europe, restrictions on the freedom of movement have historically been motivated by perennial fears over the large-scale influx of 'foreigners'. For example, the arrival of East European Jews in the UK from the 1880s provoked the passing of various restrictive pieces of legislation (see Cesarini 1996: 62). Following the First World War, passport restrictions that had been allowed to lapse since the late eighteenth century, were re-imposed by the French authorities in order to forcefully distinguish French citizens from foreigners (Torpey 2000: 112). Further afield in China, the Manchu Dynasty (1644–1912) had periodically refused to admit foreigners in order to limit foreign influence to a few coastal trading enclaves (Wolf 1982: 252–254). However, few places were perhaps as restrictive as colonial Cuba, where individuals risked the death penalty during the early sixteenth century for leaving the island without permission of the Spanish colonial authorities (Marshall 1987: 13)! More recently, attitudes have been determined by the vicissitudes of ideological conflict and diplomatic relations between states, as well as the demand for labour (and indeed tourists) in emerging economies, as a means to stimulate industrial growth and economic development.

Until the collapse of Communist rule in 1989, restrictions on both the mobility of inbound foreign tourists and the outbound movement of national citizens were enforced throughout the Eastern bloc states. Such restrictions were closely tied to the ideology of the ruling Communist regimes and their desire to tightly regulate the leisure time of their citizens, as well as to minimize any possible contact with 'outsiders', thereby limiting the influence of 'alien values' (i.e. capitalist-bourgeois) and preventing the incubation of subversive ideas among the population (Hall 1990: 38). The official stance towards tourism in authoritarian Communist states was also reflected in the monopoly exercised over inbound tourism by the state tourist agencies, such as *Intourist* in the Soviet Union, and in some cases the state-sanctioned surveillance of foreigners. In such states the individualized movement of people was inherently ascribed with mistrust and subject to a panoply of ideological constraints and draconian regulatory controls on mobility and other related rights, including the freedom of association.

The collapse of Communism subsequently brought about wholesale transformation in the border regimes of Eastern European states, together with their integration into the market economies of the West. By 2007 a majority of former Eastern bloc states (i.e. non-USSR) had joined the European Union with the most recent being Croatia, which became a full member on 1 July 2013. Draconian restrictions on the freedom of movement nevertheless remain in place in a minority of authoritarian states, including Saudi Arabia and the Democratic People's Republic of Korea (North Korea). Saudi Arabia retains strict controls on the entrance of foreign citizens, as well as the movement of its own citizens (particularly women), for reasons relating to the preservation of conservative Islamic values. North Korea is one of the few remaining states placing strict limits on the freedom of movement for more overtly ideological reasons rooted in the geopolitical entanglements of East Asia. Despite official US government warnings advising against travel to North Korea, since 2010, US citizens have nevertheless been able to enter the country with a valid passport and visa. However, they can only do so through the North Korean embassy in Beijing as there are no North Korean diplomatic or consular services in the US. Travel is organized by a limited amount of tour operators and agents, and subsequent movement within North Korean territory is closely monitored by the state. This situation nevertheless represents a modest advancement on the previous state of affairs, where US citizens were only allowed to visit North Korea during the Arirang Mass Games in Pyongyang.[1]

While routine travel from South Korea to North Korea is currently prohibited, it has been possible to do so for those travelling on official or government-authorized business. Since the late 1990s it has also been possible to travel from the south to the North on group bus tours as part of the reconciliation programmes organized by the Korean firm Hyundai (see Chapter 6). However, travel has been restricted to regions such as Mount Kumgang, Baekdu Mountain and Kaesong. At the time of writing, North Korea's retaliatory stance towards joint US-South Korean military exercises during late March 2013 not only further strained diplomatic relations between North Korea and South Korea (and the US) but also prompted Chinese tour companies – which provide the majority of tourists to North Korea – to withdraw their operations from the country (Fisher 2013).

Elsewhere, in Cuba, since the 1959 Revolution, the freedom of movement of Cuban citizens and the rights to travel and leisure have been subordinated to the values of hard work, patriotism and egalitarian socialist ideals. In 1991, subsequent to the collapse of the Soviet Union and the loss of its preferential trading relationship with the Communist bloc, the Cuban regime found itself with an urgent need to generate hard currency. To do so, Cuba opened its doors to foreign investment and tourism – an industry that had been all but abandoned since 1959 on the basis that it represented a potent symbol of US imperial dominance of the Caribbean – while continuing to maintain the segregation of Cuban citizens and foreign tourists (Sánchez and Adams 2008: 32). The internal movement of Cuban citizens thus remained subject to numerous restrictions. The segregation of Cubans and foreign tourists was motivated by an attempt to limit the adverse impact of tourism on Cuba's revolutionary ideals as well as the need to generate hard currency. While international hotels and restaurants request that foreigners pay in dollars rather than pesos – indeed many holiday packages are pre-paid by the tour operators – Cubans themselves, even those with US dollars, have until recently been prohibited from staying in these hotels except when honeymooning or in receipt of a state award for particular achievements (Sánchez and Adams 2008: 35).

Paradoxically, given the continuing espousal of socialist ideology at a state level, tourism in effect converted Cubans into 'second-class' citizens. For example, Carter's (2008: 244–245) ethnographic research in Cuba reveals how the state's control over the mobility of its citizenry has been a central feature of its project of economic modernization through international tourism since the early 1990s. Cubans are thus passive recipients of tourism and tourism commodities in their own right. Carter also suggests that principles of restrictive mobility also apply at other all-inclusive resorts in the Caribbean region (see Gregory 2007):

> Generally, all-inclusive resorts restrict the entry of non-registered guests to these controlled spaces. In the larger resorts, colour-coded plastic wrist bands and constant surveillance control who wanders about freely and who is turned away at the front door. Race and class often mark who does and does not gain entry.
>
> *(Carter 2008: 245)*

Restrictions on the internal mobility of Cuban citizens clearly contradict the socialist ideals of equality and national self-determination that mark Cuban citizenship and which have been espoused by the revolutionary regime since 1959 (Bobes 2005). At a recent gathering of Cuban students, delegates harangued the President of the Cuban National Assembly, criticizing the restrictions on the ability of Cubans to enter tourism areas on the island, as well as the draconian restrictions on foreign travel that remained in place at the time. In response, the President of the National Assembly invoked spurious concern for the environmental well-being of the planet in a crude attempt to conceal the groaning contradictions in the regime's continued restrictions on the freedom of movement of Cuban citizens: 'If everyone in the world, all six billion inhabitants, were able to travel wherever they pleased, there would be a tremendous traffic jam in our planet's airspace. People who travel are really in the minority' ([Authors' translation] El País 2008).

More recently, in response to a series of consultations with Cuban citizens undertaken by the new Cuban leader Raúl Castro, who in 2008 stepped in for his ailing brother and inspirational Cuban leader Fidel Castro, the Cuban authorities have moved to ease a number of restrictions on trade in certain foreign goods and services. The government also lifted the unpopular ban on Cubans entering and staying in hotels and tourist resorts previously reserved exclusively for foreigners (Vicent 2008). In January 2013, the Cuban authorities went further, easing the restrictions on exit visa requirements for Cubans wishing to travel overseas (Associated Press 2013).

In contrast to Cuba, in spite of the continued rule of the Chinese Communist Party and its ambivalence towards Western notions of democracy (see Jacques 2012: 534–535), China has taken up a more liberalized agenda to travel and tourism. Prior to the initiation of the 'Open Door' policy in 1982, tourism in China was the responsibility of the Foreign Ministry. Notably, in contrast to developing nations in which tourism was predominantly envisaged as an engine of economic growth and development, in China it was overwhelmingly regarded as a 'public relations exchange between representatives of a few friendly countries' (Jenkins and Liu 1997: 104). Travel to China by foreign nationals was severely discouraged until the 1980s by both the Communist authorities themselves as well as by many Western governments, in particular the United States. Indeed, as recently as 2006, few Western governments would grant tourist visas to Chinese citizens (Airey and Chong 2011: 212). However, by 1983 the government had begun to allow Chinese citizens to undertake private leisure travel for the purpose of visiting friends and relatives. Since then a combination of the growing affluence among the Chinese 'middle class' and new rich, in conjunction with the easing of travel restrictions following the introduction of China's Open Door policy, has stimulated dramatic growth in both outbound tourism as well as domestic travel (see Urry 2013: 125).

Today, as a consequence of the Approved Destination Status (ADS) programme initiated in 1995, Chinese tourists are able to travel to a range of foreign countries (Hall 2008: 40). The ADS programme comprises a series of bilateral agreements between China and overseas destinations that regulate and determine the issuance of tourist visas (Lim and Wang 2008: 453). The purpose of the ADS system, as Lim and Wang (2008) demonstrate, is to regulate the outflow of tourists and foreign currency while protecting and enabling the expansion of the domestic tourism sector. This system is strongly tied to China's national and foreign policy interests, and resembles many of the characteristics of the strategic state-led approach to economic development common throughout the East Asian 'tiger' economies (see Wade 2004). While Chinese tourists have traditionally travelled to the two principal special administrative regions (SARs) of Hong Kong and Macao, ADS agreements were signed with Australia and New Zealand in 1999, the first non-Asian countries to do so. By 2002, 20 ADS agreements had been signed, totalling 134 by 2008 (Inkson and Minnaert 2012: 62). Canada, however, only achieved its ADS status in 2009, after a four-year hiatus that provoked much consternation among representatives of the Canadian travel industry – since signing the Memorandum of Understanding with China in 2005 (Canada News Centre 2009).

Although the number of Chinese citizens travelling abroad as a proportion of its population is very small, the growth of outbound travel has been precipitous. Since the year 2000 Chinese outbound travel has increased at an average annual rate of 22 per cent, reaching nearly 48 million in 2009 (UNWTO 2010). As much as 90 per cent represents travel to neighbouring Asian and Pacific states, especially to China's two SARs, Hong Kong and Macao. Nevertheless, China remains on course to become one of the world's largest tourist markets, with total outbound travel – including overnight and day trips to Hong Kong and Macao – estimated to reach 106 million by 2014 (China Tourism Daily 2013). In 2012, the Chinese surpassed the Germans as the world's biggest-spending travellers, with total expenditure on foreign trips amounting to US$102 billion, a 41 per cent increase on the previous year (China Daily 2013). However, in contrast to the emergence of overseas travel in most Western societies, it has been implied that the current boom in outbound travel by Chinese citizens is not a direct consequence of greater democratic freedoms and the advancement of citizenship rights, as it was in many Western countries (Economist 2010: 54). Rather, it is argued that Chinese tourists have readily embraced the freedom to engage in foreign travel and conspicuous consumption abroad in exchange for their continued acquiescence to one-party rule. Nevertheless, perhaps as a reflection of changing attitudes towards individual consumer freedoms and aspirations, demand for independent outbound travel from China is increasing (Inkson and Minnaert 2012: 62).

Where there has been a history of animosity and diplomatic tensions between states, governments have often sought to impose strict restrictions on cross-border mobility for overtly ideological purposes, a practice that is often played out through the medium of government 'travel advisories' (see Chapter 5). As noted earlier, in the case of North Korea and the former Soviet Union, Communist and Eastern bloc states would routinely restrict entry of tourists from the West (Hall 1990: 44). In the Middle East, most Arab States, with the exception of Egypt and Jordan, with whom Israel signed peace treaties in 1979 and 1994 respectively, continue to restrict travel by their own citizens to Israel as a demonstration of their antipathy towards Israel's occupation of the Palestinian Territories. Although regulations vary and are often subject to interpretation by border officials, foreign travellers with a passport bearing an Israeli entry/exit stamp are also routinely prevented from entering many Arab and Muslim states and may in some circumstances, according to the US State Department advice on visiting Lebanon, face arrest or imprisonment. Unless sanctioned by the Ministry of Interior, Israeli law prohibits travel to what it regards as enemy states, including Lebanon, Syria and Iran, a law it has occasionally applied to restrict the movement of journalists (see Freedom House 2012). Arab travellers (with the exception of Egyptian and Jordanian passport holders) are also routinely prevented from entering Israel or the Occupied Palestinian Territories, whose ports-of-entry are controlled by Israel. Although prominent non-Arab Muslim countries maintain a public stance of solidarity with Palestine and may restrict entry of Israeli citizens, the movement of people between Israel and Indonesia, for example, does routinely occur. While Indonesia only maintains informal diplomatic ties with Israel, Israeli tourists can in fact apply for business travel visas or travel as part of a group tour to Indonesia (Adams 2012).

In the case of Libya, in 2004 the United States lifted a long-standing travel ban and other restrictions on business operations between the two countries, prompted by former President Gaddafi's promise to end Libya's nuclear programme and an admission of Libyan responsibility for the bombing of Pan Am Flight 103 in 1988 (Associated Press 2004). However, travel between Libya and many Western countries continues to be affected by strained diplomatic relations. In 2010, Libya rescinded the right of citizens from 25 European states that participate in the visa-free Schengen system to enter Libya (Traynor 2010a). This move was taken as a retaliatory response to the Swiss government for apparently 'blacklisting' more than 180 Libyan leaders from entering Switzerland, including members of the Gaddafi family. It was alleged that the source of the conflict was linked to the arrest of Gaddafi's son and wife in a Geneva hotel for apparently assaulting their servants, though no charges were made (Traynor 2010a). The Libyan case illustrates how even seemingly trivial political squabbles, no matter how insignificant or personal their origin, can escalate with implications for the freedom of movement and right to travel of citizens from particular states. The embargo did not directly affect UK and US tourists entering Libya, although the Libyan government did stipulate in June 2010 that US tourists would require a visa in order to enter the country. Following the fall of the Gaddafi regime in October 2011, European and US tourists were required to apply for tourist visas through tour operators licensed in Libya. Despite the fall of Gaddafi, the attack on the US Embassy in June 2012 ensured that US citizens continue to approach travel to Libya with a great deal of caution. In May 2013, given the continuing political instability and potential for outbreaks of violence, US citizens travelling to Libya were advised to 'limit nonessential travel within the country, make their own contingency emergency plans, and maintain security awareness at all times' (US Department of State 2013b).

Few countries, however, illustrate the complex entanglements between geo-politics, tense diplomacy and restrictions on the freedom of movement than the relationship between Iran and the West, particularly the United States. Although there have been sanctions placed on Iran since the 1979 Iranian Revolution, more recently, Iran's determined pursuit of a nuclear energy programme – launched in the 1950s under the auspices of US President Eisenhower's 'Atoms for Peace' programme – provoked a progressive tightening of economic sanctions by Western powers in the summer of 2012. The West's weak diplomatic ties with Iran have had a notable impact on tourists visiting Iran from the US and the UK. Since February 2010, like their US counterparts, British visitors have been required to provide their fingerprints in the departure state as part of the application process for entry into mainland Iran (World Travel Guide 2013). The process also requires that individuals receive a state-approved invite. Unlike UK citizens, US citizens cannot travel by independent means to Iran and must usually travel as part of a guided tour, obtaining a tour itinerary prior to travel as part of the visa conditions. Furthermore, due to the current lack of diplomatic or consular relations between the US and Iran, neither of the two governments has an embassy or consulate in the other country. US citizens must apply for a visa at the Iranian interest section at the Pakistan Embassy in Washington, DC (US Department of State 2013c). In addition, in an interesting example of vicarious diplomacy, since 1980, limited consular services have been provided to US citizens visiting Iran by the Swiss Embassy in Tehran, which has been granted the ominous sounding role of 'US protecting power' (Swiss Confederation 2013). Similarly, since the closure of the British Embassy in Tehran in November 2011, limited consular services to UK citizens travelling to Iran are provided by the Swedish Embassy.

However, such measures do not in any way match the low global value of the Iranian passport in terms of its limitations on its bearer to travel to countries without attaining a visa prior to departure (see Table 4.1, page 118). Although the ability of ordinary Iranians to participate in international travel and tourism has inevitably been constrained by Iran's ailing economy – principally, rising inflation and the falling value of the Iranian *rial* – international sanctions have also placed severe political obstacles in the way of Iranian citizens wishing to travel, including of course for the purpose of tourism. Not only have the sanctions forced many Iranians to travel to nearby countries to organize monetary transactions and process tourist visas (to the US and Canada for instance), Iranian travel agents actively arrange tours to Armenia, Dubai and Turkey so that students and young people can sit their English exams and tests due to the closure of many externally recognized tests centres (e.g. the British Council IELTS exams) in Iran (Theodoulou 2010). Recent attempts to further restrict the movement on Iranians (along with nationals of other countries) entering the US, include plans to reintroduce the Stop Terrorists Entry Program Act (STEP) into the House of Representatives, originally introduced in 2003. The intention of this decree is to modify the Immigration and Nationality Act in order to block entry of individuals from countries that the US believes to be a sponsor of terrorism (eTurboNews 2010). However, at the time of writing, the bill had not yet passed into law.[2]

The restriction on Iranian mobility rights and freedoms is also indirectly secured as a result of the sanctions that have been imposed on Iran's aviation industry and related concerns over its airline safety record. Since 1995 the US has imposed sanctions on Iran's ability to buy new stocks of Western-manufactured aircraft and spare parts, thereby directly affecting the safety record of Iran's ageing fleet (Erdbrink 2012). From 2002 to 2008 it was noted that there have been nine fatal air crashes involving Iranian aircraft, with as many as 302 killed in a single flight, and a combined death toll of nearly 700 (Loffell 2008). In echoes of the Cuban trade embargo, in 2011 the US imposed further restrictions on the ability of US companies to trade with Iran Air, which it accused of providing 'material support and services for the Iranian Revolutionary Guard' (BBC 2011a). The year before, the European Commission had controversially banned Iranian airlines from entering EU airspace citing safety concerns rather than its nuclear programme (BBC 2010b). However, this of course fails to note the obvious irony, that US sanctions on access to new technology and spare parts for Iranian aircraft undoubtedly exacerbated such safety concerns! US sanctions against Iran's airlines are contrary to the stipulations of the 1944 Convention on International Civil Aviation (or Chicago Convention as it is more commonly known), which the United States was not only party to signing but was also a key architect of the Chicago Conference at which the Convention came into effect. Article 44 of the Convention stipulates the principles of assuring 'safe and orderly growth of international civil aviation throughout the world' and 'the needs of peoples of the world for safe, regular, efficient and economic air transport'. Importantly, emphasis was placed on the need to 'avoid discrimination' between states (ICAO 1944). In order for the ban to be effective, the US government required strict compliance from industry. Accordingly, it was reported that the world's leading manufacturer of aircraft engines, General Electric, would not continue to provide services to Air France, KLM, Lufthansa and Turkish Airlines (THY), if they participated in any maintenance work for Iranian airlines with GE parts (Phillips 2005).

Understanding the 'right to tourism' and its institutional framework

Following the Second World War, support for the freedom of movement and relaxation of passport and visa controls reflected the post-war 'peace dividend' and the growing interdependence of the major capitalist economies. Notably of course, the war had triggered the increased influence of the United States in European affairs and post-war economic reconstruction, centred on the Marshall Plan (1948–1952). In order to boost the incipient travel industry that was beginning to benefit from Marshall Plan aid, the Organisation for European Economic Co-operation, which had been established by US aid, removed currency restrictions as well as simplified customs, passport and visa requirements (Goldstone 2001: 48). The Marshall Plan itself contained special provisions for the enhancement of international travel, placing particular emphasis on reforming the French hotel industry as a means of making Europe a 'more consumer-friendly' place through greater exposure to American tourists (Endy 2004: 83). The weight of American economic power indicated in the growth of US travel to France, and the desire of French government planners to expand the role of tourism as a means of earning much-needed foreign exchange in the post-war economy, were instrumental factors in the abolition of visa requirements for American tourists visiting France. However, as Endy (2004: 73) describes, this was not reciprocated by the US authorities for fear of communists entering the United States, who were indeed numerous and somewhat influential in post-war French politics!

Motivated by its monopolization of the production of aircraft after the war and keen to promote the virtues of free trade, the US government aggressively pursued the deregulation of global airline travel in the face of European intransigence (Strange 1994: 157). Advances in jet engine technology spurred the consequent expansion of the international holiday industry. Pressure from the US to open up the civil aviation market to competition led to the establishment of a framework for the negotiation of bilateral agreements between states, in what became known as the Bermuda Agreement (1946), regulating the freedom of the skies and competition between national airlines. Although Britain had already developed the first commercial jet aircraft in 1949, in the form of the De Havilland Comet, the commercial expansion of British airlines was strongly marked by 'considerations of empire' and favoured state ownership (Strange 1994: 158). In contrast, US expansion in the tourism and aviation industries was driven by the commercial force of its dominant aviation manufacturers and the growing rivalry between its major international carriers (Pan-Am, TWA and American Airlines), as well as the profitable market for domestic travel. The growth of international tourism represented an enormous opportunity for the overseas expansion of US corporate interests and the resurrection of some of its ailing aircraft manufacturers (e.g. Boeing), which had until then focused overwhelmingly on lucrative defence contracts.

Tourism and the defence of the freedom to travel overseas thus coalesced in a number of ways with the geopolitical concerns of advanced capitalist nations, and in particular US trade and foreign policy. For example, Goldstone (2001: 25–26) describes how Nelson Rockefeller, capitalizing on US fears of Nazi influence in Argentina, worked closely with the Roosevelt administration and a number of American Express executives in the period leading up to the Second World War, to expand his own hotel and tourism interests in Latin America. Later, in the aftermath of the Allied invasion of Europe, American Express and leading US hotel companies, including Hilton and Inter Continental, lobbied hard to expand their tourism operations into Western Europe. This included being granted the rights to offer sightseeing tours for US servicemen (Goldstone 2001: 34). US support for the freedom of movement and expansion of tourism overseas inevitably became closely intertwined with the growing preoccupation of the US in defending the 'free world' from the 'threat' of communism. Americans travelling to Europe were encouraged to become 'ambassadors of good will' and to promote the 'virtues of US foreign policy', and to thereby act as citizens of the 'free world' (Endy 2004: 1). Such was the fear of communism that American policymakers during the Cold War era were concerned that American tourists gave the right impression of their home country. The fear was that negative publicity would undermine attempts to steer Western Europe away from any potential alliance with communism. Thus while the American tourist was deployed as a potent symbol of freedom and prosperity, these values were not in the reach of the Soviet citizen.

It was during this period that a new 'moral ethos of "rights"' had begun to take shape, as states became increasingly concerned with the creation of a global architecture of universal *human rights*, which would protect the individual from arbitrary state authority (Faist 2009: 9). This represented a fundamental shift from the triptych of rights (civil, political and social) underpinning Marshall's conception of national citizenship and universal state welfare provision, towards a new transnational regime of rights emphasizing the universality of human rights and ideals of 'post-national' citizenship. This was mirrored by an ideological shift in many liberal and social democracies, away from an overriding concern with the rights of citizens within the confines of the nation-state, towards an emphasis on intrinsic rights conferred on all citizens, regardless of national origins, including that of the freedom of movement and the right to travel.

The notion of travel as a fundamental human right, or more specifically the universal right to the freedom of movement, is underpinned in international law by the *Universal Declaration of Human Rights*, which was adopted in 1948 by the then 58 member states of the UN General Assembly. Specifically, Article 13 (1) stipulates that everyone should be granted the right to freedom of movement and residence within the borders of each state, while Article 13 (2) stipulates that everyone should benefit from the right to leave any country, including *his* own, and to return to *his* country (United Nations 1948). The Declaration nevertheless stops short of guaranteeing the right of entrance into a foreign state. This right remains the prerogative of nationals returning home and, moreover, is one that is predominantly governed and regulated by the nation-state (Goodin 1992: 13). While the text of Article 13 (2) stipulates that *everyone* regardless of origin has the right to leave a country, it is only the nationals of particular states who are granted the automatic right to return. Hence, the right to cross from one country to another does not enjoy international legal standing (Hayter 2004: 1). Ironically, given the support for the freedom of movement and travel by the United States, the *Universal Declaration of Human Rights* was originally opposed by the US administration on the basis that its social provisions smacked of communism (Isin and Turner 2007: 8)! Nevertheless, the freedom of movement and right to travel have since become one of the hallmarks of Western liberal-capitalist democracies, in addition to being harnessed as a 'passport to development' – through tourism – for 'Third World' nations emerging from colonial rule in the 1960s and 1970s (De Kadt 1979).

In this regard, both the international legal framework and individual state policies governing the freedom of movement betray a perennial tension between the distinctive treatment accorded to migrants and other forms of coerced travel on the one hand, and tourists on the other. While states seek to justify opening their borders to tourists, largely but not exclusively because of the expected and immediate economic benefits, at the same time these very states often seek to limit and control the entrance of immigrants (below a certain income threshold), asylum seekers and other so-called 'undesirable' subjects, who are seen to contribute little or nothing to the 'host' society. In addition to the rights of mobility incorporated into the UNDHR, the right to travel and freedom of tourist movement are clearly set out in Article 7 (right to tourism) and Article 8 (liberty of tourist movements) of the *Global Code of Ethics for Tourism* (WTO 1999). The *Code of Ethics* builds on previous tourism charters produced by the WTO (now UNWTO), namely the *Manila Declaration on World Tourism* (1980), the *Acapulco Document* (1982) and the *Tourism Bill of Rights and Tourist Code* (1985), each of which reiterate the importance of enabling the rights of (tourist) mobility.

However, there is a vital distinction to be made between the right to the freedom of movement, as outlined in the UNDHR, and the right to tourism, as set out in the *Global Code of Ethics*. The right to tourism, while closely intertwined with the freedom of movement, is nevertheless beset by a number of tensions that highlight the indeterminate meaning and substance of the rights ascribed to travel and to being a tourist. Contemporary tourism discourses increasingly blur the distinction between the freedom of movement and the right to travel on the one hand, and the rights of tourists to consume other places and cultures on the other. People's right to partake in the pleasures of tourism may be encouraged and facilitated by the unfettered rights of corporate tourism businesses to compete for mobile consumers, as well as the rights of developers to buy and sell the resources upon which tourism depends. These corporate rights fundamentally evoke economic rights to profit from (and capitalize on) the economic opportunities afforded by tourism. Moreover, where the rights to tourism are privileged above others, it may hinder or prejudice the freedom of movement of locals as well as facilitate the enclosure and exploitation of such common pool resources as beachfront property, farmlands, cultural heritage and wilderness areas (see Hodal 2013). As Higgins-Desbiolles (2007: 319) forcefully states: 'We have somehow forgotten in the market era that a truly universal notion of a right to travel and tourism could only be predicated on a foundation of a right to development for all.' Here, we see a tension that has long defined liberal capitalist notions of citizenship, since its earliest origins. While citizens seek to avail themselves of their democratic rights in all areas of social and political life, the bourgeois-capitalist impulse is identified by the need to defend their interests in the field of business and enterprise (see Beck 1992: 183). Hence, we increasingly see the collapse of the distinction between the right to the freedom of movement and travel on the one hand, which implies freedom from the socio-economic conditions limiting participation in society, and the right to tourism on the other, which implies having the right credentials for travel, as well as the rights of capital to move across borders and exploit the opportunities afforded by tourism.

Prior to the Second World War, there was little coordinated public and/or inter-governmental support for tourism. The value of tourism within international trade was relatively insignificant and remained for the most part an elite activity. Soon afterwards, however, in 1947 the International Union of Official Travel Organizations (IUOTO) was established. This organization, whose origins can be traced back to an earlier association of public and private tourism bodies formed in The Hague in 1925, brought together representatives of the tourist industry and national tourist organizations to promote tourism as an item of international trade and as a tool of development for newly independent 'developing countries'. It also acted as an organization for the advancement of peace and mutual understanding between nations, a debate whose significance to citizenship will be considered in Chapter 5. It is against this backdrop that the IUOTO moved from being simply an industry-based association to an executing agency of the United Nations Development Programme (UNDP), with the establishment of the World Tourism Organization (WTO) in Madrid in 1975. In November 2003 the UNWTO was formally granted specialized agency status in the United Nations, the first time a new specialist agency had been formed since 1985 (Ferguson 2007: 558).

The full incorporation of the UNWTO into the institutional fabric of the United Nations reflects the growing weight of tourism in global trade and its embrace by an ever-expanding number of states and international development agencies. Currently, the principal remit of the UNWTO centres on a commitment to advance the Millennium Development Goals (MDGs) of poverty reduction and sustainable development 'without harming the interests of the private sector' (Ferguson 2007: 559). It harnesses tourism to the UN's global agenda and firmly embeds it within a robust inter-governmental framework for promoting the expansion of international travel and the business of tourism at a global level. Not only therefore is tourism unique among industries in proclaiming its elevation to a universal human right (Higgins-Desbiolles 2007: 317), it is the only 'industry' or economic sector that benefits from its own specialist UN agency. This reflects and reinforces an institutionalized discourse of rights attributed to tourism that bestows upon this particular form of mobility a political status equivalent to other key areas of human activity, including industry, agriculture, transport, education, health and labour (Ferguson 2007: 558).

By virtue of the fact that the decision-making structure of the UNWTO comprises a range of private-sector organizations and that its principal source of revenue is policy advice on tourism, its remit nevertheless goes beyond a technical agency offering impartial development 'advice' and 'assistance'. As demonstrated by its favourable stance on the General Agreement on the Trade in Services (GATS) and its close relationship with the staunchly anti-regulationist body, the World Travel and Tourism Council (WTTC),[3] it is an agency committed to the expansion of a globalized free market economy (Frangialli 2003). Together, these institutions constitute important centres of authority and sites of power, which disseminate, institutionalize and reproduce discourses trumpeting the right to travel and to profit from tourism. However, notwithstanding the influence of this transnational pro-tourism lobby, and the fact that the right to travel remains a cornerstone of Western notions of citizenship, the attitude and practice of states towards mobility continue to be marked by a significant degree of ambivalence and by a variety of constantly shifting diplomatic tensions. Nowhere perhaps is this more in evidence than in the form of passports and visas, which together form the necessary prerequisites for cross-border mobility and international travel.

Regulating and enabling travel: states, passports and visas

The modern passport constitutes one of the principal mechanisms used by states to regulate people's mobility. It is described by Salter (2004: 72) as nothing less than 'a vital instrument of individual international mobility' and the principal means by which 'mobile individuals are identified, tracked, and regulated'. The passport constitutes both a symbol of nationality and marker of citizenship, as well as a political instrument that codifies and regulates the boundaries between migrants and non-migrants, tourists and non-tourists, insiders and outsiders and, ultimately, citizens and non-citizens. O'Byrne (2001: 403) thus notes:

> The passport is a political tool because it allows an administrative body to discriminate in terms of who can and who cannot travel in its name. It has two subtle functions, both of which in some way uphold the principal logics, or projects, of the nation-state system throughout modernity. These are the project of territorial expansion, and the project of territorial exclusion.

According to O'Byrne (2001: 400), the existence of documents requesting safe passage to the holder dates back as far as eleventh-century Spain. Torpey (2000: 58) however, notes how the notion of a 'passport' entered legal parlance for the first time in late sixteenth-century Germany. The 'modern passport' arguably begins to take shape in the context of the transition from the feudal-monarchic order of the *ancien régime* to the bourgeois republican state, which emerged in France at the turn of the eighteenth century. Henceforth, the modern, sovereign territorial state started to acquire the power to regulate and monopolize the movement of individuals on an international scale:

> States' efforts to monopolize the legitimate means of movement have involved a number of mutually reinforcing aspects: the (gradual) definition of states everywhere – at least from the point of view of the international system – as 'national' (i.e., as 'nation-states' comprising members understood as nationals);

the codification of laws establishing which types of persons may move within or cross their borders, and determining how, when, and where they may do so; the stimulation of the worldwide development of techniques for uniquely and unambiguously identifying each and every person on the face of the globe, from birth to death; the construction of bureaucracies designed to implement this regime of identification and to scrutinize persons and documents in order to verify identities; and the creation of a body of legal norms designed to adjudicate claims by individuals to entry into particular spaces and territories. Only recently have states actually developed the capacities necessary to monopolize the authority to regulate movement.

(Torpey 2000: 7)

Prior to the role of the nation-state in monopolizing the means of movement, the right to authorize mobility was the preserve of numerous localized social groups, principally feudal landlords and slaveholders. As stated earlier in the chapter, the regulation and control of the international movement of persons really came to the fore in the period following the French Revolution, during the expansion of European colonial power and the increasingly large-scale movements of people from the mid to the late nineteenth-century onwards, facilitated by the cheapening cost of steamship transport. By this time, states had begun to monopolize the regulation and control of the freedom of movement and '"embraced" the traveler as a citizen-member of the nation-state' (Torpey 1998: 250). It is in this context that distinctive state attitudes and ideological divisions concerning the right to travel within and between states become increasingly apparent. Ironically, and in contrast to the ideals of individual rights and freedoms that constitute the hallmarks of neo-liberal globalization, the freedom of movement was in many ways far more widely enjoyed during the height of nineteenth century liberalism, as illustrated by this quotation originating from the 1889 International Emigration Conference: 'We affirm the right of the individual to the fundamental liberty accorded to him [or her] by every civilised nation to come and go and to dispose of his person or his destinies as he pleases' (cited in Harris 2002: 131).

In fact, it was British support for free trade that enabled foreign revolutionaries, including Vladimir Lenin, Karl Marx, Giuseppe Mazzini and Sun Yat Sen, to enter freely into Britain without fear of expulsion (Hayter 2004: 37). Lenin, moreover, was granted the right to travel back to Russia from his exile in Germany in 1917, free from either passport or custom requirements, in the belief that he would withdraw Russia from the First World War should the Bolsheviks come to power (Christman 1987: 9)! Nevertheless, imperial and racial attitudes towards 'colonized' subjects, and a perennial fear of 'aliens' diluting the identity of the native-born, played a part in establishing progressive restrictions on immigration in countries such as the UK during the early twentieth century, as the passing of the draconian Aliens Act (1905) and Aliens Restriction (Amendment) Act (1919) amply demonstrates (see Cesarini 1996: 60–63). From the early twentieth century, passports were increasingly introduced across Europe as the state increasingly took on responsibility for the welfare of 'its own citizens', further separating national citizens from foreigners, immigrants and refugees (Desai 2004: 152). The outbreak of the First World War in particular brought an end to the pre-war era of free movement, as passport controls and increased documentary requirements for domestic citizens were brought in across the continent (Torpey 2000: 111).

British citizens were not, however, required to be in possession of a passport for overseas travel until the passage of the Defence of the Realm Act in 1915 (O'Byrne 2001: 401). Elsewhere, in the United States the right to travel represents a consti-tutional right and cornerstone of liberal freedoms, exemplified when in 1958 the US Supreme Court struck down the US government's decision to prevent sus-pected Communists from holding a US passport (Torpey 2000: 171). Nevertheless, many states reserve the right to grant or deny a passport to its citizens. In 1982, for example, the South African government announced that access to a passport was a privilege rather than a right (Torpey 2000: 162), which further strengthened the subordinate status of black South Africans as their movements within South Africa and overseas were heavily repressed by the apartheid government.

At times, attempts by the state to regulate, restrict or otherwise hinder tourists' right to travel can conflict with the interests of the travel industry and its support-ers. When in 1968, President Johnson urged American citizens to 'postpone "all but essential travel" outside the Western hemisphere' in response to a ballooning balance of payments deficit, representatives of the US travel industry and their supporters in Congress launched a spirited defence of the inalienable right of American citizens to travel (Endy 2004: 182). In particular, it was Johnson's proposed tax on foreign travel – designed to stem the flow of US dollars overseas – that received the most vehement denunciations. As Endy's detailed analysis of the historical record shows, the arguments ranged from the accusation that the proposed tax was akin to a 'Communist-like' restraint on foreign travel (2004: 197), to upholding the rights of Black Americans to participate in foreign travel in response to their inability to travel safely at home (2004: 194)!

Endy (2004: 40) also describes how the American Society of Travel Agents in 1952 took a principled stand against the anti-Communist McCarran Act (1950), otherwise known as the Internal Security or Subversive Activities Control Act,[4] in support of the freedom of travel. Indeed, the US has not been averse to lobby-ing for other states to remove restrictions on the freedom of travel as well as other hindrances to the activities of overseas commerce by US business representatives, while simultaneously maintaining tightly controlled borders and restrictions on the entrance of 'undesirable' foreigners. Such was the stance adopted by the chair of the infamous House of Un-American Activities Committee in the late 1950s, for fear that waiving visa requirements on foreign tourists entering the US could potentially allow 'subversive' elements into the country (Endy 2004: 185). Thus, state policies concerning the freedom of movement and right to travel have veered between the desire to keep borders open for those groups deemed necessary for economic growth, notably tourists and highly skilled migrants, while restricting the entrance of those groups perceived to be undesirable and a threat to or burden on the host state; namely, 'terrorists' and/or 'illegal' immigrants. The symbolic value and practical scope given to different modalities of movement often depend upon the perceived level of threat or benefit presented by mobile peoples to the destination state. As Bach (2003: 227) reminds us: 'The first action that governments typically take when faced with a crisis is to close their borders. States seem intent on gaining security by stopping the world from moving.'

While such 'threats' consisted of counter-revolutionaries in the case of revolutionary France or 'foreign spies' in the case of Prussia (Torpey 2000), contemporary discourses reinforcing divisions between 'legitimate' and 'illegitimate' travellers are strongly influenced by media-fuelled scares regarding the mobility of 'illegal immigrants', 'economic migrants' and 'bogus asylum seekers'. Once again, in the UK, the issue of 'excessive' immigration and concerns regarding the movement of people from poor to rich states occupies centre stage in public discourse, as the current coalition government seeks to tighten restrictions on the entrance of those whose presence in the UK is considered 'unsustainable' and too expensive (see Soames and Field 2013). Elsewhere, in the US, the passage of the anti-(illegal) immigration law (SB1070) by the state government of Arizona in April 2010 seeks to ensure that failure to carry mandatory immigration documents is a criminal offence and that the police have the power to detain anyone suspected of being in the country illegally (Archibold 2010). In Europe, the controversial deportation of around a thousand Roma gypsies from France to the EU states of Bulgaria and Romania in September 2010 suggests a strong correlation between race – in this case 'Roma' – and unequal citizenship rights. In addition, the expulsion constituted an apparent breach of the EU ban on ethnic discrimination (Traynor 2010b). While these illustrations refer specifically to immigration, they reinforce an increasingly stark distinction between 'us' and 'them' in the public mindset. Hence, despite attempts by progressive politicians to argue the case for a greater tolerance of migrants entering the country, such discourses still fall into the trap of inscribing the distinction between favourable (i.e. tourism) and unfavourable (i.e. immigration) forms of cross-border movement.

Draconian restrictions on travel are often justified by states in exceptional or extreme circumstances. There has been perhaps no better illustration of this than the reaction of the United States to the 9/11 attacks. Following the attacks, the Federal Aviation Administration imposed a shutdown of US airspace which lasted until 14 September 2001. By the end of the following month, the draconian Patriot Act had passed through Congress. This act paved the way for the creation of the Department of Homeland Security, which oversaw a number of changes to the American passport regime in order to enhance border security and expand procedures for identifying 'high-risk' travellers (Salter 2004: 76–77). Although, as Salter points out, not only were each of the 9/11 hijackers in possession of valid passports issued by their own governments, there is no evidence that 'altered American passports have ever been used successfully by terrorists in circumventing the border security regime' (2004: 77). However, this has not stopped the US nor indeed non-Western countries, including Indonesia, from imposing stricter visa policies in the name of fighting terrorism (see Cole 2008: 282).

As already indicated, long before 9/11 created a pretext for the introduction of numerous new restrictions on cross-border mobility, states had periodically abrogated the right to travel on the grounds of 'national security'. Perhaps one of the most famous cases concerns the American actor-singer-activist Paul Robeson, whose right to travel overseas was severely curtailed along with several other leftist activists during the 1950s. Under the auspices of the 1950 McCarran Act, despite President Truman's veto, several members of the US Communist Party were denied the right to hold a passport. Robeson himself was asked to hand his over to the State Department. After all, the passport is not the property of the holder but rather that of the issuing state, notwithstanding the fact that this seemed to contradict other areas of both domestic constitutional law (e.g. US Bill of Rights) and inter-national legal frameworks that underpin the right to travel (see Salter 2004: 73). No other reason was provided for withholding his US passport, other than the claim that 'travel abroad by an individual would be contrary to the best interests of the United States' (Duberman 1989: 389). Ironically, such restrictions on the liberty of individual movements contrasted sharply with earlier attempts by US officials to emphasize US support for the inalienable right to travel and freedom of movement in contrast to the many rights and freedoms that were, at that time, being denied to the citizens of the Soviet Union.

Although there have been periodic attempts at developing a 'world passport' (O'Byrne 2001: 412), the issuance of a passport remains the sole responsibility of the nation-state. Numerous multilateral frameworks facilitating passport-free, cross-border travel have also been implemented by the European Union, and agreed by those states involved in other economic unions in such regions as the East African Community (Kenya, Uganda and Tanzania) and the CA-4 (Central America), which comprises El Salvador, Honduras, Guatemala and Nicaragua (Hall 2008: 43–44). Nevertheless, these initiatives remain at the behest of the nation-state, exemplified by the continued reluctance of the UK to incorporate itself into the EU's Schengen zone (see below), and the fundamental desire of states to maintain authority for control over their borders and ports-of-entry.

States have nevertheless been reliant upon the co-operation and compliance of private companies in order to manage, regulate and restrict the movement of 'undesirable' subjects. During the late nineteenth century, for example, European governments required steamship companies to oversee whether or not certain people should be permitted to travel to their chosen destination (Torpey 2000: 10). More recently, this has embroiled commercial airlines in controversial deportations of 'failed' asylum seekers, leading to a number of airlines pulling out in protest at such measures (Verkaik 2007). In 2004, the EU concluded an agreement with the United States Department of Homeland Security, requiring airlines operating to and from the EU to hand over 19 pieces of personal information on each passenger to the US authorities. Despite objections from the European Court of Justice (see Court of Justice of the European Commission 2006), the Passenger Name Records (PNR) system, as it is known, enables the US security services to identify potential terrorist 'threats', after which time the data is stored for 13 years and used to profile terrorist suspects. Alone among all 28 member states of the EU, the UK wanted the PNR system to be extended to rail and sea, as well as to include international and domestic flights within the EU (Traynor 2008a). Controversially, in order for the US to achieve its objective of acquiring passenger data, it used the threat of the withdrawal of EU states from its Visa Waiver Program to exert pressure on them to comply with its demands (Traynor 2008b).[5]

Passports, visas and other associated travel documentation (e.g. letters of invitation from host country 'sponsors') are the principal means through which states seek to control and regulate the freedom of movement and the right of non-nationals to enter their borders. States also of course have the right to alter passport and visa regimes, subject to the provisions of any multilateral agreements to which they are signatories. Although there are various reasons for changes to passport and visa regulations, the foreign policy and security priorities of the issuing state are often prime determinants. For example, the 9/11 attacks prompted the US authorities to make wholesale changes to visa regulations in order to tighten the security of their external frontiers. The US also eliminated the 'Transit without Visa' scheme in response to the attacks, creating havoc for millions of passengers who were merely transiting American territory with no intention of entering the country. Since 25 October 2004, visitors entering the US from any one of the 27 countries (now 37) participating in the Visa Waiver Program have been required to present a 'machine-readable passport' to border officials. Travellers without a biometric passport are required to apply in advance for a visa from the Department of Homeland Security, and then are fingerprinted and photographed once they arrive at US ports-of-entry (Department of Homeland Security 2011). However, in retaliation to this requirement, Brazil imposed similar measures on US tourists passing through its own borders (Guardian 2004). The US authorities have also co-operated with Japan in order to assist in the implementation of a similar scheme in 2007. However, in this instance, the Director of the American Civil Liberties Union's Program on Technology and Liberty expressed concern over the fact that all visitors to Japan would be entered into a biometric database in much the same way as they are in the US, questioning its efficacy in genuinely combating terrorism (Hongo 2007).

The possession of a passport together with a valid visa, where it is a requirement of entry, is a necessary though by no means a sufficient instrument of international cross-border mobility. Since 12 January 2009, in addition to being in possession of a valid passport, travellers from Visa Waiver Program countries must complete the Electronic System for Travel Authorization (ESTA) prior to departure in order to receive authorization to travel to and enter the United States (Department of Homeland Security 2011). Yet an approved travel authorization does not automatically entitle one to entry. This prerogative falls to the border security officials at the port-of-entry. The US also operates a scheme allowing fast-track entry and exit for 'low-risk' travellers, authorizing travel as part of the Trusted Traveler Program (Department of Homeland Security 2013). By undergoing a series of rigorous background checks and a personal interview, superior rights of mobility are bestowed upon these so-called 'trusted travellers'. The deployment of fast-track 'trusted traveller' schemes affords members privileged rights of travel and free movement, thus raising the spectre of 'multiple grades of state citizenship' based upon different levels of security clearance (Coles 2008a: 67). One of the various trusted traveller programmes run by the US Customs and Border Protection agency, the Global Entry Program, had screened 3 million passengers in the first year of operation (Rosenbloom 2012). Unsurprisingly, there has been close co-operation between luxury travel providers (e.g. Loew Hotels & Resorts) and the US authorities in order to provide elite clientele with preferential access to such schemes, further reinforcing the 'superior' entitlement to travel among high-income travellers.

In addition to close co-operation between myriad private firms offering such services to governments, analysts have noted that the border itself is indeed becoming significantly 'delocalized' (Salter 2006). Moreover, Rumford (2006: 160) states that: 'Whereas borders were once singular and only existed at the boundary of politics, they are now multiple and are dispersed throughout societies.' Thus while many border control functions have been outsourced to private firms, borders themselves have become increasingly differentiated, in tandem with the proliferation of various bilateral and multilateral visa agreements (see Hall 2008). In this regard, Australia established Advanced Passenger Information (API) systems in some regions in the Middle East and Asia-Pacific, and placed immigration officials at key points of transit en route to Australia. As stated by Wilson and Weber (2008: 129), these initiatives illustrate that the 'Australian Government has therefore created a formidable offshore network which operates to sort, immobilize and pre-empt unwanted arrivals at the physical border'.

The differential mobility entitlements afforded to the citizens of different nations are clearly reflected in the Henley Visa Restrictions Index. This Index comprises a global barometer ranking the passports of different states according to the degree of visa-free travel enjoyed by citizens of these countries. The results from the August 2012 survey revealed a clear division in the degree of travel freedoms enjoyed by the citizens of different states. The seventeen countries enjoying the least amount of visa-free travel are ranked below, whereby the country ranked the lowest (Afghanistan) faces the most restrictive passport and visa regimes.

TABLE 4.1 A global ranking of countries whose citizens are least able to travel without applying for a visa in advance

Rank	Country
103	Afghanistan
102	Somalia
101	Iraq
100	Palestinian Territories[6] and Pakistan
99	Eritrea
98	Lebanon and Nepal
97	Sudan
96	Angola, Djibouti, Ethiopia, Iran, Kosovo, Myanmar (Burma), Syria and Sri Lanka

Source: Henley and Partners Visa Restrictions Index (2012).

TABLE 4.2 A global ranking of countries whose citizens are most able travel without applying for a visa in advance

Rank	Country
1	Denmark
2	Finland, Germany and Sweden
3	Belgium, France, the Netherlands and United Kingdom
4	Italy, Luxembourg and the United States
5	Ireland, Japan, New Zealand, Norway, Portugal and Spain

Source: Henley and Partners Visa Restrictions Index (2012).

In contrast, the citizens most able to travel with a minimum of passport and visa hindrances, are those belonging to the world's wealthiest states with significant political standing and global influence. Unsurprisingly, only three countries in the top 17 places are non-European states. Thus, while Afghani citizens can only enter 26 countries, Pakistanis 32 countries and Iranians 37 countries without the need to apply for a visa in advance, Danes can enter 169 countries, Americans 166 countries and the Spanish 163 countries. Although one might expect the United States to be ranked highest, those countries ranked higher have a more 'neutral' foreign policy stance and thus perhaps enjoy better diplomatic standing than the more belligerent, albeit wealthier states, as in the case of the US and the UK. The top 17 countries are ranked accordingly (see Table 4.2).

It is not merely the recipient states, however, but tourist-generating countries themselves that periodically adopt measures to restrict the mobility of their *own* citizens, for reasons linked to their own diplomatic and foreign policies. For example, despite the relaxation of certain restrictions by the Obama administration on US citizens travelling to Cuba, the fifty year long economic embargo remains in place. US citizens also still require clearance from the US authorities to visit the island.[7] In 2011, despite the easing of certain restrictions on 'purposeful travel' (i.e. travel that supports civil society and/or people-to-people contact) between the US and Cuba by President Obama's administration, the apparent desire of the US to remove such mobility restrictions is overwhelmingly motivated by a desire to promote the independence of Cubans from the Cuban authorities, rather than a genuine desire to integrate Cuba into a wider democratic framework of travel mobility (MacAskill 2011). A recent trip to Cuba by the US celebrity pop star couple Jay-Z and Beyoncé sparked significant public outcry, demonstrating the extent to which travel to the island remains loaded with potent symbolism. Although the trip was formally sanctioned, as it was deemed educational, some members of the US political community, notably Republican politicians representing US Cuban exiles, believed that the visit could be seen to endorse an oppressive regime (Kozinn 2013). Despite the fury aroused by the trip, Jay-Z capitalized on the aftermath by producing the rap song, 'From Havana to Atlanta' through which he expresses his right to travel to Cuba.

US companies have also faced severe penalties if they contravene the travel ban, which has also had repercussions for tourists from other countries wishing to visit Cuba. For example, credit cards and travellers' cheques are not accepted if they are issued by US firms, regardless of whether or not they are issued by their UK divisions (Jones 2008). In 1996, the Helms–Burton Act tightened the economic embargo on the island, and led the UK-based travel firm Thomson Holidays to drop its package holidays to Cuba for fear of falling foul of even tighter restrictions imposed on companies trading with Cuba. Although at the time Thomson was owned by the Canadian Thomson Corporation, prior to its purchase by the German firm Preussag in 2000, which shortly thereafter became TUI AG, the parent firm generated the majority of its profits from other commercial activities in the US and was thus exposed to potential recrimination under the terms of the Act (Calder 2008). Predictably, Cuba's visa-free ranking is quite low, with only 56 countries allowing visa-free entry for Cuban citizens. In contrast, the socialist state of Venezuela is higher on the list in 34th position, whose citizens are able to enter 115 countries without the need for a visa. Its economic status as a rich oil-producing nation may have some leverage on other states, enabling greater freedom of mobility despite the fact that many powerful Western states, the US in particular, have been fiercely resistant to the populist-socialist regime in Caracas. On the other hand, notwithstanding the improved status and mobility of Chinese tourists in recent years, the People's Republic of China is ranked low, in 92nd position. Currently, Chinese citizens benefit from 'visa-free' access to only 41 countries (Henley and Partners Visa Restrictions Index 2012).

Passports and visas, in addition to being prerequisites (but not sufficient) for entry into a given state, also serve to assist border security officials in making on-the-spot judgements in their attempt to codify and stratify different nationalities according to predetermined rankings of 'risk' and 'danger'. Individual travellers and tourists are thus vulnerable to a fraught process of inquisition, particularly in the context of the wider political categorizations and cultural prejudices vis-à-vis 'risky' or potentially 'dangerous' travellers. Although such categorizations have always been present in the management of border crossings, the 9/11 attacks served to create an altogether new category of suspicion: 'flying while Arab', to the extent that a number of US pilots refused to carry passengers of Middle Eastern origin immediately after the attacks (Lyon 2003: 99). Widespread distrust towards those populations associated with Islam has emerged in the form of anti-Muslim sentiment frequently described as Islamophobia, which has been socially produced and reproduced within a global context. Inevitably this has had manifest repercussions on the tourist mobilities of Muslims. Indeed, a recent a study by the UNWTO and European Travel Commission has highlighted the degree to which anti-Arab/Muslim feeling across Europe has dampened the demand and propensity for travel by tourists from the Middle East wishing to travel to the West (Muqbil 2012). In this regard, Stephenson and Ali (2010: 249, 250, 251) note:

In the light of the current climate of 'global terrorism', however, Muslim journeys to and within the Western states are politically implicated ... However, 'global terrorism' has led to the need to reconsider matters of citizenship, especially as Muslim identities are implicated in the context of the current socio-political climate. As antiterrorist legislation and practices incriminate 'Muslims' as 'terrorists', this misidentification acts as a social impediment by restricting cosmopolitan performances and worldly experiences associated with tourism practices ... Islamophobia implicates the identities of members of the Muslim diaspora, where they are perceived to pose a serious threat to the safety and security of other tourists and host communities ... As Muslim tourists are considered to be a threat to humanity, cultural harmony, and the global order, they could perhaps be viewed as anti-cosmopolitan subjects, despite genuine intentions to travel for meaningful quests and experiences.

Two months following 9/11, it was reported that the US authorities required travellers from 26 mainly Muslim states to obtain FBI clearance before their visas could be processed at US consulates, thwarting people's travels plans and having a direct effect on business tourism and student travel (Goldenberg 2002). Poynting *et al.*'s (2004) book, sardonically entitled *Bin Laden in the Suburbs: Criminaling of the Arab Other*, illustrates how 9/11 exacerbated ways in which Muslim and Arab communities are collectively and hysterically perceived as retrogressive, barbaric and backward. These communities have arguably become the new 'folk devils' (see S. Cohen 1972) of global society, facing public opprobrium – particularly in the West – for the allegedly irreconcilable conflicts between nation-states, religions and cultures.

The ability of the nation-state to abrogate at will the right to travel of certain people, illustrates the fragile nature of the principle of free movement. Often the reasons are not entirely clear, other than the fact that those individuals who originate from outside the rich club of advanced capitalist states can be commonly treated as suspected 'terrorists' and/or 'illegal' immigrants and thus deterred from entry. The story of Mehran Karimi Nasseri, an Iranian citizen expelled from Iran in 1977 for his involvement in anti-Shah demonstrations, offers a graphic illustration of the restricted mobility freedoms experienced by many non-Western citizens, an experience that has on occasion rendered certain individuals 'stateless'. After spending six years in Belgium where he had been granted asylum in 1981, Nasseri decided to make a future for himself in the UK. While in transit in Paris he lost his refugee documentation or this information may have been stolen. Upon arrival at Heathrow he was refused entry to the UK for failing to present a passport to immigration officials. He was then sent back to Paris and arrested at Charles de Gaulle airport for attempting to enter the country illegally. He was not permitted to return to and re-enter Belgium on the grounds that he had left the state voluntarily, thus abrogating his right to asylum. Nasseri ended up 'trapped' in Charles de Gaulle's Terminal 1, living there in transnational limbo between 1988 and 2006 while his unusual case went through the French courts. In the meantime, he was unable to leave or enter France because he lacked his official documents. Although his refugee status was eventually confirmed in 1999, along with his right to remain in France and documents affirming his right to travel, Nasseri continued to live at the airport voluntarily until he was hospitalized in 2006 (Romain 2012). His life captivated journalists and filmmakers, especially inspiring Steven Spielberg's 2004 movie *The Terminal*, in which the protagonist (played by the actor Tom Hanks) finds work at the airport and falls in love, before eventually being granted the right to enter the US.

Since 9/11, there has been significant national and international dialogue concerning the adoption of various biometric technologies as a way to govern and regulate mobility and risk (Amoore 2006). For example, biometric passport (including the e-passport) contains such body-based identification systems as facial, iris and fingerprint recognition, and can be used to authenticate the identity of travellers and demarcate travellers in terms of 'low', 'medium' and 'high' risk. In Australia, the 2005 Australian Passports Act established the need for a state database of biometric information (e.g. facial recognition) on bearers of Australian passports/travel documents, epitomizing how the modern state is moving more and more towards policies and practices that reflect the 'securitization of mobility' (Wilson and Weber 2008: 135). Yet as Amoore *et al.* (2006: 98) clearly emphasize:

> The accelerating spread of biometric and other security technologies has been fueled in part by the privatization of security with its accompanying narratives of risk management and promotion of technological fixes for social problems.

In a controversial move, the European Union adopted a new regulation on biometrics in 2004, a regulation subsequently amended in 2009 (European Union 2009), requiring EU member states to include two biometric identifiers in passports and travel documents: digitized fingerprints and a face scan. These initiatives were devised for the ostensible purpose of streamlining border-crossing procedures and preventing the fraudulent use of EU passports. However, the integration of the EU regulation on biometrics across the member states has been problematic. In particular, their contribution to improved security has been questionable after reported problems concerning their fraudulent use in France and the Netherlands (European Parliament 2012). More significantly perhaps, the legality of incorporating biometrics into EU citizens' passports, in so far as it compromises EU legislation on the freedom of movement and potentially violates the right to privacy, has also been called into question (Peers 2004; Rodríguez 2012). According to Peers (2004), the urgency of introducing biometrics into EU passports was predominantly to satisfy US security concerns, and in order for EU member states to remain part of the US Visa Waiver scheme. In this instance, the EU has demonstrated its willingness to subordinate the rights of EU citizens to privacy and the freedom of movement to the security interests of the United States. Those nations which are signatories to the 1995 Schengen Treaty, which does not include Ireland and the UK, but does include the countries of the European Free Trade Association (Iceland, Liechtenstein, Norway and Switzerland), are now required to add fingerprint biometrics to their passports.

In the past decade or so, an opaque nexus of public institutions and private corporate interests, largely unaccountable to citizens, has evolved ostensibly for the purposes of improving security while simultaneously providing lucrative new income streams for security and technology companies. The widespread collection and analysis of digital data for surveillance purposes, or 'dataveillance', reflects a post-9/11 globalization of security politics and tightening of national border regimes, partly driven by an underlying commercial imperative to maximize profits from the 'threat' of global terrorism. Naomi Klein (2007: 298–302), in her dissection of 'disaster capitalism' and the emergence of the 'homeland security' industry, argues that the 9/11 attacks provided a useful pretext for the outsourcing of security to a growing web of corporations all too eager to develop, test and apply a range of sophisticated digital technologies and technical gadgetry (underwritten by public money) in the name of securing citizens at home and abroad from the nebulous threat of global terrorism. Dataveillance is big business. According to Klein (2007: 306), the homeland security industry grew larger than either Hollywood or the music business in just over half a decade since 9/11. The Biometrics Research Group Inc. estimated that over US$450 million per annum is spent by the US government on biometric research (King 2012a). In addition, the global market for biometrics is expected to rise to an estimated US$15 billion by 2015 from its estimated value of US$7 billion in 2012. The largest share of this market concerns fingerprint identification systems, which represent an estimated US$5 billion and are expected to rise to US$10 billion by 2015 (King 2012b). Also, it is estimated that funding for US homeland security and defence applications will increase from US$190 billion in 2011 to US$210 billion by 2014 (King 2012a).

The use of payment cards (e.g. credit and debit cards), reward cards (e.g. frequent flyer cards), the Internet and mobile phones produce large quantities of personal data related to the purchasing patterns of consumers. This information enables companies to match specific products and services to consumers and tourists. Although dataveillance ostensibly serves the purpose of monitoring and controlling mobile subjects in the interests of security, the analysis of such data may in fact disproportionately benefit frequent travellers. Weaver (2008: 9–10) appropriately notes:

> Poorer customers may pay more for products and services than customers who are deemed to be more desirable. Reward schemes offer more benefits to affluent customers who spend their disposable income. As a result, affluent consumers may receive more reward points, and therefore more discounts, than poorer consumers. With respect to travel and tourism, reward schemes may reinforce the division that exists between frequent travellers – some of whom may be considered 'hypermobile' individuals – and infrequent travellers who may not be as mobile because they are poor. Personally identified data can therefore exacerbate the market-driven separation of 'haves' from 'have nots'.

While the impetus for the further securitization of global travel was created by the 9/11 attacks and the US launch of the 'war on terror', the proliferation of digital surveillance and security technologies has arguably had little or no effect on the prevention of terrorism. As the figures above suggest, the climate of fear that has been perpetrated by the 'war on terror' has provided a significant boost to the lucrative market in private security and surveillance technologies (see Athwal 2006). The booming security-surveillance industry also exploits continuing fears over global terrorism in order to generate lucrative government defence and security contracts. Recent examples include plans by the Boeing Corporation and a consortium of other companies to construct a high-tech virtual border fence along the US–Mexico border, and the Automated Targeting System (ATS), which is designed to help border officials assign risk to travellers passing through the US (see Klein 2007: 302–307). Such technologies have enhanced the 'capacity to discriminate between different classes of persons, using algorithmic surveillance' (Lyon 2004: 310). The professed aim of the ATS system is to detect and filter out 'suspected terrorists' (Klein 2007: 304). It does so by highlighting suspicious patterns of passenger behaviour revealed through information provided by commercial airlines concerning ticket purchases, seat preferences, frequent flyer behaviour, number of bags carried, method of payment and even meals eaten!

In the light of the concerns surrounding the mass surveillance 'Prism program' being carried out by the US (see Milne 2013), it is clear such enhanced powers of surveillance have potentially far-reaching implications for both civil liberties and the free movement of travellers. The potential scope for error presented by the use of such data-mining techniques is exacerbated by the prejudices and half-truths circulating widely in the media, attributing suspicion and collective blame to particular ethnic groups. Indeed, there have been cases where passengers of 'Middle Eastern' or 'Muslim' appearance have been accused of acting suspiciously when travelling and in some cases even prevented from travelling (Glaister 2009; Wazir 2001). The privatization of data collection seamlessly coalesces with state imperatives to track, control and at times restrict the movement of certain categories of people deemed to lack the 'right credentials' to travel and cross international frontiers. The mobile citizen must thus constantly prove their innocence, not just at the border but increasingly within them, as every form of communication, their purchasing patterns and all manner of social interaction are placed under constant surveillance.

In a further illustration of how borders have been increasingly diffused throughout societies, Rumford (2006: 158) notes how the 2004 bombings in Madrid and the 7/7 bombings in London prompted the Italian authorities to pass new anti-terrorism legislation that requires customers to present their passports to café owners in order to access the Internet: literally, a 'passport to surf'. Such examples of proliferating borders combined with the deployment of state-of-the-art digital surveillance technologies further inculcate a climate of fear, striating mobility according to nationality, race and ethnicity, demarcating who has the right or not to enjoy freedom of movement. Attempts to 'lock down' spaces of mobility perpetuate the very fears that created the 'need' for the application of such technologies in the first place. While the neoliberal state propagates its role as the neutral and benevolent protector of 'legitimate' travellers and citizens, weeding out the 'bogus' tourist and 'risky' individual, mobile citizens are increasingly moulded into modular, individuated forms of citizenship. They are made to be fearful of the 'stranger' in the next seat and more accepting of the need to forego certain rights in the interests of making the world safe for travel.

Travel, security and citizenship in the 'global airport'

Nowhere are the politically contested and uneven patterns of cross-border mobility made more apparent than in the interacting flows of people encountered in the global airport. In many ways, the airport epitomizes many of the contradictory elements of global travel, simultaneously enabling and differentiating the continuous flow of human mobilities according to their credentials for travel, both perceived and real. Neoliberal globalization has converted the global airport into the gateway for extensive cross-border movements of people. However, not all those who pass through the airport are equal with respect to their rights and entitlements to the freedom of travel. The diverse scope and patterns of mobility serve as an indication of both the differential status of state citizenship (as indicated by the Henley Visa Restrictions Index) and the emergence of new and unequal rights of mobility bestowed upon the tourist and other privileged mobile subjects. In addition to the 'hypermobile elite' (Hannam *et al.* 2006: 6), comprising the transnational business class, politicians, diplomats, celebrities and sports personalities, most tourists pass through the airport with relative ease in contrast to the denizen, non-citizen or indeed those whose tourist credentials are deemed to be 'suspicious'.

The airport can be interpreted as a highly 'securitized' and 'technologized' institution that is being continuously shaped by the shifting imperatives of national security and commerce (Salter 2008a: xiii–xiv). Once predominantly serving as a gateway to the world, international airports increasingly resemble globalized retail hubs owned by major transnational corporations such as the Ferrovial Group,[8] which runs the former state-owned British Airports Authority. Privatized in 1986, this corporate giant has a financial stake in several European city airports as well as retail interests in various US airports (Salter 2008b: 19). The transformation of the global airport into an increasingly complex nexus of corporate capital and state power has invariably created a series of tensions between commerce and security. This transformation has thus rendered the boundaries between the citizen and consumer increasingly hard to discern (Lyon 2008a). In addition, the glamorous design and 'holiday' atmosphere inculcated within airport terminals serves to cast a veil over the underlying security imperatives and the coercive powers that lie beneath the surface (see Kellerman 2008).

Numerous writers and commentators enthusiastically celebrate the role of airports in temporarily suspending people's nationality and promoting a 'liberating' sense of placelessness. Ballard (1997), for instance, observes that 'we are no longer citizens with civic obligations, but passengers for whom all destinations are theoretically open … An easy camaraderie rules the departure lounges, along with the virtual abolition of nationality.' However, this view is contradicted by the myriad restrictions and hindrances to the mobility rights of persons that have been discussed thus far, and which are predominantly deployed at airports and other ports-of-entry. Although airports may signify a liberating sense of cosmopolitanism for some they are increasingly striated by discourses and practices of securitization, which ascribe risk to predetermined categories of travellers – placing them into different streams of mobility.

Airports are a potent example of how surveillance techniques operate to undermine democratic participation in travel and cosmopolitan notions of a borderless world. Lyon (2003: 123) emphasizes that airports are sites for 'security and surveillance practices and processes', where travellers are 'screened for eligibility to travel and for acceptability on arrival'. While highly mobile individuals, privileged travellers and other polyglot 'global citizens' (e.g. businesspersons, diplomats and celebrities) are able to undergo a swift and hasty departure from airports, enabled by the use of biometric passports and membership of trusted traveller and other loyalty schemes, the 'mobility poor' are increasingly subjected to a range of cumbersome checks and constraints brought about by the use of the same technologies. Airports are constantly updating their technologies to monitor the extensive flows of people that pass through each day. The Exit Sentry system, established by the US video surveillance firm and 'security consultancy' Cernium, is one such security device widely used at US airports, which warns security personnel if an individual walks in the wrong direction at exit lanes in secured areas (Magrath 2001). The US Department of Homeland Security has also recently introduced 'real-time' intelligence to detect potentially 'risky' travellers, involving extra passenger screening, international intelligence data checks and advanced imaging technologies. This enhanced surveillance system was prompted by a security incident on Christmas Day 2009, when a Nigerian male boarded a US-bound plane with explosive chemicals, despite being registered on a US terrorism database of 550,000 suspects (Montefinise 2009).

Repressive anti-terrorist legislation has also encouraged and facilitated the increased development and widespread use of biometric and digital surveillance technologies. The implications for civil liberties and free movement are clear, particularly where the boundaries between what constitutes a 'migrant', 'refugee', 'asylum seeker', 'criminal' or 'terrorist' are often blurred and rendered less distinct. Anti-terrorist legislation has proliferated since 9/11. In addition to the (US) Patriot Act (2001), mentioned earlier, notable examples include the Protect America Act (2007) and the (UK) Anti-Terrorism, Crime and Security Act (2001). The latter act, for instance, provided the UK government with the power to detain without trial for an indefinite period, non-British citizens suspected of 'terrorist' links (Hayter 2004: xxiii). It also legislated that airlines must make available registered information and data about their passengers to the appropriate legal authorities.

The airport is a crucial mechanism governing mobility that serves to reflect and institutionalize forms of social and ethnic stratification and segregation that exist within wider society. Codourey's (2008) analysis of Frankfurt am Main Airport exemplifies how forms of segregation are built into the physical configuration of the airport. One of the less publicized functions of the airport, including smaller regional airports or military bases located away from the gaze of the travelling public, is to act as a deportation centre for 'failed' asylum seekers. Such 'detention camps' are usually physically detached from the main terminal buildings yet still form part of the airport transit area. The privately run detention camp houses asylum seekers and refugees who are not permitted to leave the building during their stay at the camp. These spaces exist in contrast to those routinely accessible to most tourists and members of the mobile elite, who have comfortable access to waiting lounges, places of consumption and other leisure amenities. Augé (1995) interestingly describes airports, like refugee camps, service stations, motorways and train stations as *non-lieux* ('non-places'), where mundane locational experiences emerge and organic social interactions cease. 'Non-places' are perceived as places of solitude, anonymity, impermanence and alienation, as well as being bureaucratic and uniform. Although it cannot be denied that airports are permeated by officious security practices and constitute intrinsically alienating experiences for many, they are by no means places of anonymity. Rather, they are sites for the performance and interplay of top-down security, information management and data production in which individuals are systematically named, identified and documented, often in a manner unbeknown to them. The close surveillance of individuals also calls into question people's citizenship identities on racial, cultural and ethnic lines, such that: 'The contemporary journeys of "racialised others" do not always constitute legitimate touristic ventures' (Stephenson 2006: 294). In this regard, the writer and journalist Gary Younge (2000) indicates the difficulties often anticipated by non-white tourists upon arrival in EU states. In his description of a return flight to the UK, he sardonically notes:

> Ladies and gentlemen, we are about to land at Heathrow. Please stow away your tray tables, put your seats in the upright position, ensure your seatbelt is securely fastened and that your racial identity is put away carefully in a safe place as otherwise it may well pop out and cause you injury.
>
> *(2000: 274)*

The following encounter at airport immigration in France, witnessed by the African American writer, bell hooks (1992: 174), suggests that travel experiences can be terrorizing for black and other minorities:

> I was stripped searched by French officials, who were stopping black people to make sure we were not illegal immigrants and/or terrorists. I think that one fantasy of whiteness is that the threatening Other is always a terrorist. This projection enables many white people to imagine there is no representation of whiteness as terror, as terrorizing.

Observations by Stephenson (2004, 2006) and Stephenson and Hughes (2005) concerning the travel and tourism experiences of members of the black community of Caribbean origin in the UK illustrate how assumptions of individuals (e.g. as 'drug smugglers') negatively influence the perceptions of border officials. The authors emphasize that these suppositions are influenced by racial stereotyping, media-fuelled imagery and popular opinion regarding the threat presented by such ethnic minorities. Accordingly, the actions of others have a social and emotional impact on the travel experiences and habits of black (British) tourists. The movements of such tourists in Western states are prone to intense surveillance by the authorities, and are often defined and inspected by the all-defining power of the 'white gaze'. This power dichotomy arguably ensures that racial disposition and skin colour rather than simply nationality and citizenship exert a significant influence on people's right to travel and their freedom of movement. Religion too has a role to play. As indicated above in relation to the rise of Islamophobia in the post-9/11 era, men sporting beards and females wearing headscarves are frequently mistaken for 'terrorists'. Such trends often intensify when travelling to and from countries listed by the US as state sponsors of terrorism (Goldenberg 2002).

The prevailing logic of neoliberal economics has also encouraged the privatization of ports-of-entry and airport security. Thus, the imperatives of profit-making may increasingly coexist with or even challenge those of security (Salter 2008b). Indeed, the failure of the airport security systems at Boston Logan Airport to detect the 9/11 hijackers was partly attributed to the lax security arrangements linked to the outsourcing of these services to low-wage personnel hired by profit-making firms (Brelis and Carroll 2001). Such tensions between the state's desire to reconcile freedom of movement with the imperatives of security were also illustrated by the situation following the attempted purchase of six US ports by a UAE-based company in 2006. Although the sale had received clearance from the US Committee on Foreign Investment and the Department of Homeland Security, it provoked a backlash from a number of senators claimed that it would jeopardize the security of US frontiers despite the UAE's full support for the 'war on terror' (Brindis 2006). Therefore, attempts to reconcile the principle of the freedom of movement with such restrictions on mobility often expose contradictions, as well as the blurring of boundaries between citizenship and consumption. The ideal form of citizenship in the securitized world of travel is thus arguably represented by the 'depoliticized' neoliberal citizen, passively submitting to authority while going about the serious business of consumption.

Creswell (2006: 222) draws caution to the popular view that the airport is emblematic of a 'globalised world', acting as a signifier of cosmopolitan or global forms of citizenship, that is, a 'kind of transnational utopian space of flows where nationality has been abolished and class erased – where people are generally contented'. His critical reflection on Amsterdam's Schiphol Airport demonstrates ways in which people's mobilities are manufactured, differentiated and categorized according to specific politico-ideological imperatives: in the airport the 'war on terror' and 'racism' intersect. Creswell's (2006: 219–258) analysis illustrates that, in contrast to the spirit of the Schengen Agreement and freedom of movement enshrined in the various EU treaties, Schiphol in fact reproduces a series of borders. He notes the various ways in which Schiphol is designed to monitor and codify people's movements: separation of passengers into streams of non-Schengen passengers and Schengen passengers; spatial movements that are 'coded', 'ticketed' and 'authorized'; and where passengers are subject to biometric monitoring schemes. Innocent travellers and passengers have subsequently become entangled in the hardening web of state surveillance and preventive 'anti-terrorism' measures, often with tragic consequences. Following the introduction of the US Patriot Act in 2001, which contained provisions allowing for the expansion of undercover air marshals on commercial airlines, a Colombian male was shot after boarding a flight at Miami airport (Wilson 2005). Although the federal marshal insisted that the man had engaged in threatening behaviour by reaching into his rucksack, fellow passengers and his wife denied this. In fact, his wife later claimed that her husband had been mentally unwell.

The securitization of global travel and the proliferation of manifold border regimes not only undermine the expressed commitment of capitalist liberal democracies to the freedom of movement, but also diminish the apparent neoliberal aspiration towards minimal state interference in the realm of commerce and the creation of a borderless world. The increased policing of mobility and securitization of travel appear to contradict the ideal of the freedom of movement and the hedonistic pleasures of consumption that are arguably central to neoliberal globalization and the expanding tourism economy, to the extent that cumbersome security controls and extensive waits at airports around the world have led to a burgeoning of complaints and long delays (Murphy 2010). However, according to Harvey (2006: 25), the expansion of authoritarian state power is the corollary of neoliberal economics. Thus in order to remove the barriers to the free movement of capital and continuously open up new markets to the forces of capital accumulation (e.g. privatized security industries), the neoliberal state assiduously promotes the closing-down of democratic space. The shifting interface between security and mobility therefore has clear implications for the relationship between travel and citizenship. As noted by Loader (1999: 386), the burgeoning market for privatized security: 'enables individuals, organisations and communities to pursue their particularistic and self-defined security requirements without reference to any conception of common good, and free of obligations associated with the practice of democratic citizenship'.

The securitization of travel thus underscores a growing sense of the world and global tourism as 'dangerous' and 'risky' while simultaneously seeking to uphold a vision of privatized leisure consumption and individualized mobility. Not only do the simmering tensions between the freedom of movement and security pervade the neoliberal state, such contradictions are being reconfigured through the rescaling of states and the attempt to create seamless spaces of mobility at transnational levels.

Mobility, tourism and citizenship in the European Union

The freedom of movement and right to travel across international borders unhindered by cumbrous customs and visa formalities is a reality for millions of citizens of the European Union. As with national passport and visa regimes, such multilateral mobility frameworks reflect the underlying politico-ideological imperatives of member states encompassing any number of concerns ranging from security, economic development, tourism, terrorism, crime and immigration, and of course citizenship. The legal and political framework guaranteeing freedom of movement throughout the EEC (European Economic Community) and what was to later become the EU, was established as early as 1957 within the Treaty of Rome (Geddes 2000: 45). Subsequent treaty provisions reinforced this vision, with a significant bearing upon the interface between the right to travel and citizenship. However, as Coles (2008a: 59) acknowledges, although tourism constitutes one of the principal means through which EU citizens experience the benefits of EU membership, continuing restrictions imposed on the freedom of movement and travel within the EU, continues to frustrate people's access to the professed benefits of EU 'citizenship'.

The early provisions for the freedom of movement that were inserted into the foundational charter of the the European Economic Community, were envisaged principally as a means of facilitating the movement of labour into the industrializing regions of Western Europe. During this period the emphasis was on socio-economic mobility and the absorption of migrants from southern Europe into the industrial north, as part of a broader framework for consolidating the common market that would simultaneously ease labour shortages in the north and alleviate poverty in the south. It was only later, during the 1980s that the emphasis switched more forcefully towards enabling the freedom of movement in a wider sense, and of course tourism. These two pillars of EU policy increasingly became seen as fundamental prerequisites for stimulating economic development, enhancing cultural cohesion and fomenting the idea of European citizenship. The Treaty on European Union, or Maastricht Treaty (1993), which amended the Treaty of Rome, bestowed equal rights of mobility on all citizens of what was to become the EU. The freedom of movement principle was subsequently advanced by Directive 2004/38 and consolidated by both the Amsterdam Treaty (1997) and the Lisbon Treaty (2009), which introduced provisions for the removal of internal borders within the EU and formally inaugurated the concept of European citizenship (CEC 2010b). Nevertheless, as Geddes (2000: 58) notes, entitlement to EU citizenship and the right to freedom of movement was to be made subject to the prior acquisition of nationality of an EU member-state.

However, while there has been ample intellectual debate regarding the construction of European citizenship and the development of a pan-European public consciousness (Delanty 1995; Habermas 1994; Shore 2000), the relationship between European citizenship, freedom of movement and cultural identity remains somewhat ambiguous and contradictory. The EU has enacted a wide variety of tourism- and heritage-related programmes and cultural initiatives, some of which are indicated in this book (e.g. the Euro-Mediterranean Partnership and the Calypso Programme), geared towards both expanding the scope of co-operative regional alliances as well as forging an 'imagined community' of European citizens. However, as many seasoned analysts of the EU have noted, despite the proliferation of cultural actions and the attempt to construct an array of identifiable symbols, rituals and narratives of 'European-ness', it is an idea that has so far received a rather lukewarm response among the peoples of Europe, to say the least (Shore and Abélès 2004).

A number of EU analysts have firmly challenged the notion of a 'socially integrated Europe', particularly on two fronts. First, the existence of myriad 'intra-European differences' between the range of nationalities and ethnicities act as a fundamental barrier to the Europeanization of cultures and societies (Balibar 2002: 44). Second, the inherent problems of racial hostility towards immigrants and minority groups in major EU states have been counteractive to racial and indeed ethnic harmony (see Banton 1999; Keith 1995; Witte 1995). This fact also serves to frustrate the freedom of movement for many. Indeed, this view is bolstered by a semantic shift that is increasingly apparent with regard to the treatment of arrivals from new EU member-states. Many conservative EU governments and their supporters in the populist press increasingly use the term 'immigrants' as opposed to citizens or tourists, to refer to the movement of other EU citizens from one state to another, particularly those coming from new EU member-states in Eastern Europe (see Pascouau 2013). For some time, scholars such as Sivanandan (1990) have reminded us that explanations of pan-European racism ought to acknowledge the many 'interior racisms' thriving in Europe, as well as the fact that this kind of racism originates in the historical development of capitalism in Europe (see Miles 1994). Indeed, Jenkins (1987: 3) notes: 'European racism is a unique manifestation of ethnicity, historically formed by slavery, colonial expansion, 19th century evolution and 20th century labour migration.'

The foundations of a 'borderless Europe' began to take shape in as far back as the early 1970s, but was not established until June 1984 with the signing of the Schengen Agreement, an inter-governmental border agreement signed by five of the existing ten EEC member states at the time (Geddes 2000: 81). The Schengen Treaty itself took effect on 26 March 1995 under which seven of the by now 15 EU member states[9] agreed to eliminate national border controls on the internal cross-border movement of citizens among the signatory states, as well as create a passport-free travel zone. Accordingly, a 'Europe without borders' was promoted as part of the EU's continuing mission to create a sense of belonging and a stronger bond between the EU and European citizens (Samatas 2003: 147). Schengen entitles EU citizens who are members of signatory states to enter any other EU country without having to show a passport. However, Schengen member states reserve the right to curtail or restrict the right to travel and cross-border movement on grounds of public policy, public security or public health, as well as to carry out identity checks throughout their territory as part of regular police duties. Hence as Coles (2008b: 67) reminds us: 'It is all well and good to be offered the right to travel but this is meaningless if the right to entry is restricted.'

While seeming to promote freedom of cross-border movement for EU citizens, equally, the emphasis of Schengen is on security, as exemplified by the innocuous-sounding Schengen Information System (SIS). The SIS is a computerized surveillance information exchange system, which uses the latest surveillance technologies to provide a database on 'undesirable strangers', that is, mobile criminals, asylum seekers and 'illegal' immigrants. It was introduced in 1995, in tandem with the elimination of internal frontier controls, as a means of simultaneously enhancing the freedom of movement of 'legitimate' EU citizens and reinforcing Europe's external borders against criminals, asylum seekers and terrorists. Although not a Schengen signatory, Britain has opted into the SIS despite condemnation of the SIS by Amnesty International and the United Nations High Commission for Refugees, due to its attempt to impose draconian curbs on migration and the right to asylum (Hayter 2004: 61).

Increasingly the EU has given itself the almost impossible task of simultaneously filtering out the 'undesirable' subjects of mobility, who are moreover part of a continuum of illegitimate mobility in the eyes of the authorities, while encouraging the growth and spread of tourism around the EU, partly as a means of halting its declining market share in world tourism. Greece offers a particularly apposite illustration given its dependence on tourism and geographic location on 'the borders' of the EU. The incorporation of Greece into the Schengen zone in March 2000 was partly encouraged by concerns relating to Greece's strategic geographic position in Europe's south-eastern corner, an area facing significant migratory pressure, as well as ongoing friction over Turkey's territorial claims in the Aegean (Samatas 2003: 153). Schengen thus constitutes a key instrument in what has been termed 'Fortress Europe', reinforcing differential mobility entitlements: 'For Euro-enthusiasts, it is necessary for a wonderful, passport- and crime-free Europe; but for human rights activists it is a horrible, anti-democratic exclusionary system for creating a maximum-security "Fortress Europe"' (Samatas 2003: 144).

Samatas (2003) surmises that what is gained in terms of mobility freedoms and passport-free travel by European tourists and business classes is lost in terms of the introduction of a complex electronic surveillance system (SIS) and maximum-security infrastructure at the EU's external border. These systems and structures dehumanize migrants and refugees, potentially criminalizing immigration and asylum-seeking by linking these phenomena to crime and terrorism. Widespread discrimination among refugees and immigrants from 'Third World' countries has been exacerbated by the rise of 'spot checks' within the Schengen area, which tend to target 'dark-skinned people from the Third World who are treated as second-rate persons' (Samatas 2003: 148). However, as indicated earlier, ethnic minority citizens with EU passports are also profiled and vulnerable to harassment. Accordingly, Balibar (1991: 6–7) claims:

> The fact that, in Europe as a whole, a large proportion of 'Blacks' or immigrants are not foreigners in the eyes of the law merely intensifies the contradictions, and intersects with the ever more pressing question of European

identity. On the one hand, then, the emergence of a European racism, or the model of racism, raises the issue of Europe's place in a world system, with its economic inequalities and population flows. On the other hand, it appears to be inextricably bound up with questions relating to collective rights, citizenship, nationality and the treatment of minorities, where the real political framework is not each particular country but Europe as a whole.

The right to the freedom of mobility that is now a well-established principle of EU integration implies that every EU citizen is entitled to travel within and across EU territories, unobstructed by visa formalities and custom requirements at national borders. However, not only have such rights been denied to those fleeing persecution (see Babington and Papadimas 2013), nor do they apply equally to all EU citizens. For example, fears of large-scale migration and 'benefit' tourism from the AC10 states,[10] which acceded to the EU on 1 May 2004, resulted in the imposition of a number of restrictions on the entrance of new EU citizens from these states, until 2011. A further series of quotas were imposed on entrants from Bulgaria and Romania after their accession in 2007 (Coles 2008a: 61). Further to this, in September 2011, the Netherlands and Finland, as a result of pressure from right-wing populist parties, vetoed the incorporation of these two states into the Schengen area on much the same basis (Pignal 2011). This was in contrast to the previous enlargement in 1995, when three states, Austria, Sweden and Finland, which had previously been members of the *European Free Trade Association* (see fn. 9), joined the EU. These states, which have a combined GDP higher than the EU average, were not greeted with similar calls for restrictions on the mobility of rights of their citizens when joining the EU (Hall 2004: 10).

The accession of the AC10 states provided a major stimulus for inbound and intra-regional travel to destinations in the former Soviet bloc, which had to a large extent been 'off-limits', while also providing an opportunity for the citizens of these states to travel with relative freedom around the European Union. As the Communist-era restrictions on cross-border mobility ceased, a number of historic cities and heritage sites in Eastern Europe (e.g. Budapest, Kraków, Maribor, Prague, Sibiu) were quickly incorporated into European cultural tourism itineraries and circuits of capital accumulation. As part of its ongoing enlargement and integration policy in the Western Balkans, the European Union announced its intention to lift Schengen visa requirements for citizens of Serbia, Macedonia and Montenegro in possession of biometric passports, from 19 December 2009. Similarly, on 27 May 2010, the European Commission also announced proposals for visa-free travel to the EU by citizens of Albania and Bosnia, which came into effect on 8 November 2010. This would, according to the EU Commissioner for Home Affairs, Cecilia Malmström, facilitate further people-to-people contact, enhance business opportunities and provide an opportunity 'for the people of the region to get to know the EU better' (CEC 2010c). Nevertheless, the introduction of visa-free travel was accompanied with a warning from Malmström that, 'a visa-free regime also comes with responsibilities for both the governments and the people of the countries benefiting from this freedom', and that these countries should undertake their responsibilities to monitor and prevent 'unfounded asylum requests' (Sofia Echo 2010).

Paradoxically then, the EU has presided over substantial enlargement of its external frontiers while simultaneously hardening its regimes of surveillance and identity checks in the name of security and the fight against organized crime, illegal immigration and terrorism. This has frustrated the free movement of EU citizens as well as the legitimate right to travel within the EU of those from non-member states, contrary to certain provisions of EU law (see Geddes 2000: 121), a situation exacerbated by the intensification of xenophobia and anti-Muslim hysteria (see Fekete 2004). Such racialized perceptions of travel have penetrated the very heart of a multiracial Europe, affecting common notions of hospitability, which are arguably essential to the social harmony and well-being of tourism destinations. Hasan (2012) documents ways in which 'halal hysteria' is increasingly pervasive throughout Europe, spurred on by populist media scares and conservative-nationalist politicians, who misleadingly claim that Islamic slaughtering methods are inhumane and that the public is unknowingly being made to consume halal products. Such Islamophobia represents a challenge to the nurturing of welcoming environments and hospitality for travellers and citizens of emerging tourism nations. More importantly, it also runs counter to the cosmopolitan and multicultural practices that are arguably integral to the cultivation of social solidarity and the civic bonds that underpin the ideals of cosmopolitan citizenship.

Despite their right to the freedom of movement as citizens of Europe, it is arguably Europe's extensive population of Roma gypsies who are the most vilified and persecuted of all Europe's peoples. The expulsion of more than 10,000 Roma gypsies from France in 2009, mainly to Romania and Bulgaria, violated both EU and international law (Human Rights Watch 2011). The existence of a sizeable Roma community in Romania has also been used to cast doubt on Romania's acceptability for joining the Schengen area, and to retain quotas on the numbers of Romanians (and Bulgarians) able to move freely and work throughout the EU (see J. Taylor 2013). Elsewhere, outside the existing borders of the EU, the homes of Istanbul's long-standing Roma community in the historic Sulukule quarter were demolished as part of the embellishment of the city in preparation for Istanbul's stint as one of three European Capitals of Culture in 2010 (Turgut 2008). Further still, as a result of its attempts to transcend national jurisdictions over the freedom of movement and the right to travel *within* the EU's borders, the EU has in fact ceded these powers to an opaque network of unaccountable bureaucracies and private corporations (e.g. Shengen visa processing). This calls into question the ideological premises behind the enlargement of the freedom of movement and its implications for social justice and the equality of access to mobility rights.

The reconfiguration of the EU's borders together with the increasing ease of low-cost travel provides a legal framework and further practical scope to the mobility freedoms enjoyed, for the most part, by EU citizens. In addition, the entitlement by citizens of the EU member-states to draw their pensions outside the country in which they have been earned has facilitated the growth of international retirement migration, whose foundations had been laid in the context of decades of north–south mass tourism in Europe (Gustafson 2008; Williams *et al.* 1997). By the early 1970s, the trend towards settling in southern Europe was in full swing. Indeed, Young (1973: 138) confirms that it was cheaper for pensioners to spend the winter months of 1972–1973 in the Mediterranean on a £5.65 per week package provided by Sun Air Holidays, than it was to maintain them in a local authority home in the UK! By 1997, 700,000 UK government pensions were being paid to UK citizens living outside the UK, 70,000 of which corresponded to UK residents in southern Europe (Williams *et al.* 1997: 121).

O'Reilly's (2000) ethnography of the British living in the Costa del Sol challenges the popular image perpetuated by the British media that resident expatriates often live in isolated national enclaves. She demonstrates that in fact they are made up of increasingly diverse and heterogeneous groups of people, and thus do not fit into simple distinctions between 'tourists' and 'expat residents' (O'Reilly 2000: 17–22). Not only are these increasingly mobile individuals and families often younger and professionally diverse, they are often peripatetic, moving from one place to another in search of work and new lifestyles (Bianchi 2000). However, unlike immigrants from 'Third World' states outside the EU or indeed EU residents with non-EU passports, these forms of mobility tend to be relatively unconstrained by comparison. The relocation of large numbers of citizens from EU member-states in the north, many of whom first visited as tourists, to a variety of southern European regions, has nevertheless progressively changed the ethnic and social composition of local populations in certain places, most notably the Costa del Sol in Spain (see also Williams *et al.* 1997).

In municipalities such as San Fulgencio, located near Alicante in Spain, newcomers largely from Britain have eclipsed the proportion of native-born Spaniards. Without wishing to exaggerate the dichotomy between 'native born' and 'expatriates', this demographic shift has been reflected in the balance of power in municipal politics, as well as distinctive attitudes towards, among other things, taxation, security and public expenditure on local *fiestas* (Tremlett 2007: 23). The bestowal of 'equal' rights of mobility, residence and work on EU citizens from states with significantly different standards of living has also accentuated tensions between EU citizens from the relatively more affluent member-states in Western Europe, and those newly incorporated into the EU since 2004. While citizens of the wealthier EU member-states in the 'West' availed themselves of the new freedoms to move, reside and own property anywhere in the EU, in contrast, citizens of new EU member-states in Eastern Europe have moved from East to West in search of work, only to face the hostility of host populations and politicians.

Deepening and widening EU integration has of course induced new forms of tourist-related mobility, both intended and unintended, which have a series of implications for evolving constructions of citizenship. Tourism is both a beneficiary of the right to the freedom of movement (and residence) bestowed upon EU citizens, as well as a vehicle through which the EU has tried to encourage a greater sense of understanding and awareness of a pan-European sense of identity and ultimately, citizenship. Indeed, Roche (2001: 87) argues: 'The seasonal migrations of Europe's masses from the wealthier north to the relatively poorer South ... are indeed likely to be potentially powerful vehicles of cultural Europeanization in the early 21st century.'

Europe's political elite only began to take the question of tourism seriously subsequent to the accession to the then EEC, of Greece and Portugal in 1981, and Spain in 1986, whose economies were heavily reliant upon tourism. The first *Community Action Plan to Assist Tourism* was published in 1991, in which it was explicitly recognized that tourism would benefit greatly from EU enlargement. However, as Lickorish (1991) notes, EU support for the liberalization of freedom of movement and tourism took a long time coming. Among other reasons, he argues, this was due to poor policy coordination at EU level and, more pertinently, because 'tourism represents the "mobile" as distinct from the residential community' and thereby exerts less influence over policymakers (1991: 178). Subsequently, the EU has become increasingly active in this area, establishing a range of tourism-related policies, cultural programmes and itineraries in order to encourage EU citizens to travel within the EU as a means of enhancing a European sense of cultural identity and citizenship.

Although the Treaty of Rome did not assign competence to the EU in matters of culture or indeed tourism, the EU has consistently sought to forge a stronger sense of European cultural identity and develop the basis of European citizenship through a range of cultural practices and actions (Shore 2000). By reinforcing the freedom to move and reside freely anywhere in the EU, the architects of the Maastricht Treaty hoped to encourage and provide practical scope for EU citizens to explore Europe and to foster a sense of shared values and belonging. In this regard, Article 128 of the Maastricht Treaty (Art. 151, Treaty of Amsterdam) refers to the role of culture in contributing to knowledge and awareness of Europe's 'common cultural heritage'. This indicates how attempts to delineate notions of European citizenship have tended to emphasize how the cultural foundations of a pan-European identity are premised upon the fundamental values and cultural norms (e.g. tolerance, freedom of expression, and respect for religious and ethnic diversity) seemingly shared by all European citizens. One of the earliest and perhaps best-known actions in the realm of culture sponsored by the EU is the 'European City of Culture' initiative, subsequently renamed 'Capital of Culture' in 2005, initiated under the auspices of the EEC in 1985 by Melina Mercouri, who served as Greek Minister of Culture from 1981-1989. Although the rationale motivating each city to bid for such a designation (lasting a year) varies from city to city, the initiative was conceived initially as a means of moving the EU agenda towards greater emphasis on culture at a time when the predominant focus was still energy, security and industry. Subsequently, greater emphasis was placed on the Capital of Culture as a catalyst for economic and cultural development, exemplified perhaps by the 'successful' examples of Glasgow (1990), Madrid (1992) and Liverpool (2008).

Similarly, through the Euromed Heritage Programme, inaugurated in 1998 under the auspices of the Barcelona Declaration (1995), the EU has also sought to harness the heritage and culture of countries beyond the southern and eastern frontiers of the EU as constituent parts of a European identity. The Euromed Heritage Programme is a multilateral framework of co-operation that mobilizes culture and heritage as a means of strengthening civil society across the region, rooted in the interconnected histories of trade, cultural exchange and commerce in the Mediterranean (CEC 2002a). Moreover, it reflects the desire by the EU to draw its 'neighbours' into a web of economic, political and cultural exchange as a means of 'establishing a common cultural basis for a European *demos*, transcending national boundaries' (Scott 2005: 227). However, the attempt to delineate such fundamental European values tends to privilege an identity that draws upon predominantly Greco-Roman and Judeo-Christian cultural and political reference points. Similarly, the notion of a 'common Euro-Mediterranean heritage' draws upon age-old discourses of the Mediterranean as the 'cradle of European civilization', though remaining silent on the fact that the Mediterranean has become a battleground between the various border security forces throughout the EU and desperate refugees and migrants trying to reach the hallowed ground of Europe.

Nonetheless, Europe continues to absorb the largest concentration of tourists in the world, and its history and heritage are necessary components of its wider destination image. The Council of Europe's Cultural Routes programme offers a further apt illustration of how Europe is seeking to represent certain cultural commonalities through touristic-based projects focusing on a series of special routes, for instance: Viking Routes, Santiago de Compostela Pilgrim Routes and the Mozart Route (Verstraete 2010: 42–43). The Council's recent inauguration of the Roma Cultural Route (Grauman 2010), which is based on a tourism itinerary of museums, shows and activities across nine countries, seemingly speaks volumes for the wider social recognition of this marginalized group. However, it seems remarkably out of sorts with the common attitude and perception towards the Roma communities across Europe. One wonders therefore if its implicit objective is to merely work towards a sort of multicultural policy of 'recognition', as opposed to genuine political engagement, or whether it is an attempt to try and counterbalance the existing policies of exclusion that prevail in European states.

Indeed, the eastward expansion of the EU, coupled with the continued reservations among certain quarters regarding the possible future accession of Turkey, reveals a number of tensions that mark the differential entitlements to mobility and modalities of citizenship that inhere within the EU, expressed poignantly here by Verstraete (2010: 28–29):

> As civilization proceeds and modern Europe expands its fantasies to its faraway colonies, Europe's idealized past is disseminated all over the world in a process that gets ever more mythological as its materiality and diversity increase. The prime instrument of the European cosmopolitan view becomes

nothing less than the mythology produced through colonialism and its twen-
tieth-century counterpart, the travel industry.

While Delanty (1995) rightly argues that any attempt to establish a genuinely
post-national, European citizenship must transcend linguistic, religious and/or
national moorings, so far the EU has failed to prevent age-old prejudices, whether
cultural, linguistic, religious or nationalist, from permeating the debate over what
constitutes a 'legitimate' standard of European identity and citizenship. These tensions have led to the accusation of double standards being displayed by the EU
with regard to the desire it has demonstrated to facilitate visa-free travel by the
citizens of Western Balkan states, as compared to Turkish citizens, who still require
visas for entry into the EU (Tezcan 2010). At the time of writing, negotiations
between Turkey and the EU over visa-travel into the EU for Turkish citizens, were
still in progress. Hence, while the EU may invoke an aspiration to bring the citizens of the wider circum-Mediterranean together in order to celebrate their common cultural *roots*, increasingly the *routes* into the EU from non-member states are
subject to a proliferation of borders, surveillance and security checks. These stipulations prevent the liberty of movement and entrance of those whose identity and
cultural origins signify the very genesis of a cosmopolitan European citizenship.

Conclusion

This chapter has illustrated how the relationship between travel and citizenship was
increasingly played out on an international stage in the aftermath of the Second
World War. As the post-war political and economic order began to take shape, driven
by the United States and the resurrected liberal capitalist democracies of Western
Europe, questions of the freedom of movement and the right to travel increasingly
took centre stage. Fuelled by rising disposable incomes and cheap energy, this gave
rise to an unquestioned sense of entitlement to travel among the inhabitants of rich
states, and one that was extended to the masses through the advent of the cheap
package holiday in Western Europe. The right to the freedom of movement and the
associated right to travel thus became increasingly wedded to the growing demand
for international travel and the exercise of individual rights to consume a range of
tourist destinations worldwide.

   This chapter also drew attention to how the rise of the modern nation-state
that emerged in the wake of the French Revolution, gave birth to the modern
passport and early support for the freedom of movement as a fundamental right of
all citizens. Notwithstanding the expansion of international travel, both during the
interwar years as well as after the Second World War, as the state consolidated its
monopolization on the issuance of passports and visas, notions of 'national citizen'
and 'foreigner' became increasingly marked. Thus while states such as the US were
keen to embrace international travel as a symbol of Western freedoms and corporate prowess, countervailing tendencies soon emerged characterized by a much

more ambivalent stance towards the mobility of 'foreigners' vis-à-vis 'national citizens'. Such ambivalence continues to mark the state's attitude towards the movement of foreigners, and in some cases its own citizens, and is one that fuels tensions surrounding the politics of borders, passports and visas.

Thus, contrary to the pervasive discourses of freedoms and individual rights associated with neoliberalism and capitalist globalization, this chapter has argued that many states remain fundamentally ambivalent towards different modalities of movement. Moreover, while international travel is said to be uniquely able to foster peace, development and social harmony among human beings, neoliberal discourses of 'tourism as freedom' and by association, free trade, simultaneously underplay and exacerbate the material inequalities and unequal power relations that determine people's ability to enjoy the freedom of movement and right to travel. The chapter also considered the politico-ideological forces and social practices of discrimination that work to regulate and frustrate the freedom of movement and right to travel of those deemed to lack the right credentials for travel. Particular attention was given to the role of the global airport, where commerce, state power and surveillance technologies converge to filter and restrict the movement of people, sorting them into different tiers of citizenship based on their nationality, ethnicity, race and religious backgrounds.

Finally, this chapter considered the implications of certain multilateral frameworks governing the freedom of movement and right to travel, notably that of the European Union, for the mobility rights and freedoms enjoyed by tourists and other mobile peoples, both within the EU and between third countries and the EU. In conclusion, it has demonstrated the deeply politicized nature of international travel and tourism, and the implications for enabling and constraining the free movement of people. It has raised a number of concerns related to the closely aligned nexus of state and corporate power that increasingly fuels the expansion of tourism worldwide, while simultaneously working to constrain and prevent the movement of those deemed 'risky' and lacking the appropriate credentials for travel. These issues will continue to be addressed in the next chapter in relation to the securitization of global travel and its entanglement within a constellation of geopolitical forces. In doing so, it will identify how notions of tourism as peace have been contested by violent reprisals in particular geographical contexts, thus challenging our understanding of the new discourses and practices of citizenship associated with tourism.

Notes

1 The Arirang ('Kim Il Sung's people') Mass Games is a gymnastics and artistic festival, starting in early August and ending around 10 September. The objective of the mass games is to represent and signify the cultural and unified values of North Korean nationalism (see Jeon 2011).
2 At the time of writing the bill had been referred to the Subcommittee on Immigration, Citizenship, Refugees, Border Security, and International Law (see http://www.govtrack.us/congress/bills/111/hr4441, accessed 19 May 2013).

3 The former Chairman of Green Globe21 and ex-President of the WTTC, Geoffrey Lipman, was appointed as Special Advisor to the WTO Secretary-General on Trade in Tourism Services in 2002 and subsequently held the position of Assistant Secretary-General from 2006 until 2010.

4 The McCarran Act was motivated by US fears of a worldwide Communist conspiracy. Those deemed to be in violation of this Act could not only have their mobility rights restricted but they could also be stripped of their citizenship or be denaturalized, on the basis that they had in effect repudiated their allegiance to the United States (for the full text see http://www-rohan.sdsu.edu/dept/polsciwb/brianl/docs/1950InternalSecurityAct. pdf, accessed 14 May 2013).

5 The Visa Waiver Program is a US programme enabling visa-free travel for up to 90 days to the US for citizens of 37 European countries that have been granted 'clearance' by the Department of Homeland Security (see http://travel.state.gov/visa/temp/without/ without_1990.html, accessed 14 May 2013).

6 Since the Oslo accords of 1995, the Palestinian National Authority took over responsibility for issuing the Palestinian passport, albeit under licence from the Israeli Civil Administration, which oversees the Occupied Territories. In addition to the low global ranking of the Palestinian passport, as a result of the continuing Israeli stranglehold on the Palestinian Territories, Palestinians are subject to a range of additional restrictions on their movements, both within their 'borders' as well as across them (see Halper 2005).

7 US economic aggression against Cuba dates back to the US Trading with the Enemy Act of 1917, which was designed to prevent aid from being sent to Cuba. Travel by US citizens to Cuba for reasons other than those licensed by the US Treasury Department (e.g. educational, religious and scientific) has been technically illegal since President J. F. Kennedy imposed an economic embargo on the island in 1963. In 1992, the Cuban Democracy Act (otherwise known as the Torricelli Act) further tightened sanctions against Cuba subsequent to the collapse of the Soviet Union. In 1996 the Cuban Liberty and Solidarity Act (otherwise known as the Helms–Burton Act), which was passed in response to the downing of an aircraft piloted by two members of a US-based anti-Castro organization, increased the penalties for US citizens who travel to Cuba illegally (Canally and Carmichael 2006).

8 Total revenue in 2009 for the Ferrovial Group was €12 billon (http://memoria2009. ferrovial.es/en/index.asp, accessed 18 February 2011).

9 This has now been extended to include 26 out of the current 28 EU member states along with the 4 non-EU EFTA (*European Free Trade Association*) states (Iceland, Liechtenstein, Norway and Switzerland). EFTA was set up in 1960 to encourage closer economic co-operation and free trade among European states.

10 The AC10 states include the Republic of (South) Cyprus, the Czech Republic, Estonia, Hungary, Latvia, Lithuania, Malta, Poland, Slovakia and Slovenia.

5

TOURISM, POLITICS AND THE BATTLEGROUNDS OF COSMOPOLITAN CITIZENSHIP

> Travel has become one of the great forces for peace and understanding in our time. As people move throughout the world and learn to know each other's customs and to appreciate the qualities of individuals and of each nation, we are building a level of international understanding which can sharply improve the atmosphere for world peace.
>
> *(John F. Kennedy, cited in O'Grady 1990: 16)*

As improved living standards, plentiful supplies of cheap oil and technological advances in transport fuelled the expansion of international travel for the citizens of Europe and North America in the aftermath of the Second World War, the belief in the universal right to travel became increasingly marked throughout advanced industrialized societies. Furthermore, government-led attempts to stimulate economic growth in Western Europe were framed by discourses of peace, co-operation and economic development, overseen by a range of new international institutions among whose remit it was to engineer a stable international political and economic order via the US Marshall Plan. The subsequent worldwide expansion of international tourism signalled the consolidation of economic prosperity and political stability among the liberal democracies of the 'West', reinforced by liberal discourses of citizenship premised upon the freedom of movement and the right to travel throughout an international order 'made safe' by the *Pax Americana*.[1]

This chapter considers the notion that tourism is uniquely able to foment peaceful relations between states with specific regard to the implications for the relationship of tourism to discourses of cosmopolitanism and global citizenship. It then examines the contradictions that have emerged where the freedom of movement and right to travel become enmeshed within a wider geopolitics, leading to the curtailment, restriction or indeed violent reactions to such mobility. In this regard, the discussion highlights the problematic relationship between the support for the freedom of movement and right to travel by governments and the tourism industries alike, and the violent challenge to such rights presented by terrorism and political violence. The chapter concludes by reflecting on the disjuncture between the freedom of movement and right to travel on the one hand, and the rights of destination populations to development and livelihood security on the other. Indeed, as the argument indicates, destination populations may not only have their livelihoods threatened by certain exploitative forms of tourism (or lack of opportunity to engage in the potential for work afforded by it), but also are likely to suffer disproportionately from the pervasive climate of (in)security that is perpetuated by the global 'war on terror' and its aftermath.

Tourism, peace and citizenship

The idea that international tourism has an intrinsic capacity to foment peaceful relations between states has preoccupied a number of tourism researchers (Askjellerud 2003; Blanchard and Higgins-Desbiolles 2013; Brown 1989; D'Amore 1988; Litvin 1998; Moufakkir and Kelly 2010; Var *et al.* 1994). This premise revolves around a set of assumptions that tourism represents more than merely an instrument of trade and economic development, but is able to foster knowledge, empathy and cross-cultural understanding, leading to greater tolerance of other cultures. Accordingly, tourism is seen to warrant its own specialized UN agency in the form of the UN World Tourism Organization (UNWTO), which sets it apart from other areas of economic activity. While the relationship between tourism and peace has been the subject of much debate and dispute, few have sought to consider the conceptions of citizenship encapsulated within these discourses. Indeed, Chapter 2 implied the significance of tourism in developing forms of travel and socio-cultural exchange rooted in cosmopolitan principles, which hints at ways in which tourism could be viewed as a vital component in the nurturing of global citizenship.

The concept of tourism as peace has a long history. The British Travel and Holidays Association had declared 'Travel for Peace' as the theme of its inaugural meeting in 1929 (Honey n.d.). This ideal was echoed in earlier international attempts to build inter-governmental institutions capable of guaranteeing collective security and world peace, exemplified by the ill-fated League of Nations, established in 1919 at the Paris Peace Conference, and its successor the United Nations, established in 1948. Enshrined within the institutional ethos of such organizations were ideas of 'world citizenship' and 'cosmopolitanism'. The antecedents of contemporary discourses of tourism as peace can also be found in the 'civilizing discourses' underscoring the expansion of international travel, especially during the period in which European colonial rule reached its zenith towards the end of the nineteenth century. The spectacular growth of Thomas Cook & Son was to a significant extent underscored by the protective mantle of British imperial power, enabling the firm to expand its operations further into the Levant by the first decade of the twentieth century (Hazbun 2008: 82). Direct co-operation between

Thomas Cook & Son and British imperial power ensued when John Cook – who by the early 1880s had taken over from his father – arranged for a relief force to rescue Captain Charles Gordon, who was besieged in the Arabi Pasha's revolt in Khartoum (Brendon 1991: 189). By this time Thomas Cook & Son was also running trips to the battlefield at Omdurman (now a suburb of Khartoum) in Sudan, the pacification of which by Lord Kitchener's forces in 1898 was described by the firm's in-house magazine, the *Traveller's Gazette*, as having brought 'civilization' to Khartoum (Brendon 1991: 252).

Thomas Cook had seen in tourism the potential for not only bringing travel to the masses but as a means of spiritually empowering those who suffered from the drudgery of work and the evils of drink. John Cook later proclaimed that 'Ours is a "business of peace" as well as "pleasure"' (Brendon 1991: 189). Nevertheless, the business of peace continued to contribute to the business of war in the Pacific during the Second World War, where US landings on enemy territory were facilitated by briefings and photographs provided by the successors of Thomas and John Cook (Brendon 1991: 280). As befits a Victorian businessman, Thomas Cook was a firm believer in the benefits of free trade and its potential to reduce prices and spread peace, essential preconditions for travel to flourish (Brendon 1991: 35). This echoes views articulated by other prominent Victorian liberal thinkers, including Richard Cobden and Lord Willoughby Dickinson, a former secretary-general of the World Alliance for International Friendship, who envisaged a global system of free trade in which states would become 'knitted in the peaceful rivalry of trade' (cited in Brennan 2001: 79).

To an extent, contemporary advocates of 'tourism as peace' wilfully ignore both the politicized nature of travel and the manner in which tourism affects the distribution of wealth and power across different societies (Shanks 2009). For the most part, studies of tourism and politics tend to reduce the question of tourism's interaction with different political systems to a technical matter of policy or, indeed, 'crisis management' (see Wilks *et al.* 2006). Such high-minded and often well intentioned rhetoric also forms part of the established diplomatic lexicon of policymakers and the representatives of international tourism organizations worldwide. The alignment between tourism and both colonialism and neo-colonialism is of course well documented (Turner and Ash 1975). What is perhaps less documented is how these forces came to shape the identities of colonized peoples and emergent conceptions of citizenship beyond the metropolitan centres of power. Thus, while to varying degrees and in different historical geographical contexts tourism was envisaged as a civilizing force and an instrument of peace, it also became enmeshed within evolving views of national identity in both colonial and postcolonial epochs. For example, Hazbun (2008: 5) illustrates how tourism was harnessed to the project of French colonialism in Tunisia. During this period, French citizens were encouraged to travel to the colonial territories in order to encourage settlement and identification with 'their' empire. Subsequently, upon the demise of French colonial rule, post-colonial governments typically used tourism for political ends. In this instance, the objective was the reverse: to convert colonial subjects into national citizens. In post-independence Tunisia after 1956, conflicting visions of national citizenship were reflected in different approaches to tourism. Initially, the secular government of President Habib Bourguiba, in contrast to emergent ideas of radical pan-Arabist nationalism, sought to deploy tourism as an instrument of economic modernization and employment; integrating Tunisia within the orbit of the capitalist world system (Hazbun 2008: 6). In a harbinger of things to come, Bourguiba's enthusiastic promotion of tourism brought him and the government into conflict with the religious and socially conservative sectors of Tunisian society, which rejected the materialism and secularizing forces associated with tourism (Hazbun 2008: 46–50).

President Bourguiba's stance on tourism contrasts sharply with the attitude of Tanzanian academics and policymakers towards tourism development. Similar to Tunisian intellectuals and religious traditionalists, they saw tourism as an instrument of neo-colonialism (Shivji 1973). Seen in this way, international tourism was regarded as being incompatible with the aspirations of independent statehood, economic sovereignty and Tanzanian citizenship, as evidenced in the Ujamaa programme of economic self-reliance overseen by President Julius Nyerere between 1967 and 1985. Shivji (1973: 10), drawing on the work of Frantz Fanon (1968), accused tourism of turning the Mediterranean and Caribbean islands into the 'brothels of the world'! Putting aside the somewhat outdated and over-blown rhetoric, there is evidence pointing to the alignment between tourism and low levels of economic development in the 'Third World' (see Brohman 1996; Reid 2003). In turn, this has undermined the ability of low-income states to provide for the basic needs and to guarantee full citizenship rights, particularly social rights, for all citizens (see Faist 2009: 20–21). The relationship between tourism, nation-building and citizenship rights also continues to be problematic in transition economies. As indicated in Chapter 4, the development of tourism in Cuba in the aftermath of the Soviet Union's collapse has given rise to new forms of inequality and reignited racism among Cubans themselves, undermining the government's stated support for the core values of social justice and equality (Sánchez and Adams 2008).

The International Institute for Peace through Tourism (IIPT), established during the UN's International Year of Peace in 1986, explicitly proclaimed the idea of tourism as the world's first 'peace industry' at the inaugural Global Conference on Tourism: A Vital Force for Peace, which was held in Vancouver (Canada) in 1988. According to D'Amore (1988: 152), 'there is a growing realization of the role of international travel in promoting understanding and trust among people of different cultures'. The notion that tourism is uniquely able to foster harmonious relations through cross-cultural contact between people, regardless of class, ethnicity, gender, sexual orientation, religion and nationality, has been a key mantra of the IIPT since its establishment. While D'Amore (1988: 154) was careful to specify that only a 'properly designed and developed' tourism industry can contribute to building peace and prosperity, the institutional apparatuses of global tourism and its representatives consistently repeat vague platitudes and hyperbolic claims to promote the view that tourism and peace are inseparable. For example, in his address to the Third Prime Ministerial Conference for Tourism to Israel, held in Jerusalem in 2004, UNWTO Secretary-General Francesco Frangialli (2004: 6) made the following rather grandiose claim:

> History shows that the forces unleashed by tourism are so powerful that they can change apparently irreversible situations and bring about reconciliation where none was considered possible. Tourism and peace are inseparable; together, they can often reverse the course of things.

The concept of tourism as peace echoes Kant's notion of 'perpetual peace', which influenced later writings on cosmopolitanism and cosmopolitical democracy (Archibugi and Held 1995; Vertovec and Cohen 2002), in which he contends that all human beings are part of a common humanity and thus endowed with a unique capacity for reason and moral behaviour. Accordingly, it is our status as 'world citizens' that compels us to empathize with others (Heater 2002: 35). Although international tourism is predominantly driven by the imperatives of trade and commerce, as well as an intrinsic need to develop human relations and gain first-hand knowledge of the wider world, it is often invoked in relation to such notions as world or global citizenship and cosmopolitanism (e.g. Bianchi and Stephenson 2013); D'Amore 1988; Germann Molz 2005). In many ways, the concept of tourism and peace, as well as the international regime of rights underpinning the freedom of movement and right to travel, can be seen as the embodiment of Kant's cosmopolitan law and thinking on world citizenship. This idea is furthermore rooted in the notion of universal hospitality, specifically, 'the right of a stranger not be treated with hostility when he arrives on someone else's territory' (Heater 2002: 99). These principles encapsulate many of the complex (and often contradictory) discourses circulating throughout international tourism. On the one hand, such notions of cosmopolitanism could be seen to lend implicit support to the view that the right of tourists to travel must be privileged (over locals), while on the other it could also be interpreted in terms of the right of tourists to be able to travel free from discrimination and harassment.

After the Second World War, numerous efforts were made on behalf of the leading Western powers to construct a secure, stable and prosperous post-war order, underpinned by various international agreements and legal frameworks. Of these, the United Nations – in whose remit it is to foster peace, cultural exchange and mutual understanding among the peoples of the world – declared 1967 as International Tourism Year, accompanied by the slogan 'Tourism: Passport to Peace'. In tandem with the universality of human rights, the freedom of movement was envisaged as the cornerstone of a peaceful and secure post-war order. These rights became enshrined in the UNDHR (1948) and numerous subsequent international conventions, and were deemed intrinsic to all individuals on the planet regardless of race, nationality or creed. One of the principal beneficiaries of this new international architecture of rights and framework of inter-governmental co-operation was of course, international tourism.

During the Cold War attempts were made by the major powers to harness tourism as part of a rapprochement between the West and the Soviet bloc. The Helsinki Accords (1975) represented a commitment by the signatories to the inviolability of international frontiers and respect for the territorial integrity of states. The Accords set in motion the path to *glasnost* and *perestroika* instigated by Soviet leader Mikhail Gorbachev, and referred explicitly to 'the contribution of international tourism to the development of mutual understanding among peoples' (Organization for Security and Cooperation in Europe 2013: 31). Some years later, in a joint statement following the 1985 Geneva Summit, US President Reagan and President Gorbachev affirmed the role of tourism in breaking down the ideological barriers between East and West, and promoting international understanding and peace.

One of the first international conventions to explicitly integrate the practice of tourism with peace was the *Manila Declaration on World Tourism* (WTO 1980). This Declaration, signed by 107 states in Manila on 27 October 1980, asserted that tourism 'can be a vital force for world peace and can provide the moral and intellectual basis for international understanding and interdependence'. The Declaration made explicit reference to tourism's role in eliminating 'the widening economic gap between developed and developing countries' and sought to mobilize these ideals in the pursuit of a more peaceful and egalitarian world order. Although it contained echoes of the progressive ideals underpinning the Non-Aligned Movement, it was ironic that the Declaration was signed in a state where the President of the Philippines, Ferdinand Marcos, had declared martial law in 1972 (lifted in 1981) and whose regime had attacked many of the basic citizenship rights of ordinary Filipinos during his period of office. His reckless pursuit of national aggrandizement and personal enrichment through tourism, combined with mismanagement of the industry, left an economy in ruins and an impoverished populace, part of which took up arms against the tourism industry in protest at his ruthless and inept regime (Richter 2000: 52–74). Nevertheless, the lack of any substantive evidence to support claims that tourism has in fact produced a meaningful resolution of conflict or engendered long-term peace between nations has not diminished the enthusiasm of policymakers, and the UNWTO in particular, for reaffirming tourism's innate ability to foster peace in numerous charters and declarations. These include the WTO *Acapulco Document* (1982), the UNWTO *Global Code of Ethics for Tourism* (1999) and the *Amman Declaration on Peace and Tourism* (2000).

Similar ideals are espoused by the UN specialist agency for Education, Science and Culture (UNESCO), established in 1945, and indeed in other initiatives such as the World Heritage Programme. Adopted in 1972, the World Heritage Convention encourages states worldwide to protect and conserve built, cultural and natural sites, via their inscription onto the World Heritage List. Numbering close to a thousand properties worldwide, these sites reflect UNESCO's desire to reinforce humanity's responsibility towards the upkeep of such heritage, regardless of nationalist imperatives, as well as the right of all to experience such sites deemed of 'global significance' (Urry 2000: 174). The World Heritage Programme conforms to UNESCO's wider aim of creating 'the conditions for dialogue among civilizations, cultures and peoples, based upon respect for commonly shared values' (UNESCO n.d. *Introducing UNESCO*) through the medium of culture. Culture and of course heritage are deeply intertwined with all manner of tourist activities. As was noted in Chapter 4, the European Union has sought to harness the diverse cultural heritage of its member states, as well as fund a range of cultural initiatives, in an attempt to stimulate tourism development and bind European citizens together through a sense of common cultural identity and citizenship (Smith 2003b: 62–80). More recently, the EU has sought to extend this process beyond its external frontiers. The Euro-Mediterranean Partnership (EMP), discussed briefly in Chapter 4, finances a number of initiatives in order to harness and mobilize the historic cultural links between Europe and the Mediterranean region, especially to build a 'new model of international exchange' premised upon mutual respect and cultural dialogue (CEC 2002b: 7). The EMP reflects the liberal cosmopolitan ideology that lies at the heart of the EU. Here, cosmopolitanism is invoked as a 'quasi-moral force' and mobilized through such programmes of cultural intervention (Scott 2008).

Different waves of migration and the various histories of travel have been essential ingredients in the fluid and complex ethnic and cultural layerings of the Mediterranean and Europe for centuries, from the shores of the Black Sea to the Atlantic. Yet the connection between cosmopolitanism and citizenship alluded to in such EU programmes is rendered problematic by the proliferation and securitization of borders, as discussed in Chapter 4. The attempt to develop an increasingly sophisticated range of deterrents to the cross-border movement of migrants from outside the EU (and, increasingly, from new EU entrants) serves to restrict access to the full rights and benefits of citizenship. Moreover, the professed link between culture, heritage and economic development, much less peace and understanding, that is articulated in the various programmes financed by the EMP, is somewhat undermined by the logics of neoliberalism that inform its overall outlook (see Bianchi 2005). Indeed, the Euro-Med Heritage programme, one of several initiatives financed by the EMP, views cultural heritage-led development in the Euro-Mediterranean as a potential facilitator of the 'difficult transition towards a modern free market economy' (CEC 2002a: 13), as well as a possible alleviator of the destabilizing effects of the very liberal economic reforms that are being promoted by the EU.

While there is little disputing the fact that tourism usually thrives under conditions of peace and political stability, there is scant evidence to suggest that tourism has an *intrinsic* relationship to peace and cultural understanding. Indeed, it has been argued that in some cases tourism may in fact engender a worsening of attitudes towards the places and people visited (see Pizam 1996)! Moreover, contends Salazar (2006: 330): 'It seems contradictory, then, that an industry which is so laden with conflict claims to be in a privileged position to foster world peace.'

Without a hint of irony, dictatorships that have presided over exploitation and human rights abuses against their own populations, such as Myanmar (Burma), have not been averse to proclaiming the ability of tourism as a means of 'strengthening friendships' and 'reinforcing a sense of national identity' (Henderson 2003: 108–109). However, tourism is more often than not a *consequence* of peace and the restoration of normal diplomatic relations between states, or more instrumentally, an outcome of national security. Lisle (2007: 342) thus questions the conceptual separation of tourism and conflict, and argues that the 'orbits of security and tourism collide in explicit ways' to the extent that tourists, terrorists and soldiers may often occupy the same space. As Richter's (2000) landmark survey of tourism and politics demonstrates, states do of course see tourism as a potent political force and often seek to harness its potential across different areas of government activity, with diverse ramifications for diplomatic relations and citizenship rights. Whether tourism is deployed by states in the service of nationalism, or as a means of conveying legitimacy on a particular regime and countering external criticism, as in the cases of Fascist Spain (1939–1975) and the Philippines under President Marcos demonstrate (Richter 2000: 53–54), it can reinforce state-sanctioned citizenship narratives as well as indirectly serve to marginalize other citizenship rights. These rights could include the rights of minority communities to the freedom of cultural expression, the right to work and the associated rights of workers to collective bargaining.

Certain scholars have also explored how states of different ideological persuasions have deployed tourism as a means to project narratives of ethnicity and cultural identity, as part of the process of nation-building and the reinforcement of official state-sanctioned notions of citizenship. It is not uncommon for states, democratic or authoritarian, to harness tourism (and heritage) to the imperatives of nationalism. As Hitchcock (1998) demonstrates, examples include 'folk culture villages' in East and South-East Asia. These were influenced by European traditions of open-air museums and have been linked to the early growth of tourism in countries such as Indonesia while still under colonial rule. In the case of *Taman Mini* in Indonesia, after independence such attractions continued to be developed for the purpose of tourism, in the process reconceptualizing the country's ethnic, cultural and linguistic diversity in order to project an image of a 'united nation state' (Hitchcock 1998: 129). A coherent sense of national identity may be reconstructed and communicated in more nuanced ways, via the experience of heritage tourism at sites of national cultural-historical significance, as noted earlier in Chapter 2. In Belize, from the late 1990s, the People's United Party actively pursued a number of initiatives to celebrate ethnic diversity through tourism. One among various strategies to promote ethnic diversity was the establishment of Houses of Culture in four distinct ethnic regions of Belize: the Mestizo region in the north, the Garifuna region on the southern coast, the Creole population on the central coast and the Maya region in the west. The purpose of these institutions was to attract international tourists and domestic tourists from each ethnic region, where members of each group could educationally interact with other ethnic cultures, as well as to contribute to a wider programme of 'nation-building':

> [T]ourism is one important context in which the production of citizenship occurs in Belize. The construction of touristic ethnicity in particular provides a venue for the regulation of a civil conduct and thus is one means by which

local Belizeans are managed and come to understand themselves as, above all, ethnic citizens of Belize.

(Holmes 2010: 166)

Occasionally, authoritarian regimes have cynically manipulated tourism to enhance their national image and political legitimacy, and to divert attention from internal repression. The Marcos regime, for instance, under the auspices of his 'New Society' programme, developed a promotional campaign around the slogan, 'Where Asia Wears a Smile', to present an image of a contented and hospitable populace. This image was brutally shattered by the kidnappings of Japanese tourists and selected attacks on regime-owned hotels, including a bomb attack on the Manila hotel in which the American Society of Travel Agents (ASTA) was due to hold its annual convention (Richter 2000: 56, 64). Indeed, as part of the obligations of national citizens, the state may strongly encourage hospitality and courtesy towards tourists (Holmes 2010). In the case of Singapore, a cosmopolitan city-state characterized by a peculiar blend of liberal economics and authoritarian politics, the state has reconfigured and mapped diverse ethnic identities onto specific urban enclaves for the purpose of constructing a relatively sanitized national image based on a rather weak and depoliticized form of cosmopolitanism. This sanitized projection of national identity also helps to communicate Singapore's diverse and fluid cultures in easily digestible chunks for tourist consumption (Leong 1989).

India is a tourism destination that is currently undergoing significant challenges, in the wake of recent events, in terms of trying to reassure international tourists that it remains a credible destination to visit, or 'incredible' as the destination slogan claims: 'Incredible India' – a popular logo established over a decade ago. Specifically, this challenge concerns a series of sexually motivated group attacks on local women, most recently the rape and murder of a young female student in New Delhi in 2012, which drew the attention of the world's media. Similar attacks have also been directed at foreign tourists, including a British woman who was injured jumping out of a hotel window in Agra, fearing that a group of men were about to break into her room, and a violent sexual assault on a Swiss woman in Madhya Pradesh, which led to her death (McLain and Taylor 2013). These attacks have inflamed the public outcry concerning patriarchal violence and male attitudes to women in India. In turn, they have drawn widespread opprobrium and provoked a 'moral panic' that is having a serious effect on the image of the country and India's tourism industry. According to India's Associated Chambers of Commerce and Industry, visits to India by women declined by 35 per cent in the first three months of 2013 as compared to the same period for 2012 (Aparis 2013: 7). Despite the negative repercussion for the tourism industry and the wider economy, this issue also raises significant questions concerning women's freedom of mobility, both nationally and internationally. Moreover, it raises crucial questions concerning the gendering of citizenship and illustrates the problems facing women in terms of gaining access to full and equal social rights (including rights to tourism) in a world where male dominance of social space and male aggression towards women prevails (see Listner 2012).

On an ideological level, tourism was closely associated with the strategic imperatives of US foreign policy in the aftermath of the Second World War. It was utilized, for instance, as a means of highlighting the lack of freedoms and democracy in the Soviet bloc. Conversely, in response to the US boycott of the Moscow Games in 1980, the Soviet Union sought to undermine the 1984 Los Angeles Olympic Games by encouraging other socialist countries not to participate. This followed previous attempts by successive US governments during the 1950s and 1960s, to hold up American tourists as symbols of freedom and the superiority of American capitalism. Endy (2004: 145) demonstrates how US President Eisenhower, in his speeches on foreign relations, would utilize references to tourism as a means of reinforcing the 'patriotic duty' of US citizens travelling overseas to represent a positive image of America as a 'peace loving nation living in the fear of God'. Both he and President Kennedy embraced the potential of tourism to advance the cause of peace, particularly to inculcate a positive attitude overseas towards American cultural values. To further these aims, Eisenhower set up the People-to-People Foundation (1956) while Kennedy later established the US Peace Corps (1961). While the former sought to encourage private-sector initiatives, JFK represented a more hands-on government-directed approach to cultural diplomacy (Endy 2004: 148). However, the Peace Corps initiative took place against the backdrop of growing US military involvement in Vietnam. This event was to define the cultural politics of American identity for decades to come, as well as influencing the expansion of new, 'alternative' forms of international travel among discontented American citizens in protest against the war. In an early indicator of the transformative ideological force of tourism, these examples also illustrate how overseas travel and volunteer assistance were deployed as a counter-weight to growing animosity towards US imperialism.

It was not just the state but corporations too that mobilized the ideological power of tourism to promote a vision of peace and freedom, often for commercially expedient reasons. Leading members of the US travel industry, notably Pan American World Airways, espoused a form of 'populist internationalism' to underline how Pan Am's expansion of affordable air travel for ordinary working Americans was closely aligned to the US values of freedom and democracy (Endy 2004: 42). Conrad Hilton, the founder of the Hilton Hotel chain, also declared that 'we are doing our bit to spread world peace, and to fight socialism' (Hilton 1957, cited in Higgins-Desbiolles 2012: 636). Indeed, following the prescriptions of the Marshall Plan itself, through which American business practices were exported to Europe (Cox 1987: 215), the hotel industry in particular served a vital ideological function. By encouraging French hotels to adopt a more 'customer-friendly approach' to appeal to middle-class American tourists, and the rationalization of labour practices (against the will of the Communist-backed hotel and restaurant unions), the architects of the Marshall Plan sought to use tourism to extend American business practices into the heart of Europe (Endy 2004: 84).

The idea that tourism and peace are intrinsically connected betrays both a central tenet of functionalist international relations theory, whereby close economic integration through tourism lessens the prospect for conflict (Shanks 2009), as well as the notion that peaceful coexistence between states and global security is best served by liberal democracy and a globalized free market (Lisle 2007: 339). According to such logic, if tourism requires political stability in order to prosper, and liberal democracies offer the best guarantee of such peaceful coexistence, then the preferred politico-ideological settings point in one direction, to that of liberal-capitalist democracy. Discourses of tourism as peace not only reflect this underlying liberal premise, they also constitute a reductionist approach to human relations, in which complex social phenomena are reduced to quantifiable and comparable indices (see Nyaupane *et al.* 2008). As Askjellerud (2003: 743) notes, 'world peace does not depend on individuals' but emerges out of the interplay between complex social, economic and political forces. The normative outlook of the 'tourism as peace' model thus reflects an underlying liberal premise, whereby people of different ethnic, religious, national and socio-economic backgrounds can meet, interact and exchange on relatively equal terms in the ostensibly neutral meeting grounds of tourism. Such notions also assume a clear separation between tourism and conflict, in which the former exists as a benign social force abstracted from the complex economic and political realities in which it exists (Lisle 2007: 340–341).

International tourism embodies many of the major attributes of liberal-democratic notions of cosmopolitanism and citizenship, whereby a global order of peaceful states can be built upon a foundation of free trade, consensual diplomacy and cross-cultural exchange. However, the platitudes associated with notions of tourism as peace tend not to embrace the mobility of those deemed too risky to travel, or whose mobility is motivated by the search for work or escape from persecution. Unless of course such mobility benefits capital and the neoliberal state, as in the form of plugging labour shortages and/or combating inflation by exerting downward pressure on wages, then it must be hindered or constrained. What is more, to proclaim the intrinsic value of tourism as a harbinger of peace ignores the degree to which tourism is implicated in the geopolitical strategies of states, and the socio-economic polarization arising from neoliberal globalization. The myriad forms of cross-border mobility evinced by international tourism thus raise a number of questions regarding tourists' inherent right to travel and the concomitant need of states to ensure their safety, versus the obligation of destination states to secure the livelihoods and adequate developmental circumstances of their own, often poor, citizens.

'Making the world safe for tourism':[2] security, risk and the geopolitics of travel

In the 'West' the dawn of a new era of unprecedented peace, stability and prosperity after the Second World War saw the populations of the industrialized capitalist economies liberated from at least half a century or more of large-scale political conflict and economic uncertainty. The strengthening of universal welfare programmes in Western Europe further insured the populations of these states from the risk of disease, illiteracy and unemployment, enabling them to put aside disposable income for the purposes of holiday travel and in some cases benefit from enlarged social tourism programmes. These changes, together with falling transportation costs combined with advances in transport speed, comfort and safety, helped to expand overseas travel to a range of new destinations in (what became known as) the 'Third World' (Turner and Ash 1975). In South-East Asia alone, international tourism arrivals increased 18-fold between 1960 and 1976 (Wood 1979: 274).

Encouraged by a series of reports that extolled the virtues of tourism, commencing with the *Checchi Report* in 1958, international tourism held out the promise of economic modernization and social advancement to the newly independent citizens of 'Third World' states (Wood 1979: 277). In effect, by promoting a transfer of surplus disposable income in the rich 'North' to low-income states in the developing economies of the global South, tourism became seen as one of the essential ingredients of nationhood and national sovereignty in newly independent states such as Tunisia (Hazbun 2008). Despite generating considerable foreign exchange and improving local employment prospects in parts of Africa, the Caribbean and the Pacific, by the late 1970s critics began to describe international tourism as a new form of imperialism, sustaining unequal patterns of trade and structural dependence on foreign corporations (Britton 1982; Pérez 1980). Although seemingly less invasive, the emergence of new, niche forms of travel in the 1980s, such as eco-tourism, designed to enhance local economic benefits and empower 'Third World' citizens, also did little to transform the overall balance of power in global trade between high and low-income states (Mowforth and Munt 2009). As a result of governments' inability to satisfactorily deal with many of these underlying contradictions, tourism became the focus of resentment and hostility across a number of 'Third World' destinations (Lea 1993).

Prior to the 1960s – at a time when travel was still a relatively elitist and altogether less regulated pursuit – politically motivated violence against tourist establishments and the targeting of tourists by organized 'terrorist' groups were all but non-existent. Tourists were exposed to certain risks, mainly crime and kidnappings, which became more frequent as international tourism became increasingly accessible to those on modest incomes by the 1970s. Some of these incidents were well publicized, as in the case of the murders committed by the notorious Charles Sobhraj, otherwise known as the 'bikini killer', who murdered over 15 Western tourists throughout South-East Asia during the 1970s (Blackden 2003). Any notion of international travel and tourism as a 'politics-free' zone was soon shattered by a series of high-profile incidents, especially the hijacking of five Western airliners by the Popular Front for the Liberation of Palestine (PFLP) in September 1970, as part of its struggle for an independent Palestinian state. By the mid-1970s, tourism was increasingly drawn into the maelstrom of politically violent conflicts between states and various dissident organizations worldwide. From a series of arson attacks and bombings of hotels in the Philippines and Tunisia in the 1980s to multiple attacks against European airports in 1985, it was clear that the era of relatively 'unregulated' travel was coming to an end. By the end of the 1980s, the bombing of UTA Flight 772 in 1988 and the downing of Pan Am Flight 103 over

Lockerbie in 1989 signalled a profound shift in the vulnerability of aviation, as tougher security and greater degrees of surveillance increasingly became the norm (Rekacewicz 2013).

By the 1980s, politically motivated terrorist attacks on tourism had moved from the periphery of the world economy to its very centre (Richter and Waugh 1986). Nevertheless, for many analysts in the West, the demise of the ideological order of the Cold War and disintegration of the Soviet Union in 1991 were a sure sign that the world was witnessing the end of ideological conflict. The ushering in of a new era of peace and prosperity was accordingly seen as the basis for the worldwide embrace of capitalist free markets and liberal democracy (Fukuyama 1989). However, this optimism soon faded as a spate of kidnappings and attacks against tourists and tourism resorts was carried out throughout the 1990s and into the 2000s in a variety of geographic locations, including Bali, Colombia, Egypt, Kashmir, Kenya, Mexico, Morocco, the Philippines, Tunisia and Yemen. The specific targeting of foreign tourists by organized militant groups was illustrated most tragically by the killing of 58 Western tourists and 4 Egyptians by Islamic militants at Luxor in 1997, while the wider upsurge in global instability was further underlined by the dramatic 9/11 terrorist attacks in New York City and Washington, DC. These attacks were an indication that the peaceful spread of liberal democracy and worldwide expansion of capitalist markets, deemed to be a precursor to the emergence of a globalized borderless world (see Ohmae 1990, 1995), were somewhat premature and perhaps flawed altogether.

This renewed globalized form of terrorist violence further unsettled the mutually reinforcing calculus at the heart of the neoliberal global order, that is, the peaceful coexistence between states, the unfettered expansion of global capitalism and the unhindered mobility, upon which the freedom of movement and right to travel of international tourists depend. To some extent, global travel in the late twentieth century has served to remove the protective veil of modernity that shields most tourists from the day-to-day insecurity that afflicts the lives of many inhabitants in low-income states and politically volatile destinations. Such attacks, however atrocious, are a bleak reminder that the universal right to travel and consume different cultures may be deeply intertwined with hegemonic state practices, geopolitical entanglements, and the pervasive inequalities and myriad injustices that continue to exist at global and national levels. Contrary also to the normative view that posits the modernity (and, one could argue, cosmopolitanism) of tourism, in contrast to the 'medieval paradigm' of global terrorism (Tarlow 2006), such forms of contemporary terrorist violence are in many ways quintessentially *globalized* phenomena. Not only are terrorists themselves continuously 'on the move' (Steiner 2007: 170), as they travel across international borders, often undetected (e.g. the 9/11 bombers) as ordinary business travellers or tourists, the passport itself (particularly those of powerful Western states) constitutes a vital commodity facilitating the transnational and clandestine mobility of international terrorists (Rudner 2008).[3] This then illustrates a quandary with which states are still grappling: how to keep borders open for tourists while ensuring that 'terrorists' do not slip through. The result has been to reinforce not only the 'ambiguous status of the traveler' but also the inherently political nature of travel itself (Shanks 2009: 364). Hence, the shifting demarcations of who is or is not afforded the status of tourist, and the mobility rights that come with it, is one that is deeply informed by the broader ideological and geostrategic context within which tourism occurs.

Needless to say, terrorist groups rarely 'represent', in any meaningful sense, the interests of those in whose name they carry out such acts. Nevertheless, somewhat perversely, transnational terrorist groups can be seen as engaged in a struggle over citizenship, however violent their acts and reactionary their goals. Indeed Beck (2005: 10) refers to them as 'NGOs committed to violence'. Furthermore, in her analysis of the lethal attacks against various tourist targets in Egypt during the early 1990s, Aziz (1995: 91) claims that such incidents were 'a reaction to irresponsible tourism development', which was promoted by the World Bank and other donors as part of President Sadat's Open Door Policy, initiated in 1974. This position casts doubt on the generalized view, as often implied in some quarters of the media, that tourist attacks are the outcome of a visceral and culturally determined hatred of foreigners. She also observes that attacks on the tourism industry in 1986 were not perpetrated by so-called 'Islamic' terrorists but by disgruntled soldiers doing their military service, who were living in miserable conditions alongside luxurious new hotel developments. Richter (1995: 22), nevertheless, states that in Egypt tourists and tourism have been explicitly targeted by 'fundamentalist political organizations' by virtue of being associated with the secularism of Egypt's former regime under President Mubarak.

The reasons why tourists are sometimes seen as 'legitimate' targets in the eyes of the antagonists are thus complex and varied, and have been widely discussed in the literature (Hall and O'Sullivan 1996; Richter and Waugh 1986; Sönmez 1998). Although such attacks are seen as being related to local animosity among certain conservative/religious groups towards the Westernized culture of tourists, more often than not they are due to the elevated 'exchange value' of tourists in a highly mediatized global economy, who thus become worthwhile targets for kidnappings and other forms of violence (Phipps 1999: 84). Often they do not constitute explicit attacks on tourism and tourists at all, but rather, are designed to highlight internal socio-economic injustices as part of a wider political struggle. For example, this was the case in Spain and Turkey during the final two decades of the last century, where Basque (ETA) and Kurdish (PKK) separatist movements respectively targeted tourism in their protracted and violent conflicts against the central state in these two countries. Similarly, in the UK, the Provisional Irish Republican Army (IRA), a paramilitary Irish republican organization, waged a bombing campaign against the British state from 1969 to 1997 as part of a long-standing struggle for a unified Ireland, and is believed to have been responsible for the bombing of the Tower of London in 1974, killing one person and injuring 44 others (BBC 1974). These attacks on tourists, although springing from quite diverse political contexts, nevertheless convey an attempt, however crude or violent, by dispossessed and disenfranchised groups to be accepted as bona fide citizens of the state, or to reject its legitimacy altogether.

Prior to the rise of politically motivated terrorist attacks on tourists in recent decades, there was little in the way of a formal security apparatus surrounding international tourism. For the most part passage through major ports-of-entry was relatively unencumbered by the lengthy security queues and panoply of checks and filters that have been increasingly devised to screen 'risky' travellers in response to the rise of a more footloose, globalized terrorism. Perceptions of risk nevertheless vary according to diverse national, ethnic and cultural attitudes towards travel and risk themselves (see Henderson 2003: 113). Often the fear of travel is conditioned by experiences and perceptions of racism, as was noted in Chapter 4. Nevertheless, the perceptions of insecurity that are associated with international travel are often disproportionate to the actual scope and magnitude of risks faced by tourists. For example, in 1985, of the 28 million American citizens who travelled overseas during that year, a total of 163 were either killed or injured as a result of terrorist violence. Despite a probability of less than 0.00057 per cent of becoming a victim of terrorist violence, 1.8 million American tourists changed their travel plans for the following year (Sönmez 1998: 438).

As already noted, the period from the mid-1990s into the first decade of the twenty-first century did in fact witness an upsurge of terrorist attacks on Western tourists and destinations frequented by Westerners. Destinations such as Yemen have experienced a sharp decline in tourist arrivals, as much as 60 per cent, together with a flight of investment, as a result of a decade and a half of terrorist attacks against mainly foreign targets, and the recent political unrest related to the wider 'Arab uprisings' (Al-Muraqab 2012). Yet, in spite of the often sensationalist media coverage of such incidents, the evidence suggests that, prior to the Arab Spring and recent outbreak of violence in Syria, the world had entered an unprecedented era of global stability in terms of the limited incidence of armed conflict worldwide. In 2004, notwithstanding the invasions of both Afghanistan and Iraq, the number of armed conflicts worldwide had reached its lowest point since the early 1970s (see Harbom and Wallensteen 2005: 624). In 2001, which was the single most deadly year in recent history, a US citizen was five times more likely to die from HIV/ AIDS and 25 times more likely to have been killed in a traffic accident – not to mention deaths committed by the use of firearms – than from global terrorism (Abbott et al. 2007: 40). Despite a spike in terrorist incidents in 2003 and 2004, these were predominantly associated with attacks against on-duty US forces in Iraq and political disturbances in South Asia (Kashmir), neither of which involved attacks on foreign tourists (Mack 2005: 44). In addition, as in the case of India where nearly a thousand people were killed in sectarian violence between 2001 and 2011, the victims were predominantly domestic civilians as opposed to foreign tourists (see Al-Jazeera 2011).

The selective media focus on the global dangers associated with terrorism has, in part, been driven by the rise of a veritable industry of media pundits and corporate security industries, particularly since 9/11 propagating a sense of perpetual insecurity and an exaggerated climate of fear (Toolis 2004). In today's hyper-connected (virtual) world, a 24-hour news service, the web and social media rapidly produce, spread and exacerbate these fears throughout tourist-generating societies. The impulse to contain and control subversive forces deemed threatening and 'alien' to society is not of course new, as was noted in relation to the introduction of the passport. Davis (2001: 41), however, sees rather darker forces at work whereby the 'current globalization of fear' and accompanying securitization of societies that was ratcheted up in the wake of 9/11 can be regarded as akin to 'the quest for the bourgeois utopia of a totally calculable and safe environment'. State impulses to 'secure' borders and territories, particularly in the light of concerns discussed in Chapter 4, not only contribute to exaggerating such fears but have been a key factor in shifting the focus of public anxieties onto the immigrant 'Other', with severe implications for the freedom of movement of ethnic minority citizens.

In his celebrated analysis of risk, Beck (1992) makes the convincing claim that industrial societies have entered a key transitional phase in global human relations, in which the world has become increasingly exposed to (and aware of) a range of unprecedented and diverse risks. The growth in the scale and scope of these risks can, he argues, be attributed to a number of factors associated with globalization, urbanization, migration and technological innovation, each of which have exacerbated human vulnerability and insecurity. Central to his thesis is the idea that the 'risk society' has eclipsed the 'class society' which defined the era of industrial capitalism. Whereas the class society was organized by the need to eliminate *scarcity*, which in turn is informed by the ideal of equality, the 'risk society' is organized around a constant quest for *security* (Beck 1992: 49). This prompted widespread organizational transformations and the expansion of regulatory frameworks designed to anticipate, pre-empt and manage such risks. More recently, Beck (2005: 12) notes that the heightened climate of fear has dissolved the boundaries separating 'suspect' from 'non-suspect'. As a consequence all citizens are increasingly under suspicion and must continuously prove they do not pose a threat to 'national' security. This climate of fear and prejudice permeates contemporary media and public discourse and in many ways reinforces demarcations between 'legitimate' and 'illegitimate' forms of mobility, which are furthermore being shaped by the disruptive forces of capitalist globalization. Accompanying this transition to a more insecure global order, a new paradigm of 'neoliberal global governance' has emerged, geared increasingly towards containing the effects of endemic poverty and political instability rather than challenging their underlying causes (Wilkin 2002). Central to this framework of global governance is the prioritization of security and corporate business interests over those of the poor in the disbursement of development aid (WDM 2013). Thus, for example, the marketization and securitization of development aid from the UK has increasingly targeted areas of conflict (e.g. in the Horn of Africa) as part of a wider process of managing the threat of terrorism, as well as 'securing the dominant status of neoliberalism as an expansive global framework for economic and social policy' (Moore 2012).[4]

Given the spate of attacks against international tourists in Egypt throughout the 1990s and early 2000s, the 9/11 attacks and similar attacks in Madrid (2004) and London (2005), the securitization of global tourism took an altogether dramatic

PLATE 5.1   An armed scout accompanying a visitor to Awash National Park, Ethiopia. Photo: R. Bianchi, April 2012.

turn as discourses of development and security increasingly converged. It has since become conventional wisdom that the world has entered a new era of globalized insecurity and, in addition, that international tourism is facing a period of uncertainty and unprecedented risk (Santana 2001; Tarlow 2006). The 'impending threat of international terrorism is impeding greater permeability of borders for tourism', halting a trend towards borderless regions and transnationalism that was seen as vital to the future of international tourism and indeed the freedom of movement (Sofield 2006: 117). As discussed at length in Chapter 4, the securitization of global travel has ushered in a panoply of new encumbrances to mobility, to help identify and pre-empt security risks among people seeking to cross international borders. In addition to the common practice of having 'tourist police' and even military personnel stationed around major resorts (Goldstone 2001: 62; Rogers 2002: 2–3), the WTTC (2003) even backed calls for the tourist industry itself to work closely with the security industries to help with the security profiling of employees (Plate 5.1).

Paradoxically, the affluent in general and international tourists in particular, are more shielded from violence and disaster than ever, especially given the widespread adoption of travel insurance and use of credit cards. Although tourists are often very much aware of the potential risks of travel, given the saturated media coverage of high-profile incidents, places of violence and conflict are more accessible than ever (Lisle 2007). Unlike the majority of tourists, when faced with natural disasters, drought, disease, civil war, systemic poverty or the risk of economic ruin as a result of global market turbulence, the vast majority of inhabitants in low-income destinations do not benefit from 'the economic clout to spend their way out of difficulty or hardship' (Mowforth and Munt 1998: 198). Moreover, in the face of kidnappings or political unrest tourists are often able to call upon a range of diplomatic, legal and financial instruments in order to minimize risk, and in some cases seek damages from host destinations and the tourism industry. In 2005, for example, a lawsuit was filed on behalf of 100 foreign tourists who died in the 2004 Indian Ocean *tsunami* (McGirk 2005). The lawsuit was filed against the Thai government and the US *tsunami* warning base in Hawaii for failing to give adequate notice to evacuate the afflicted areas. Nevertheless, the vast majority of the estimated 230,000 people who died were local inhabitants of the stricken coastal regions in Thailand, Indonesia, Sri Lanka and the Maldives. In a similar case, although in response to political violence rather than a natural disaster, the father of one of the victims of the 1997 Luxor massacre, a Japanese lawyer, was partially successful in his attempt to prosecute a tour company for ignoring a warning that tourists should avoid Egypt, issued a month prior to the attacks by a known 'terrorist' organization (Day 2002: 27m 42s). These incidents point to the increasingly complex alignments of mobility, power and citizenship in a world criss-crossed by manifold movements of people, and the increasingly blurred boundaries between national and transnational jurisdictions regarding the safety and security of mobile citizens (Lisle 2007: 340). In addition, it also begs the question, to what extent the safety and security of tourists may be deemed more important than that of other mobile subjects? Often the answer to this question seems to imply a straightforward cost-benefit calculus: international tourism represents both a temporary movement of foreigners from their home country to the destination and a source of considerable export revenue. However, is there not an equally compelling *moral imperative* to protect all mobile peoples regardless of the purpose of travel?

The evacuation of British expatriates employed by Western oil multinationals in Libya offers a stark illustration of the relationship between citizenship and differential mobility rights. In February 2011 these British citizens were evacuated by the SAS at the expense of British taxpayers. In contrast, thousands of migrant workers from neighbouring African countries and beyond were left stranded at the border in search of a means of escape from the hostilities. Miles (2011: 21) comments:

> What intrinsic merit does someone who happens to hold a British passport have in this situation over a Bangladeshi or a Guinean? … But in a globalised world, where people work overseas, flitting from country to country, following contracts, what makes them British citizens?

In addition, Miles contrasts the experience of the British oil executives in Libya, many of whom, she argues, pay no tax in either the UK or the host country, whom she describes as 'global corporate citizens', with that of a British backpacker accused of drug smuggling in Brazil, left to fend for herself with no diplomatic assistance. Similarly, immediately after their release from prison in Iran, three US hikers, held by the Iranian authorities for allegedly straying into Iranian territory during a tour of Iraqi Kurdistan, spoke of the numerous other political detainees in US and Iranian prisons, who did not have the benefit of a globally publicized campaign for their release (BBC 2011b). Whether for reason of class or nationality, such cases serve to illustrate how emergent notions of global citizenship are considerably premised upon existing political citizenship rights and economic power.

As Chapter 4 illustrated, the fears of 'terrorism' and the globalization of insecurity, reflected in concerns over the safety of travel, have become increasingly aligned with those of a global security politics. In response, there has been a move among private security firms and technology companies, and indeed aircraft manufacturers (e.g. Boeing), to capitalize on the growing demand among states and corporations alike for increasingly sophisticated (and discreet) security systems (see Corporate Europe Observer 2002). Nevertheless, such trends were already apparent at the time of the signing of the North American Free Trade Agreement (NAFTA)[5] in 1994, which coincided with massive government expenditure in the US on increased border patrols and other technological means of surveillance, including technologies to strengthen the restriction of cross-border movement from Mexico into the US (Wilkin 2002: 636).

Tensions between the commercial imperatives of the corporate tourism industries and the security imperatives of the state have also become increasingly apparent. Representatives of the travel industries and other commercial sectors dependent on tourist revenues have often campaigned against what are deemed to be unnecessary visa restrictions and regulatory encumbrances to the free movement of tourists. Recently, the discrepancy between the length and complexity of the UK visa application process in comparison to the Schengen Visa[6] was highlighted by the British media in response to what was perceived to be a burdensome visa application process for Chinese tourists. While wealthy Chinese tourists represent the single largest market of overseas shoppers in London, the mobility of other Chinese – as illustrated by the Morecambe cockle-picker tragedy in 2003, in which 23 Chinese undocumented migrant workers drowned (see Watts 2007) – continues to be viewed with some suspicion in other areas of government (Barrett 2011).[7] Criticisms regarding the complexity and restrictiveness of the UK visa application process prompted the Secretary of State for Culture, Media and Sport in the UK (whose Department also has responsibility for Tourism) to announce measures to simplify the visa application process to facilitate inbound tourism, particularly for high-spending Chinese nationals (UK Visa Bureau 2012). Following this, during a high profile diplomatic visit to China in October 2013, the UK Chancellor of the Exchequer anounced the introduction of a new, simplified visa system that would facilitate travel by business leaders and wealthy tourists from China, to the UK (Watt, 2013). It is striking, however, that such a move is framed in terms of improving the efficiency of border regimes and the commercial imperatives of boosting international tourism arrivals and economic growth, rather than recognizing any civic or transnational responsibility towards the advancement of equitable mobility freedoms and rights (see Blanke and Chiesa 2011: 90). Conversely, very few politicians or indeed representatives of the tourism industries would argue for a similar liberalization of visa restrictions to facilitate the freedom of movement for citizens of African states into Europe.

A new paradigm of neoliberal global governance, in which the imperatives of security increasingly outweigh those of long-term development assistance, has thus brought the differentiated experiences of mobility into sharp relief. While the mobility of migrants, refugees and terrorists are often conflated by media and state discourses of security, so as to appear as a uniform threat to global order, the mobility of capital and of course tourists – who for the most part accept the need for tightened security or remain oblivious to its effects on those deemed to be illegitimate tourists – are seen as intrinsic to the advancement of peace, prosperity and stability. The stark contrast in the mobility freedoms enjoyed by tourists compared to the impoverished masses seeking asylum in the West can often collide in the most tragic of circumstances. This point was tragically illustrated by the event surrounding the case of Angolan asylum seeker Jimmy Mubenga, who died on a BA plane at London's Heathrow airport as he was being deported. One of the passengers, who witnessed Mubenga's death during a struggle on board the aircraft with three private security guards, spoke out against official accounts of his death released by the Home Office and the private security firm G4S. He candidly claimed:

> For the rest of my life I'm always going to have that at the back of my mind – could I have done something? That is going to bother me every time I go to sleep ... I didn't get involved because I was scared I would get kicked off the flight and lose my job. But that man paid a higher price than I would have.
>
> *(Lewis and Taylor 2010)*

Although the tectonics of global inequality are by no means uniform (see UNCTAD 2012: 52–60), neoliberal globalization has spawned a new era of unequal and regulated mobility rather than ushered in a world of universal mobility rights and the democratization of travel. The combined forces of material deprivation and poverty have also fuelled the growth of multiplex border regimes, particularly in the rich states of the global North. These forces have been exacerbated by neoliberal programmes of debt restructuring and market liberalization in regions such as sub-Saharan Africa, and the imperatives of security that are central to the new paradigm of neoliberal global governance. Border regimes purposefully filter out the 'terrorist', the 'criminal' and the 'illegal migrant', each of whom are deemed to represent an existential threat to the virtuous circle of consumer capitalism and liberal democracy, and in some cases the cultural integrity of the nation-state itself (Harris 2002: 63–68). This not only contradicts the wave of optimism that followed the fall of the Berlin Wall and the ostensible sustainable turn presaged by the 1987 *Brundtland Report* (WCED 1987), it places considerable doubt on the inclusiveness of the mobility rights supposedly shared by all humanity, as well as the material and political foundations of contemporary citizenships that are associated with participation in travel and being a tourist.

The securitization of travel highlights the degree to which the kind of attenuated cosmopolitanism often associated with global tourism seemingly ignores the vast discrepancies in people's ability to participate in global travel. Such notions of cosmopolitanism also lack the shared moral purpose and architecture of transnational solidarity without which an active global citizenship is all but a vague ideal, a point further discussed in the final chapter. A question repeatedly faced by governments and the tourism industries is: how can tourists be shielded from the range of new dangers to which they are exposed in a globalized but volatile world, without excessively restricting their freedom of movement? Also, at what point does the reconciliation of mobility freedoms and security lean in favour of security to the extent that it ends up perpetuating perceptions of danger and insecurity?

The politics of security, travel advisories and the challenge to the freedom of movement

Government travel advisories are periodically issued by tourism-generating countries in response to specific security threats at destinations. In addition, the travel advice contained in popular travel guides may further exacerbate the perception of risk and danger associated with travel to certain places, particularly Africa (see Carter 1998). In a review of travel advisories on 46 African countries issued by the US State Department in 1998, Harrison (2000: 41) notes that the overwhelming impression given was of a region that tourists should largely avoid. Similarly, regional ties among Arab states have been severely tested and familial ties disrupted by the violence in Syria, which has led to numerous Gulf states advising their citizens not to travel to Lebanon (Sherif 2012). Edmonds and Mak (2006) reveal how closely linked are the perceptions of insecurity, the ethno-religious characteristics of tourists and patterns of global and regional travel. The combined effects of the 9/11 attacks and subsequent 'war on terrorism', in conjunction with the 2002 Bali bombings, led to a dramatic reduction in foreign visitor arrivals to Malaysia. Edmonds and Mak (2006: 4) suggest that being a predominantly Muslim country, Malaysia was seen as a far riskier destination than neighbouring Singapore, for example, where levels of foreign visitor arrivals recovered far more quickly. However, Stephenson's (in press (2014b)) observations of the Emirate of Dubai note that, despite significant levels of conflict and terrorism in the Middle East and Gulf region over the past three decades, including recent civil unrest in nearby Bahrain, the numbers of international tourists have continued to rise dramatically, reaching well over the 9 million mark in 2011. Not only has Dubai formed strong and enduring diplomatic relations and economic alliances with the West, it has been able to successfully differentiate itself as a safe and secure microstate within the broader context of the wider United Arab Emirates, and the Middle East as a whole.

In the Middle East, it is not only the perception of insecurity that functions as a periodic deterrent to foreign travel into the region, but the cross-border movements of those living within the region are also marked and shaped by the geopolitical rivalries and diplomatic relations between the various regional powers. In the aftermath of the 1994 peace agreement between Israel and Jordan, travel between Israel and Jordan became routinely possible once again. The normalization of diplomatic relations between the two states opened up the borders and stimulated travel between these two states for the first time since 1948, as well as marking Jordan's integration into the wider global tourism economy and flows of investment capital (Hazbun 2008: 133–135). Stein (2001: 526), however, notes that prior to the normalization of diplomatic relations and opening up of cross-border travel, Israeli travellers had long participated in clandestine travel to visit the historic site of Petra, a place 'immortalized in Israeli myth'. Nevertheless, she recounts how, once normal travel had resumed, the popular Israeli media soon began to depict the Jewish-Israeli tourist as a 'heroic traveller, freely traversing borders into Arab lands' (Stein 2001: 517).

In contrast, Jordanian tourists, many of whom were of Palestinian origin with a tangible historical relationship to the disputed territories of Israel and Palestine, were portrayed in the Israeli media as objects of anxiety (Stein 2001: 517). Such was the level of concern among the Israeli authorities that Jordanians of Palestinian origin travelling on tourist visas would in fact seek to reclaim their 'homeland', that in 1995, the Israeli Ministry of Tourism declared that Muslim tourism to Jerusalem would not be encouraged (Stein 2001: 534–535). Jordanian media narratives, on the other hand, reflected growing frustration with the dividends of the 'peace process' and the political stalemate between Israel and Palestine (Hazbun 2008: 174). Against a backdrop of growing Palestinian and Jordanian distrust of Israel and growing suicide attacks against Israeli targets by Palestinian militants, the border once again began to harden. In 1996, Israel began to issue cautionary travel advisories for its citizens travelling to Jordan. Tragically, this step was followed soon afterwards by the killing of seven Israeli schoolgirls by a Jordanian soldier in 1997, at the 'Island of Peace' on the Israeli-Jordanian border (Hazbun 2008: 181–185).

Government travel advisories rarely, however, provide visitors with a dispassionate assessment of the prevailing security conditions in a particular country. They are often underscored by the prevailing ideological stance of the issuing government, as well as the status of the diplomatic relations between it and the destination authorities. As a result, the citizens and businesses of the issuing state may have their right to travel and freedom to engage in commercial transactions across borders constrained or prevented altogether – in accordance with the broader geopolitical imperatives of their government and its allies. Tourists may therefore have their freedom of movements and right to travel restricted due to a combination of political and/or moral reasons (Lovelock 2008: 339). For example, in 1968 sanctions were imposed on Rhodesia by the UN Security Council, urging states to restrict the entry of Rhodesian passport holders into their territories and preventing financial transactions with tourist enterprises in Rhodesia, in response to the Unilateral Declaration of Independence and white minority rule by renegade leader Ian Smith (Strack 1978).[8] More often than not, the motives are overtly political. As Linda Richter (1994: 13) states, 'Countries ideologically close to the United States require a much higher level of danger to US citizens' before cautionary travel warnings are issued. Thus, traditionally, severe travel warnings to staunch US allies have rarely been issued (Richter 1995). For example, despite long-term civil unrest and political violence, the Philippines rarely received negative travel advisories while the US Clark Air Force Base and Subic Bay Naval Base were in operation there.

The threat of sanction using the abrogation of travel rights, which thereby affects revenues that flow from tourist expenditures, is one frequently used by the US on states seen as hostile to its geostrategic interests. During the 1970s, the US deterred American tourists from visiting the island of Jamaica in an attempt to undermine support for the moderate left-wing government led by Michael Manly. Among the socialist policies enacted by Manly, his government nationalized much of the Jamaican hotel industry as well as refusing to implement many of the conditions attached to IMF structural adjustment loans (Bastin 1984: 86–87). In the nearby island of Grenada, the rise to power in 1979 of a revolutionary left-wing government led by Maurice Bishop provoked a US-led invasion in 1983. This situation was inflamed by the West's assumption, albeit later falsified, that the small island was building an international airport not for the tourism industry and transportation of cargo (which was the actual intention) but for harbouring a Soviet and Cuban military base. This had a clear and dramatic impact on the island's tourism industry. According to Pattullo (1996: 30), tourist arrivals dropped by 25 per cent overall, while the US share of the market decreased by 77 per cent between 1978 and 1982. Furthermore, it was the firm belief of Bishop's government that travel agents in the US were giving out 'hostile information' to potential tourists. Such was the scale of the US invasion that the Cuban government was certain that the US invasion force was heading for them. Accordingly, it was claimed that plans were drawn up to prevent tourists from leaving their hotels and, if necessary, to arm them (Marshall 1987: 90–91)!

Whereas Chapter 4 considered the various restrictions on the right to travel of Cubans imposed by the Cuban authorities, Cuban mobility has of course been inhibited by the United States. Since 1963, in an act of ideological and economic aggression against the revolutionary government of Fidel Castro, the United States effectively banned its citizens from travelling to Cuba under the auspices of the *Trading With the Enemy Act* (1917) and *Foreign Assistance Act* (1961), followed by numerous subsequent laws passed by the US Congress. Any attempt to breach the US embargo on travel by US citizens to Cuba can result in hefty fines being imposed: in 2005, 307 US citizens were fined up to US$7,500 each for making unauthorized trips to Cuba (Arrington 2005). US policy to inhibit travel to Cuba and prevent US-owned corporations doing business with Cuban counterparts has even extended into the sovereign territory of other states. In 2006, the Mexico City branch of the US-owned Sheraton hotel chain was fined for hosting a delegation of Cuban businessmen, who were due to meet a group of US businessmen opposed to the US embargo against Cuba (BBC 2006).

There have nevertheless been persistent calls over the years by representatives of the US travel industry to relax the US-imposed trade embargo. Currently, the embargo places US companies at a commercial disadvantage compared to their European counterparts, such as Sol Meliá, which by virtue of being a European company is free to operate on the island (Steinmetz 2009b). Despite the recent relaxation of travel to Cuba, little has changed with regard to the freedom of movement between both countries. In 2009, the *Freedom to Travel to Cuba Act* was introduced to Congress, which proposed to remove remaining restrictions on travel to Cuba by all US citizens. However, at the time of writing, the Act has not yet been enacted, and the broader economic embargo preventing US companies from entering the Cuban market remains in place. Although former leader Fidel Castro publicly renounced Cuba's support for communist insurgencies in Latin America in 1992, Cuba nevertheless continues to be listed by the US as a 'state sponsor of terrorism'. This is despite the fact that the US itself has orchestrated a series of both overt and covert military operations designed to unseat the Cuban regime since the early 1960s, including the bombing of a Cubana Airlines flight in 1976 and a series of bombings against tourism facilities as recently as 1997 (Weinglass 2006). More recently, Cuba's opposition to the 'war on terror', and its friendly diplomatic relations with Iran and former Venezuelan President Hugo Chávez, have provided the justification for continued blacklisting by the US. After the collapse of the Soviet Union, attitudes towards Cuba among US policymakers in fact hardened in order to isolate the Cuban regime even further. This resulted in many sanctions that had been eased since the 1960s being restored and the introduction of harsher penalties for illegal travel to the island (Canally and Carmichael 2006).

What is more, Sharpley *et al.* (1996: 6) note that negative travel advisories imply a withdrawal of the diplomatic 'means of travelling' and a 'contravention of international agreements supporting the facilitation and development of tourism'. They imply the curtailment of tourists' right to travel as well as the possible infringement of the rights of the tourist industry (local and foreign) to engage in business. Travel advisories thus point to a complex and potentially contradictory relationship between the right to travel and development rights.[9] Higgins-Desbiolles (2007: 318) appropriately states that 'a universal right to tourism and travel have no meaning when the vast majority of the world's population must struggle to secure their own survival'. Similarly, given the fact that many low-income states have few other options than to develop tourism for the purposes of generating much-needed foreign exchange and employment, negative travel advisories may have a severe impact on local livelihoods. This was demonstrated most notably in 1994, when the British government issued warnings against travel to The Gambia in response to a bloodless coup (see Sharpley *et al.* 1996), and again in 2003 in response to what it termed a 'credible terrorist threat to Western interests in Kenya', leading to the suspension of all British Airways flights to the country (Tourism Concern 2003: 7).

The problem lies not only in their inconsistency – both in relation to the level of travel advice issued by other major markets and the uneven application of warnings to different states – but also the fact that travel bans may not be removed until months after the 'threat' has subsided. This can result in a significant loss of tourism revenue and local employment, as workers are often laid off (Sharpley *et al.* 1996: 3). It was estimated that the Kenyan tourism industry lost up to US$30 million as a result of the 2003 travel warnings and subsequent suspension of flights from the UK by British Airways, in response to attacks on an Israeli-owned hotel and charter flight in November 2002 (Dunn 2004: 483). Although blanket travel bans are no longer issued for countries as a whole, following further criticism in 2008 regarding the excessive severity of such bans, Kenya has continued to suffer from periodic outbreaks of political violence, particularly around election time, fuelling cautionary travel advisories and cancellations (Rice 2008). Often the response to political violence in developing countries by Western governments is invoked in support of further security measures, further reinforcing colonial-era anxieties regarding the dangers associated with travel to Africa. Following the attacks in November 2002, the US urged the Kenyan authorities to push through anti-terrorism legislation in return for relaxing the restrictions on travel (Mbogo 2003; Whitaker 2007: 1023–1024). However, following a storm of protest from opposition MPs and civil society, the legislation was blocked as it was seen to unfairly target Muslim minorities.

The new global development security agenda has thus paved the way for the realignment between the ideological interests of capital and corporate business on the one hand, and impoverished populations on the other. As noted earlier, this alignment is mirrored by the ideological values that frame the UNWTO's (1999) *Global Code of Ethics for Tourism*. This charter posits an equivalence between the right to the freedom of movement and travel and the right to tourism, when in fact these imply two quite distinct practices characterized by a series of unresolved tensions, noted earlier in Chapter 3. In addition, as pointed out in Chapter 3, the organization explicitly invokes such freedoms in the same breath as support for the 'market economy, private enterprise and free trade' (WTO 1999: 3). This ignores the degree to which the enjoyment of the right to tourism may both be premised upon and indeed indirectly contribute to the inequalities that impede most members of the planet from asserting their own right to travel freely across borders. It also conceals the very manner in which tourism is implicated in the consolidation of neoliberal globalization and a pervasive global security politics. Moreover, the right to tourism is the only area of rights that relates specifically to the commercial interests of a particular industry. This predisposes the UNWTO to promote the expansion of tourism and private-sector interests that seek to profit from tourism, as opposed to an agency that seeks to protect the right to the freedom of movement of humanity as a whole.

Cosmopolitan globalism and violence against mobile citizens

Some time ago, the headline in *The Independent on Sunday*, a left-of-centre British newspaper, posed the question: 'Is anywhere in the world safe?' (Moreton 2003). Listing at least a dozen countries where tourists had recently been the target of terrorist bombings (e.g. Bali, Kenya and Morocco) and subject to negative FCO travel advisories, the article – which was accompanied by a graphic illustration of the world's 'danger zones' – gave the distinct impression that the global village was becoming a less welcoming and increasingly dangerous place for tourists. In addition, the fact that a considerable number of attacks had taken place in Arab states with predominantly Muslim populations and/or had been perpetrated by self-confessed militant Islamic organizations, only serves to further reinforce the wider association of Islam with fundamentalism and irrational violence. A list compiled by the *Al-Jazeera* news channel shows that 17 separate attacks took place in Egypt between 1992 and 2009, leading to the deaths of around 150 foreign tourists and 85 Egyptians (Al-Jazeera 2009). The most devastating of these involved the killing of 58 tourists and four Egyptians at Luxor in 1997, and the explosion of car bombs at the Red Sea resort of Sharmel-Sheikh in 2005, which killed nearly 90 people, mostly Egyptians, many of whom were workers gathered in the Old Market.

On 26 November 2008, Islamist militants laid siege to the commercial and tourist centre of Mumbai, killing 120 people and taking several people hostage. Although the majority of victims were Indians, a number of symbolic locations frequented by foreign tourists, including the Taj Mahal Palace, the Oberoi Trident Hotel and the Cafe Leopold,[10] were specifically targeted by the gunmen. In her reaction to the attacks, the Bollywood actress Maninee Misra expressed understandable outrage at the killing of innocent people, stating that the 'cosmopolitan heart of this city is destroyed' (Misra 2008). Evoking Mumbai's long-standing reputation for cosmopolitanism, she also expressed concern over the restrictions on being freely able to visit the luxurious hotels and shopping malls in the city centre that were likely to ensue as a result of these events. While her reaction was perhaps understandable, it nevertheless reveals a wilful ignorance of the deeply iniquitous socio-economic conditions and social injustices that prevent the majority of Mumbai's residents from enjoying the benefits of its much praised economic boom and cosmopolitan 'way of life'.[11] As if to highlight the kind of attenuated cosmopolitanism evoked by her response, shortly after the attacks took place a public interest lawsuit was filed in Mumbai's high court charging the Indian government with having failed to protect its citizens (Sengupta 2008). What is striking about this move is the fact that it was filed by members of Mumbai's financial elite, including the Bombay Chamber of Commerce. As Sengupta (2008) notes, there is a tragic irony in the fact that it those who have profited most from the retreat of the state and the opening of India to global markets, who now invoke their citizenship rights, specifically, demanding that the state do more to protect them and their assets.[12]

In an equally revealing evocation of liberal cosmopolitanism, the mother of one of three US hikers detained in July 2009 by the Iranian authorities for entering into Iranian territory illegally while hiking in Iraqi Kurdistan, emphasized that these young tourists were 'intentionally being global citizens' (BBC World Service 2010: 11m 4s). As if to reinforce this view, not only was it claimed that they had strayed unwittingly into Iranian territory (although the facts are not clear), it was also stressed that they were taking a break from their jobs teaching English to refugees in Syria as part of a more general concern with Middle Eastern affairs. In contrast, Iran, already something of a pariah state in the eyes of the US and her allies, was popularly constructed as a state devoted to the pursuit of an agenda that is antithetical to not only peaceful inter-state dialogue, but also to cosmopolitan globalism itself. While the hikers may have been naive victims of wider geopolitical tensions, some reports have cast doubt on their claims not to have known that they were near the Iranian border, or aware of the problems of straying into this territory (Bahari 2010). Nevertheless, the discourse circulating in the Western media overwhelmingly portrayed the US hikers as global citizens with a keen interest in improving the well-being of others – at least two of the hikers are also well-known activists in the US. Such discourses implicitly reinforce the West as the site of cosmopolitanism in contrast to Iran, the locus of a reactionary regime rooted in an anti-globalist and narrow worldview. Such notions of cosmopolitanism implicitly express a Western and at times elitist worldview, as exemplified by the reactions to the Mumbai attacks cited above (see Calhoun 2002). More importantly, the relative freedom of movement of the hikers as citizens of the US contrasts starkly with respect to the difficulties experienced by Iranian citizens seeking to enter foreign countries, as noted in Chapter 4.

Reactions to such random and seemingly irrational acts of violence against tourists and other symbolic sites of conspicuous hedonism are often expressed in terms of an attack on the ideals of cosmopolitanism and freedom. These ideals are regarded as inherent in contemporary globalization and integral to the workings of international tourism. Hence, the 'terrorist' is seen to be a manifestation of an atavistic social force, hell-bent on the destruction of the alleged prosperity that has been built by globalization, market capitalism and the opening up of the world to international tourism. As if to reinforce this notion, despite the fact that many of their fellow citizens had also been killed in the attacks, the Islamist militants who carried out the bombing of Paddy's Bar and Sari's Bar in Bali's Kuta Beach on 12 October 2002 were adamant that they had done so out of their hatred for Western decadence associated with such well-known tourist hangouts (Hitchcock and Nyoman Darma Putra 2010). Such tropes have often been expressed in the aftermath of terrorist attacks against Western targets, whether tourist-related or against Western business or military installations in the Middle East and Gulf regions (Cockburn 2004). Clearly, these were horrific acts of violence perpetrated against innocent people. While the indiscriminate killing and kidnapping of tourists or civilians cannot be condoned under any circumstances, this should not however absolve us from the responsibility to look deeper into the ideological framing of such acts and to think through the wider socio-political processes at play where such violent incidents occur. It is therefore important to probe the extent to which tourists and more specifically the tourism industries are actually 'innocent of the implications of global geopolitics' (Phipps 1999: 76), and to consider what this can tell us about the differential citizenship entitlements of tourists as opposed to those who are less mobile or altogether denied access to travel. Indeed, such questions have already been raised in relation to an earlier period of international travel. As noted by Richter and Waugh (1986: 237): 'To the extent that the tourist industry in most developed and developing nations is controlled or managed by socioeconomic and political elites, tourists and facilities may be targeted by any group in opposition to capitalist resort owners.'

To accept uncritically the notion of tourism as a force for peace or to attribute the ideals of cosmopolitanism and global citizenship to international tourism without deeper scrutiny of the context in which such attacks arise, may conceal deeper structural forms of violence and injustice throughout the global order. Rojek's (1998: 291) claim, 'we don't think of tourism as a citizenship right until our freedom to travel is threatened', poignantly encapsulates how the rights of mobility and the sense of entitlement to travel that are intrinsic to tourism have increasingly become mediated by heightened concerns of risk and security. While the response of the media to attacks on tourists implicitly reinforces the status of the tourist as a privileged mobile subject able to invoke the universal right to travel, it also serves to illustrate how the right to travel has implicitly worked its way into discourses of cosmopolitanism and global citizenship. To challenge the untrammelled right to travel is interpreted in some quarters as a challenge to the progressive potential of tourism as means of development and indeed, modernity itself (see Butcher 2003: 24).

The conflation of progressive values with narrow corporate agendas is also a well-trodden path in global trade diplomacy,[13] as well as tourism. As noted previously, during the early post-war period representatives of the US travel industry firmly associated international travel with high-minded ideals of freedom and world citizenship as they sought to establish a foothold in Western Europe. More recently organizations such as the UNWTO and WTTC often portray the liberalization and globalization of tourism as synonymous with the values of democracy, peace and freedom. The claim that international tourism represents an intrinsic force of democratization as well as peace has almost come to be seen as self-evident to the governments, corporations and international agencies involved in the business of promoting tourism investment and development. In this regard, James Robinson III, CEO of American Express from 1977 to 1993 and founder of the WTTC, once remarked that 'the American tourist plays a vital role in the economies of all free nations' (cited in Goldstone 2001: 44).

In addition to proclaiming the virtues of tourism as an instrument of peace and prosperity, Goldstone (2001: 87) also notes how the WTTC, whose remit includes the forceful promotion of corporate-led tourism worldwide, claims a strong ideological identification with such democratic rights such as the right to freedom of assembly. In a speech to the annual meeting of the International Council of Tourism Partners in 2005, the founding president of the WTTC and advisor to the UNWTO Secretary-General, Geoffrey Lipman, went so far as to evoke the African notion of *ubuntu* in the context of promoting the expansion of the tourism export sector throughout Africa. This is an indigenous Nguni term from South Africa denoting a sense of shared belonging and common humanity, which even the Archbishop Desmond Tutu suggests is 'difficult to render into a Western language' (Tutu 1999: 54)! While tourism may well serve some of the goals associated with poverty alleviation and other Millennium Development Goals, as suggested in Lipman's speech, such discourses again confirm the conflation of the right to travel with that of the commercial imperatives of the tourism industries, as expressed in the UNWTO's *Global Code of Ethics*.

The claim that tourism is synonymous with the values of freedom and democracy is nevertheless a powerful one, and one that is moreover consistently reinforced through a variety of discourses that circulate throughout public policy, the media and the commercial spheres of tourism. For example, in his book, *Travel as a Political Act* (2009), well-known American travel journalist and intrepid traveller Rick Steves (2009: 161) invokes the metaphor of the tourist as 'jester', that is, someone who is in a unique position to bear witness to internal repression and speak out on issues that would otherwise go unnoticed or ignored by states. In this regard tourism is seen to consist of more than a mere expression of the right to travel and the freedom of movement, but rather, is regarded as an instrument of progressive political change aligned with local peoples' aspiration for citizenship, a theme to which we will return in the final chapter. While in a minority of cases tourists have borne witness to local political violence and even lent assistance to pro-democracy activists, as occurred in Tibet in October 1987 (Schwartz 1991),[14] there is little if any evidence to suggest that the influence of tourism on processes of democratization and/or long-term political change is anything other than marginal or indeed non-existent.

Similarly, the claim that tourism and the right to travel can foster democracy is one that has also been made with regard to the democratization of former Communist bloc states in Eastern Europe. While demands for the right to the freedom of movement were no doubt encompassed within the popular struggles against Communist rule, Steves (2009) makes the somewhat unsubstantiated claim that travel to the Soviet Union by citizens of the West helped to diffuse tensions between East and West during the latter stages of the Cold War. What can nevertheless be stated with some degree of certainty, is that, tourism was deployed by the architects of the transition as a means of integrating the former Soviet satellite states into the mainstream of European society and the expanding reach of global capitalism, a process that has been continued through subsequent EU enlargement. As noted by Derek Hall (2004: 8), the focus of the transition from Communist state-planned societies to free market liberal democracy in the former USSR was 'markedly Eurocentric' despite the fact that the USSR was a predominantly Asian country, with an 'ideological driving force that was strongly trans-Atlantic'.

Despite sporadic acts of political violence directed at tourists or that claim the lives of tourists, the vast majority of international tourists come to no harm and are rarely in fact ever targeted by militant organizations. Rather, it is the very inhabitants of such poor and politically unstable destinations who are exposed to perpetual insecurity and risk. For example, numerous terrorist attacks in India between 2001 and 2008 killed approximately 700 Indian civilians, including seven bombings at railway stations and packed commuter trains in Mumbai, which killed around 180 people on 11 July 2006 (Al-Jazeera 2011). As in the case of Kenya, the Balinese too faced a severe downturn in their livelihoods in the wake of the 2002 bombings in Kuta. Indeed, Hitchcock and Nyoman Darma Putra (2005: 67) claim that the 2002 Bali attacks led to 'arguably the worst crisis in tourism since Indonesia closed its doors to foreigners in the wake of the massacres that followed the alleged Communist coup of 30 September 1965'. The uneven social and territorial distribution of risk was also starkly demonstrated by the 2004 Indian Ocean tsunami, which claimed approximately 230,000 lives, including 2,000 foreign tourists, injured a further half a million people and left 2.5 million people homeless. Despite the unprecedented humanitarian response, which raised approximately US$10 billion, many poor coastal inhabitants have since been marginalized and displaced by the subsequent attempts of developers, aided by governments, to appropriate and enclose the lucrative coastal lands that were laid to waste by the destructive force of the *tsunami* (see Rice 2005).

The right to travel and relative prosperity of most tourists continues to exist in stark contrast with the day-to-day living and working conditions in the impoverished communities and shanty towns adjacent to popular tourist destinations and resort areas in poorer countries. Despite a period of unprecedented prosperity and the accelerated expansion of global travel in the period following the end of the Cold War and leading up to the 2007–2008 financial crisis, it is not uncommon to encounter large pockets of poverty and deprivation adjacent to major tourism destinations areas. In the coastal town of Mombasa, for instance, which accounts for over half of all accommodation in Kenya, 60 per cent of residents lack basic amenities (Akama and Kieti 2007: 740). Elsewhere, the World Heritage town of Oaxaca in Mexico, built by Spanish colonialists and famed for its pre-Columbian archaeological heritage, is described by Mexican journalist Hernández Navarro (2006) as a 'Mexican tourist enclave, surrounded by poverty where people survive on remittances sent by migrant workers abroad'.

In some cases, however, inequalities and social deprivation do provide a breeding ground for the kind of political violence witnessed in certain major tourism destinations. For example, Kenya, one of sub-Saharan Africa's major tourist destinations, has suffered from a troubled image due to periodic outbreaks of political violence. At least in part, this violence has taken place against a backdrop of disputes over land rights, and in some cases the loss of lands to make way for tourism development (Economist 1997). Elsewhere, despite the economic importance of Mexico's international tourism industry, it is estimated that up to 40 per cent of residents in Cancun are without sewerage or running water and are lucky if they earn US$10 per day (Kraul 2003). Meanwhile, in 2006, tourism in the state of Quintana Roo accounted for US$3 billion of revenue, one-third of Mexico's annual income from tourism revenue (Hawley 2006).

As if to underline the degree to which the right to tourism may often override other rights and freedoms, in 2007, former President Maumoon Abdul Gayoom of the Maldives sought to attribute part of the blame for a bomb attack in Male, which injured 12 foreign tourists, to the *Friends of Maldives*. This is a UK-based civil society organization that had been calling for a boycott of the Maldives' tourism industry in the course of campaigning for democracy and political reforms in the Maldives (Carter and Ramesh 2007). Prior to this, Amnesty International (2004) had accused his tenure of being characterized by repressive political rule, multiple abuses of human rights and corruption, a reality that is rather at odds with the image of the Maldives as a tourist paradise. Such examples demonstrate how tourism and specific destinations are easily drawn into the complex maelstrom of global geopolitics, where domestic politics, local grievances and global conditions intersect. Moreover, globalization and increased technological interconnectedness have further highlighted deep schisms within the fractured global citizenry, accentuating the perceived and material differences between tourists and deprived local communities. A combination of tourism, satellite TV and the Internet comprise a portal through which the 'knowledgeable poor' are pressed up against the virtual shop window of the global village (see Nahdi 2002), inflaming what security analyst Rogers (2002: 86–87) refers to as a 'revolution of unfulfilled expectations'.

Conclusion

In this chapter, we have seen how the expansion of international travel and tourism was premised upon the peaceful coexistence between states and, with the exception of the Soviet bloc, the emergence of an international order of states underpinned by Western values of liberal democracy, free market capitalism and human rights. International tourism was thus one of the prime beneficiaries of the post-war 'peace dividend'. It was also a central plank of post-war European reconstruction and soon became embraced by newly independent states in the 'Third World' as a principal mechanism of nation-building and economic modernization. With vague echoes of Kantian notions of perpetual peace and world citizenship, international tourism seemed to foretell a coming era of growth, prosperity and peaceful relations among citizens of the world, partly premised upon access to cheap, international travel.

However, the notion of tourism as uniquely able to foster peace as well as representing an aspect of commerce worthy of elevation to the status of a human right is deeply problematic. As the discussion in this chapter has demonstrated, the extent to which tourism can be seriously considered as a panacea to global conflict much less a marker of global and cosmopolitan forms of citizenship can be seriously questioned. By the 1980s international travel and tourism became increasingly unsettled by political violence and insecurity that has often been levelled directly at tourists themselves. However, while such attacks served to reinforce the idea of tourism as a form of cosmopolitanism and citizenship that was being threatened by those who sought to destabilize the post-Cold War neoliberal order of states, they also throw up a number of of questions regarding the notion of tourism as a universal right, particularly in the face of widespread and growing inequalities and injustices.

Notwithstanding moves towards the incorporation of sustainability, poverty allevi-ation and human rights agendas into mainstream tourism thinking, the imperative to 'make the world safe' for tourists and the business of tourism often takes pre-cedence over the more complex and long-term efforts to improve the livelihoods and quality of life of destinations. The securitization of travel has thus become increasingly aligned with neoliberal global governance in which security impera-tives and market-based development 'solutions' increasingly go hand in hand. This issue points to a profound contradiction between the global framework of rights underpinning the right to the freedom of movement vis-à-vis those claimed by tourists, as well as between the right to profit and the impoverished development rights of low-income countries.

While the idea that tourism is uniquely able to nurture world peace and facili-tate inter-cultural understanding is a contentious one, such discourses do nonethe-less articulate a sense of cosmopolitanism and hint at the possibility of harnessing tourism to ideas of global citizenship. However, without an understanding of social justice the notion of tourism as a force for peace and inter-cultural understand-ing ignores the extent to which it is implicated in patterns of global and regional inequalities and caught up in the geopolitical entanglement between states. We must therefore continue to remain sceptical towards narrow neoliberal interpret-ations of rights and freedoms in which the individual right to travel is aligned with the right to consume, at the expense of dealing with the rights of develop-ment upon which universal participation in travel partly depends. The relation-ship between neoliberal discourses of rights and emerging notions of citizenship, specifically those related to transnational civil society activism, will be further explored in the final chapter. Attempts to challenge and contest existing forms of tourism, as well as to develop 'alternative' models of tourism development framed by discourses of ethical travel, potentially indicate new pathways towards the align-ment of the right to travel, development rights and citizenship.

Notes

1 The *Pax Americana* refers to the post-war balance of power in which the United States assumed a leading role. Key to this post-war geopolitical order was the unrivalled dom-inance of the US outside the sphere of influence controlled by the Soviet Union, into which Western Europe, Japan and much of the 'Third World' were incorporated, albeit on unequal terms (see Cox 1987: 211–219).
2 See Goldstone (2001).
3 The sixth edition of the *Rough Guide to Turkey* (2007: 89) explicitly warns Britons with Latin or Asian surnames to be wary of the thriving trade in stolen EU passports that resulted in a number of Britons being killed in Turkey during the 1990s.
4 In March 2011, the UK's Department for International Development (DfID) reallocated development assistance using a methodology that prioritizes funding for those multi-lateral organizations that follow market-oriented policy prescriptions. In addition, the 2010 Strategic Defence and Security Review has made it clear that aid will be focused on fewer and 'more fragile' areas, with the explicit intention of managing the threat of terrorism and thereby reducing the cost of future intervention (Moore 2012).

5 The NAFTA is a trilateral agreement negotiated by the United States, Canada and Mexico, whose goal it was to establish a new trading bloc that would eliminate barriers to capital mobility between these three states. See Klein (2001) and Marchand (2005) for a more detailed discussion of the role of this treaty and other ideas in forging new coordinates of resistance to neoliberal globalization.

6 At the time of writing, the UK visa application is 26 pages long, and many sections are only available in English, while in comparison, the Schengen Visa is only eight pages long and allows the holder to visit 25 other European countries as part of the Schengen Arrangement (UK Visa Bureau 2012).

7 It is estimated that visa liberalization in the UK alone could generate £2.8 billion in additional tourist expenditure (BBC Radio 4 2012).

8 Efforts to impede the rights of Rhodesian passports to travel overseas were somewhat undermined by the fact that many of them held dual nationality (see Strack 1978: 190–200).

9 The United Nations Declaration on the Right to Development was adopted by the UN General Assembly on 4 December 1986. The declaration proclaims the 'right to development' as an inalienable right, and states that everyone is 'entitled to participate in, contribute to, and enjoy economic, social, cultural and political development, in which all human rights and fundamental freedoms can be fully realized' (https://www.un.org/en/events/righttodevelopment/declaration.shtml, accessed 13 September 2013).

10 Both of these iconic hotels trace their origins back to British colonial rule in India. The Tata family, which built the Taj, were closely associated with the British Raj and made much of their early fortune supplying British military expeditions into Abyssinia, while the founder of the Oberoi group, M. S. Oberoi, started life as a bellhop in a hotel in Simla, the summer retreat of the British colonial classes (Jack 2008). Ironically, according to Mehta (2008: 7), the construction of the Taj in 1903 was in fact triggered by an earlier form of discrimination when Jamshetji Tata, a prominent Parsi industrialist at the time, was denied entrance into the colonial Watson's Hotel in Bombay.

11 In Mumbai, an estimated one in five of the inhabitants live in extreme poverty and 60 per cent live in slums (Baliga 2011).

12 Chomsky (2013: 18–22) notes how India has been steered towards ever-closer geopolitical alignment with the United States and neoliberal economics by the current Prime Minister, Manmohan Singh, a key architect of India's liberalization policy in his role as finance minister in the early 1990s.

13 In the aftermath of the 9/11 attacks, US Trade Representative Robert Zoellick (2001–2005) supported President George W. Bush's attempt to fast-track the controversial Free Trade Agreement of the Americas (FTAA) through the US Congress. This piece of legislation would significantly reduce the ability of Congress to scrutinize global free trade agreements, in support for which Zoellick explicitly harnessed the ideals of democracy and freedom to the defence of global market capitalism and a corporate free trade agenda (Kelsey 2008: 54–55).

14 The Dalai Lama has always maintained that foreigners *should* travel to Tibet in order to witness the results of Chinese repression and inform others of their experiences (Free Tibet Campaign, http://www.freetibet.org, accessed 13 September 2013).

6

TOURISM AS A 'FORCE FOR GOOD'?

Ethical travel, civil society and global citizenship

> The key political tensions in the coming era will be between the forces of neoliberal economic globalization, seeking to expand the freedom of capital, and the forces of social resistance, seeking to preserve and to redefine community and solidarity.
>
> *(Gills 2000: 3)*

Introduction

This chapter examines how various interpretations of global citizenship are being defined and extended through the actions of civil society groups and social movements that have mobilized against exploitative forms of tourism development. It also considers discourses of cosmopolitanism and global citizenship and associated notions of environmental citizenship that increasingly mark tourists' participation in 'ethical' and 'responsible' forms of travel. It asks whether such forms of travel genuinely imply the exercise of a global civic responsibility and a moral commitment towards the people, places and cultures they visit. It also examines how the emergence of the idea of the 'ethical' traveller as a putative 'global citizen' has increasingly aligned itself with seemingly responsible tourism businesses, which have deployed a stance of corporate social and environmental responsibility towards destinations. Finally, the discussion returns to the notion of tourism as peace discussed in the previous chapter, to explore how similar ideals have shaped attempts to build civic models of citizenship and seek reconciliation through tourism in the aftermath of conflict. Through its consideration of the various 'progressive' ideas of citizenship that underscore 'ethical' and 'altruistic' forms of travel, the chapter considers whether in fact such forms of travel have the potential to build forms of solidarity and citizenship that are not reducible to neoliberal ideas of ethical consumption and consumer citizenship.

Ethical tourism: a pathway to global citizenship?

Despite the precipitous worldwide growth of tourism in recent decades, fuelled in part by the considerable expansion of corporate investment in tourism and the rise of emerging markets, there exists a diversity of other forms of travel that can be described as 'socially transformative' types of tourism (Higgins-Desbiolles 2006a: 1201). These encompass the kinds of social tourism programmes that emerged in Europe in the early to mid-twentieth century, as discussed in Chapter 1, as well as more recent developments concerning a variety of alternative types of tourism, notably 'volunteer tourism' (Wearing 2001) and 'pro-poor tourism' (Ashley *et al.* 2001), and more overtly political forms of travel, namely 'solidarity' or 'justice tourism' (Scheyvens 2002). There are parallels here too with religious pilgrimages. However, despite the fact that many 'alternatives' to mainstream travel were given impetus by religious distaste towards the corrupting nature of mass tourism in the 'Third World', there are a number of contrasts between pilgrimages and distinctly secular forms of alternative travel. Not least of which are the values – for example, global citizenship, social justice and environmental stewardship – which seemingly give direction to more recent, altruistic forms of travel. In addition, unlike pilgrimages, both the organizational form and nature of participation in contemporary ethical forms of travel are marked by neoliberal globalization, often but not always as a counter point to the marketization of societies, and the resultant socio-economic transformation within advanced consumer societies.

Alternatives to what were regarded as mainstream forms of tourism began to emerge in the context of the upsurge in counter-cultural movements and popular protests in the 1960s, and the subsequent transition towards a globalized, post-industrial society in the advanced capitalist countries. Radicalized middle-class citizens of Western industrialized societies began to express their discontent with the materialism and militarism of Western capitalist societies, not least through various forms of political agency as well as overseas travel to peripheral and isolated places in search of authenticity and indigenous cultures, including, for example, places such as the small island of La Gomera in the Canary Islands (see Macleod 2004). Where once 'non-institutionalized' travel constituted little more than self-conscious acts of individual rebellion against the mainstream, increasingly the idea of an *ethical* 'alternative' to corporate mass tourism is guided by an explicit moral agenda and harnessed to the advancement of progressive socio-economic and environmental outcomes in destination communities.

Socially and environmentally motivated forms of tourism, while bearing some similarities to social tourism in so far as they are geared towards the fulfilment of wider social goals rather than profit-making, are orientated towards the empowerment of disadvantaged communities that are visited by tourists rather than those who are excluded from the opportunity to participate in tourism. This is mirrored in the distinction posed by Minnaert *et al.* (2007) between 'visitor-related' and 'host-related' forms of social tourism. While visitor-related social tourism in Western Europe developed from the early twentieth century onwards as a means of enabling low-income and working-class families to travel and take holidays, the intended beneficiaries of host-related social tourism, or rather ethical travel, are the marginalized and oppressed communities inhabiting parts of the 'Third World'. The protagonists of the former usually comprise the underprivileged residents of ostensibly rich states, who are dependent upon the interventions of the state and other agencies in order to participate in holidays and travel, whereas the protagonists of the latter overwhelmingly comprise the professional, 'new middle classes' from within these very societies (see Carroll 2008; Mowforth and Munt 2009: Ch. 5).

These two socially transformative variants of travel also imply a distinctive relationship between tourism and citizenship. The former (visitor-related tourism) is rooted in the advancement of social rights and the welfare state in rich nations, discussed in Chapter 1. Conversely, the latter (host-related tourism) is more closely aligned to emergent notions of global citizenship. In turn, this distinction highlights a further paradox, and one that is raised by Haulot (1981): while charitable organizations and governments in advanced capitalist states are able to draw upon funds to help reduce travel disparities between privileged and less privileged groups in these societies, few developing countries have the resources to do so. Many also depend a great deal upon foreign charities and international aid to deliver much-needed social programmes and in many cases to initiate tourism development schemes (see Martin 2008). To put it simply, while the less privileged citizens of rich states can achieve the right to travel and benefit from the social citizenship rights that accrue from state-funded welfare programmes and the work of other charitable agencies, it is through host-related forms of social tourism that impoverished or marginalized communities in poor states are sometimes able to reap the benefits of tourism in terms of creating opportunities for employment and sustainable livelihoods in the absence of other alternatives.

As the volume of international tourist arrivals continued to increase throughout the 1980s and into the early 1990s, particularly into Africa and the Asia-Pacific region (see WTO 2006), calls for a more sustainable form of tourism that would be developed in harmony with destination environments and local cultures began to gather momentum (Eber 1992). The urgency of the need to move tourism towards a more sustainable and ethical platform was underlined by a series of prominent media reports on the destructive effects of industrialized, mass package tourism, epitomized by, among other examples, the environmental degradation brought about by large-scale tourism development on the Spanish coastlines (Rice 1991). Inspired by the 1987 *Brundtland Report*, which arguably brought the idea of sustainable development into the political mainstream, and the subsequent 1992 Earth Summit in Rio de Janeiro, a plethora of NGOs and a minority of travel companies themselves began to develop a series of initiatives and travel products to start to address these issues. These developments, it was claimed, would advance the cause of sustainability and encourage tourists to see themselves as purveyors of a new ethical travel imperative (see Butcher 2003: 67–73). By the end of the twentieth century, such efforts had culminated in the publication of the UNWTO's *Global Code of Ethics for Tourism*, signalling the apparent consolidation and institutionalization of an ethical movement in tourism that had commenced several decades earlier.

In contrast to the idea of international tourism as a corrupting force and a form of 'neo-colonialism', which was prevalent throughout much of the 1960s and 1970s (see Turner and Ash 1975), these days it is rare to find a form of tourism that does not proclaim either its green or ethical credentials. The claim that 'tourism can be a vehicle for the common good of humankind' has increasingly achieved significant consensus within the industry and academia alike (Swain and Hall 2007: 99). However, there is considerable disagreement over the philosophical foundations of ethical behaviour in tourism and no agreed definition of ethical tourism. Claims regarding the moral foundations of travel are of course nothing new. However, as Smith and Duffy (2003: 54) observe, whereas participation in the Grand Tour was rather more to do with one's 'personal moral betterment', contemporary forms of ethical tourism lay claim to the potential for the advancement of social justice in the places that encourage ethical forms of tourism development. Hultsman (1995: 555) instructively notes how a 'just' form of tourism implies limits on the freedom of tourists in the interest of 'social conduct', thus implying the antithesis of Butcher's (2003) staunchly libertarian perspective. Typically, the consumers of such ethical tourisms are seen as discerning travellers who are more concerned than other tourists with the environmental effects of travel and keen to engage in more meaningful contact with host cultures. Already, by 1993, acclaimed pioneer in the field of sustainable tourism Jost Krippendorf suggested that the percentage of German tourists interested in purchasing 'ecological goods and services' was approximately 20 per cent (Krippendorf 1993: 56). While not all analysts are in agreement with the ethical claims of these seemingly distinctive forms of travel (see Butcher 2003; Wheeler 1993), since the early 1990s there has been a proliferation of travel products that lay claim to a 'higher moral purpose' (Butcher 2003: 28). While these ethical forms of tourism encompass various types of travel – eco-tourism, community tourism, responsible tourism, fair trade tourism, pro-poor tourism and, more recently, slow tourism and volunteer tourism – all lay claim to the potential for progressive change in regards to the creation of a new kind of concerned tourist and the stimulation of a range of positive socio-economic and environmental outcomes in the destination itself. In contrast to the 'mainstream' mass tourist who is merely interested in 'having fun in the sun, shopping duty-free, and cashing in frequent flyer miles' (Steves 2009: 12), the ethical tourist is said to be motivated by an 'ethic of care' for other peoples, cultures and environments. It is these tourists who have the potential to advance progressive changes in tourism practices and destinations, demonstrating their claims to cosmopolitan political ideals and notions of global citizenship (Plate 6.1). Tourism can thus no longer be considered an 'innocent pleasure' but rather as part of an emerging global civil society that seeks to harness travel to progressive ends (Lyons *et al.* 2012: 363).

Many have argued that globalization has stimulated increased cultural connectedness across borders, producing new understandings of nationality and citizenship (Nash 2000: 52–53). According to Germann Molz (2005), an increasingly globalized world has given rise to new kinds of mobile, deterritorialized conceptions of global citizenship. Liberated from the hierarchical bonds of duty to the nation-state, a

PLATE 6.1 A staff member at Awash Lodge, Ethiopia, with t-shirt emblazoned with the slogan: 'We tourism unite the world together'. Photo: R. Bianchi, April 2012.

global form of cosmopolitan citizenship is premised upon transnational, fluid and, ultimately, mobile social relations. In return for a series of rights, including 'the right to be mobile' and to consume commodities from across the world, global citizens are duty-bound 'to be informed about the state of the world, to live in an ethical and sustainable manner, to act in the interest of the global public' (Germann Molz 2005: 522). In addition, and in contrast to Calhoun (2002: 90–91), for whom cosmopolitanism is ultimately grounded in a Euro-centric worldview, Turner sees travel as a 'significant mode of attaining a cosmopolitan appreciation for other cultures' (cited in Germann Molz 2005: 521).

Following this line of argument, globalization and the expansion of global travel have stimulated a growing awareness among certain groups of tourists of the consequences of their movements and the consumption of fragile environments and non-industrialized cultures. This has of course been encouraged by the proliferation of codes of conduct and certification schemes, and the work of campaigning NGOs such as *Tourism Concern*, founded in the UK in 1989. The increasing support for 'sustainable tourism' across the tourism industries has also helped advance such environmental awareness among tourists and destinations alike. Influenced by numerous and widespread interventions by various actors, from NGOs to local grass-roots community activists across a number of destinations, certain forms of travel have contributed to a growing concern with defining the principles of responsible travel and what can best be described as the globalization of tourist ethics. The search for a common ethical ground between tourists and members of destination societies has nevertheless also brought with it tensions regarding the commensurability of universal citizenship rights and culturally sanctioned inequalities, such as those existing between the status of men and women in some societies (see Kennedy 2004). In this regard, Smith and Duffy (2003: 37) ask whether tourists have some sort of responsibility to understand and perhaps even form a critique of the 'morally problematic background' of certain places and cultures they visit.

The WTO (1980) *Manila Declaration* makes an explicit reference to the role of tourism in the development of one's 'civic responsibilities' (Article 22). In a recent interview, founder of the IIPT Louis D'Amore (2005) stated that tourists, particularly the young, represent not only peace ambassadors but also the first generation of 'global citizens'. While the tone of the charter reflects a rather anachronistic state-led benevolence that seems out of synch with today's fluid, globalized and individuated societies, it does invoke a civic republican discourse in which tourism and tourists can and indeed should become actively engaged in the creation of better societies, at home as well as through their travels. Although encompassing many different forms and organizations, ostensibly ethical forms of travel do in many ways reflect a cosmopolitan 'politics of morality' (Hirst and Thompson 1999: 263) that eschews either a statist or collective politics of emancipation in favour of an approach that combines individual ethical agency and lifestyle-driven consumption. The question remains: to what extent can new ethical forms of travel and tourism claim to be the vanguard of a global citizenship?

Accordingly, the participants in such forms of travel lay claim to not only being good tourists, but also committed global citizens. Steves (2009) proclaims the importance of travel to broaden one's personal, cultural and political horizons, but also to become better citizens in our daily lives. Germann Molz's (2005) discussion of the narratives of 'round-the-world' travellers supports this position. These travellers not only assert their right to mobility by virtue of having the right credentials for travel (in this case, US and Canadian passports), as well as for the most part comprising relatively affluent members of the middle classes, they nonetheless view their participation in global travel as part of acquiring the attributes of cosmopolitanism: openness, tolerance and cross-cultural understanding. The potential for travel to cultivate a cosmopolitan ethic and global citizenship can be advanced by the medium of the Internet. Various online travel fora, including *Drive Around the World*,[1] are frequently seen as a democratic medium through which travellers can communicate across physical, political and cultural boundaries, enacting a form of transnational civic engagement and fulfilling the promise of global citizenship (Germann Molz 2005: 525). Significantly, in the light of the strained relationship between tourism and the right to travel, brought about by terrorism and the securitization of travel, she further argues that travellers use such online fora to counteract negative images of their own country abroad and the demonization of other states by their own governments.

This then begs the question: which notions of global citizenship are constituted through participation in tourism and which kinds of ethical travel in particular are conducive to the advancement of such ideals? Global citizenship through travel can imply merely behaving as a responsible tourist, one who seeks genuine interaction with local culture while taking due care with the local environment and ensuring respect for local customs and norms of behaviour (McMillan 2004). In this regard ethical forms of tourism can be seen as a marked expression of cosmopolitanism. For example, this association is famously invoked by Mark Twain's pithy remark in *Innocents Abroad*: 'Travel is fatal to prejudice, bigotry, and narrow-mindedness' (1869: 650). More specifically, it may function as a means through which tourists exercise a global civic responsibility and moral commitment towards the people, places and cultures they visit, albeit one that is enacted through the market. In her preamble to the celebrated *Ethical Travel Guide*, produced by Tourism Concern, writer Polly Pattullo (2006: 13) goes even further, stating that 'globalization has also made us aware of our responsibilities as global citizens'. In her view, ethical travel constitutes the vanguard of a movement that has coalesced around a loose coalition of 'thoughtful travellers, campaigning NGOs, farsighted tour operators and radical organizers'. Through travel their actions are said to not only bear witness to the dark underbelly of globalization and the corporate exploitation of resources in poor countries, but to quite literally bring us together as human beings regardless of faith, ethnicity, politics and other barriers to cross-cultural understanding.

The desire to actively contribute to improving the well-being of the planet reflects a growing global consciousness brought about by the increasing awareness of trans-planetary risks and concern over the depletion of 'global public goods', particularly the ozone layer and the biosphere itself (Valencia Sáiz 2005: 164). In response, transnational advocacy coalitions have emerged beyond the narrow sphere of state–citizen relations, encouraging the formation of a 'new public sphere' (Morris-Suzuki 2000: 65). Although the politics of environmentalism encompass a number of different strands, from radical anti-systemic movements (e.g. Earth First) and global NGOs (e.g. Greenpeace and Friends of the Earth) to a more moderate green parliamentarianism in many European countries, green politics has played a significant role in extending notions of citizenship in two specific ways. First, environmental citizenship emphasizes an ethic of care towards nature, demanding a new paradigm of thinking about the relationship between the individual and the planet's natural environments. In this regard, it implies attributing status and indeed rights beyond the sphere of human relations altogether, to nature and the biosphere itself (Falk 1994; Steward 1991). Second, the scale and scope of environmental risks *transcend* national borders thus highlighting the inadequacy of existing national policy frameworks and challenging statist models of citizenship (Valencia Sáiz 2005). Although a number of transnational and multi-level institutional responses to environmental threats have worked towards building strategies for a sustainable future, epitomized in the *Brundtland Report* and subsequent global environmental strategies to address climate change (e.g. the Kyoto Protocol), the growth of a grass-roots environmental politics indicates the inadequacy of market-based and statist solutions alone. This underlines a paradigm shift towards new conceptions of citizenship based on the agency of global civil society, an issue to which we return below. Indeed, Urry (2000: 186) suggests that environmentalists derive their sense of identity and citizenship from bearing witness to the destruction of nature on behalf of humanity as a whole, as opposed to membership of any given state.

The emergence of greener forms of tourism in the 1980s gave rise to a new dimension in global environmental politics, as tourists began to seek out pristine environments and indigenous cultures in a range of 'Third World' countries (Mowforth and Munt 2009: 154). There is some evidence to suggest that citizens in general and tourists in particular are becoming increasingly concerned with the state of the environment, as well as the impact their travel choices and behaviour has on particular ecosystems. In 2011, for instance, 93 per cent of readers of the upmarket *Condé Nast Traveller* magazine stated that travel companies should be responsible for protecting the environment. The 2010 TUI Travel Sustainability Survey listed the following issues in order of their importance to tourists: pollution (71 per cent), biodiversity and animal protection (64 per cent), climate change and carbon emissions (63 per cent), fair trade and labour standards (62 per cent), and social and community issues (61 per cent) (Center for Responsible Travel 2013). However, being an 'eco-conscious' traveller does not automatically equate with a form of environmental citizenship. As this role often implies someone with an above-average annual income, it undermines a sense of citizenship predicated on reducing inequalities of wealth and power. This contradiction is eloquently summarized by Chip Ward, the caretaker of a tourist lodge and environmental activist near Utah's Great Basin Desert:

> I was tired of answering enthusiastic questions from guests over dinner about the 'beautiful' geology and ecology they had just encountered on hikes and jeep tours, only to discover later how heavily invested they were in resort condo developments, or the sale of strip-mining machinery, or drilling for oil and gas, or on and on.
>
> *(Ward 1999: 34)*

There are many examples of where green politics and discourses of environmental citizenship are closely aligned with tourism. However, support for environmentally sustainable forms of travel encompasses a broad and diverse spectrum of tourists and organizations alike. Indeed, eco-tourism, once seen as the forerunner of new and more responsible forms of travel designed to promote local economic development and conservation, has increasingly come under attack for opening up nature to capital accumulation and 'high-end' luxury eco-tourism (Duffy 2002). Nevertheless, the proliferation of self-conscious forms of ethical travel and responsible travel providers reflects wider socio-political transformations within post-industrial capitalist societies that are less structured by the traditional politics of

left and right. Increasingly, argues sociologist Anthony Giddens (1990, 1991), individuals are eschewing formal channels of political agency and collective forms of
emancipatory politics in favour of a more reflexive 'politics of individual lifestyle'
(Nash 2000: 67). Accordingly, while there is an almost universal acceptance of capitalism and market economics among all but the most radicalized sectors of society,
individuals increasingly look to affirm progressive lifestyle choices by making ethical consumption choices.

With the aid of ethical travel guides, certification schemes, eco-labels, NGOs,
charities and travel companies, consumers are keen to contribute to the places
they visit as tourists and can increasingly do so through careful selection of the
travel company, type of holiday and other travel products. Of the various new
forms of ethical travel that lay claim to advancing a higher moral agenda, volunteer tourism or volun-tourism, whereby tourists participate in a range of conservation and development projects in poor countries, is one form of altruistic travel
that is particularly associated with the attributes of global citizenship (see Butcher
and Smith 2010; Lyons *et al.* 2012). Although sharing certain traits with ethical
travel, volunteer tourism is distinguishable from other forms of alternative travel
by the 'altruistic desire to volunteer' (Mustonen 2005: 165). It also overlaps with
earlier government-sponsored volunteering programmes such as Voluntary Service
Overseas in the UK, and of course the US Peace Corps, established in 1961, whose
purpose is 'to serve their country in the cause of peace by living and working in
developing countries' (Peace Corps 2013).

Participants arguably share a common distaste for the commoditization of tourism and a desire to contribute to the host communities through their participation in
a range of conservation, educational and other projects designed to reduce poverty
and improve self-reliance. Significantly, volunteering aims to not only make a positive contribution to local livelihoods, but also to foster a more tolerant and socially
inclusive global outlook among the volunteers themselves (Wearing 2001).

Volunteer tourism is associated with the growing phenomenon of 'gap year',
tourism, whereby young Western tourists who are often in transition between
school and further study take a year off to travel overseas and volunteer on a range
of philanthropic projects in poor countries. Gap year travel is no longer the preserve of traditional not-for-profit organizations such as Voluntary Service Overseas
and Raleigh International, but has now become a major industry with a range of
commercial companies, including STA Travel, involved in selling gap year holidays.
In the UK and Australia, where gap year travel is firmly established, it is seen as a
means of broadening one's horizons as well as potentially contributing to a more
ethical approach to one's own society and indeed business (Simpson 2004). In this
regard volunteer tourism and gap year travel lay claim to developing a sense of cosmopolitanism among participants, providing a pathway towards global citizenship.
Nevertheless, campaigning organizations such as Tourism Concern have raised a
number of concerns regarding the genuine benefits provided by the proliferation of
volunteer tourism schemes and companies to local communities in poor countries,
while others have accused them of reinforcing a paternalism or even neo-colonial

relationship between the volunteer tourists and receiving community (see Barkham 2006). Although the accusation of neo-colonialism that has been levelled at new forms of ethical travel is perhaps exaggerated, there is little doubt that participation in volunteer tourism or gap year travel is more often than not motivated by improving one's CV and marketability in the fiercely competitive labour market of neoliberal capitalism (Halpenny and Caissie 2003). Accordingly, from this perspective, it has less to do with a progressive form of politics or development intervention, and much less a form of global citizenship. The following extract from the website of the Year Out Group, an association of leading gap year organizations in the UK, appears to confirm this view: 'City firms such as Deloittes and Slaughter & May welcome applications from graduates who have a wide range of experiences, including a productive gap year' (Year Out Group n.d.).

According to Butcher and Smith (2010: 34), the claim that volunteer tourism amounts to a more progressive and enlightened form of travel is 'symptomatic of a degradation of the discourse of development', as well as a 'retreat from the social understanding of global inequalities and the poverty lived by so many in the developing world'. If the discourses of cosmopolitanism and global citizenship associated with gap year travel and volunteer tourism serve to attribute an explicit moral purpose to what is little more than a form of niche travel, what scope is there then for tourism to lay claim to being an avenue through which to build more robust forms and understandings of global citizenship? Despite claims that volunteer tourism may provide a platform for decommodified exchanges between tourists and other stakeholders, as well as bring about a more egalitarian form of exchange between tourists and host communities, many remain circumspect with regard to its contribution to local societies, let alone global citizenship.

Volunteer tourism, argues McGehee (2012), much like tourism as a whole, may in fact reflect and reinforce the hierarchy of power/knowledge between predominantly Anglo-European volunteers and non-Western host communities. In this regard, volunteer tourism can also be interpreted as a manifestation of the wider asymmetries of mobility in the global order. Increasingly, the proliferation of volunteer tourism programmes organized by profit-making commercial organizations, including corporate giants TUI, has further undermined any association that might exist between volunteer tourism and global citizenship (Lyons et al. 2012; Tomazos and Cooper 2012). Ultimately, claim Dalwai and Donegan (2012: 21), volunteer tourism is shaped by the unequal structures of racism and global capitalism, which determine 'access to resources, travel possibilities and the direction of volunteer tourist traffic from the global North to the global South'. Equally, writers such as Gordon (2006: 20) are convinced that such new ethical forms of travel, whether volunteer tourism or eco-tourism, amount to little more than a means of acquiring cultural capital and a display of conspicuous consumption.

Although one could perhaps be forgiven for dismissing such forms of travel as an expression of post-ideological consumerism or lifestyle politics, ethically motivated travel cannot be simply interpreted as a selfish act of individual self-gratification and fulfilment. Whether or not ethical forms of tourism result in robust, long-term socio-economic or political transformation in the host societies and the betterment of the lives of local residents, they can stimulate a sense of being part of a globalized fellowship of like-minded individuals, many of whom may be members of the same international charities and NGOs. However, despite the fact that numerous surveys carried out by sectors of the tourism industry (e.g. Association of British Travel Agents), charities (e.g. Tearfund) and green tourism advocacy organizations (e.g. Center for Responsible Travel 2013) testify to tourists being genuinely concerned how tourism and their own behaviour impact upon the societies they visit (Pattullo 2006: 32–33), such responses tell us little about the rights and duties of tourists as global citizens nor the material foundations of such cosmopolitan forms of tourist citizenship.

Ethical tourism in many ways epitomizes the transition to a world increasingly configured around a new lifestyle politics through which a sense of cosmopolitanism and global citizenship can be derived from consuming ethical travel products and experiences. In her proclamation of ethical tourism as a nascent 'global consumer movement', Pattullo (2006: 5) unwittingly perhaps illustrates one of the principal contradictions that lie at the heart of the idea that ethical travel implies a more enlightened form of travel and passport to global citizenship. ETOA (European Tour Operators Association) director Tom Jenkins argues that the tourism industry will only adopt sustainable practices, defined simply as 'environmentally sound' holidays, if the consumer demands it (McGrath 2004). This view underlines a predominantly market-led discourse of consumer citizenship whereby progressive change can be brought about by consumers making ethical consumption choices. However, such choices by consumers may take place in the absence of attempts to tackle underlying structural inequalities of trade and development, which leads us to question the progressive credentials of so-called ethical tourism altogether. In addition, this also of course assumes an ability to afford certain types of ethical holidays, many of which are priced at a premium.

The business of ethical tourism and corporate citizenship

There is a logical step from ethical travel consumption to the issue of whether businesses themselves can be considered as responsible corporate citizens. In this regard, it is felt that corporations should balance their freedom to trade and responsibility to shareholders with a set of wider social and environmental obligations to the communities in which they operate (at home and abroad), and thus consider the 'wider public good' (Sklair 2001: 171). Often corporations are spurred into action only as a response to accusations of corporate malfeasance from activists. In 1998, when the global energy giant Shell published a report outlining its commitment to a range of core ethical principles, it was widely believed that this move was galvanized by the execution of nine human rights activists in the Niger Delta by the Nigerian government in 1995,[2] as well as the campaign against the dumping of the Brent Spar oil platform in the North Sea, halted by Greenpeace activists in that same year (Sklair 2001: 184–191).

Some time before corporate social responsibility became a relatively common business practice, Henderson (1968) posed the question: should corporations do more than seek to maximize profits, and develop a responsibility to society and the environment? In her article she cites the view of an economist as an example of the conventional wisdom at the time: 'The only responsibility of corporations is to make profits, thus contributing to a prosperous economic system' (Hacker 1963, cited in Henderson 1968: 80).

Corporate citizenship can take any number of forms, ranging from conspicuous acts of charity to the incorporation of environmentally and socially responsible principles across all areas of their business operations. Notably, the Caux Principles, established in 1986 as an international network of businesses working to promote 'moral capitalism', emphasize that the first purpose of business should be to society and that profit is the reward for serving society with integrity. On this basis, the tourism industry should fundamentally serve the interests of society and the wider environment and oppose any measures or developments that have potentially negligent outcomes. Where tourism is concerned, recognition of the pressing need to incorporate the principles of corporate social and environmental responsibility gathered momentum in the wake of the campaign by NGOs against child sex tourism in Asia in the late 1980s.[3] The arrest of a number of offenders in South-East Asia was later followed by a series of declarations and measures to combat the pervasive practice of child sex tourism, including the 1995 WTO *Statement on the Prevention of Organised Sex Tourism* and more recently, the 2006 *Child Protection Code* promulgated by a range of leading tourism industry representatives (De Man 2013). More importantly, campaigners succeeded in bringing about changes in national laws in the sending countries, including the UK and Switzerland, to enable tourists and travel companies to be prosecuted for participating in, procuring or encouraging sex tourism in receiving countries (see Keefe and Wheat 1998).

However, despite the fact that tourism has often come under scathing attack due to myriad adverse economic, environmental and socio-cultural consequences attributed to it (see Mowforth and Munt 2009), there are numerous examples where tour companies themselves have sought to boycott reckless and irresponsible forms of tourism development that may damage ecosystems or impose too great a burden on local societies. For example, in 2006 a group of seven tour operators successfully lobbied the Zambian government to halt plans to develop luxury tourism facilities in close proximity to Victoria Falls (Marks 2006/7: 6). In addition, numerous corporate and environmental responsibility reports and charters produced by global tourism businesses do in fact seek to demonstrate a lasting commitment to the communities affected by tourism. Perhaps one of the most proactive in this regard is the Swiss-based tour operator Kuoni Travel, which, in its Code of Conduct, stakes its claim to being the 'most admired leisure travel company' in the world, but also possesses a 'reputation for professionalism, integrity and fairness in its dealings with all its stakeholders' (Kuoni 2011: 3).

The commitment to sustainability and corporate social responsibility would now appear to be widespread across the tourism industries. Moreover, it is no longer restricted to specialized niche tour operators represented in the UK, for instance, by the Association of Independent Tour Operators (AITO) (Mowforth and Munt 2009: 188–193). TUI Travel, the world's largest tour operator, with an annual turnover of £15 billion, outlined its approach to the wider environment in its recent Sustainability Holiday Plan (2012–2014). The report indicates TUI's commitment to 'responsible leadership in the travel sector', the environment and the planet (through reducing carbon emissions), local communities (through charitable work and support for community projects), businesses with whom it trades, and of course its customers (TUI Travel 2012). TUI has also taken a leading role in the Global Sustainable Tourism Council (GSTC), which is working towards the establishment of a universal set of global sustainable tourism criteria, and is one of the first companies to commit to working with GSTC-recognized standard businesses. In fact, there is practically no area of its business untouched by a stated commitment to what can best be described as global corporate responsibility and citizenship.

It often makes 'good business sense' for tourism companies to take account of the potentially adverse consequences of their activities on the environment and local communities (Forsyth 1997: 271). However, critics have argued that the newfound enthusiasm for voluntary self-regulation[4] and corporate citizenship was largely based on an attempt to pre-empt further and tougher government regulation of business activities (Finger and Kilcoyne 1997). This view is supported by Noel Josephides (1994), managing director of UK tour operator Sunvil Holidays, and a pioneer in challenging the UK tourism industry to adopt tougher standards on sustainability in tourism. However, the responsible credentials of major tourism organizations are sometimes regarded with suspicion as a result of their actions elsewhere. This occurred in the case of ABTA (Association of British Travel Agents), which stresses its need 'to be seen to be a good citizen' where the destination is concerned (Hammond 2004: 16). However, in 2002 ABTA reportedly threatened to withdraw its annual convention from Mallorca in response to the imposition of the Balearic eco-tax, on the grounds that it would deter visitors from the island – mistakenly, as it happened. This was in spite of the fact that ABTA's own research indicated that a majority of tourists would be willing to pay more for their holidays if they were certain it would contribute to better working conditions and environmental practice in the tourism industry (Kalisch 2002). Worse still, the president of the renowned Sol Meliá hotel group, which like many others trumpets its corporate social responsibility credentials, referred to the eco-tax as an 'atrocity' (Bungay 1999b). More recently, ABTA has once again voiced its opposition to the imposition of environmental taxes in the Balearic Islands, this time in relation to a levy on car hire that was announced in November 2012. While ABTA argued that 'Taxing tourists does more harm than good in the long term', without clearly specifying how, Spain's Minister of Tourism also denounced the tax as 'unfair' (I. Taylor 2013).

Ultimately, as Josephides (1994) clearly states, voluntary self-regulation is non-binding and fails to adequately deal with many of the problems that are exacerbated by the competitive structure of the global tourism industries. While praiseworthy, corporate social and environmental responsibility initiatives do not constrain the freedom of companies to pursue profits. Power ultimately resides with corporate shareholders whose overriding concern is with profitability. There is little doubt that there has been a substantive shift in the way in which many of the major corporate players in the tourism industry envisage the relationship of their business to both society and nature. However, these endeavours constitute neither a radical critique of consumption nor do they alter the fundamental imbalance between the position of the world's privileged citizens who have the right and freedom to travel, and the position of those low-income groups in poor states who have little development rights and/or the 'wrong' credentials for travel. Specifically, the corporate shift towards social responsibility ignores the ways in which the vastly unequal distribution of wealth and power, which continues to underpin the working of the global tourism industries and shape the asymmetrical patterns of cross-border mobility, could be effectively challenged and overturned.

Citizenship and social movements

The end of the Cold War culminated in the dramatic events in Berlin on the evening of 9 November 1989, as the citizens of East Berlin broke through the concrete barrier that had divided them from their Western counterparts for nearly three decades. This highly symbolic moment signalled a fundamental shift in the coordinates of popular struggle. In many ways it also marked a revival of interest in notions of citizenship and the transformative potential of civil society (Mayo 2006). The citizens of former Communist states in the East sought to 'build a culture of citizens instead of comrades' (van Steenbergen 1994: 141), while also claiming new rights to the freedom of movement and travel from which they had long been excluded. At the same time a new momentum was set in motion bringing like-minded citizens together across borders to contest the hubris of Western analysts, who proclaimed the triumph of capitalist free markets and liberal democracy as the Communist bloc began to disintegrate (see Fukuyama 1989).

Despite the fact that the history of popular struggle can be traced back to the nineteenth-century anti-slavery movement and the trade union movement, and the campaign for women's suffrage at the turn of the twentieth century, the origins of contemporary social movements lie more specifically in the anti-systemic movements of the 1960s and 1970s. These include urban community organizations, youth groups, civil rights, women's and gay rights movements, as well as the campaign for peace and nuclear disarmament, and last but not least, the environmental movement. Although diverse and often characterized by a 'vague sense of collective purpose', these early oppositional movements were united in their hostility towards 'established authority and white middle-class lifestyles' and, more specifically, the growing corporate takeover of democratic politics in advanced industrial societies (Boggs 1986: 38). Moreover, social movements, whether in terms of dealing with issues concerning women's rights or environmental degradation, evolved to raise serious concerns over the definition and advancement of citizenship rights (Turner 1986).

The expansion of popular struggle during the twilight years of the Cold War in the 1980s, demonstrated most poignantly by the decade-long protest by the women's peace movement against nuclear missile deployment at Greenham Common in the UK, marked an important shift in the nature of contentious politics and the realignment of popular struggle along increasingly differentiated and transnational axes (Tarrow 2005). Boggs (1986: 4) argues that such movements were instrumental in the development of a democratic and egalitarian politics, premised upon 'a new paradigm of oppositional discourse' no longer grounded in the values and discourses of the labour movement. This point is also relevant for understanding different forms of contestation that have arisen in the context of tourism, many of which have either taken place or are concerned with issues that affect the less industrialized states on the European periphery and Mediterranean, as well as the 'Third World', where the labour movement has traditionally been weak, fragmented or, indeed, altogether absent.

The emergence of a radicalized transnational politics of resistance to neoliberal globalization arguably came of age on 1 January 1994 in the southern Mexican state of Chiapas, marked by the Zapatista uprising against the imposition of the North American Free Trade Agreement (NAFTA). This protest was spearheaded by the Zapatista National Liberation Army (EZLN), a peasant army rooted in a long history of indigenous struggles against colonialism, genocide and oppression by the Mexican state and, more recently, resistance to US support for South American dictatorships (see Castells 1997: 72–83). However, what made this movement particularly noteworthy was the manner in which it provided the first coordinated focus of resistance to neoliberal economics by a diverse alliance of groups, encompassing concerns relating to the environment, democracy, human rights, indigenous rights and women's rights (Marchand 2005: 112). Henceforth, the so-called 'anti-globalization' movement was born whose defining moment arguably came at the World Trade Organization summit in Seattle on 30 November 1999. On this day around 50,000 activists from around the world, including 'Third World' peasant farmers, trade unions, environmentalists and human rights groups, converged on the summit and brought the talks to a halt despite violent police repression (St. Clair 1999). The now infamous 'Battle of Seattle' was followed by a series of regular protests at global trade summits and set in motion the momentum for the creation of the Word Social Forum (WSF), inaugurated at Porto Alegre in Brazil in April 2001. The WSF subsequently became a rallying point for a loose, transnational network of social movements, including NGOs, trade unions, church groups and civil society groups, to formulate progressive alternatives to global capitalism (Sader 2002).[5] Recent gatherings have also attracted a number of activist organizations involved in tourism. At the 2009 WSF meeting at Belém do Pará in Brazil, a collection of civil society groups issued a statement calling upon 'all citizens of the world' to contribute to bringing about just, sustainable, community-based forms of tourism, 'through their organizations and as conscious consumers' (Tourism Concern 2009).

While the capacity of the nation-state to shape global politics and economic affairs has increasingly been undermined by global movements of capital and the actions of transnational corporations, there is little question that globalization has enlarged the scope of democratic activism and provided a platform for movements to 'enact a new type of politics' (Isin and Wood 1999: 156). New social movements and transnational advocacy groups have therefore sought to resist the depoliticization and marketization of mainstream politics. Accordingly, through their actions they seek to contribute to a revitalized conception of the public sphere, and to pave the way for the development of new ideas of citizenship that both challenge and transcend the nation-state. Some analysts have thus interpreted the emergence of these transnational social movements and advocacy networks as contributing to the emergence of a 'global civil society' through which a 'new class of global citizenship' has begun to take shape (Sader 2002: 93).

As states have become increasingly transnationalized, notions of citizenship have been extended beyond the confines of the nation-state, most notably in the case of attempts by the European Union to construct a sense of pan-European identity and citizenship, as discussed in Chapter 4. Globalization has also opened up new spaces of contestation and demands for citizenship through what Beck (2005: 6) refers to as the 'counter-power of global civil society'. Beck (2005: 8) tellingly refers to the cosmopolitan orientation exhibited by such movements in so far as they reflect the 'new humanism of civil society', which has supplanted the labour movement in its ability to call capital to account and challenge the actions of transnational corporations. Moreover, transnational social movements imply a loose coalition of activists encompassing both producers, such as organized labour and farmers, as well as consumer groups and other concerned groups of citizens involved in the environmental movement and, indeed, tourism justice movements. At risk of oversimplifying the diversity of earlier forms of political agency, these movements are concerned neither with the political objectives of a particular class, that is, the working class, nor with taking over the reins of power:

> Most people in these movements are not against trade or industrial development. What they are fighting for is the right of local communities to have a say in how their resources are used, to make sure that the people who live on the land benefit directly from its development.
>
> *(Klein 2001: 88)*

In contrast to many popular struggles, however, these movements are motivated by their belief in people's rights to the 'commons' (see Ecologist 1995). In this sense, contemporary social movements are involved in struggles that imply a transformation in the very meaning of citizenship, towards one that challenges concentrations of state and/or corporate power. Furthermore, these struggles have gained impetus in the context of the myriad exclusions imposed on the entitlements to citizenship in the United States and various European states since 9/11, and the corporate assault on the public sphere driven through by neoliberal policies (Susser 2006: 216–217). These social movements nevertheless encompass a wide variety of ideological positions and organizational forms, marked by the contrast between radical anti-systemic movements and institutionalized NGOs (see Mayo 2006: 3–4). Arguably, however, with the exception of right-wing populist and religious nationalist organizations, such as those in the United States (see Castells 1997: 96) – they are for the most part united in their opposition to the 'privatization of everyday life, and the transformation of every activity and value into a commodity' (Klein 2001: 82). Importantly, they do not seek to replace one form of authority with another, nor do they have the means to do so. Rather, as Beck (2005: 239) asserts, they seek to highlight the inner contradictions of the system and to delegitimize both state and corporate actors through 'advocatory strategies of public awareness'.

As we shall see in the following section, the rise of new social movements has emboldened civil society opposition to certain forms of tourism development. Many of these new social movements are also indicative of 'a shift in emphasis from struggles over material resources and physical security towards conflicts over culture, meaning and identity' (Morris-Suzuki 2000: 67). Although one must take care not to exaggerate the declining significance of class-based struggles over the distribution of surpluses in the workplace (see Callinicos 1989: 127), it is fair to say that new social movements are as much concerned with the politics of cultural contestation and recognition as they are with struggles over the material conditions of life. Indeed, the two are often deeply intertwined. Although in Scott's (1990) view, the principal aim of new social movements is to bring about a change in values and develop alternative lifestyles, where indigenous demands for cultural recognition are concerned, these forms of social mobilization 'from below' imply much more than questions of lifestyle politics. Rather, they involve struggles over the scope and application of citizenship rights within and beyond the state.

A plethora of social movements and global advocacy NGOs have stepped into the vacuum left by the retreat of the state from many areas of politics and the concomitant rise of individual rights-based activism in Western, neoliberal societies (Harvey 2006: 51). Governments and corporations are increasingly challenged by a plethora of civil society and consumer groups as the power of collective bargaining by trade unions on behalf of workers continues to wane. The counter-power of civil society to which Beck (2005: 6–7) refers, draws its strength from an authoritative discourse of human rights as well as the ability of consumers themselves to exercise influence on corporate activities through discriminatory consumption and consumer boycotts of particular firms that breach certain environmental or other ethical standards. Most notably, this occurred in the campaign by Greenpeace in 1995 to stop the dumping of the Brent Spar oil platform in the North Sea (Lofstedt and Renn 1997). Equally, there have been periodic boycotts against certain tourism destinations (e.g. Bali, Burma, China (Tibet), Turkey) where close links between human rights abuses and tourism have been uncovered, or simply as a means of bringing pressure to bear on the host governments to address any number of wider concerns regarding the nature of their rule (see Hitchcock 1999). Going on strike implies the loss of pay and the risk of redundancy, and potentially also the threat of physical violence for the workers involved. In contrast, in a world saturated by consumerism, where global corporations are keen to protect their brand reputation, 'unethical' firms are particularly vulnerable to the scrutiny of activist-consumers. As Beck (2005: 7) states: 'not even all-powerful global corporations can make their consumers redundant'. Equally, multinational corporations may be exposed to public scrutiny from consumers, the media and civil society organizations, to the extent that global business actors increasingly take their responsibilities to consumers and citizens alike, seriously.

Notwithstanding the many schisms that often divide relatively well-financed global NGOs based in the rich 'North' from their counterparts and other local grass-roots activists in developing countries, the growth of transnational activist coalitions has arguably fostered new solidarities among a globally dispersed network of like-minded citizens. Thanks to the creative use of communications technologies, new social movements are able to mobilize public opinion across borders and engage in multiple institutional contexts in ways unimaginable a generation ago. Although there is a danger of exaggerating the democratizing potential of the Internet and new digital media (see Morozov 2011), there is ample evidence to suggest that such technologies have helped to facilitate new forms of political mobilization and transnational advocacy, stitching together both offline and online social movements at different scales (Castells 2012: 220–221). The place-bound struggles of impoverished peasant and indigenous communities, which may have previously gone unnoticed, are, thanks to the mobilizing potential of the Internet and social media, increasingly conjoined with a broader politics of mobilization against predatory corporations and neoliberal globalization (Fraser 2005: 71–72).

While there are certainly many examples of NGO and grass-roots protests against the enclosure and commodification of resources for tourism, the relationship between new social movements and tourism is one that has, with notable exceptions, been largely ignored in the literature (see Botterill 1991; McGehee 2002). If considered at all, this relationship tends to be conceptually encompassed within the framework of tourism's impact on host communities and the dichotomy of the empowered tourist versus the disempowered host. However, the varying forms of civil society mobilization against tourism are more complex and cannot be simply understood as 'anti-tourism' movements. Not only does opposition to tourism encompass a variety of actors and discourses, grass-roots resistance to tourism and certain forms of justice tourism may succeed, whether intentionally or not, in contesting and redefining citizenship rights as well as extending these rights to encompass new and more inclusive interpretations.

Tourism, civil society and citizenship: sustainability, justice and reconciliation

The damaging consequences of tourism development have been somewhat overshadowed by the corporate misdemeanours and the polluting side effects of heavy industries in the 'Third World', such as the Union Carbide chemical disaster at Bhopal in India in 1983 (see Sklair 2001: 182–183). Yet, in some parts of the world at this time, tourism itself began to take centre stage as both the target of citizens' protest as well as becoming mobilized in the context of advancing the cause of sustainability and social justice. As international tourism began to consolidate itself within the major capital cities and coastal resorts of various 'Third World' societies in the 1980s, cracks began to appear in the broad consensus regarding tourism's contribution to the economic prosperity of such societies, if not at government level then within the broader arena of civil society. Early critiques of international tourism were inspired by a combination of ecumenism and anti-colonial ideologies, casting tourism in the role of an exploitative tool of Western hegemony. One such critic, Koson Srisang, a former executive director of the Ecumenical Coalition on Third World Tourism (ECTWT), now the Ecumenical Coalition on Tourism (ECOT), a church-based civil society network founded in Bangkok in 1982, forcefully stated that:

> In short, tourism, especially Third World tourism, as it is practised today, does not benefit the majority of people. Instead, it exploits them, pollutes the environment, destroys the ecosystem, bastardises the culture, robs people of traditional values and ways of life and subjugates women and children in the abject slavery of prostitution. In other words, tourism epitomises the present unjust world economic order where the few who control the wealth and power, dictate the terms. As such, tourism is little different from colonialism.
>
> *(Srisang 1992: 3)*

Regardless of this highly critical view of tourism, many newly independent 'Third World' states enthusiastically embraced international tourism as a means of state-managed economic development and modernization, as they sought to consolidate the gains of national self-determination. Gleaming new hotels, built by the state or with international financial assistance, began to sprout in a variety of downtown areas in 'Third World' capital cities, including Nairobi, Addis Ababa and Tunis. These temples of a new cosmopolitan modernism welcomed expatriate businessmen, members of the former colonial 'settler class' and the new African elites, who were able to mix as relative equals for the first time.

However, early critics of 'Third World' tourism development emphasized that international tourism reinforced inequalities between citizens of the sending countries and those living in the destinations, and thus did little to improve people's livelihoods (see Bugnicourt 1977; Pérez 1980). In addition, others have accused tourism of marginalizing indigenous groups, who were themselves disenfranchised citizens within the newly independent states, while simultaneously exploiting their culture for economic gain, as in the case of the Maasai in Kenya (Bruner and Kirshenblatt-Gimblett 1994). Hence, tourism expressed a rather unusual paradox: it made manifest accumulated citizenship gains of Western tourists for whom travel was fast becoming an unquestioned right, underpinned by the right to paid holidays and rising disposable incomes, while proving only partially able to advance the benefits of social and economic citizenship in the periphery. At worst, it served to exacerbate the material inequalities between developed and developing nations, as well as reinforce differentiated access to the newly-acquired rights of citizenship between post-colonial elites and the various marginal indigenous groups within 'Third World' states, most notably in East Africa (see Abbink 2000; Sindiga 1996; Turton 1987). While the expansion of international tourism in sub-Saharan Africa partially integrated many tribal peoples into the formal capitalist economy, they were often portrayed as 'noble savages' living in a 'pristine' state of nature, seemingly untouched by modernity (see Abbink 2000; Bruner and Kirshenblatt-Gimblett 1994). Such patterns of exploitation are not of course restricted to non-industrialized societies. As Saarinen's (1999) research on the indigenous Sami communities of northern Finland demonstrates, indigenous peoples on the periphery of Europe have also struggled to simultaneously challenge the 'exoticization' of their cultural practices and claim their rights to benefit economically from tourism.

Despite, or rather, perhaps as a result of, the demonstrable advances associated with decolonization – not least the emancipation of hitherto colonized peoples who could now have a say in the economic destiny of their incipient nations – members of the radicalized 'Third World' intelligentsia and others began to challenge Western discourses of tourism and economic modernization. Accordingly, tourism increasingly became seen as an integral cog in an unjust world economic order and symbolic of a corrupt 'Western' morality (see Lea 1993). By the late 1970s and early 1980s growing disquiet among 'Third World' intellectuals and ecumenical organizations over the environmentally and culturally damaging effect of tourism in 'Third World' destinations prompted the establishment of a number of civil society activist groups in the global 'South' as well as in Europe (see Lea 1993). Curiously, although Thailand was one of the first major countries within which popular resistance to tourism was to emerge, it had 'no colonial past from which to escape' (Elliott 1983: 390). Moreover, according to Elliott, outright rejection was often muted due to the deferential structure of Thai society. Nevertheless, resistance to sex tourism as well as the enclosure of coastlines and damage to ecosystems resulting from the construction of large-scale tourism facilities soon began to spread from Asia throughout a global network of churches into the tourism-sending countries themselves (De Man 2013).

By the early 1980s, the ECTWT had spawned an established network of development aid agencies, churches and solidarity groups throughout Europe (e.g. *Third World Tourism Ecumenical European Net*), as well as North America and Japan, which have been actively engaged in campaigns to raise awareness of the effects of tourism on people of the 'Third World' from within the context of unequal 'North–South' relationships (TEN 1984). In India and Goa, *Equations* (founded in 1985) adopted a rather more radical stance towards tourism, driven by hostility to state corruption and the opening up of India to global markets through trade liberalization. At around the same time a growing number of citizens in the rich world, who had witnessed at first hand the injustices of tourism in the 'Third World', began to organize and raise awareness of these issues in their home countries. Initially their focus was on working with schools and colleges to educate citizens in the generating countries about the detrimental aspects of tourism (Stancliffe and Barnett 2010). Significantly, despite the presence of a range of committed development organizations working on behalf of the poor and dispossessed in places such as East Africa, few of them at the time recognized that the source of their impoverishment lay partly or wholly with tourism (Barnett 2008: 998).

A dispersed yet loosely integrated global network of grass-roots activists and advocacy NGOs works to inform and mobilize civil society across borders. They seek not to reject tourism altogether, although this is not unheard of (see Muse 2011), but rather to assert claims to a range of existing and new citizenship rights that have been denied or put in doubt as part of the dominant discourses and practices of tourism development. According to its former director, Tourism Concern explicitly set out to shine a light on the 'underbelly of tourism' as well as to create a platform for those marginalized and displaced by tourism to be heard (Barnett 2008: 995–996). Founded in 1988, it quickly evolved from a small fledgling organization comprising a few committed activists and scholars, to a globally networked campaigning NGO with 450 donors, 200 friends and 9,000 supporters (Watson 2013), known worldwide for its action on a range of issues under the umbrella of ethical and fair trade tourism.

Through its various campaigns Tourism Concern works as part of a global network of NGOs and activists, seeking to build solidarity with communities adversely affected by and marginalized by tourism. It appeals to an alternative set of values (based on 'sustainability', 'fairness' and 'justice' rather than 'profit', 'growth' and 'competitiveness'), in order to bring about change across the global tourism industries through challenging dominant thinking and practices. Organizations such as ECOT, Equations, Tourism Concern and TEN have brought together a diverse configuration of concerned citizens and tourists, linking up popular struggles against the damaging effects of tourism in the 'Third World' with a global network of activists in rich economies, raising awareness and campaigning on a range of issues. These encompass the negative environmental and socio-cultural impacts of tourism, to a broad spectrum of issues encompassed under the mantle of human rights, including child sex tourism and prostitution, women's rights, displacement, working conditions and water rights.

As the momentum of civil society and NGO advocacy grew, activists increasingly focused on the application of universal human rights[6] in a challenge to the abuses of state and/or corporate power. Where previously the emphasis of international charters relating to tourism had emphasized the rights of tourists to rest, leisure and the freedom to travel, increasingly the UNWTO's *Global Code of Ethics*, among numerous other charters, sought to balance the rights of tourists with those affected by tourism through explicit reference to the promotion of human rights (Smith and Duffy 2003: 74). Concern over the distribution of material resources, development rights, cultural preservation and cultural autonomy within host societies has accentuated this discursive shift. The mobilization and the attempted application of such rights came to the fore in the context of campaigns in the mid-1990s against the displacement of Maasai and Samburu pastoralists from their lands in East Africa, as well as the campaign to boycott travel to Burma as a result of human rights abuses being perpetrated by the Burmese military regime (Barnett 2008).

Resistance to tourism: environmental and cultural citizenships

One of the principal characteristics of the recent wave of new social movements is the manner in which they mobilize civil society and in so doing bring together a range of intertwined citizenship issues linked, for example, to the rights of nature, social justice and cultural rights. In this sense, the locus of oppositional struggle has to some extent moved out of the workplace and into the 'capillaries of the lived world' (Morris-Suzuki 2000: 84). As stated earlier, civil society protest movements encompass everything from small localized groups of disaffected activists to large global advocacy NGOs, campaigning on a range of different albeit often inter-related issues. Although these movements display significant differences in terms of their origin and their social make-up, new social movements and grass-roots protests, particularly those originating among indigenous communities in non-industrialized societies, often mobilize in defence of certain key rights that encom-pass struggles related to land rights, livelihoods and cultural identities. These rights have variously been threatened by a range of adversaries in the form of repressive or undemocratic states, often acting in collusion with corporate capitalist interests. Although diverse in origin and nature, indigenous struggles against the displace-ment and forcible removal of pastoralists from their ancestral lands in the name of wildlife conservation and tourism in East Africa (Jones 2006; Yale 1997), as well as widespread mobilizations in defence of the Mediterranean coastline from the ravages of speculative real estate-driven tourism development (Kousis 2000; Selwyn 2004), for instance, imply struggles over the use and organization of public space as much as they do questions of environmental rights and cultural identity (Plate 6.2). In this regard, tourism can be seen as a vehicle through which myriad citizenship rights are contested, claimed and redefined, rather than simply viewing such strug-gles through the lens of a pro- and anti-tourism dichotomy.

Given the manner in which tourism has frequently resulted in the enclosure of spaces that are vital to the livelihood of local communities, altering traditional ways of life and sanitizing local cultures, it is unsurprising that particular forms of tourism become embroiled within citizens' struggles 'concerning the meaning and representations attached to particular places and the identities of those folks who live in such places' (Routledge 2001: 222). In some cases, tourism itself has been embraced by indigenous communities in their struggle for *recognition* as well as *access* to and custodianship of sacred or ancestral lands. Such forms of indigenous social mobilization concern not only questions of cultural citizenship rights, but are closely associated with struggles for economic rights and the very survival of indigenous ways of life, such as those associated with pastoralism in East Africa. Accordingly, the struggle for 'cultural property' often concerns conflict over rights

PLATE 6.2 A large-scale public demonstration against excessive urban and tourism development in Mallorca, Balearic Islands. The signs being held aloft by several protesters are adorned with the slogan, in Catalan: 'Qui estima Mallorca no la destrueix' (Whoever loves Majorca does not destroy it). Photo: Morell and Franquesa, 2004.

to customary and common lands and/or resources that are integral to the sustaining of local livelihoods, which may be threatened and/or cosseted by developers. Following Pakulski's (1997) interpretation of cultural rights, noted in Chapter 2, such claims for representation may also include concerns over the way in which such groups are embodied in (and signified by) the commercialized tourism/entertainment economy, something that has been a long-standing concern of indigenous Hawaiians (Buck 1994) and the Sami in Finland (Saarinen 1999).

Conversely, tourism, particularly through the display of indigenously produced cultural artefacts and heritage, may open up new avenues of political agency through which indigenous peoples invoke their demand for rights, where they may have previously lacked the political means to do so on the basis of historic forms of exploitation, racial discrimination or other forms of oppression. This, for example, has been the experience of the native Ngarrindjeri in Australia, who have adopted low-key forms of tourism as part of wider attempts to foster 'reconciliation' between Aboriginal peoples and majority 'White' Australian society (Higgins-Desbiolles 2006b). These very issues help us to think about the new and diverse conceptions of citizenship that are being shaped by, and expressed within, the tourism and heritage industries. Cultural tourism for the Embera in Panama, an ethnic group originally from neighbouring Colombia, has also become an important source of economic exchange and a mechanism through which cultural traditions and representations are being revived (e.g. music, dance and cultural artefacts). Informatively, Theodossopoulos (2010: 121–122) indicates that tourism development for the Embera, especially since the late 1990s, has transformed the community from being commonly perceived as 'Chocoes' (Indians from Choco in Lowland Colombia) and 'marginal' to wider Panama society, to a conception of a community that has now 'become emblematic of "indigenous" Panama'. The Embera are now an integral part of the national tourism campaign and have a wider involvement in mainstream society.

The Ainu are an ethnic minority on the island of Hokkaido that has long lived in the shadow of the unitary Japanese state (Friedman 1994: 110). Inspired by the mobilization of indigenous groups elsewhere, the Ainu had already been active in campaigning for land rights and self-determination since the 1960s (Morris-Suzuki 2000: 79). From this period onwards, increased interest in their culture among Japanese tourists provided them with another avenue of mobilization. Henceforth they began to embrace tourism as a vehicle for indigenous self-expression through the production and display of their handicrafts and traditional village lifestyles, while eco-tourism has enabled them to secure greater accesses to land and waterways. Through lobbying initiatives at national and international levels, in 2008 the Ainu Association of Hokkaido received official recognition from the government as an indigenous people of Japan. The Ainu also sought strong recommendations from the International Union for Conservation of Nature that Shiretoko National Park should involve Ainu as co-stewards, given its newly acquired status as a World Heritage site (Lewallen 2011). Elsewhere, in a radical departure from a history dominated by the uprooting of the community and appropriation of their lands by the state, the Tsou, an aboriginal people in southern Taiwan, have been able to assert their territorial rights and retain control over natural resources for, among other reasons, the purposes of developing eco-tourism in the Tanayiku National Ecology Park (Hipwell 2007). Although tourism is often seen as an alienating force, enclosing lands and placing stress on traditional cultures, these examples illustrate how indigenous peoples have embraced and sought to claim ownership over cultural, heritage and nature-based tourism. Accordingly, tourism may offer minority ethnic groups and indigenous peoples alternative avenues to express their cultural identities and affirm their citizenship rights, where previously there had been few opportunities to do so.

In his study of grass-roots resistance to tourism development in Goa, Routledge (2001) deploys the concept of 'resistance identities', which implies forms of struggle by 'actors that are in positions/conditions devalued or stigmatised by the logic of domination' (Castells 1997: 8). During the 1980s, a network of activists and citizens' protest movements arose in reaction to the enclosure of lands for large-scale tourism development and the loss of cultural integrity brought about by tourism. These campaigns have been orchestrated by two organizations with overlapping aims. On the one hand, the *Goa Foundation* (GF) is an environmental lobby group that challenges the large-scale and often illegal hotel construction threatening Goa's coastal ecology, while on the other, the *Jagrut Geoncarachi Fauz* (JGF) or 'Goan vigilante army', founded in 1987, has adopted a more militant perspective that stresses the exploitation faced by Goan villagers and hotel workers in the context of tourism development (Routledge 2001: 231). In the course of these struggles, these organizations have also forged extensive ties with wider, national and international networks of activists and NGOs. Notwithstanding their ideological differences, both the GF and the JGF have sought to mobilize village communities adversely affected by tourism, in defence of Goan livelihoods and the resources upon which these have been based (see Noronha 1999). Elsewhere, the indigenous Rapa Nui of Easter Island, a territory of Chile annexed in 1888, have also protested vigorously against tourism. On two occasions in 2010, the Chilean government commissioned the military police to remove demonstrators occupying a public building that was to be converted into a luxury hotel by both American and Chilean investors. In the previous year, the protestors had blocked the airport for two days, proclaiming that formal restrictions should be placed on tourists' length of stay on the island. The main concerns of the Hanga Roa town council are not to oppose tourism altogether, realizing that is an essential component of their economy, but to critically acknowledge that if unregulated it will continue to have a detrimental effect on the fragile ecosystem. Although there currently seems to be a political stalemate on this issue, this case nevertheless illustrates the degree to which marginalized people deploy proactive protests to make their case against the exploitative nature of tourism (Legrand 2013).

Similarly, across Spain, particularly in regions that had experienced significant levels of tourism development since the late 1950s, various environmental movements emerged in the wake of democratization and the death of Franco in 1975. They protested against a range of issues related to the damaging and exploitative aspects of large-scale tourism development. In the Canary Islands, in addition to the loss of natural habitats and pollution, more recently, their concerns have revolved around public access to and the organization of space along the littoral. During the tourism boom of the 1990s, previously undeveloped coastal areas continued to be enclosed in order to make way for the construction of extensive resort infrastructures (see Bianchi 2004a). In the 1980s, a small group of committed activists came together on the island of La Gomera, despite the fact that the island remained outside the circuits of mainstream mass tourism until well into the 1990s. This group of activists began to raise concerns over threats to the environment posed by tourism, and in particular creeping urbanization and property speculation in coastal enclaves where tourism had begun to establish itself (see Macleod 2004). They have also been instrumental in revitalizing and maintaining a number of pre-Hispanic cultural traditions through effective lobbying and the mobilization of islanders in defence of these cultural traditions and historic landscapes (see Bianchi 2004b). Moreover, these concerns were also linked to a sense of emotional disconnection felt by many rural inhabitants from the island's central uplands, or 'mountain' (*el monte*) as it is known locally, as a result of the restrictions imposed on agrarian livelihoods in the decades leading up to the designation of Garajonay National Park in 1981 (see Bianchi 2002). While tourism is seen by environmental activists as a threat to the island's landscape, heritage and environment, it has served to bring the wider population into the debate regarding stewardship of the environment and the region's cultural heritage. In addition, increased tourism has also brought into focus the question of the appropriate balance of rights and duties that should prevail between tourism and tourists on the one hand, and Canary Island citizens on the other.

Elsewhere, in the Mediterranean during the 1990s, growing environmental concern among the Maltese reflected the increasing importance of 'post-materialist' values brought about in part by economic modernization and rising living standards, paradoxically, as a result of tourism, in Maltese society (Bramwell 2003). Despite a long history of colonial ties to the UK and the continued influence of conservative Catholic values on social life, the emergence of a Maltese environmental movement in opposition to unregulated construction and large-scale tourism development, particularly along the littoral, challenged tourism's association with values of modernity and progress. Significantly, this fact appears to have been lost on those advocating the unrestrained freedom of movement and right to tourism (see Butcher 2003: 10–11). Notably, the activities of the environmental movement came to head in response to proposals by the Hilton to extend the development of luxury facilities and a marina along the foreshore in St. Julian's (see Boissevain and Theuma 1998). Although the proposals were eventually passed by the island's planning authority, the environmentalists succeeded in underlining the importance of the environment not just for its own sake but also as a vital public asset and an integral component of their cultural heritage, as well as strengthening the voice of civil society itself.

The civil society struggles against tourism in Spain and Malta, albeit rooted in distinctive political contexts – civil society protests against tourism in Spain are deeply influenced by regional nationalisms (see Bianchi 2004b) – share a number of common traits, namely a concern with maintaining territorial integrity, enhancing democratic practices, together with preserving and enhancing regional and/ or island cultural identities. These struggles have also served to develop and promote the values associated with various conceptions of environmental citizenship. Moreover, both examples illustrate how the littoral, in addition to being a fragile ecological space, constitutes a vital public asset and one that is often imbued with deep cultural significance (see Bramwell 2003; Sabaté Bel 2001). In the case of the Balearic eco-tax referred to previously, on the one hand it constituted a straightforward fiscal measure designed to moderate the impact of tourism on the ecological and cultural environment of the archipelago (Palmer and Riera 2003). On the other hand, however, this ostensible restraint on the rights of the tourism industry to pursue its interests without due concern for the natural and cultural environment of the islands was defended in some quarters as a means of reinforcing autonomous regional control over sovereign Balearic territory in the face of 'external' interference from the conservative-led central government and foreign tour operators, as well as the corrupt and unaccountable practices of certain regional developers and politicians (Morell 2001: 56). The vociferous and often vitriolic debate for and against the eco-tax also served to ignite further civil society intervention in the debate regarding the interrelationship between the democratic use of territory, environmental rights and regional cultural identity (Valdivielso 2001).

The embracing of the language of human rights by social movements and activists in order to counter the injustices perpetrated by global capitalism reflects the search for a new language of resistance that was not rigidly informed by the ideological climate of the Cold War. Such is the importance of human rights in global policy discourses that Smith and Duffy (2003: 74) claim 'rights discourses are now part of the vernacular of international affairs'. However, others have posed questions regarding the degree to which human rights-based advocacy constitutes a sufficiently robust challenge to the political and economic dynamics of capitalist globalization (Harvey 2006). Leftist critiques of such liberal rights-based activism argue that the foregrounding of rights-based discourses and concomitant shift from the realm of politics to law reflects the triumph of neoliberalism, and signals the retreat from a more radical anti-capitalist politics to the terrain of legalistic pragmatism (Kamat 2004). Conversely, other progressive writers emphasize the significance of rights-based struggles for those oppressed minorities who have been historically excluded from mainstream rights discourses and political enfranchisement (Blomley 1994: 411). Furthermore, although human rights are derived from our common humanity and deemed to be universal and inalienable, they can only be enforced by the nation-state and guaranteed through national citizenship (Isin and Wood 1999: 69). Hence, while NGOs and advocacy groups seek to defend the human rights of minority groups and those disenfranchised by tourism, without support or co-operation from the state in which these groups reside, such rights are meaningless.

Many advocacy NGOs, including Tourism Concern, have worked closely with governments as well as representatives of the tourism industries in order to encourage dialogue between them and the communities affected by tourism, as well as to hold them to account where certain rights are being neglected or diminished as a result of a particular tourism activity. For example, in partnership with the international trade union movement, Tourism Concern has challenged the industry for neglecting labour rights and working conditions in their commitment to developing corporate social responsibility policies (see Beddoe 2004). While such interventions inevitably imply a degree of compromise with the politic-economic status quo, these actions have nonetheless served to advance the citizenship rights of various minority groups and people struggling to defend their territories and livelihoods against enclosure and the disruption that is often brought about by tourism development. However, as if to illustrate the complex and ambiguous nature of rights-based struggles, the international campaign against travel to Burma in the 1990s led to an often acrimonious clash between civil society organizations and a diverse coalition of voices in the media, tourism industry and academia, centring on the relationship between the right to travel and the human rights of the domestic population. In the course of the public debate that ensued, tourists' right to travel to Burma was severely questioned in the light of the human rights abuses perpetrated against Burma's population by its own government. Nowhere perhaps has the divide between the rights and freedoms enjoyed by the planet's more privileged citizens (i.e. tourists) and the paucity of rights enjoyed by place-bound populations, in this case Burmese citizens, perhaps been more starkly illustrated and debated.

Tourism, freedom of movement and human rights in Burma

From 1988 Burma was ruled by a military dictatorship, known as the State Law and Order Restoration Council (SLORC) which was subsequently changed to the State Peace and Development Council (SPDC) in 1997, until its dissolution in 2011. In 1990, the National League for Democracy (NLD), led by Nobel Laureate, Daw Aung San Suu Kyi, won a landslide victory in the country's first general elections to be held since 1960. However, the results were promptly annulled by the military rulers. A brutal crackdown ensued and Aung San Suu Kyi was placed under house arrest for 15 years until her definitive release in November 2010 (BBC 2010c). Henceforth, an international campaign for human rights and democracy led to a boycott against travel to Burma, spearheaded by the Burma Campaign UK and Tourism Concern (Plate 6.3). What marked Burma out as a special case in the eyes of these and other civil society groups worldwide (see Info Birmanie 2013) was not merely the severity and extensiveness of human rights abuses committed by the regime, but the fact that such widespread abuses of human rights were inextricably linked to the regime's desire to develop international tourism (Keefe and Wheat 1998: 22). As the principal justification for boycotting travel to Burma, Human Rights Watch, the International Labour Organization and civil society organizations, together with a wealth of evidence from Amnesty International, pointed to the systematic links between the forcible removal of people from their homes and the use of forced labour, including child labour, to build hotels and other infrastructure necessary for tourism (Tourism Concern 1995).

The calls for a boycott appealed explicitly to the defence of the Burmese people and pointed to the systematic abuses of human rights committed by the military regime, many of which were directly linked to tourism. From the perspective of the civil society groups supporting calls for a boycott, the abrogation of tourists' right to travel to Burma was therefore justified. In their view, the negative repercussions for the rights of tourists and the tourism industry were inconsequential in comparison to the human rights abuses that were perpetrated as part of the regime's desire to expand tourism, as well as the fact that the benefits of tourism were overwhelmingly monopolized by the military regime (Keefe and Wheat 1998). Indeed, the travel boycott was announced by the NLD in response to the anouncement by the military regime that 1996 was to be declared 'Visit Myanmar Year'. This was seen as a blatant attempt to use tourism as a means of generating foreign

The cost of a holiday could be someone's life

BUR

There are times when travellers
have to take a stand...
This is one:

BOYCOTT LONELY PLANET

Lonely Planet have produced a new edition of their guide to Myanmar
(Burma). They are encouraging more people to visit Burma, despite
knowing the many ways that tourism lends support to one of the
world's most brutal dictatorships.

- tourism development causes severe human rights abuses
- tourist dollars boost the coffers of a vicious military regime
- the democratically elected party has asked all tourists
  not to visit Burma until democracy is restored

DON'T LET THEM GET AWAY WITH IT

Boycott Lonely Planet Guides until they have
withdrawn their Burma Guide

SIGN AND SEND THE POSTCARD ATTACHED TODAY

PLATE 6.3 A 'Boycott Burma' campaign postcard produced by Tourism Concern. With
the permission of M. Watson.

exchange, predominantly to finance military expenditure. It was also claimed (with
considerable justification) that army generals and members of their families owned
and had economic interests in much of the tourist facilities (see National League
for Democracy 2011). The travel boycott was endorsed by Aung Suu Kyi, who

had communicated numerous statements to the press and campaigners during her house arrest (see Boynton 2000). She declared:

> It's not good enough to suggest that by visiting Burma tourists will understand more. If tourists really wanted to find out what's happening in Burma – it's better if they stay at home and read some of the many human rights reports there are.
>
> *(Aung San Suu Kyi, cited in Tourism Concern 2000)*

Responses to the travel boycott from the tourism industry were mixed. While some voluntarily withdrew, citing a combination of ethical and/or commercial reasons (e.g. lack of demand), others agreed to stop promoting Burma or withdrew as a result of the negative publicity from the campaign (Travelmole 2003a, 2003b). Notably, however, a number of leading tour operators were adamant that the right to travel should be upheld both in support of tourists' right to make up their own minds, as well as in defence of ordinary Burmese citizens and their livelihoods, arguing that tourism provides a lifeline to many local inhabitants and their families (Brock 2000; Melzer 2000). When accused by Burma pro-democracy campaigners of using hotels linked to Burma's military regime, a spokesperson for UK-based travel company Pettits Travel retorted that 'our clientele is literate and educated and more than capable of making up their own minds' (Bleach 2009). In the words of Jost Krippendorf (1993: 56), these tourists can be seen as 'a kind of special consumer' with a strongly held belief in the total freedom and liberty to do things they would not do at home, bolstered by a firm belief in the inherent right to travel. Similarly, a number of up market travel companies invoked vague notions of freedom in defence of their decision to continue promoting tours to Burma:

> We are probably Britain's leading specialists for Burma, firmly believing that contact with the free world does more good than isolation. In spite of a number of good new private sector hotels and new airlines, Burma remains a destination for the traveller rather than the tourist, but the rewards are great, with splendid scenery, magnificent monuments, and a warm and smiling welcome from the Burmese themselves.
>
> *(Coromandel 2000, cited in Mowforth and Munt 2009: 332)*

Notwithstanding the attempt to single out Burma as 'off limits' to travel on the basis that it would lend succour and legitimacy to a brutal and murderous regime, the calls for a boycott of those companies that continued to promote tours to Burma were greeted by a surprising level of vitriol by much of the tourism industry and members of the media, including the publishers of the well-established Lonely Planet guidebook. Campaigners urged Lonely Planet to withdraw the seventh edition of its guide to Burma, published in January 2000, citing numerous inconsistencies and factual errors in the guide which, in their view, underplayed the severity of human rights abuses and their links to tourism. In addition, it was argued that the publication of the guidebook itself indirectly lent legitimacy to the military dictatorship.

In contrast to its main rival, Rough Guides, which cited the NLD's support for the boycott as the reason for not publishing its own guide to the country, Lonely Planet refused to withdraw the publication. In support of this action, the publisher made the somewhat disingenuous claim that tourists should have the right to make up their own minds whether or not to travel to Burma. It also pointed out that regular abuses of human rights also took place in many other countries that did not face a travel boycott. Lonely Planet's decision was vigorously defended by well-known travel journalists as well as a number of tour operators that refused to withdraw from Burma. One travel journalist in particular went as far as to portray the travel boycott as an attack on the fundamental freedom to travel and the right to 'self-indulgence':

> But aren't holidays supposed to be carefree times, for suntans and self-indulgence? Is it really such a crime to seek out somewhere you can simply enjoy yourself? Is spreading on factor 10, rather than reading up on the local medieval history and contemporary political systems, the sign of a lesser mortal soul?
>
> *(Birkett 2000: 24)*

It is instructive to note that the voices calling for a boycott on travel to Burma were confined for the most part to the West, not least the UK and the European Union. Here, civil society action was supported by calls from the UK Foreign Office that tourists should consider avoiding Burma, while the EU placed severe restrictions on trade and investment with companies known to be linked to the Burmese regime (Tourism Concern 2008). In contrast, tourists from Burma's other main source markets, notably Singapore, remained undeterred by the accusations levelled against the regime and continued to visit the country throughout the period of Aung San Suu Kyi's detention. This illustrates the degree of influence on patterns of international travel exercised by the distinctive coordinates of diplomatic relations between states. It also illuminates the manner in which the cultures or rather traditions of citizenship diverge, as well as questioning the extent to which human rights are universally understood and applied (Henderson 2003: 113).

Although Aung San Suu Kyi has been released and civilian rule restored in 2011, there has not been a marked improvement in the human rights situation. Following advice from the NLD, the Burma Campaign UK no longer supports a blanket ban on travel to Burma but rather supports a targeted boycott of large-scale package tourism and luxury hotels, which continue to benefit members of the former ruling dictatorship and their families (Burma Campaign UK 2010). However, despite restoration of civilian rule in Burma, Human Rights Watch has released evidence of ethnic cleansing and crimes against humanity that continue to be perpetrated against the ethnic Rohingya, a Muslim minority group that has long resided in Burma's Arakan state (Mepham 2013). Although the Burma Campaign has highlighted this issue, the fact that it is no longer deemed socially unacceptable to travel to Burma suggests that the persecution of stateless or ethnic minority groups does not carry the same weight as did the incarceration of a highly educated international political figure in terms of justifying calls for a travel ban.

The point here is not to consider the arguments for and against the boycott/travel ban to Burma during this period. Indeed this has been well covered elsewhere (see Henderson 2003: 111–113; Rajendra 1999). Rather it is to highlight how, even in cases where the right to travel is challenged on such seemingly irrefutable moral grounds, there are those who will argue that the freedom of movement and right to travel must be upheld under any circumstances. It is true that many of those who defended the right of tourists to continue travelling to Burma did so on the basis that it was the Burmese people, not the dictatorship, that would suffer most from a boycott.[7] However, the degree of invective aimed at the campaigners suggests a far more deep-rooted ideological defence of freedom, interpreted as 'our' right to travel where and when 'we' please. The reaction also betrayed something of a contradictory interpretation of rights and their relationship to issues of citizenship. On the one hand, the right to travel to Burma was defended on the grounds of individual choice and the right to literally 'have fun', while on the other it was also viewed in explicitly *moral* terms and heralded as a means of applying pressure on the dictatorship to democratize.

The defence of tourists' right to decide for themselves whether or not to travel to Burma was further backed by the claim that any attempt to define ethical boundaries of travel is tantamount to, at best, paternalism, and at worst, totalitarianism (see Cohen 2000: 6)! This follows the line of argument pursued by Butcher who vigorously defends the position that 'attempts to morally regulate leisure travel in the name of cultural and environmental sensitivity will only make for guilty tourists and erect new cultural barriers between people' (2003: 63). Conversely, according to the Malay poet and human rights lawyer, Cecil Rajendra, travel to such places does little 'to uplift the dignity of the human being' (Rajendra 1999: 7). Although Aung San Suu Kyi and the majority of her compatriots were denied freedom of movement, and widespread human rights abuses against the population had been well-documented, representatives of the tourism industry and many in the media still felt that the cause of freedom and social justice were best served by allowing individuals, tourists and businesses to make up their own minds whether or not to travel to Burma. Although invoking the defence of Burmese interests, support for tourists' right to travel on such grounds nevertheless constitutes a crude instrumentalist defence of human rights, which echoes the defence of consumers' rights and market freedoms.

Reconciling citizens and building social justice through tourism

Tourism, is perhaps, one of the most potent apparatus for peace and justice in our world. It provides the basis for building a global community based on notions of global citizenship – one that transcends barriers of class, ethnicity, religion, nationality…

(Khid-arn 2005)

As we have seen in the previous section, while certain forms of 'predatory' tourism have been singled out for civil society opposition, in a number of other contexts tourism has been mobilized as a tool of justice and reconciliation. For example, it has been embraced in the context of struggles for land rights as well as a tool of reconciliation between the indigenous and non-indigenous inhabitants of Australia (Higgins-Desbiolles 2006b). In a different context altogether, in the Occupied Palestinian Territories, tourism has been deployed by a number of civil society groups and grass-roots operators as a means of overcoming the economic isolation that is reinforced by the Israeli occupation, and simultaneously advancing the wider struggle for Palestinian freedom and political self-determination (Kassis 2005). Elsewhere, as we noted above, heritage tourism has also been used as a means of reclaiming land rights and as a tool of political-cultural recognition by indigenous minority peoples, such as the Ainu in Japan (Cheung 2005; Lewallen 2011) and the Tsou in Taiwan (Hipwell 2007). Thus, in contrast to the libertarian defence of the right to travel, a rather more vigorous defence of tourism in relation to social justice and civic ideas of citizenship can be made, involving the active engagement of tourists in educational and transformational forms of travel in order to high-light injustices and advance the rights of indigenous and/or other marginalized communities (Scheyvens 2002). By doing so, justice tourism seeks to contribute to the advancement of mutual understanding, solidarity and equality between tourists and specific communities that have historically been or continue to be entangled within myriad webs of injustice.

There is of course a close alignment here with many of the ethical forms of travel, in particular volunteer tourism, referred to earlier. Indeed, beyond providing a channel for tourists to consume 'with a conscience', one might reasonably ask, what if any aspects of citizenship, particularly global citizenship, are revealed through par-ticipation in justice tourism? Arguably, what sets many justice tourism organizations (e.g. US NGO *Global Exchange* and the French *Tourisme et Développement Solidaires*) apart from corporate-run responsible tourism, or indeed mainstream volunteer-ing organizations, is their close alignment with social movements and the explicit desire to 'foster transformations that are intended to spark changes for a more just and sustainable order' (Higgins-Desbiolles 2008: 357). Often such organizations are guided by a specific set of ideological goals and are directly implicated in the 'global justice movement' and other forms of oppositional protest. There is thus a strong affinity between civil society and alternative ways of producing and organizing tourism that are not run according to the principles of profit maximization. Indeed, the worker co-operatives that emerged in the wake of the Argentine economic collapse in 2001–2002, including the Hotel Bauen discussed by Higgins-Desbiolles (2012), point the way to the emergence of new forms of economic democracy and strengthening of citizenship rights centred on workers' rights and solidarity among diverse communities (see Restakis 2010: 200–202).

One notable organization that actively works in the arena of 'justice tourism' is the Alternative Tourism Group (ATG), based in the town of Beit Sahour in the Palestinian West Bank. Since its inception in 1995, the ATG has comprised a small group of activist-entrepreneurs who have mobilized tourism as a vehicle for highlighting the injustices perpetrated by the 46-year Israeli occupation by offering a range of tours throughout the West Bank and into East Jerusalem (the latter remains off limits to Palestinians without the appropriate residency permit). By doing so the ATG seeks to counter the often distorted and stereotypical portrayal of Palestinians in the mainstream Israeli and global media, to provide the residents of the West Bank with an economic livelihood that has been curtailed as a result of the military occupation, as well as to diversify tourism away from its overreliance on pilgrimage tourism, which continues to account for the majority of all visits to the West Bank. Notwithstanding the Israeli withdrawal from Gaza in 2005, since 1967 the organization of Palestinian tourism has been largely determined by Israel's ongoing military occupation. As a result, Israel continues to monopolize the economic benefits resulting from tourist flows into Israel, as well as into the West Bank itself. This is due mainly to its control over the issuing of visas and the numerous constraints imposed on the mobility of tourists, which often leaves Palestinian hotels struggling to attract clientele (Isaac 2010: 27).[8] The Occupation restricts the movement of Palestinians within and between the West Bank and Israel, and indeed between Gaza and the West Bank. Long delays and questioning of tourists by the Israeli army at border controls and checkpoints act as a further deterrent for foreign visitors, inhibiting the attempts of Palestinians to build a functioning and viable tourism economy.

Working in conjunction with other NGOs, church groups and political organizations in Palestine and overseas (e.g. Hebron Rehabilitation Committee, Jerusalem Tourism Cluster and ECOT), as well as academics, students, diplomats, journalists and activists, the ATG brings tourists into contact with the everyday lives of Palestinians. Tourists are taken into both Palestinian refugee camps as well as Israeli settlements in the West Bank in order to make them aware of the political realities on the ground. It is hoped that by bringing tourists into contact with the various people and organizations caught up in the struggle for Palestinian justice and ordinary residents alike, this form of tourism will help to challenge the framework of injustice and inequality that blights Palestinian lives. The ATG thus aligns itself with a wider struggle for Palestinian autonomy, statehood and identity. It is also a locally run tourism enterprise seeking to develop a sustainable grassroots form of tourism in alliance with a network of civil society organizations, volunteer associations, small businesses and Palestinian refugees displaced from Israel in 1948. One particularly significant way it does this is through lending assistance to local farmers excluded from their lands as a result of the Occupation, helping them to cultivate their harvests (see Plate 6.4). According to Rami Kassis, the Executive Director of ATG, through their work they endeavour to transform tourists and pilgrims into advocates for justice and democracy, enabling them to fulfil their civic duties across borders and thus to affirm their 'common humanity' (Kassis 2013).

PLATE 6.4 Tourists picking olives on a 'solidarity tour' in the West Bank. Photo: R. Kassis, ATG, October 2012.

A small number of Jewish organizations comprising mainly European and North-American-based Jews and Christian Zionists have also mobilized tourism for political ends (Brin 2006). In this case, however, visiting Israel is cast in terms of a religious calling as well as a means of demonstrating support for Israel and thus, by implication, its policy of military occupation and the Zionist claims to the lands of 'Judea and Samaria' (West Bank). Such organizations, including the Evangelical Christian Zionists (ECJ) and several settlers' groups actively involved in the expansion of Israel's illegal settler colonies in the West Bank, employ distinctive and exclusivist discourses of citizenship in support of their tourism initiatives (and the wider goals these support) in contrast to the inclusive, non-sectarian and cosmopolitan discourses reflected in Palestinian justice tourism. Selwyn (2009) draws attention to how such exclusivist religious-nationalist narratives have underpinned the (successful) struggle by right-wing Jewish settlers' organizations to claim and expropriate the contested holy site of Rachel's Tomb in Bethlehem for exclusively Jewish use, and subsequently annexing it to the municipality of Jerusalem. This was despite the fact that for centuries this site has paid host to Jewish and Muslim visitors alike. However, not all Jewish tour organizations and Jewish tourists align themselves with the politics of the Occupation. Accordingly, Selwyn's (2009: 51–52) discussion concerning the progressive Jewish voices appealing to the cosmopolitan narratives and traditions surrounding Rachel's Tomb clearly demonstrates this point. In addition, the ATG and other Palestinian-based organizations, work alongside progressive Israeli organizations and human rights groups such as B'Tselem and the Israeli Committee Against House Demolitions (ICAHD), in order to achieve an end to the Occupation and advance the goals of Palestinian liberation.

Many such initiatives are heralded as part of the so-called 'peace process'. Nevertheless, the 1993 Oslo accords did little to reduce the restrictions on Palestinian mobility. In many cases the restrictions on mobility were in fact increased via the imposition of a complex system of checkpoints and barriers throughout the Palestinian Territories, as well as the continued expropriation of Palestinian lands and property throughout Palestinian-controlled areas (Halper 2005: xii). As if to emphasize the diminishing spaces of mobility to which Palestinians have been subject since the advent of the various 'peace initiatives', Mitri Raheb, a Lutheran pastor in the Palestinian town of Bethlehem, talks of a time prior to 1989 (around the time of the first *intifada*) when Palestinians were in fact much freer to travel to Jerusalem and around the West Bank. At this time, it was possible for Palestinians to drive to Beirut for lunch then on to Damascus in the afternoon: 'It sounded to me like paradise – a life without borders where people could travel for hours without permit, and where people and goods could move freely from one place in the Middle East to another' (Raheb 2004: 73). Today, such a journey would be unthinkable for Palestinians. Even foreign tourists would find such a journey fraught with difficulties (even before the recent Syrian civil war broke out). Palestinian mobility, both within and between Palestinian areas in the West Bank and Gaza, and into Israel itself and overseas, is subject to stringent controls and limitations, reinforcing an ethnic hierarchy of mobility in which Palestinians occupy the lowest rung.[9] Nonetheless, even members of the Palestinian National Authority and other dignitaries are often forced to wait for hours alongside ordinary Palestinian workers and families at Israeli military checkpoints.

Notwithstanding the commonly held yet somewhat vague notion that tourism is uniquely able to foster peace, there have been a number of initiatives to deploy tourism and heritage in order to overcome the legacy of conflict and bring about peaceful reconciliation between divided communities (Butler and Mao 1996). Nowhere is this perhaps more poignant (and timely given the escalating tensions between North and South Korea at the time of writing) than the Mt. Kumgang tourism project in the Korean peninsula. This programme of cross-border reconciliation tourism grew out of earlier failed attempts to advance North–South co-operation through tourism in the 1980s, and was formulated in the late 1990s as part of South Korean President Dae Jung Kim's (1998–2003) policy of rapprochement, or 'Sunshine Policy'. The principal aim of this policy was to advance 'peaceful, mutually rewarding, and constructive dialogue and exchanges' between North and South Koreans (Kim and Prideaux 2003: 679).

Mt. Kumgang's appeal lay in both its location in the south-east corner of North Korea, close to the border that has separated North and South Korea since 1945, and the fact that it is the only non-militarized arena of contact between North and South Koreans. Moreover, the land has symbolic and religious value to all Koreans, and is admired because of its natural beauty. Additionally, one of the key protagonists of the programme was the founder of the Hyundai Group, who was born near Mt. Kumgang itself, and whose own family had been separated by the division of the country (Kim and Prideaux 2003: 680). However, despite substantial investment in tourism facilities around Mt. Kumgang and the initial goodwill created by the cross-border tourism programme, it has been overshadowed by continuing military tensions between the two countries. In July 2008, tours to Mt. Kumgang were suspended after the fatal shooting of a South Korean tourist by North Korean guards, followed in 2011 by the seizing of assets at the resort by North Korea (BBC 2011c). Although Kim and Prideaux (2003) do not address the citizenship implications of this programme directly, their analysis demonstrates that in spite of their cultural, religious and linguistic ties, Korean citizens continue to be polarized along nationalist and ideological lines. For now, tourism's potential for fostering peace, let alone in enabling separated families to be reunited and to build a new and shared sense of 'Korean-ness', appears to be far from becoming a reality.

In terms of mobilizing heritage and tourism in the name of post-conflict reconciliation and the healing of wounds left by inter-ethnic conflict, there are perhaps few images more poignant than the rebuilding of the sixteenth-century bridge at Mostar in Bosnia-Herzegovina. The bridge, which spans the Neretva River linking two sides of this Muslim-Croat town, was destroyed by Bosnian Croat forces in 1993 in the midst of the fierce fighting between Bosnian Croats and Muslims, which took place in the former Yugoslavia from 1992 to 1995. The project to rebuild the bridge, which reopened in July 2004, is part of a series of processes designed to reconstitute, at least in part, aspects of Bosnian multiculturalism that were erased by the wars and to some extent hindered by simmering tensions in the post-war political order (Causevic and Lynch 2011).

In contrast to the generic proclamations associated with discourses of 'tourism as peace', the link between tourism and reconciliation often involves mobilizing explicit political support and financial resources along with the development of specific and sensitive forms of tourism conducive to countering negative stereotyping and fostering direct contact between divided peoples. Such initiatives have in common a number of aspects that reveal further layers of tourism's relationship to notions of citizenship: first, to seek to overcome past or, indeed, simmering hostilities through combating entrenched xenophobia and racism; second, to develop longer-term bonds of bi-communal solidarity; third, mutual co-operation and a desire to transcend recriminations and blame for past misdeeds. These initiatives imply dissolving, transcending and/or healing prevailing divisions, symbolic and material, whether based on race, religion or nationalist discourses, and contributing to the constitution of civic forms of citizenship. The key to the success of any attempt to harness tourism to the goal of peace and, more specifically, post-conflict reconciliation requires transcending entrenched politico-ideological positions and doing more than promoting economic revitalization, to effecting institutional change through the medium of 'civil society structures' (Scott 2012: 2118).

Both tourism and heritage have been harnessed by the state in an attempt to redefine the meaning of citizenship in post-apartheid South Africa. After its election in 1994, the ANC government set about to use tourism and heritage as a means of building a post-racial South African identity based upon a new civic conception of citizenship (Flynn and King 2007; Goudie et al. 1999). Iconographic heritage, sites of commemoration and museums were mobilized in the name of building the new post-apartheid nation and reconciling the divided white and black South African communities. Tourism was also identified as a central plank in the ANC government's strategy of combating poverty and reducing the socio-economic gulf between black and white South Africans (Mathers and Landau 2007). The circulation of discourses of a new post-racial South African identity was also mirrored by the removal of previous restrictions on the mobility of black South Africans. Amidst these changes, Robben Island,[10] whose universal significance as a symbol of the struggle against oppression was recognized in 1999 when it was inscribed on the World Heritage List, came to symbolize the process of atonement and reconciliation in post-apartheid South Africa (Deacon 2004). However, the success of these programmes is clouded by the continued legacy of apartheid and deep-seated economic inequalities among South Africans (Seekings and Nattrass 2005). The domestic travel experiences of black South Africans and their attempts to reclaim membership of the South African nation on equal terms continue to be marred by a landscape bearing the scars of apartheid. According to Mathers and Landau (2007: 527), the unequal experiences of mobility for black as compared to white South Africans are most poignantly reflected by the game parks in which tourist lodges evoke South Africa's imperial past and whose existence was 'made possible by a colonial history of land grabbing'.[11]

Although such initiatives are defined by their context, they represent an attempt to construct and nurture new forms of citizenship, transcending the fragmentation and divisions that are often derived from sub-national ethnic, cultural and religious allegiances (Chatterjee 1993). Indeed, in their discussion of the role of tour guides in Sarajevo and Mostar, Causevic and Lynch (2011) explain how the guides divert the emphasis of their narratives away from the war itself onto the seemingly more 'mundane' aspects associated with the everyday experiences of 'ordinary citizens' in the case of Sarajevo or, in the case of Mostar, the physical and aesthetic features of the bridge. Such initiatives may not appear to be directly implicated in the issue of tourists' mobility, yet the questions of borders (and who controls them), the freedom of movement and the degree to which the relationship between national cultural heritage and citizenship is related to a territorially fixed notion of identity, highlight the fragile tectonics of citizenship that are often played out in the context of tourism and heritage politics.

The inherently political nature of tourism and its entanglement within distinctive renderings of citizenship clearly intersect at borders and within the often contested and shifting spaces of borderlands. Borders signify the territorial limits of the legitimate exercise of state sovereignty, as well as delineating the boundary between different languages, cultures and political systems (Sofield 2006). Border regimes change in accordance with prevailing geopolitical circumstances and can often harden in response to the outbreak of conflict and 'terrorist' activities, especially when the state seeks to deter foreigners deemed to be hostile to its citizens.[12] While borders function to regulate, manage and striate mobility, they may also become focal points for tourist activity and attractions in their own right. The Berlin Wall, or what is left of it, is perhaps one of the most iconic examples of a divided territory

PLATE 6.5 Tourists at a viewing gallery at the Ledra Street Crossing of the UN buffer zone in Nicosia, Cyprus. Photo: C. Morris Paris, July 2007.

in recent history, in this case marked by ideology. In what remains of the Wall, Checkpoint Charlie is now firmly established on the international tourism circuit among visitors to Germany's capital. Rather ironically, Israel's 'Separation Wall', the construction of which commenced in 2002 and was declared illegal by the International Court of Justice in 2004, has become the focus of 'alternative' tourism itineraries in the West Bank linked to educational tours and justice tourism programmes (Isaac 2009).[13]

Thus, the existence (or not, as the case may be) of tourist activity at borders often carries a deeper symbolism beyond the mere fact that tourists may attribute different meanings to their desire to visit such places and consume the heritage and/or attraction of borders. Borders themselves are either contested or in a process of flux and constant realignment (e.g. Cyprus). Hence the movement of people and tourists across borders is shaped by changing geopolitical circumstances, which in turn may reflect and further reinforce debates concerning national identity and citizenship. The East European popular uprisings culminating in the fall of Berlin Wall in 1989 were of course about much more than the right to travel. Nevertheless, the freedom of travel and to walk across the city of Berlin was indeed a key symbolic and political element of the democratic revolution that brought about the end of Communist rule (Burstein 1991: 54–55). While the fall of the Wall supplied the impetus for the reunification of Berlin, it also opened up a series of tensions around the process of reconstructing Berlin's rich and often controversial monumental heritage, and a heritage of atrocity and war associated with the Nazi regime. These tensions have emerged in the context of wider debates regarding national identity and citizenship that had already begun during the late 1970s (see Till 2005).

On the divided Mediterranean island of Cyprus, tourism and the associated claims to the right to the freedom of movement across the 'Green Line' that separates the Turkish Republic of North Cyprus from the Republic of Cyprus in the south, is implicated in questions of territorial power, shifting borders and multiple notions of citizenship (Plate 6.5). During the period 1974–2003, travel across the 'Green Line' by Cypriots all but came to a standstill, while limited crossing for non-Cypriots was permitted (Webster and Timothy 2006: 169). In 2003, in the wake of the failed UN-sponsored peace talks and a week after Cyprus signed the EU accession treaty (Cyprus joined the EU on 1 May 2004), restrictions on the cross-border movement of Cypriots and tourists were relaxed. Scott (2007) notes how foreign tourists unwittingly became protagonists in wider geopolitical strategies to realign the borders of the EU as they sought to invoke their right as EU citizens to the freedom of movement and to visit the island as a whole. Nevertheless, despite a continuing lack of a formal political agreement at government level, in a recent study Scott (2012) demonstrates the transformative potential of tourism through the experience of working on a joint eco-village project in Cyprus that sought to offer village tourism experiences to tourists on both sides of the border. Despite ongoing suspicions of bi-communal initiatives on both sides, and the failure to include a village from the Republic of Cyprus in the south, the project has managed to forge a space of dialogue and avenue of co-operation between Greek and Turkish Cypriots. It has thereby establish the potential for the building of civil society ties across the border through tourism, regardless of the failure of the respective governments to overcome entrenched nationalist discourses.

Conclusion

This chapter has sought to reflect on the diverse ways in which tourism has emerged as a means through which varying claims to global citizenship have been advanced. These range from participation in ostensibly ethical or responsible forms of travel, whether in defence of the environment or the empowerment of destination communities, to civil society mobilizations *against* certain destructive forms of tourism development. In this light, we have also considered the active embrace of tourism in order to promote social justice and/or reconciliation between divided peoples. Participation in such forms of travel are seen by tourists and the organizations involved in putting such tours together as part of a wider commitment to the exercise of global civic responsibility across borders, physical and symbolic. However, it has also been argued that the relationship between responsible forms of tourism, much of which is increasingly indistinguishable from certain niche packages sold by multinational tourism companies, and notions of a cosmopolitan and global citizenship, is rather weak.

On the one hand, such forms of travel may enable tourists to enact certain forms of cosmopolitanism through active engagement in a variety of projects designed to improve the livelihoods of low-income populations. On the other hand, however, responsible tourism often implies little more than an ethically minded form of consumption whereby a range of progressive outcomes are conjoined with the simple pleasures of travel, involving little if any additional sacrifice or effort on the part of the tourist. At worst, volunteer tourism has been accused of elitism, thus reinforcing, rather than overcoming, political-economic inequalities of power between volunteer organizations and host communities. As long as such forms of ethical tourism are predicated on a 'rush of guilt' (Hickman cited in Pattullo 2006: 29), it will remain in a privileged enclave of middle-class travel that is ultimately based on turning guilt itself 'into a commodity form' (Hutnyk 2011).

This chapter has also considered how tourism has been directly harnessed for the purpose of promoting social justice and reconciliation. Justice tourism comprises a form of travel concerned with highlighting and potentially overcoming specific forms of injustice. It can thus be understood as an attempt to reconcile the rights of individuals to travel with distributive justice for the world's poor and those inhabiting the margins of destination economies. Moreover, these forms of tourism are often organized along lines that are not exclusively based on profit motive, or which may run counter to capitalist social relations. In this regard, such forms of tourism do perhaps signal one of a number of pathways towards the strengthening of the ties of transnational solidarity upon which a robust form of global citizenship arguably depends. What marks out justice tourism, and in some cases attempts to mobilize tourism for the purpose of reconciliation, from other forms of responsible travel its explicit political orientation. In addition, participation in such tours implies both the material act of crossing borders that were previously closed to the respective participants, as well as transcending the socio-ethnic divisions and/ or political animosities that previously prohibited travel between or within these particular territories.

Notes

1 One could also include here Lonely Planet's Thorn Tree internet forum (http://www. lonelyplanet.com/thorntree/index.jspa) as well as the many travel blogs (e.g. http:// www.jumpamonkey.com/) and 'couch-surfing' sites (e.g. http://globalfreeloaders.com) that can be found on the Internet.
2 In one of the largest legal payouts in a case involving a multinational corporation accused of complicity in human rights violations, Shell paid out nearly £10 million in compensation to relatives of the executed activists (Pilkington 2009).
3 One of the leading organizations involved is ECPAT International *(End Child Prostitution, Child Pornography and Trafficking of Children for Sexual Purposes, formerly, End Child Prostitution in Asian Tourism)*, based in Bangkok, Thailand (see http://www.ecpat.net/EI/ index.asp).
4 Two well-known schemes include the International Hotels Environment Initiative (IHEI) set up in 1993, now renamed the International Tourism Partnership (http:// www.tourismpartnership.org), and the Green Globe Programme established by the WTTC in 1994 (see Mowforth and Munt 2009: 194–202).
5 Transnational advocacy networks and social movements range from radical 'anti-globalization' movements (e.g. ATTAC, The Ruckus Society), transnational alliances of peasant farmers (e.g. La Via Campesina) and landless peasants (e.g. Movimento Sem Terra), and more recently the Occupy Wall Street movement (Gitlin 2012), to international advocacy NGOs.

6 For a more thorough analysis of the philosophical underpinnings of human rights and social justice, as they pertain to tourism, see Smith and Duffy (2003: Chs 4 and 5).

7 This argument was also put forward against the 1999 'Boycott Bali' campaign in New Zealand, which was also supported by the British Guild of Travel Writers in the UK, in protest against the violent suppression of moves towards independence in East Timor by Indonesian military forces (see Cole 2008: 284). Despite the undoubted brutality of the Suharto regime (1966–1998), whose family members were believed to control many of the luxury tourism assets in Bali, the island was largely unaffected and there was no evidence of human rights abuses directly attributed to the development of tourism (as was the case in Burma) (Hitchcock 1999).

8 Approximately two-thirds of the Occupied Palestinian Territories are under Israeli military control (allocated to Area 'C' under the Oslo accords), while Israel is the only recognized sovereign state in the world without officially declared borders (see Said 2005: 5–12). According to Israeli human rights organization B'Tselem, the Separation Wall, built by Israel under the pretence of improving security, and declared illegal under international law by the International Court of Justice in 2004, when completed, will enclose 9.5 per cent of the West Bank, containing 60 Israeli settler colonies on the Israeli 'side', isolating it from Palestinian towns and villages in the rest of the West Bank (http://www.btselem.org/separation_barrier/map, accessed 27 March 2013). The planned extension of the Wall also threatens an ancient agricultural landscape, as well as Palestinian attempts to develop eco-tourism in the rural village of Battir that lies just to the west of Bethlehem, adjacent to the 1949 armistice line (Sherwood 2012).

9 In January 1991, the system that had allowed residents of the Palestinian Territories to move with relative freedom between the West Bank, Israel and Gaza since 1972 was revoked. Palestinian ID holders resident in the West Bank who wish to enter Jerusalem, or indeed any other part of Israel (1948 territories) or Gaza, must apply to the Israeli authorities to receive authorization in advance. Such permission will not usually be granted without evidence of a work contract or a certificate from a hospital, or indeed any other 'good reason'. Of course having a 'good reason' to visit friends or relatives for instance, to go to Jerusalem or other places in Israel, does not guarantee that such permission will be granted. Where overseas travel is concerned, most Palestinians living on the West Bank must travel through Jordan via the main land border crossing at the Allenby/King Hussein Bridge, which, like all other ports of exit/entry, is controlled by the Israeli forces. In a minority of cases, some Palestinians are able to travel via Tel Aviv's international airport (pers. communication, R. Kassis, ATG). Needless to say, such restrictions on Palestinian mobility are in contravention of Article 13 of the UNDHR, as well as the 1966 International Covenant on Economic, Social and Cultural Rights (see http://www.btselem.org/freedom_of_movement).

10 Long used as a place of banishment and exile, Robben Island is best known as the site of the former prison where Nelson Mandela was imprisoned for 18 years out of the 27 years he served, between 1964 and 1982, along with other black male members of the banned ANC (see http://www.robben-island.org.za).

11 For this reason, Mathers and Landau (2007: 527) point out that the 'reality tours' run by the US NGO and justice tourism organization Global Exchange consciously avoid game parks.

12 In Israel's case, both reasons are used to justify the continued clampdown on Palestinian mobility as well as the construction of the Separation Wall, which commenced in 2002.

13 For an entertaining yet politically informative perspective on the Wall, see Mark Thomas's account of his ramble along the controversial barrier in his book: *Extreme Rambling: Walking Israel's Barrier for Fun* (2011, Ebury Press). See also the clip showing a group of European tourists being arrested for straying too near the Separation Wall near the town of Bethlehem, during a tour organized by the ATG (http://www.youtube.com/watch?gl=GB&v=aK6ePKRmffM).

CONCLUSION

Thinking through global reconfigurations of tourism and citizenship

We commenced our exploration of tourism and citizenship in this book by questioning the assumption that participation in international tourism is becoming simultaneously more widespread and democratic. Indeed, in spite of the temporary downturn in 2008–2009, largely due to the 2007–2008 financial crash, international tourist arrivals have once again started to increase. In 2012, the total volume of travellers worldwide exceeded one billion for the first time. Despite significant signs that the centre of gravity of global economic power is shifting eastwards, and to some extent towards the south, the asymmetries of international travel and cross-border mobility are nevertheless still glaringly apparent. Inequalities of movement and participation in tourism continue to be associated with unfolding patterns of regional and global economic inequalities, and conditioned by the geopolitical imperatives of powerful states. While the framework of 'North–South' relations is no longer adequate for understanding and explaining the uneven patterns of global travel, closer examination of these disparities informs us that the pathways towards the globalization and democratization of travel remain encumbered with myriad obstacles. To be a tourist still remains a privilege denied to the majority of the world's inhabitants for varying reasons, albeit one that is no longer aligned predominantly along the axes of the political-economic power that emerged in the aftermath of the Second World War. Yet, as the book has also clearly demonstrated, the mobility of tourists themselves is hampered and constrained by forces linked to the wider entanglements of geopolitics and diplomacy, as well long-standing forms of prejudice and discrimination.

In this book, we have sought to interrogate the basis upon which tourists are able to claim the right to travel and the degree to which it can be considered as an inalienable human right and hence a marker of citizenship. Although tourism is popularly seen as little more than a prosaic pastime associated with innocence and fun, from another perspective it is perceived as a vital social need warranting a status alongside other human rights. We have thus seen how tourists are for the most part ascribed rights superior to that of other mobile human beings, notably immigrants, migrant workers and refugees. In fact, the hyper-mobility of tourists belies a world in which international travel is extensively stratified and is premised upon different gradations of rights and freedoms.

The citizenship entitlements that enable international tourism mobility involve both the right to travel and the associated frameworks governing the freedom of movement, as well as the means to consume the diversity of different experiences and destinations on offer, unhindered by 'unjust' and/or 'arbitrary' political impediments. From the early days of international leisure travel in the nineteenth century, a taken-for-granted sense of entitlement to cross borders and enter new territories took root among the citizens of wealthier societies, marked by the expanding reach of colonial trade and imperial power, presaging the later emergence of what certain scholars of 'Third World' tourism development would refer to as the neo-colonial enterprise of international tourism. As discussed in Chapter 1, towards the mid-twentieth century access to leisure and holidaymaking was extended to the masses in Western Europe through the mechanism of paid holidays and state-sponsored social tourism schemes, underpinned by a welfare ethos, although with some notable differences between states in terms of the degree of material support and the political motivations behind such provision. As the discussion has made clear, although the provision of social tourism and state support for subsidized tourism may in fact represent an attempt to construct an enduring form of social citizenship rights, it can also signify attempts by the state to encourage citizens to be duty-bound to the political and ideological endeavours of the nation-state. The state-led leisure and tourism programmes developed in Fascist Germany and Italy during the 1930s exemplify this claim. As further indicated in Chapter 1, state-planned social tourism programmes in Communist Eastern Europe were designed not only to ensure that everyone had access to leisure opportunities and limited forms of international travel *within* the Communist bloc, but equally, they were motivated by a desire to inculcate a commitment to the ideals of 'socialism' among all citizens of these territories. Therefore, although states have the option to confer such social citizenship entitlements to their citizens, they often do so with degrees of political bargaining, however subtle or implicit. In fact, some advanced capitalist states such as the UK may only envisage social tourism provision as an act of state benevolence afforded to those in marginal circumstances, whereby the welfare system designates those considered to be in 'real need' or 'deserving' of leisurely respite. Accordingly, social citizenship entitlements as expressed through tourism are selectively applied and often come at a price.

In the aftermath of the Second World War, access to cheap and plentiful oil, rising disposable incomes and technological advances in transport arguably did more to democratize tourism and to extend the possibilities of international travel to the populations of the Western capitalist democracies than anything that had preceded it. At the same time, the benefits of international tourism for the citizens of the advanced industrialized states – in terms of the recuperative potential of being able to temporarily leave one's home environment simply for the purpose of pleasure and discovery – were harnessed to the developmental objectives of 'less developed' states seeking to establish and build their nations in the wake of decolonization and independence. Such notions of citizenship thus implied the ability of wealthier Western tourists to move with relative ease across national boundaries and take advantage of the rights of access and entry to a range of spaces and places that were integrated into the circuitry of global tourism. At this point tourism clearly began to reflect the accumulated citizenship rights of Western industrialized nations, where for many citizens international travel was soon to become the norm, while extending the promise of nationhood, economic development and social mobility through tourism for those living in receiving societies. However, in an age marked by public austerity, deepening and widening socio-economic deprivation and the continued attack on notions of universal rights to welfare in the advanced capitalist states of Europe, it is imperative that we remain alert to the uneven ways in which rights (including those of mobility) continue to be distributed and applied across an ethnically diverse and highly unequal population.

In Chapter 2, we considered the scholarly view that tourism can also be perceived as an indicator of global and cosmopolitan citizenship, generating new currencies of value for those who have the capacity and political freedom to travel and indeed consume a constantly expanding spectrum of places, cultures and environments, often accessible at the click of a mouse. In this regard, we spoke of the emergence of a 'new' elite transnational class, a transformation that is reflective of the reconfiguration of states and their relationship to capital. Such individuals and groups have a negligible relationship to the state and are often afforded a range of rights and unprecedented freedoms. Nonetheless, we are reminded by Hannerz (1990: 241) that, 'being on the move ... is not enough to turn one into a cosmopolitan'. It is essential to be aware of the pitfalls surrounding any simplistic associations of tourism with the attributes of a cosmopolitan or global citizenship. This is even more the case where forms of travel and international tourism reflect and signify 'rootless' rather than 'rooted' forms of engagement with the peoples and localities through which they transit.

More importantly, as indicated in Chapter 3, the right to travel is far from being universally enjoyed or regarded in all societies as a fundamental cornerstone of citizenship rights, as it has been in most Western democracies for the past half century or so. Moreover, while international tourism has been a significant force fuelling the globalization of societies, closely intertwined with transnational flows of communication and large-scale movements of people, capital and labour, the right to travel and to be a tourist remains fundamentally grounded in state–citizen frameworks. Thus, while the global landscape of travel has become more populated as consumers in emerging economies continue to travel in increasing numbers, international tourism continues to expand in an uneven and differentiated manner, including some and excluding others. At the same time, and as this chapter indicated, international tourism has increasingly come to be regarded as a marketized commodity shaped by discourses of market individualism, consumer freedoms and

the unfettered right to travel. Accordingly, it has drawn attention to the alignment between tourism and increasingly market-based renderings of citizens as consumers. We thus need to remain sceptical of the claim that international tourism has
become increasingly democratized and is founded upon an equitable distribution
of the rights and freedoms upon which access to travel is based.

Consequently, the book takes issue with both business-centred assumptions
concerning tourism, in which tourism is considered as a privatized and individualistic form of consumption by 'free' and 'rational' consumers, and associated neoliberal conceptions of citizenship in which individuals are 'free' to play and construct an infinite array of social bonds and identities, through differentiated acts
of consumption. This book also contends that we should remain sceptical towards
notions of tourism citizenship in which the consumption of travel is equated with
empowerment, and the right to travel is elided with the right to tourism. Whatever
the future for global mass tourism, scrutinizing the flows of international travel
mobility through the lens of citizenship and power enables scholars to think critically about the balance of power and forms of citizenship that emerge within the
striated spaces of global travel. Consequently, it is the authors' aspirations that this
book will contribute towards establishing a framework through which progressive
solutions to the asymmetrical relations of tourism mobility and tourism immobility can be further analyzed, debated and proposed. Furthermore, such solutions
should be guided by the premise that the universal right to travel can and should
be commensurate with a radical, redistributive politics that promotes social justice
and development rights for all.

In contrast to many of the ideas that have underpinned theories of globalization and neoliberalism, Chapter 4 demonstrated the extent to which states retain
a significant apparatus at their disposal in order to manage, regulate and control
the cross-border movements of people, and to determine their freedom of movement: from the issuing of passports and visas to the increased use of technologically
advanced systems of digital surveillance. Indeed, cross-border travel in its current,
highly differentiated form would be impossible without the panoply of controls,
regulatory constraints and forms of surveillance imposed by the state. A number
of tourism analysts often talk with genuine passion about the rooted citizen with
worldly intentions passing freely through borders with a social or cultural mission
to be a good and responsible global citizen, or perhaps rather more dispassion-
ately about persons travelling around the world because they have the economic
or political power to do so. Yet, as Chapter 4 emphasized, the right to travel across
borders and frontiers must be legitimized by the state or indeed supra-national
entities such as the European Union. In addition to both the financial capacity
to travel and the purpose of travel, the freedom of movement and the ability to
travel with ease are stratified in relation to nationality, ethnicity, race and religion.
The problem is compounded by the fact that there are no globally transparent or
standardized criteria to determine who can or should be able to freely travel across
borders. Rather, the border remains the last bastion of state power, as economic
decision-making has shifted increasingly towards unaccountable multinational

corporations and financiers to whom states appear increasingly beholden. In addition, as Chapter 5 demonstrated, cross-border mobilities are deeply entangled in regional and global webs of power and geopolitics. Such entanglements continue to exercise considerable influence over the implicit and explicit criteria regarding who counts as a 'legitimate' as opposed to an 'illegitimate' traveller and tourist.

Considerations of global insecurity and crisis management have also reinforced a trend towards the securitization of international travel, ushering in a world of increasingly regulated and constrained mobility. This has been underpinned by an interlocking, state–corporate nexus designed to control, manage and constrain cross-border mobility through restrictive passport and visa regimes, the proliferation of border controls, and the application of new digital surveillance and security technologies to the varying arenas of international travel. Since 9/11, as the acclaimed journalist and writer Naomi Klein (2007) poignantly notes, the fear of terrorism increasingly began to outweigh concerns regarding living in societies under constant surveillance. Such digital surveillance technologies, developed by some of the world's leading corporations, many of which having been tried and tested elsewhere, for example in 'predictive policing' (see Morozov 2013), are likely to be deployed further and become more widespread in the years to come, in order to make the world safe for travel. Such technologies are being continuously deployed in the context of border surveillance and aviation security, through the use of optical scanning, biometric IDs and the analysis of commercial databases provided, for example, by airlines to detect patterns of suspicious travel behaviour. Accordingly, these technologies pose a threat to civil liberties as well as reinforcing the securitization of international travel and related inequalities of mobility. Perhaps most worrying of all, as indicated by Morozov, citizens have no way of knowing the extent to which discriminatory biases have been built into the sophisticated algorithms used by companies and state agencies to 'mine' data, given that the technology developed by large corporations may remain exempt from public scrutiny.

The privatization of security and associated securitization of travel have profound implications for state–citizen relations. Not only are the primary targets and victims of such technologies often migrants as opposed to 'terrorists', such moves are likely to further reinforce a kind of modular, neoliberal form of citizenship whereby we are simultaneously sold the myth of personal freedom and autonomy while being subject to increasingly draconian and often invisible forms of digital surveillance and security profiling. Following Beck's (2005: 12) comments on global terrorism, in a world in which we have all become potential suspects, though some more than others, citizens (to whom we could add tourists) are constantly required to prove their innocence, not least while on the move. This further erodes notions of privacy and associated ideas of civil rights in the name of security, and in turn this gives rise to a climate of heightened fear and suspicion, dividing mobile peoples into 'legitimate' and 'illegitimate' travellers, striating movement and ultimately eroding the quality of our association with others. What makes these trends even more paradoxical is the manner in which the hyper-connectedness of global populations, through transnational networks of social media and 24-hour telecommunications, has greatly enhanced worldwide awareness of the disparities of wealth and income and perhaps, as a result, magnified local grievances. Accordingly, at a time when the world's populations are connected as never before through multiplex virtual networks, the material pathways of travel and cross-border mobility are increasingly regulated, managed and often restricted altogether for those without the right credentials for travel.

Tourism expresses a 'mobility paradox'. It is a social force that articulates closely with the progressive values underpinning the freedom of movement and right to travel, while at the same time constituting a vehicle of corporate profit-making and capital accumulation for transnational enterprises and corporate investors, which may serve to undermine the development rights of low-income and marginalized communities in destinations. Hence, tourism is regarded as being a unique privilege in so far as it is seen as a right akin to the right to work, leisure and rest. However, as we have argued throughout the book, like many other rights, the right to travel is by no means universally enjoyed. Furthermore, doubts also remain as to whether the right to tourism itself should be considered as a public good. Notwithstanding nationally based social tourism programmes, transnational social tourism initiatives or socialist-based models of tourism, it is difficult to imagine the appropriate institutional framework through which universal and democratic access to the right to travel can be fully achievable. Continuing global inequalities of wealth and power, let alone politico-ideological differences between states, renders this task highly unlikely given current circumstances. Although the less well off and socially disadvantaged in advanced capitalist states may at least be able to benefit partially from state-funded (welfare) schemes and other charitable programmes in order to participate in leisure travel, such provision remains a distant hope for the majority of the world's inhabitants. Nevertheless, as we have shown in this book, conceptualizing the relationship of tourism through the lens of citizenship enables us to recast the right to travel in terms of having the capacity to travel, rather than being construed simply as the right to travel free from 'excessive' or 'unnecessary' political hindrance. Through an understanding of tourism's manifold relationships to the discourses and practices of citizenship, we should seek to align the right to travel and indeed to be a tourist with a broader canvass of development rights, and the capacity for all citizens to partake in travel and tourism, free from material constraint and discriminatory restrictions.

Despite optimistic pronouncements following the collapse of communism, the kind of integrated and borderless world that has been envisaged by neoliberals and hyper-globalists has not fully materialized. Far from extending the possibilities of freedom of movement and the concomitant capacity to enjoy such freedoms, the effects of neoliberal restructuring of advanced capitalist economies, the reorganization of the social democratic state and its withdrawal from many areas of public expenditure, and rising inequalities continue to put a brake on widening participation in international tourism. Those who are on average to low incomes, let alone the close to 60 per cent of the world's population that continue to live in poverty or near poverty, are not able to fully experience the right to travel or associated touristic freedoms. Additionally, given the prevailing inequalities in the global order, one's right to travel freely for the purpose of touristic consumption may be another person's toil and burden. Some of the less guarded predictions surrounding the continued growth of outbound travel from emerging economies significantly underplay the impact of rising inequalities within these states as well as the potential for economic reversal, not least given their dependence on oil imports to fuel such growth. Significantly, the emphasis on the removal of restraints on the mobility of capital, information and people (notably tourists) has in no way entailed a comparable strengthening of mobility rights for labour nor indeed migrants and refugees. To some extent then, claims regarding the democratization of tourism are based largely on the continued expansion of outbound tourism from new and emerging markets. Nor does the seemingly more widespread participation in travel necessarily constitute evidence of the universal spread of the idea that tourism equates with a form of mobile citizenship. Indeed, ethnographic research would no doubt enable deeper and richer interpretation of the meaning and purpose of such travel in relation to ideas of citizenship, for the newly mobile consumers from emerging markets.

In Chapter 5, we identified how in the aftermath of the Second World War tourism was embraced by the world's leading power, the United States, as a vehicle for the internationalization of the values of capitalism, along with the post-war reconstruction and reconsolidation of liberal democracy in Western Europe. In vague echoes of Kantian notions of perpetual peace and cosmopolitanism, international tourism was envisaged as an integral cog in a peaceful global order of states bound together through capitalist enterprise. However, we also drew attention to the manner in which tourism often becomes deeply intertwined with geopolitical rivalries concerning disputed borders and contested territories. In some cases, tourism has been used as an overt political tool to expropriate territory, as well as to striate and constrain the movements of citizens from neighbouring or 'hostile' states. Such divisions were shaped by Cold War *realpolitik*, in as much as they were also determined by the circumstances of regional conflicts between states. Tourism was heralded by the architects of the post-war order, and continues to be lauded by a range of institutions as a global force for spreading the ideals of peace, freedom and democracy worldwide. However, as we have seen, it has become deeply entangled within the securitization of global and regional politics and more specifically the politics of anti-terrorism, which serve to fuel racialized distinctions between 'legitimate' and 'illegitimate' travellers.

Further to the constraints on travel implied by persistent global inequalities and the geopolitical rivalries between states, the differentiated and uneven distribution of the right to travel and the 'means of movement' (Torpey 2000) has been further exacerbated by the criminalization of the mobility of ethnic and other minority citizens in recent years. Although discrimination against ethnic minorities in the course of travel is nothing new, such trends have been reinforced in the wake of the 9/11 terrorist attacks. Fears that the West, including tourists, were increasingly under threat from international terrorism have further strengthened these trends. These attacks, whatever their origin or specific cause, served to shatter the fragile consensus surrounding the role of tourism as an instrument of peace, and associated rights and freedoms of mobility that underpin this, reinforcing the securitization of travel and tightening of international borders. Such attacks also raise a number of issues relating to the appropriate balance between open borders and secure frontiers, as well as the hegemonic practices of states that serve to identify and target certain subjects as 'risky' and thus deemed unworthy of being able to move freely. Random attacks and political violence against tourists have reconfigured the geographies of international travel along new axes of risk and security, exposing the fragility of discourses of 'tourism as peace' advocated by such globally minded institutions as the UNWTO and the IIPT. Furthermore, they have cast doubt on tourism's supposedly unique ability to promote peace, mutual understanding and cultural exchange. Nevertheless various international tourism organizations, representatives of the major corporate tourism industries and to some extent governments continue to expend a great degree of effort and resources to ensure that countries remain open for business and safe for travel. However, global responses to the periodic attacks on tourists reinforce the extent to which there is a sense of entitlement surrounding the right to travel among the world's 'mobility rich' citizens. At the same time, this tension further illuminates, somewhat tragically, the disproportionate emphasis on the right to travel claimed by those with the legitimate credentials for travel, and the lack of rights enjoyed by the world's 'mobility poor' for whom the right to shelter, food, sanitation and work are far more pressing concerns.

The universal right to travel and the widening of democratic participation in tourism are undoubtedly noble and worthwhile ideals. However, the libertarian defence of the right to travel unhindered by the attempts of states and NGOs to 'morally regulate' individuals and the collective behaviour of tourists may, at worst, lend tacit support to authoritarian regimes and human rights abuses. However, at best, it may serve to reinforce support for the rights of private property and the rights of capital against the rights to development of indigenous or low-income populations. It can be argued, therefore, unlike most other arenas of international trade, tourism significantly blurs the differentiation between the spheres of commerce and human socio-cultural relations in such a way as to render distinctions between the right to *travel* and the right to *tourism* difficult to interpret and define. However, muddying the distinction between the freedom of movement and the right to travel and participate in tourism serves to provide a convenient ideological cover for governments and developers alike seeking to open up and exploit new markets for the tourism industries. Thus, the contradiction within tourism between the right to the freedom of movement and the universal right to travel remains unresolved.

More optimistically, Chapter 6 observed how notions of global and/or cosmopolitan forms of citizenship are expressed and extended in the context of new, 'alternative' forms of tourism. Such forms of travel, encompassed broadly under the mantle of responsible and/or ethical tourism, espouse a set of ideals akin to a kind of global citizenship and a liberal cosmopolitan outlook motivated by a shared 'ethic of care' for the planet, local environments, indigenous peoples and other vulnerable communities brought into the orbit of international tourism. However, if we are to interpret responsible tourism as little more than consuming ethical travel 'products', it is unclear what (if any) notions of citizenship can be developed out of passive forms of solidarity articulated through the mechanism of market exchange. There is also something of an irony when relatively well-off tourists participate in what are deemed to be progressive, 'community-based' forms of tourism. As commendable as these may be in serving to provide employment opportunities in low-income 'Third World' communities, one wonders what conception of citizenship is being advanced when tourists express a greater awareness or concern for the environment and ways of life in distant places, yet know little about or are impervious to the poverty and social deprivation that exists in their own societies. Moreover, ethical forms of tourism often attract predominantly well-off tourists who have most likely benefited from a secure and lucrative position within the neoliberal order. As we have argued, such examples of ethical travel express a diluted, liberal cosmopolitanism and weak bonds of global citizenship, which afford little in the way of a challenge to the dominant framework of globalizing capitalism and contemporary inequalities of wealth and power.

For the most part, the discourses of global citizenship and cosmopolitanism that circulate through the capillaries of ethical and responsible forms of travel, whether promoted by concerned travellers, campaigning NGOs, enlightened policymakers or corporate philanthropy, avert our attention from the systemic nature of inequality that is linked to the 'smooth functioning of our economic and political systems' (Žižek 2009: 1). That is not to suggest that any and all attempts to advance forms of ethical tourism are complicit in such patterns of exploitation, but rather to point to the fact that in many cases the discourses of ethical travel and global citizenship have become increasingly aligned with (and difficult to differentiate from) the dominant logics of neoliberalism and corporate capitalism. Indeed, the critique presented in Chapter 6 concerning the links between ostensibly ethical or responsible forms of tourism and global citizenship does indicate that such notions often constitute little more than a form of personal consumer choice and are therefore firmly grounded in neoliberal ideals of consumer citizenship.

Nevertheless, even if the ties of global citizenship are weaker and less grounded than those attributed to place-bound national forms of citizenship, participants in certain forms of volunteer and justice tourism do exhibit a set of ideals that go further than merely consuming ethically branded travel services. A growing body of scholarly opinion has proclaimed such forms of tourism as evidence of an active engagement by tourists in the struggles of marginalized and less fortunate peoples than themselves, in a manner that affirms ties of solidarity across borders. To some extent, therefore, it can be claimed that they are guided less by profit and more by a desire to rebalance the unequal relations of power between mobile and immobile populations. Volunteer and justice tourism, for example, represent more than simple acts of charity or ethically minded forms of consumption. Rather, they speak to emergent ideas of civic cosmopolitanism and global citizenship denoting an active concern and engagement with the well-being of those in the wider global order, beyond one's national environment. However, irrespective of such isolated and 'micro-scale' initiatives, unless we are able to identify, nurture and somehow institutionalize a sense of shared norms, reciprocal obligations and mutually reinforcing ties of solidarity between tourists and the inhabitants of less fortunate destination communities, the prospects for the advancement of meaningful forms of global citizenship through tourism appear rather slim.

We have also seen how large-scale, environmentally damaging and often culturally insensitive forms of tourism development have engendered a broad spectrum of civil society resistance from transnational advocacy NGOs to local grass-roots activists. In most if not all cases, they have mobilized civil society, often through transnational, networked fora in order to both defend existing citizenship rights as well as extend notions of citizenship that are in some way being threatened by excessive and/or inappropriate forms of tourism. Through their actions, advocacy NGOs have worked closely with marginalized destination communities, invoking notions of human rights in defence of traditional livelihoods, the protection and stewardship of local environments, as well as the cultural rights and self-recognition of indigenous peoples, all of which may be deeply intertwined. Where such forms of contestation have sought to act as a constraint on untrammelled and harmful forms of tourism development, it has brought many of the implicit assumptions guiding the development and expansion of tourism, not least the unquestioned right to travel and to engage in tourism, out into the open, as in the case of the boycott against travel to Burma.

Rights-based struggles have been at the centre of manifold struggles by civil society groups and social movements against different forms of exploitative and unjust tourism development. Such struggles illustrate how the contestation of tourism cannot be understood simply in terms of a conflict over the spoils of tourism. Rather, they imply a deeper, more complex set of issues and debates concerned with the use and organization of public and/or customary lands, implying multiple readings of citizenship. Moreover, it is an arena of struggle in which the rights to travel and to profit from tourism are often posited against the rights to development of low-income/indigenous communities, from the Mediterranean littoral to the savannahs of East Africa. It is through such struggles that notions of citizenship and the role played by tourism, in either inhibiting or advancing the rights associated with different notions of citizenship, are increasingly crystallized, applied and extended throughout different political-geographical domains. However, a more circumspect view is that such advocacy campaigns reflect the splintering of social activism into specialized interests since the 1960s, and the lack of a cohesive set of values and institutional structures through which to build genuine and lasting forms of transnational solidarity that can act as a robust counterweight to concentrations of corporate and political power. Nevertheless, such 'rights-based struggles', from the grass-roots contestation of tourism development to globally orchestrated campaigns against specific issues (e.g. child sex tourism), do hold out the possibility for a more progressive politics – aptly described by Blomley (1994: 412) as the 'political promise of citizenship'.

Global citizenship remains a vague and problematic notion, not least given the impracticability of a global polity with the ability and legitimacy to be able to impose its will at a global level (see Gamble 2009: 156–159). However, some analysts have suggested that the material foundations of *cosmopolitan* citizenship, as distinguished from global citizenship (which implies a form of world government or global state) could be brought about by a 'mobility and transaction tax' (Isin and Turner 2007). Such a tax could take a variety of forms (e.g. a tourist tax on aviation fuel, a mobility tax on people entering other countries and a sport tax on people travelling to watch major sporting events) and applied on 'global movements and transactions' (Isin and Turner 2007: 15). Importantly, it would apply in principle to all human beings, helping to generate the necessary funds to compensate vulnerable or less well-off populations from the vagaries of both a natural (e.g. earthquakes, tsunamis, hurricanes) and human (financial crises, political instability) genesis. More importantly, by making people 'pay for their rights and to contribute through taxation to a common good at a global level' (Isin and Turner 2007: 16), it would make real the cosmopolitan duties of global citizens and importantly provide the resources with which to underpin a global civic culture, bolstered by an adequate and effective institutional framework.[1] Given the disproportionate contribution of the world's wealthiest industrialized states to greenhouse gas emissions, such a levy would go some way to addressing the imbalance between the polluting rights of rich states (which by implication implies tourists from these and rapidly emerging nations) and the development rights of low-income states. Despite the obvious practical difficulties and political obstacles such a proposal presents – certainly these are considerable if the Balearic eco-tax experiment is anything to go by – it opens up an interesting avenue, one where it is possible to explore the construction of new, transnational forms of solidarity and institutional mechanisms of cohesion that could form the basis of a robust and meaningful form of civic solidarity across borders as well as between mobile and immobile peoples.

If tourism is developed along democratic, just and sustainable principles, it has the potential to become a valuable tool of economic development and poverty alleviation. However, this does not absolve organizations such as the UNWTO and WTTC, the cheerleaders of a liberalized and corporate-run tourism industry, and whose fervent support for tourism and the right to travel often amounts to little more than a convenient cover for the rights of business and capital to exploit the ever-expanding potential of this lucrative area of commerce. More importantly, in a world in which other mobile subjects face constant harassment, persecution and containment, we cannot think about the mobility rights of tourists in isolation from the rights of those who do not have the right credentials for travel, or indeed have little access to the consumer economy.

The purpose of this book has been to conceptualize and examine the multiplex relations between tourism and citizenship with particular attention to the interplay between the discourse and practices that underscore the freedom of movement and the right to travel, and by implication tourism. It is not our concern to put forward a singular conception of *tourist citizenship* or even advance the case for or against the right to travel and the right to tourism, no matter how desirable that may be. It is our belief, however, that it is essential to interrogate the ideological norms that continue to nourish discourses pertaining to the right to travel and the right to tourism, as well as scrutinize the fluid dynamics of wealth and power that lubricate the engine room of global capitalism that is driving the corporate expansion of tourism. If tourism analyses fall short or fail to consider these elements then the genuine potential for travel as a progressive force will be left to simplistic moral pronouncements that fall within a narrow spectrum of neoliberal discourse, constrained by the imperatives of security and the interests of commerce.

One particular issue to which we have not been able to devote much attention, not least due to the demands of space, relates to the growing contradiction between humanity's carbon-fuelled, mobile lifestyles and the onset of global climate change, and the implications for the alignments of tourism and citizenship. Undoubtedly, as Urry (2013) considers in his lucid analysis of the coming energy crisis, the world is on the precipice of significant and far-reaching changes to the ways in which we work, travel and go about our lives, as a result of the 'perfect storm' arising from peak oil, global climate change and water shortages. Yet, although there are indications that demand for air travel is peaking and in some cases falling away in rich industrialized states (Urry 2013: 209), it is likely that the aspiration and enthusiasm for international travel will continue unabated in the short to medium term. Indeed, as we have indicated, not only does the UNWTO (2013) estimate that by 2030 international tourist arrivals will have reached 1.8 billion, it is likely that much of this growth will increasingly originate outside the advanced capitalist states, in the BRIC and other emerging economies.

Ultimately, this of course raises a philosophical conundrum regarding the unfolding relationship between the freedom of movement, right to travel, democracy and citizenship. While it may become increasingly socially unacceptable to travel among certain groups in the advanced capitalist states, as evidenced by the rise of radical climate change activism, to suggest that the rising middle classes in emerging economies suppress their desire for travel, given that global carbon emissions have resulted overwhelmingly from industrialization and the expansion of capitalism in the West, places us on considerably difficult and contradictory ethical grounds. Immanuel Kant, who is regarded as a founding thinker on 'cosmopolitanism', was no traveller himself, thus giving the lie somewhat to the notion that one has to engage in travel in order to become a global citizen. Given the increasing threats faced by the planet, many of which are linked to our carbon-fuelled mobile lives and economies, it could be argued that to develop a meaningful conception and practice of global citizenship requires precisely the opposite: travelling less and more locally! As to whether international travel and participation in tourism can fulfil its progressive potential and engender new forms of citizenship will depend upon the battle of values and ideologies in the global system over the course of the twenty-first century. Moreover, the unfolding relationships between tourism and notions of citizenship will continue to revolve around and be determined by shifts in the global distribution of wealth and power. These changes may create for some the acquisition of the trappings of citizenship from which they have long been excluded. However, the extent to which the rights of the planet outweigh these newly acquired rights and freedoms of mobility is one of many pressing questions with which tourism analysts and policymakers will continue to grapple for some time to come.

Notes

1   Such a tax is similar to the proposed Tobin Tax on cross-border financial transactions, as well as reflecting some of the principles applied in the Balearic eco-tax, on a transnational scale. Indeed, one such proposal already exists: the International Air Passenger Adaption Levy (Scott and Becken 2010: 287). If implemented, this levy would theoretically provide up to US$8 billion per year to fund costly climate adaptation schemes in low-income countries.

REFERENCES

Abbink, J. (2000) 'Tourism and its discontents: Suri–tourist encounters in southern Ethiopia', *Social Anthropology*, 8(1): 1–17.

Abbott, C., P. Rogers and J. Sloboda (2007) *Beyond Terror: The Truth About the Real Threats to Our World*, revised edition, London: Rider.

Adams, K. J. (2012) 'Indonesia to informally upgrade its relations with Israel via ambassador-ranked diplomat in Ramallah', *Times of Israel*, 6 July. Available at http://www.timesofisrael.com/indonesia-to-informally-upgrade-its-relations-with-israel-via-ambassador-ranked-diplomat-in-ramallah/ (accessed 10 June 2013).

Adler, J. (1985) 'Youth on the road: reflections on the history of tramping', *Annals of Tourism Research*, 12(3): 335–354.

Aguilar, F. and L. Siruno (2004) 'A community without kidney: a tragedy? Analysis of the moral and ethical aspects of kidney organ donation', paper presented at the 5th Asian Bioethics Conference (ABC5) and 9th Tsukuba International Bioethics Roundtable (TRT9) at the University of Tsukuba, Tsukuba Science City, Japan, 12–16 February.

Airey, D. and K. Chong (2011) *Tourism in China: Policy and Development Since 1949*, London: Routledge.

Akama, J. and D. Kieti (2007) 'Tourism and socio-economic development in developing countries: a case study of Mombasa resort in Kenya', *Journal of Sustainable Tourism*, 15(6): 735–748.

Al-Jazeera (2009) 'Timeline: bombings in Egypt', Al-Jazeera.net, 23 February 2009. Available at http://www.aljazeera.com/news/middleeast/2009/02/20092221901217811.html (accessed 10 December 2012).

Al-Jazeera (2011) 'Timeline: attacks on India', Al-Jazeera.net, 7 September 2011. Available at http://www.aljazeera.com/news/asia/2011/07/2011713201019508329.html (accessed 10 December 2012).

Allcock, J. (1995) 'International tourism and the appropriation of history in the Balkans', in M.-F. Lanfant, J. Allcock and E. Bruner (eds) *International Tourism: Identity and Change*, London: Sage, pp. 100–112.

Allcock, J. and K. Przeclawski (1990) 'Introduction', *Annals of Tourism Research* (Special Issue on Tourism in Centrally Planned Economies), 17(1): 1–16.

Allsop, K. (1967) *Hard Travellin': The Hobo and His History*, New York: New American Library.

Al-Muraqab A. (2012) 'Aden's future uncertain now all tourists are gone', *Yemen Times*, 8 October. Available at http://www.yementimes.com/en/1614/report/1498 (accessed 1 March 2013).

Alsharif, M. J., R. Labonte and Z. Lu (2010) 'Patients beyond borders: a study of medical tourists in four countries', *Global Social Policy*, 10(3): 315–335.

Al Tamimi, J. (2013) 'Southern countries rise as major powers', *Gulf News*, 15 March, p. 27.

Ambrose, I. (2012) 'European policies for accessible tourism', in D. Buhalis, S. Darcy and I. Ambrose (eds) *Best Practice in Accessible Tourism: Inclusion, Disability, Ageing Population and Tourism*, Bristol: Channel View Publications, pp. 19–35.

Amnesty International (2004) *Amnesty International Report 2004 – Maldives*, 26 May 2004. Available at http://www.unhcr.org/refworld/docid/40b5a1fbc.html (accessed 5 March 2013).

Amoore, L. (2006) 'Biometric borders: governing mobilities in the war on terror', *Political Geography*, 25(3): 336–351.

Amoore, L., S. Marmura and M. B. Salter (2006) 'Editorial: Smart Borders and Mobilities: Spaces, Zones, Enclosures', *Surveillance and Society*, 5(2): 96-1-10.

Anderson, B. (1991) *Imagined Communities: Reflections on the Origins and Spread of Nationalism*, London: Verso.

Andrews, H. (2002) 'A theme park for the Brits behaving badly', *Times Higher Education*, 19 July. Available at http://www.timeshighereducation.co.uk/features/a-theme-park-for-the-brits-behaving-badly/170527.article (accessed 19 September 2005).

Aparis, C. (2013) 'Repeated rapes in India put woman tourists off', *Gulf News, Business*, 12 June, p. 7.

Appadurai, A. (1995) 'The production of locality', in R. Fardon (ed.) *Counterworks: Managing the Diversity of Knowledge*, London: Routledge, pp. 204–225.

Appiah, K. A. (2006) *Ethics in a World of Strangers*, London: Allen Lane.

Archibold, R. C. (2010) 'Arizona enacts stringent law on immigration', *New York Times*, 23 April. Available at http://www.nytimes.com/2010/04/24/us/politics/24immig.html?ref=us&_r=0 (accessed 24 December 2012).

Archibugi, D. (2000) 'Cosmopolitical democracy', *New Left Review*, II, 4: 137–150.

Archibugi, D. and D. Held (eds) (1995) *Cosmopolitan Democracy*, Cambridge: Cambridge University Press.

Arremberi, J. (2009) 'The future of tourism and globalization: some critical remarks', *Futures*, 41: 367–376.

Arrington, V. (2005) 'Less US travel prompts Cuba to lash out', *Travelwire News*, 29 September. Available at http://www.travelwirenews.com (accessed 29 September 2005).

Ashley, C., D. Roe and H. Goodwin (2001) *Pro-Poor Tourism Strategies: Making Tourism Work for the Poor*, Pro-Poor Tourism Report No. 1, Nottingham: Russell Press.

Askjellerud, S. (2003) 'The tourist: a messenger of peace?', *Annals of Tourism Research*, 30(3): 741–744.

Associated Press (2004) 'U.S. lifts Libya travel restrictions after 23 years', NBCNEWS.com, 26 February. Available at http://www.nbcnews.com/id/4381087/ns/world_news/t/us-lifts-libya-travel-restrictions-after-years/#.UYztgkpv9EM (accessed 10 May 2013).

Associated Press (2013) 'Cuba relaxes travel restrictions for citizens', *The Guardian*, 15 January. Available at http://www.guardian.co.uk/world/2013/jan/15/cuba-relaxes-travel-restrictions (accessed 2 February 2013).

Ateljevic, I. (2000) 'Circuits of tourism: stepping beyond the "production/consumption" dichotomy', *Tourism Geographies*, 2(4): 369–388.

Athwal, H. (2006) 'The emergence of a European security-industrial complex', *Independent Race and Refugee News Network*, 11 May. Available at http://www.irr.org.uk/2006/may/ha000016.html (accessed 20 May 2006).

Augé, M. (1995) *Non-places: Introduction to the Anthropology of Supermodernity*, London: Verso.

Aziz, H. (1995) 'Understanding attacks on tourists in Egypt', *Tourism Management*, 16(2): 91–95.

Babington, D. and L. Papadimas (2013) 'Fleeing war, Syrians face new misery in Greece', *Reuters*, 10 March. Available at http://www.reuters.com/article/2013/03/10/us-greece-syria-idUSBRE92907920130310 (accessed 12 June 2013).

Bach, R. L. (2003) 'Global mobility, inequality and security', *Journal of Human Development*, 4(2): 227–245.

Bahari, M. (2010) 'Iranian ex-officials: U.S. knew hikers were seized in Iraq', *Newsweek International*. Available at http://www.thedailybeast.com/newsweek/2010/10/28/iranian-ex-officials-u-s-knew-hikers-were-seized-in-iraq.html (accessed 25 February 2013).

Balibar, E. (1991) 'Racism and the politics in Europe today', *New Left Review*, II, 186: 5–19.

Balibar, E. (2002) *Politics and the Other Scene*, London: Verso.

Baliga, L. (2011) '1 in 5 Mumbaikars below poverty line', *The Times of India*, 23 September. Available at http://articles.timesofindia.indiatimes.com/2011–09–23/mumbai/30193453_1_bpl-population-bpl-survey-poverty-line (accessed 12 January 2013).

Ballard, J. G. (1997) 'Going somewhere?', *The Observer*, 14 September. Available at http://www.jgballard.com/airports.htm (accessed 5 July 2010).

Banton, M. (1999) 'National integration and ethnic violence in Western Europe', *Journal of Ethnic and Migration Studies*, 25(1): 5–20.

Baranowski, S. (2004) *Strength Through Joy: Consumerism and Mass Tourism in the Third Reich*, Cambridge: Cambridge University Press.

Barkham, P. (2006) 'Are these the new colonialists?', *The Guardian*, 18 August. Available at http://www.guardian.co.uk/society/2006/aug/18/internationalaidanddevelopment.education (accessed 21 February 2013).

Barnett, T. (2008) 'Influencing tourism at the grassroots level: the role of NGO Tourism Concern', *Third World Quarterly*, 29(5): 995–1002.

Barrett, C. (2011) 'Simplify visas for Chinese tourists', *Financial Times*, 30 January. Available at http://www.ft.com/cms/s/0/ae31f484–2c9d-11e0–83bd-00144feab49a.html (accessed 7 January 2013).

Bastin, R. (1984) 'Small island tourism: development or dependency?', *Development Policy Review*, 2: 79–90.

Batty, D. (2009) 'Uluru visitors face climbing ban', *The Guardian*, 8 July. Available at http://www.guardian.co.uk/world/2009/jul/08/uluru-climbing-ban-plan (accessed 13 November 2012).

Bauman, Z. (1993) *Postmodern Ethics*, London: Routledge.

Bauman, Z. (1996) 'From pilgrim to tourist – or a short history of identity', in S. Hall and P. de Guy (eds) *Questions of Cultural Identity*, London: Sage, pp. 18–36.

Bauman, Z. (1998) *Globalization: The Human Consequences*, Cambridge: Polity.

Bauman, Z. (2003) 'The tourist syndrome: an interview with Zygmunt Bauman', *Tourist Studies*, 3(2): 205–221.

Bauman, Z. (2007) *Consuming Life*, Cambridge: Polity.

BBC (1974) '1974 bomb blast at the Tower of London', On This Day 1940–2005. Available at http://news.bbc.co.uk/onthisday/hi/dates/stories/july/17/newsid_2514000/2514429.stm (accessed 27 December 2012).

BBC (2006) 'Mexico fines US hotel in Cuba row', 6 March. Available at http://news.bbc. co.uk/1/hi/world/americas/4778268.stm (accessed 6 March 2006).

BBC (2010a) 'Both sides say they are winning in BA strike', 21 March. Available at http:// news.bbc.co.uk/1/hi/business/8578568.stm (accessed 19 July 2010).

BBC (2010b) 'EU imposes flight ban on Iran Air over safety', 6 July. Available at http://www. bbc.co.uk/news/10529236 (accessed 13 May 2013).

BBC (2010c) 'Burma releases pro-democracy leader Aung San Suu Kyi', 13 November. Available at http://www.bbc.co.uk/news/world-asia-pacific-11749661 (accessed 23 March 2013).

BBC (2011a) 'US imposes economic sanctions on Iran Air', 23 June. Available at http:// www.bbc.co.uk/news/world-us-canada-13897272 (accessed 13 May 2013).

BBC (2011b) 'Iran frees jailed US hiker "spies" Bauer and Fattal', 22 September. Available at http://www.bbc.co.uk/news/world-middle-east-15000563 (accessed 11 August 2012).

BBC (2011c) 'North Korea seizes South's Mt. Kumgang resort assets', 22 August. Available at http://www.bbc.co.uk/news/world-asia-pacific-14611873 (accessed 4 April 2013).

BBC Radio 4 (2012) 'Open for tourist business?', *Face the Facts*, broadcast 11 July 2012. Available at http://www.bbc.co.uk/programmes/b01kmjj6 (accessed 12 July 2012).

BBC World Service (2010) 'Nora Shourd: a mother's plea', 14 July. Available at http://www. bbc.co.uk/worldservice/programmes/2010/07/100714_outlook_hikers.shtml (accessed 10 August 2012).

Beck, U. (1992) *Risk Society: Towards a New Modernity*, London: Sage.

Beck, U. (2003) 'Rooted cosmopolitanism: emerging from a rivalry of distinction', in U. Beck, N. Sznaider and R. Winter (eds) *Global America? The Cultural Consequences of Globalisation*, Liverpool: Liverpool University Press, pp. 15–29.

Beck, U. (2005) *Power in the Global Age*, Cambridge: Polity.

Beck, U. (2006) *Cosmopolitan Vision*, Cambridge: Polity.

Beddoe, C. (2004) *Labour Standards, Social Responsibility and Tourism*, London: Tourism Concern.

Bell, D. and G. Valentine (1997) *Consuming Geographies: We Are What We Eat*, London: Routledge.

Benhabib, S. (1998) 'On European citizenship: replies to David Miller', *Dissent*, 45: 107–109. Available at http://www.yale.edu/polisci/sbenhabib/papers/On%20European%20 Citizenship.%20Replies%20to%20David%20Miller.pdf (accessed 12 January 2013).

Berlin, I. (2002) *Liberty: Incorporating Four Essays on Liberty*, H. Hardy (ed.), Oxford: Oxford University Press (first published in 1969, Oxford University Press).

Bianchi, R.V. (2000) 'Migrant tourist-workers: exploring the contact-zones of post-industrial tourism', *Current Issues in Tourism*, 3(2): 107–137.

Bianchi, R.V. (2002) 'The contested landscapes of World Heritage on a tourist island: the case of Garajonay National Park, La Gomera', *International Journal of Heritage Studies*, 8(2): 81–97.

Bianchi, R.V. (2004a) 'Tourism restructuring and the politics of sustainability: a critical view from the European periphery', *Journal of Sustainable Tourism*, 12(6): 495–529.

Bianchi, R.V. (2004b) 'Heritage, identity and the politics of commemoration on "Columbus Island" (La Gomera, Canary Islands)', *Working Papers in Tourism and Culture*, Sheffield Hallam University, Centre for Tourism and Cultural Change.

Bianchi, R.V. (2005) 'Euromed heritage: culture, capital and trade liberalisation – implications for the Mediterranean city', *Journal of Mediterranean Studies*, 15(2): 283–318.

Bianchi, R.V. and M. L. Stephenson (2013) 'Deciphering tourism and citizenship in a globalised world', *Tourism Management*, 39: 10–20.

Billett, M. (1997) *Highwaymen and Outlaws*, London: Orion Publishing Co.

Birkett, D. (1991) *Spinsters Abroad: Victorian Lady Explorers*, London: Victor Gollancz Ltd.

Birkett, D. (2000) 'Trouble in the paradise industry?' *The Guardian* (Comment section), 1 June, p. 24.

Bishop, M. (1983) *Selected Speeches 1979–1981*, Havana, Cuba: Casa de las Americas.

Blackden, P. (2003) *Tourist Trap: When Holiday Turns to Nightmare*, London: Virgin Books.

Blanchar, C. (2012) 'Cicatrices de ladrillo', *El País Semanal (Magazine)*, No. 1,880, 7 October, pp. 50–57.

Blanchard, L. and F. Higgins-Desbiolles (2013) *Peace Through Tourism: Promoting Human Security Through International Citizenship*, London: Routledge.

Bland, A. (2011) 'Paris bans Muslim street prayers after far-right protests', *The Independent*, 17 September. Available at http://www.independent.co.uk/news/world/europe/paris-bans-muslim-street-prayers-after-farright-protests-2356115.html (accessed 26 April 2013).

Blanke, J. and T. Chiesa (2011) *The Travel and Tourism Competitiveness Report: Beyond the Downturn*, Davos: World Economic Forum. Available at http://www3.weforum.org/docs/WEF_TravelTourismCompetitiveness_Report_2011.pdf (accessed 27 December 2012).

Bleach, S. (2009) 'Tour operators refuse to cut links with Burmese regime', *Sunday Times Travel*, 22 February, p. 2.

Blomley, N. K. (1994) 'Mobility, empowerment and the rights revolution', *Political Geography*, 13(5): 407–422.

Bloomberg (2013) 'Billionaires worth $1.9 trillion seek advantage in 2013', *Bloomberg.com*. Available at http://www.bloomberg.com/news/2013-01-01/billionaires-worth-1-9-trillion-seek-advantage-in-2013.html (accessed 5 February 2013).

Bobes, V. C. (2005) 'Citizenship and rights in Cuba: evolution and current situation', in J. S. Tulchin, L. Bobea, M. P. Espina Prieto and R. Hernández (eds) *Changes in Cuban Society since the Nineties*, Washington, DC: Woodrow Wilson Center for International Scholars, pp. 61–80.

Boggs, C. (1986) *Social Movements and Political Power: Emerging Forms of Radicalism in the West*, Philadelphia: Temple University Press.

Boissevain, J. and N. Theuma (1998) 'Contested space: planners, tourists, developers and environmentalists in Malta', in S. Abram and J. Waldren (eds) *Anthropological Perspectives on Development*, London: Routledge, pp. 96–119.

Boorstin, D. J. (1963) *The Image*, Harmondsworth, Middlesex: Penguin Books.

Botterill, T. D. (1991) 'A new social movement: Tourism Concern, the first two years', *Leisure Studies*, 10: 203–217.

Boyes, R. and J. Carr (2010) 'Safe haven for your cash? Germans call on Greece to sell off its islands', *The Times*, 5 March, p. 4.

Boynton, G. (2000) 'Should we boycott Burma?' *The Telegraph*, 17 June.

Bramwell, B. (2003) 'Maltese responses to tourism', *Annals of Tourism Research*, 30(3): 581–605.

Breen, M., A. Haynes and E. Devereux (2006) 'Citizens, loopholes and maternity tourists: media frames in the citizenship referendum', in M. P. Corcoran and M. Peillon (eds) *Uncertain Ireland: A Sociological Chronicle 2003–2004*, Dublin: Institute of Public Administration, pp. 59–70.

Brelis, M. and M. Carroll (2001) 'FAA finds Logan security among worst in US', *Boston Globe On-line*, 26 September. Available at http://web.archive.org/web/20010927100927/www.boston.com/dailyglobe2/269/nation/FAA_finds_Logan_security_among_worst_in_US+.shtml (accessed 8 July 2010).

Brendon, P. (1991) *Thomas Cook: 150 Years of Popular Tourism*, London: Secker & Warburg.

Brennan, T. (1997) *At Home in the World: Cosmopolitanism Now*, Cambridge, MA: Harvard University Press.

Brennan, T. (2001) 'Cosmopolitanism and internationalism', *New Left Review*, II, 7: 75–84.

Brenner, R. (2003) *The Boom and the Bubble: The US in the World Economy*, London and New York: Verso.

Briassoulis, H. (2002) 'Sustainable tourism and the question of the commons', *Annals of Tourism Research*, 29(4): 1065–1085.

Brin, E. (2006) 'Politically-oriented tourism in Jerusalem', *Tourist Studies*, 6: 215–243.

Brindis, T. (2006) 'United Arab Emirates firm may oversee 6 US ports', *Washington Post*, 12 February. Available at http://www.washingtonpost.com/wp-dyn/content/article/2006/02/11/AR2006021101112.html (accessed 23 February 2006).

Britton, S. G. (1982) 'The political economy of tourism in the third world', *Annals of Tourism Research*, 9(3): 331–358.

Britton, S. G. (1991) 'Tourism, capital and place: towards a critical geography tourism', *Environment and Planning D: Society and Space*, 9: 451–478.

Brock, A. (2000) 'View from the tour operator', Burma: Your Views (Letters page), *Telegraph Travel (The Telegraph)*, 8 July, p. 13.

Brohman, J. (1996) 'New directions for tourism in the third world', *Annals of Tourism Research*, 23(1): 48–70.

Brown, F. (1989) 'Is tourism really a peacemaker?', *Tourism Management*, 10(4): 270–271.

Bruner, E. and B. Kirshenblatt-Gimblett (1994) 'Maasai on the lawn: tourist realism in East Africa', *Cultural Anthropology*, 9(4): 435–470.

Buck, E. (1994) *Paradise Remade: The Politics of Culture and History in Hawai'i*, Philadelphia: Temple University Press.

Bugnicourt, J. (1977) 'Tourism with no return!', *Development Forum*, 5(5): 1–2.

Buhalis, D., S. Darcy and I. Ambrose (2012) *Best Practice in Accessible Tourism: Inclusion, Disability, Ageing Population and Tourism*, Bristol: Channel View Publications.

Bungay, S. (1999a) 'A very taxing issue for the general public', *Mallorca Daily Bulletin*, 6 August, p. 9.

Bungay, S. (1999b) 'Escarrer labels ecotax an atrocity', *Mallorca Daily Bulletin*, 14 August, p. 8.

Burma Campaign UK (2010) 'Burma tourism boycott now targeted at package tours', press release, 4 November. Available at http://www.burmacampaign.org.uk/index.php/burma/about-burma/about-burma/tourism-campaign (accessed 23 March 2013).

Burstein, D. (1991) *Euroquake: Europe's Explosive Economic Challenge Will Change the World*, New York: Simon and Schuster.

Butcher, J. (2003) *The Moralisation of Tourism: Sun, Sand … Saving the World?* London: Routledge.

Butcher, J. and P. Smith (2010) '"Making a difference": volunteer tourism and development', *Tourism Recreation Research*, 35(1): 27–36.

Butler, R. W. and W. Mao (1996) 'Conceptual and theoretical implications of tourism between partitioned states', *Journal of Tourism Research*, 1(1): 25–34.

Caire, G. (2011) 'Social tourism and the social economy', in S. McCabe, A. Diekmann and L. Minnaert (eds) *Social Tourism in Europe: Theory and Practice*, Clevedon: Channel View Publications, pp. 80–94.

Calder, S. (2008) 'These Boots rules are made for Washington', *The Independent Traveller* (supplement to *The Independent*), 27 December, p. 3.

Calhoun, C. (2002) 'The class consciousness of frequent travellers: towards a critique of actually existing cosmopolitanism', in S. Vertovec and R. Cohen (eds) *Conceiving Cosmopolitanism*, Oxford: Oxford University Press, pp. 86–109.

Calhoun, C. (2008) Cosmopolitanism and nationalism, *Nations and Nationalism*, 14(3): 427–448.

Callinicos, A. (1989) *Against Postmodernism: A Marxist Critique*, Cambridge: Polity.

Callinicos, A. (2003) *An Anti-Capitalist Manifesto*, Cambridge: Polity.

Canada News Centre (2009) 'China grants Canada Approved Destination Status', 3 December. Available at http://news.gc.ca/web/article-eng.do?m=/index&nid=500169 (accessed 22 June 2010).

Canally, C. and B. A. Carmichael (2006) 'A political economy of destination image: manufacturing Cuba', paper presented to Conference: *The Critical Turn in Tourism Studies Promoting an Academy of Hope?* Second International Critical Tourism Studies Conference, Split, Croatia, 20–23 June 2007.

Capgemini and RBC Wealth Management (2012) *16th World Wealth Report*, Paris: Capgemini Consulting. Available at http://www.capgemini.com/services-and-solutions/by-industry/financial-services/solutions/wealth/worldwealthreport/ (accessed 18 September 2012).

Carroll, R. (2008) 'The Sandalistas who never left', *The Guardian* (G2 supplement). Available at http://www.guardian.co.uk/world/2008/feb/12/11 (accessed 11 August 2012).

Carruthers, D. V. (1996) 'Indigenous ecology and the politics of linkage in Mexican social movements', *Third World Quarterly*, 17(5): 1007–1028.

Carter, H. and R. Ramesh (2007) 'Bomb that injured newlyweds blamed on dissidents', *The Guardian*, 1 October, p. 7.

Carter, S. (1998) 'Tourists' and travellers' social construction of Africa and Asia as risky locations', *Tourism Management*, 19(4): 349–358.

Carter, T. F. (2008) 'Of spectacular phantasmal desire: tourism and the Cuban state's complicity in the commodification of its citizens', *Leisure Studies*, 27(3): 241–257.

Cassen, L. (1994) *Travel in the Ancient World*, Baltimore: Johns Hopkins University Press.

Castells, M. (1997) *The Power of Identity*, Oxford: Blackwell.

Castells, M. (2012) *Networks of Outrage and Hope: Social Movements in the Internet Age*, Cambridge: Polity Press.

Castles, S. and A. Miller (2000) *Citizenship and Migration: Globalization and the Politics of Exclusion*, London: Macmillan.

Causevic, S. and P. Lynch (2011) 'Phoenix tourism: post-conflict tourism role', *Annals of Tourism Research*, 38(3): 780–800.

CEC (Commission of the European Communities) (2002a) *Euromed Heritage: Creating a Future that Cares for the Past*, Luxembourg: Office for Official Publications of the European Communities.

CEC (Commission of the European Communities) (2002b) *Dialogue Between Cultures and Civilisations in the Barcelona Process*, Luxembourg: Office for Official Publications of the European Communities.

CEC (Commission of the European Communities) (2010a) *Calypso Widens Europe's Travel Horizons*, DG Enterprise and Industry, Tourism Unit. Available at http://ec.europa.eu/enterprise/sectors/tourism/files/docs/calypso/leaflets/leaflet_calypso_en.pdf (accessed 27 May 2013).

CEC (Commission of the European Communities) (2010b) *EU Citizenship Report 2010: Dismantling the Obstacles to EU Citizens' Rights*. Available at http://ec.europa.eu/justice/citizen/files/com_2010_603_en.pdf (accessed 19 May 2013).

CEC (Commission of the European Communities) (2010c) 'European Commission proposes visa free travel for Albania and Bosnia and Herzegovina', press release. Available at http://europa.eu/rapid/pressReleasesAction.do?reference=IP/10/621&type=HTML (accessed 25 June 2010).

Center for Responsible Travel (2013) *The Case for Responsible Travel: Trends and Statistics*, Washington, DC: CREST. Available at http://www.responsibletravel.org/resources/marketing-reports.html (accessed 10 September 2013).

Cesarini, D. (1996) 'The changing character of citizenship and nationality in Britain', in D. Cesarini and M. Fulbrook (eds) *Citizenship, Nationality and Migration in Europe*, London: Routledge, pp. 57–73.

Chanlett-Avery, E. (2008) 'North Korea's abduction of Japanese citizens and the Six-Party talks', *CRS Report for Congress*, Washington, DC: Library of Congress. Available at http://www.fas.org/sgp/crs/row/RS22845.pdf (accessed 11 January 2013).

Chatterjee, P. (1993) *The Nation and its Fragments: Colonial and Postcolonial Histories*, Princeton: Princeton University Press.

Chen, S. (2009) 'Ease Cuba travel restrictions? Some Americans hope so', *eTurboNews, Global Travel Industry News*, 4 February. Available at http://www.eturbonews.com/7585/ease-cuba-travel-restrictions-some-americans-hope-so (accessed 13 August 2009).

Cheong, S.-M. and M. L. Miller (2000) 'Power and tourism: a Foucauldian observation', *Annals of Tourism Research*, 27(2): 371–390.

Cheung, S. C. H. (2005) 'Rethinking Ainu heritage: a case study of an Ainu settlement in Hokkaido, Japan', *International Journal of Heritage Studies*, 11(3): 197–210.

Chin, C. B. N. (2008) 'Labour flexibilization at sea', *International Journal of Feminist Politics*, 10(1): 1–18.

China Daily (2013) 'Chinese move to top in tourism spending', *China Daily*, 12–18 April, p. 6.

China Tourism Daily (2013) 'China to reach 100 million outbound travellers', *China Tourism Daily*, 26 August. Available at http://www.tldchina.com/EN/WebSite/yudu.aspx?FID=454&id=2345 (accessed 9 September 2013).

Chomsky, N. (2013) *Power Systems: Conversations with David Barsamian on Global Democratic Uprisings and the New Challenges to US Empire*, London: Hamish Hamilton.

Christman, H. M. (ed.) (1987) *Essential Works of Lenin: 'What is to be Done?' and Other Writings*, New York: Dover Publications.

Clarke, J. and C. Critcher (1985) *The Devil Makes Work: Leisure in Capitalist Britain*, London: Macmillan.

Clifford, J. (1992) 'Travelling cultures', in L. Grossberg, C. Nelson and P. Treichler (eds) *Cultural Studies*, London: Routledge, pp. 96–116.

Cockburn, P. (2004) 'We only want to hurt the Westerners. Where can we find them?', *The Independent*, 31 May, p. 4.

Codourey, M. (2008) 'Mobile identities and the socio-spatial relations of air-travel', *Surveillance and Society*, 5(2): 188–202.

Cohen, E. (1972) 'Toward a sociology of international tourism', *Social Research*, 39(1): 164–182.

Cohen, E. (1973) 'Nomads from affluence: notes on the phenomenon of drifter-tourism', *International Journal of Comparative Sociology*, 14(1–2): 89–103.

Cohen, E. (1979) 'A phenomenology of tourist experiences', *Sociology*, 13: 179–201.

Cohen, G. (2010) 'Protecting patients with passports: medical tourism and the patient protective-argument', *Iowa Law Review*, 95(5): 1467–1576.

Cohen, N. (2000) 'Burma's shame', *The Observer*, 4 June, p. 6.

Cohen, S. (1972) *Folk Devils and Moral Panics: The Creation of Mods and Rockers*, London: MacGibbon and Kee.

Cole, S. (2008) 'Living in hope: tourism and poverty alleviation in Flores,' in P. Burns and M. Novelli (eds) *Tourism Development: Growth, Myths and Inequalities*, Oxford: CABI, pp. 272–289.

Coles, T. (2008a) 'Citizenship and the state: hidden features in the internationalization of tourism', in T. Coles and C. M. Hall (eds) *International Business and Tourism: Global Issues, Contemporary Interactions*, London: Routledge, pp. 55–69.

Coles, T. (2008b) 'Telling tales of tourism: mobility, media and citizenship', in P. M. Burns and M. Novelli (eds) *Tourism and Mobilities: Local–Global Connections*, Oxford: CABI, pp. 65–80.

Coles, T. and D. J. Timothy (2004) *Tourism, Diasporas and Space*, London: Routledge.

Conrad, D. (2012) 'Survival in the dumps', *Gulf News*, 25 May, pp. 8–9.

Conversi, D. (2000) *The Basques, the Catalans, and Spain: Alternative Routes to Nationalist Mobilisation*, Reno: University of Nevada Press.

Corporate Europe Observer (2002) 'TABD takes up arms: post-September 11, major EU and US arms producers take a leading role in the ailing group', Issue 11, May. Available at http://www.corporateeurope.org/observer11/tabd.html (accessed 15 May 2003).

Court of Justice of the European Commission (2006) 'The Court annuls the Council decision concerning of an agreement between the European Community and the United States of America on the processing and transfer of personal data and the Commission decision on the adequate protection of those data', Press Release No. 46/06, 30 May 2006, Luxembourg.

Cox, R. (1987) *Production, Power and World Order*, New York: Columbia University Press.

Creswell, T. (2006) *On the Move: Mobility in the Modern Western World*, London: Routledge.

Creswell, T. (2010) 'Towards a politics of mobility', *Environment and Planning D: Society and Space*, 28: 17–31.

Crompton, J. (1979) 'Motivations for pleasure vacation', *Annals of Tourism Research*, 6(4): 408–424.

Curran, G. and M. Gibson (2013) 'WikiLeaks, anarchism and technologies of dissent', *Antipode*, 45(2): 294–314.

Curtis, M. (2003) *Web of Deceit: Britain's Real Role in the World*, London: Vintage.

Daga, R. (2013) 'Sky's the limit? Southeast Asia budget airlines bet big on growth', *Reuters*, 23 March. Available at http://www.reuters.com/article/2013/03/24/us-southeastasia-airlines-idUSBRE92N02F20130324 (accessed 15 April 2013).

Dalwai, S. and B. Donegan (2012) 'From travellers to global citizens? Practitioner reflections on an activist volunteer tourist project', *Journal of Tourism Consumption and Practice*, 4(1): 5–29.

D'Amore, L. (1988) 'Tourism – a vital force for peace', *Tourism Management*, 9(2): 151–154.

D'Amore, L. (2005) 'The Ecoclub Interview', *International Ecotourism Monthly*, Year 6, Issue 67, January 2005. Available at http://ecoclub.com/news/067/interview.html (accessed 6 July 2012).

D'Andrea, A. (2006) 'Neo-nomadism: a theory of post-identitarian mobility in the global age', *Mobilities*, 1(1): 95–119.

Dann, G. M. S (1977) 'Anomie, ego-enhancement and tourism', *Annals of Tourism Research*, 4(4): 184–194.

Davis, A. (2013) 'Estonia's capital made public transit free to make people give up driving', *Business Insider*, 3 January. Available at http://www.businessinsider.com/tallinn-estonia-makes-public-transit-free-2013-1 (accessed 27 April 2013).

Davis, M. (2001) 'The flames of New York', *New Left Review*, II, 12: 34–50.

Davis, M. (2004) 'Planet of slums: urban involution and the informal proletariat', *New Left Review*, II, 26: 5–34.

Davis, M. (2005) 'The predators of New Orleans', *Le Monde Diplomatique*, October, pp. 1–3.

Day, P. (2002) 'Massacre in Luxor', BBC documentary, 8 December 2002. Exec. Producer: Alison Rooper. Available at http://www.youtube.com/watch?v=QeSFdjbhL84 (accessed 6 December 2012).

Deacon, H. (2004) 'Intangible heritage in conservation management planning: the case of Robben Island', *International Journal of Heritage Studies*, 10(3): 309–319.

Deakin, N. (2001) *In Search of Civil Society*, Basingstoke: Palgrave.

Defoe, D. (1972) *Robinson Crusoe*, J. D. Crowley (ed.), Oxford: Oxford University Press.

De Grazia, V. (1981) *The Culture of Consent: Mass Organization of Leisure in Fascist Italy*, Cambridge: Cambridge University Press.

De Kadt, E. (1979) *Tourism: Passport to Development? Perspectives on the Social and Cultural Effects of Tourism in Developing Countries*, Oxford: Oxford University Press.

Delanty, G. (1995) *Inventing Europe: Idea, Identity, Reality*, Basingstoke: Palgrave Macmillan.

Delanty, G. (2000) *Citizenship in a Global Age: Society, Culture, Politics*, Buckingham: Open University Press.

De Man, F. (2013) 'Personal communication', Founder of Dutch NGO RETOUR (Netherlands) and Chair, United Nations Working Group on Tourism, UN Commission on Sustainable Development, 1999.

Department of Homeland Security (2011) 'Electronic system for travel authorization', US Customs and Border Protection. Available at http://www.cbp.gov/xp/cgov/travel/id_visa/business_pleasure/vwp/ (accessed 26 April 2011).

Department of Homeland Security (2013) 'Trusted traveler programs', US Customs and Border Protection. Available at http://www.cbp.gov/xp/cgov/travel/trusted_traveler/ (accessed 15 May 2013).

Desai, M. (2004) *Marx's Revenge: The Resurgence of Capitalism and the Demise of State Socialism*, London: Verso.

Deveaux, M (2003) 'A deliberative approach to conflicts of culture', *Political Theory*, 31(6): 780–807.

Diekmann, A. and S. McCabe (2011) 'Systems of social tourism in the European Union: a critical review', *Current Issues in Tourism*, 14(5): 417–430.

Diekmann, A., S. McCabe and L. Minnaert (2011) 'Social tourism today: stakeholders, supply and demand factors', in S. McCabe, L. Minnaert and A. Diekmann (eds) *Social Tourism in Europe: Theory and Practice*, Clevedon: Channel View Publications, pp. 35–47.

Dimireva, I. (2012) 'Russia: country overview', *EU Business*, 4 September. Available at http://www.eubusiness.com/europe/russia (accessed 28 March 2013).

Dube, S. (1999) 'Travelling light: missionary musings, colonial cultures and anthropological anxieties', in R. Kaur and J. Hutnyk (eds) *Travel Worlds: Journeys in Contemporary Cultural Politics*, London: Zed Books, pp. 29–50.

Duberman, M. B. (1989) *Paul Robeson*, London: The Bodley Head.

Duffy, R. (2002) *A Trip Too Far: Ecotourism, Politics and Exploitation*, London: Earthscan.

Dunn, K. C. (2004) 'Fear of a black planet: anarchy anxieties and postcolonial travel to Africa', *Third World Quarterly*, 25(3): 483–499.

Eber, S. (1992) *Beyond the Green Horizon: A Discussion Paper on Principles for Sustainable Tourism*, London: Tourism Concern.

Ecologist (1995) 'The commons: where the community has authority', *The Ecologist*, in J. Kirkby and P. O'Keefe (eds) *The Earthscan Reader in Sustainable Development*, London: Earthscan, pp. 227–237.

Economist (1997) 'War on the coast', *The Economist*, 23–29 August, pp. 44–45.

Economist (2010) 'A new Grand Tour', *The Economist*, 18–31 December, pp. 54–56.

Edmonds, C. and J. Mak (2006) 'Terrorism and tourism in the Asia-Pacific region: is travel and tourism in a new world after 9/11?', *East West Center Working Papers*, No. 86 (February). Available at http://www.eastwestcenter.org (accessed 7 May 2007).

Eggers, D. (2010) *Zeitoun*, London: Hamish Hamilton.

Ehrkamp, P. and H. Leitner (2003) 'Beyond national citizenship: Turkish immigrants and the (re)construction of citizenship in Germany', *Urban Geography*, 24(2): 127–146.

El País (2008) 'Ojalá pudiéramos viajar y ver el mundo real', *El País*, 8 February. Available at http://www.elpais.com/articulo/internacional/Ojala/pudieramos/viajar/ver/mundo/real/elppgl/20080208elpepuint_14/Tes (accessed 31 August 2008).

Elliott, J. (1983) 'Politics, power and tourism in Thailand', *Annals of Tourism Research*, 10(4): 377–393.

Elliot, L. (2012) 'New-wave economies going for growth', *The Guardian*, 18 December. Available at http://www.guardian.co.uk/world/2012/dec/18/booming-economies-beyond-brics?intcmp=239 (accessed 19 December 2012).

Endy, C. (2004) *Cold War Holidays: American Tourism in France*, Chapel Hill: University of North Carolina Press.

English Tourist Board (ETB) (1989) *Tourism for All: A Report of the Working Party*, London: ETB.

Enloe, C. (1989) *Bananas, Beaches and Bases: Making Feminist Sense of International Politics*, London: Pandora Press.

Erdbrink, T. (2012) 'Iran's aging airline fleet seen as faltering under US sanctions', *New York Times*, 13 July. Available at http://www.nytimes.com/2012/07/14/world/middleeast/irans-airliners-falter-under-sanctions.html?_r=0 (accessed 20 March 2013).

eTurbo News (2010) 'US Congressman to reintroduce legislation barring travel from Iran', *eTurboNews, Global Travel Industry News*, 8 January. Available at http://www.eturbonews.com/13727/us-congressman-reintroduce-legislation-barring-travel-iran (accessed 17 May 2013).

eTurbo News (2011) 'Tourism author delivers inspirational keynote address to TAFI', *eTurboNews, Global Travel Industry News*, 22 December. Available at http://www.eturbonews.com/27054/tourism-author-delivers-inspirational-keynote-address-tafi (accessed 22 December 2011).

Euromonitor International (2011) 'Impact of the Western European debt crisis on global outbound tourism', *Passport GMID*, 3 October. Available at https://www.portal.euromonitor.com/Portal/Pages/Magazine/IndustryPage.aspx (accessed 8 October 2011).

Euromonitor International (2012) *World Travel Market Global Trends Report 2012*. Available at http://www.wtmlondon.com/Content/WTM-2012-Reports (accessed 23 April 2013).

European Parliament (2012) 'MEPs question Commission over problems with biometric passports', *European Parliament, News*. Citizens' Rights. 19 April. Available at http://www.europarl.europa.eu/news/en/headlines/content/20120413STO42897/html/MEPs-question-Commission-over-problems-with-biometric-passports (accessed 24 December 2012).

European Union (2009) 'Regulation (EC) No 444/2009 of the European Parliament and of the Council of 28 May 2009 amending Council Regulation (EC) No 2252/2004 on standards for security features and biometrics in passports and travel documents issued by Member States', *Official Journal of the European Union*, L 142, 6 June 2009, pp. 1–4. Available at http://eur-lex.europa.eu/LexUriServ/LexUriServ.do?uri=OJ:L:2009:142:0001:01:EN:HTML (accessed 24 December 2012).

Evening Standard (2011) 'Unions have jumped the gun, claims minister', *Evening Standard*, 30 June, p. 1/5.

Ewing, K. (2010) 'Yes, striking is a human right', *The Guardian*, 26 March. Available at http://www.guardian.co.uk/commentisfree/libertycentral/2010/mar/26/ba-strike-human-rights (accessed 19 July 2010).

Fagge, N. (2004) 'Gypsies: Britain here we come', *Daily Express*, 26 April. Available at http://www.express.co.uk/news/uk/171439/Gypsies-Britain-here-we-come (accessed 17 November 2011).

Faist, T. (2009) 'The transnational social question: social rights and citizenship in a global context', *International Sociology*, 24(1): 7–35.

Falk, R. (ed.) (1993) *The Constitutional Foundations of World Peace*, New York: State University of New York Press, pp. 127–140.

Falk, R. (1994) 'The making of global citizenship', in B. van Steenbergen (ed.) *The Condition of Citizenship*, London: Sage, pp. 127–140.

Fanon, F. (1968) *The Wretched of the Earth*, New York: Grove Press Inc.

Fearis, B. (2007) 'Industry hits back at Tory plans for "green" air tax', *TravelMole.com*, 12 March. Available at http://www.travelmole.com/news_feature.php?news_id=1116510&c=setreg&region=2 (accessed 12 March 2007).

Feifer, M. (1985) *Going Places: The Ways of the Tourist from Imperial Rome to the Present Day*, London: Macmillan.

Fekete, L. (2004) 'Anti-Muslim racism and the European security state', *Race and Class*, 46(1): 3–29.

Ferguson, L. (2007) 'The United Nations World Tourism Organization', *New Political Economy*, 12(4): 557–568.

Fiennes, C. (2009) *Through England on a Side-Saddle*, London: Penguin Classics.

Finger, M. and J. Kilcoyne (1997) 'Why transnational corporations are organizing to "save the global environment"', *The Ecologist*, 27(4): 138–142.

Fisher, M. (2013) 'Report: China may be shutting down some tourism into North Korea', *Washington Post*, 9 April. Available at http://www.washingtonpost.com/blogs/worldviews/wp/2013/04/09/report-china-may-be-shutting-down-some-tourism-into-north-korea/ (accessed 7 April 2013).

Flynn, M. K. and T. King (2007) 'Symbolic reparation, heritage and political transition in South Africa's Eastern Cape', *International Journal of Heritage Studies*, 13(6): 462–477.

Ford, C. (2009) 'A summer fling: the rise and fall of aquariums and fun parks on Sydney's ocean coast 1885–1920', *Journal of Tourism History*, 1(2): 95–112.

Foroohar, R. (2006) 'Going places', Special Report, *Newsweek International*, 15–22 May, pp. 51–58.

Forsyth, T. (1997) 'Environmental responsibility and business regulation: the case of sustainable tourism', *The Geographical Journal*, 163(3): 270–280.

Frangialli, F. (2003) Statement circulated at the 5th World Trade Organisation Ministerial Conference, Cancún, 10–14 September. Available at http://www.unwto.org/newsroom/speeches/2003/Cancun%20Mexico%2010%20September%202003.pdf (accessed 1 July 2010).

Frangialli, F. (2004) 'Hope, all the same', Address by Francesco Frangialli, Secretary-General of the World Tourism Organization, on the occasion of the Third Prime Minister's Conference for Tourism to Israel, Jerusalem, 22–24 February. Available at http://www.hospitalitynet.org/news/ (accessed 30 September 2010).

Frank, T. (2001) *One Market under God: Extreme Capitalism, Market Populism and the End of Economic Democracy*, London: Vintage.

Franklin, A. and M. Crang (2001) 'The trouble with tourism and travel theory?', *Tourist Studies*, 1(1): 5–22.

Fraser, N. (2005) 'Reframing global justice', *New Left Review*, II, 36: 69–90.

Freedland, J. (2012) 'This sacred text explains why the US can't kick the gun habit', *The Guardian*, 21 December. Available at http://www.guardian.co.uk/commentisfree/2012/dec/21/sacred-text-us-gun-habit (accessed 21 December 2012).

Freedom House (2012) 'Israel – freedom of the press'. Available at http://www.freedom-house.org/report/freedom-press/2012/israel (accessed 10 June 2013).

Friedman, J. (1994) *Cultural Identity and Global Process*, London: Sage.

Fukuyama, F. (1989) 'The end of history?', *The National Interest*, 16: 3–18.

Gamble, A. (2009) *The Spectre at the Feast: Capitalist Crisis and the Politics of Recession*, Basingstoke: Palgrave Macmillan.

Gearon, E. (2006) 'After the pilgrimage', *The Middle East*, August/September, Issue 37, pp. 44–45.

Geddes, A. (2000) *Immigration and European Integration: Towards Fortress Europe?* Manchester: Manchester University Press

Germann Molz, J. (2005) 'Getting a "flexible eye": Round-the-World travel and scales of cosmopolitan citizenship', *Citizenship Studies*, 9(5): 517–531.

Germann Molz, J. (2006) 'Cosmopolitan bodies: fit to travel and travelling to fit', *Body Society*, 12(3): 1–21.

Ghimire, K. B. (2001) 'Regional tourism and south–south economic cooperation', *The Geographical Journal*, 167(2): 99–110.

Giddens, A. (1990) *The Consequences of Modernity*, Cambridge: Polity.

Giddens, A. (1991) *Modernity and Self-Identity: Self and Society in the Late Modern Age*, Cambridge: Polity.

Gill, S. (1998) 'New constitutionalism, democratisation and global political economy', *Pacific Review*, 10(1): 23–38.

Gillett, T. (2004) 'Rich minority "fuelling air travel boom"', *Travelmole.com*, 2 November. Available at http://www.travelmole.com/news_feature.php?id=102052 (accessed 23 April 2013).

Gills, B. K. (ed.) (2000) *Globalization and the Politics of Resistance*, London: Routledge.

Gilroy, P. (1987) *There Ain't No Black in the Union Jack: The Cultural Politics of Race and Nation*, London: Unwin Hyman.

Gini, A. (2003) *The Importance of Being Lazy: In Praise of Play, Leisure, and Vacations*, London: Routledge.

Gitlin, T. (2012) *Occupy Nation: The Roots, the Spirit and the Promise of Occupy Wall Street*, New York: Harper Collins.

Gladstone, D. L. (2005) *From Pilgrimage to Package Tour: Travel and Tourism in the Third World*, London: Routledge.

Glaister, D. (2009) 'Muslim family thrown off US jet for "remarks"', *The Guardian*, 3 January. Available at http://www.guardian.co.uk/world/2009/jan/03/airtran-flight-muslim-passengers (accessed 3 January 2010).

Global Spa Summit (2010) *Spas and the Global Wellness Market: Synergies and Opportunities*. A report prepared by SRI International (www.sri.com). Available at http://www.globalspaandwellnesssummit.org/images/stories/pdf/gss_spasandwellnessreport_final.pdf (accessed 23 April 2013).

Glyn, A. (2007) *Capitalism Unleashed: Finance, Globalization and Welfare*, Oxford: Oxford University Press.

Goldenberg, S. (2002) 'Arabs and Muslims to be fingerprinted at US airports', *The Guardian*, 2 October. Available at http://www.guardian.co.uk/world/2002/oct/02/usa.september11 (accessed 7 December 2003).

Goldsmith, O. (1819) *The Citizen of the World; or, Letters from a Chinese Philosopher, Residing in London, to His Friends in the East*, London: Taylor and Hessey.

Goldstone, P. (2001) *Making the World Safe for Tourism*, New Haven and London: Yale University Press.

González Lemus, N. (1999) *El Puerto de la Cruz y el Nacimiento del Turismo en Canarias (Apuntes para una interpretación)*, Tenerife: Excmo. Ayuntamiento del Puerto de la Cruz.

Goodin, R. E. (1992) 'If people were money…' in B. Barry and R. E. Goodin (eds) *Free Movement: Ethical Issues in the Transnational Movement of People and of Money*, Pennsylvania: Pennsylvania State Press, pp. 6–22.

Gordon, R. J. (2006) *Tarzan Was an Eco-Tourist*, Oxford: Berghahn.

Goudie, S. C., F. Khan and D. Kilian (1999) 'Transforming tourism: Black empowerment, heritage and identity beyond apartheid', *South African Geographical Journal*, 81(1): 22–31.

Gould, P. (2011) 'A new middle class that likes to shop', *Financial Times*, 3 October. Available at http://www.ft.com/cms/s/0/4c5f8804-e852-11e0-ab03-00144feab49a.html#axzz28k0MZIBb (accessed 15 October 2012).

Graburn, N. H. H. (1989) 'Tourism: the sacred journey', in V. L. Smith (ed.) *Hosts and Guests: The Anthropology of Tourism*, second edition, Philadelphia: University of Pennsylvania Press, pp. 21–36.

Graham, S. and D. Wood (2003) 'Digitizing surveillance: categorization, space, inequality', *Critical Social Policy*, 23(2): 227–248.

Grauman, B. (2010) 'Will Roma cultural route help bypass prejudice?', *Global Post*, 30 May. Available at http://www.globalpost.com/dispatch/europe/091218/gypsy-roma-cultural-route (accessed 21 June 2013).

Gregory, S. (2007) *The Devil Behind the Mirror: Globalisation and Politics in the Dominican Republic*, Berkeley: University of California Press.

Guardian (2004) 'Brazil takes prints from US tourists', *The Guardian*, 2 January. Available at http://www.guardian.co.uk/world/2004/jan/02/brazil.usa/print (accessed 20 January 2005).

Gustafson, P. (2008) 'Transnationalism in retirement migration: the case of north European retirees in Spain', *Ethnic and Racial Studies*, 31(3): 451–475.

Habermas, J. (1994) 'Citizenship and national identity', in B. van Steenbergen (ed.) *The Condition of Citizenship*, London: Sage, pp. 20–35.

Halimi, S. (2013) 'Tyranny of the one per cent', *Le Monde Diplomatique*, May, No. 1305: 1–3.

Hall, C. M. (2005) *Tourism: Rethinking the Social Science of Mobility*, Harlow: Prentice Hall.

Hall, C. M. (2008) 'Regulating the international trade in tourism services', in T. Coles and C. M. Hall (eds) *International Business and Tourism: Global Issues, Contemporary Interactions*, London: Routledge, pp. 33–54.

Hall, C. M. and V. O'Sullivan (1996) 'Tourism, political stability and violence', in A. Pizam and Y. Mansfeld (eds) *Tourism, Crime and International Security Issues*, Chichester: John Wiley, pp. 105–121.

Hall, D. R. (1990) 'Stalinism and tourism: a study of Albania and North Korea', *Annals of Tourism Research*, 17: 36–54.

Hall, D. R. (2004) 'Introduction', in D. Hall (ed.) *Tourism and Transition: Governance, Transformation and Development*, Wallingford: CABI, pp. 1–24.

Hall, D. R. and F. Brown (2012) 'The welfare society and tourism: European perspectives', in S. McCabe, L. Minnaert and A. Diekmann (eds) *Social Tourism in Europe: Theory and Practice*, Clevedon: Channel View Publications, pp. 113–127.

Hall, M. (1907) *A Woman's Trek from the Cape to Cairo*, London: Methuen.

Halpenny, E. and L. Caissie (2003) 'Volunteering on nature conservation projects: volunteer experiences, attitudes and values', *Tourism Recreation Research*, 28(3): 25–33.

Halper, J. (2005) *Obstacles to Peace: A Re-framing of the Palestinian–Israeli Conflict*, Bethlehem, Palestine: Palestinian Mapping Centre.

Hammond, R. (2004) 'The interview: Ian Reynolds', Chief Executive of ABTA, *Tourism In Focus*, Spring, No. 49/50: 16–17.

Handler, R. (1988) *Nationalism and the Politics of Culture in Quebec*, Madison: University of Wisconsin Press.

Hannam, K., M. Sheller and J. Urry (2006) 'Editorial: mobilities, immobilities and moorings', *Mobilities*, 1(1): 1–22.

Hannerz, U. (1990) 'Cosmopolitans and locals in world culture', in M. Featherstone (ed.) *Global Culture: Nationalism, Globalization and Modernity*, London: Sage, pp. 237–251.

Haq, F. and H. Y. Wong (2010) 'Is spiritual tourism a new strategy for marketing Islam?', *Journal of Islamic Marketing*, 1(2): 136–148.

Harbom, L. and P. Wallensteen (2005) 'Armed conflict and its international dimensions', *Journal of Peace Research*, 42(5): 623–635.

Harding, L. (2007) 'Oligarch buys up French hotels', *The Guardian*, 27 March. Available at http://www.guardian.co.uk/business/2007/mar/27/france.russia (accessed 8 October 2012).

Hargreaves, J. (2000) *Freedom for Catalonia? Catalan Nationalism, Spanish Identity and the Barcelona Olympic Games*, Cambridge: Cambridge University Press.

Harris, N. (2002) *Thinking the Unthinkable: The Immigration Myth Exposed*, London: I. B. Tauris.

Harrison, D. (2000) 'Tourism in Africa: the social and cultural framework', in P. U. C. Dieke (ed.) *The Political Economy of Tourism Development in Africa*, New York: Cognizant, pp. 37–51.

Harron, S. and B. Weiler (1992) 'Ethnic tourism', in B. Weiler and C. M. Hall (eds) *Special Interest Tourism*, London: Belhaven Press, pp. 83–94.

Harvey, D. (1989) *The Condition of Postmodernity*, Oxford: Blackwell.

Harvey, D. (2006) *Spaces of Global Capitalism: Towards a Theory of Uneven Geographical Development*, London: Verso.

Hasan, M. (2012) 'Halal hysteria', *New Statesman*, 9 May. Available at http://www.newstatesman.com/politics/politics/2012/05/halal-hysteria (accessed 25 July 2012).

Haukeland, J. V. (1990) 'Non-travellers: the flip side of motivation', *Annals of Tourism Research*, 17(2): 172–184.

Haulot, A. (1981) 'Social tourism: current dimensions and future developments', *International Journal of Tourism Management*, September, pp. 207–212.

Hawley, J. (2006) 'Darkness beyond Cancun's beaches: Mexico's model resort city hides an undercurrent of crime and poverty', *East Carolina University News*, 12 June. Available at http://www.ecu.edu/cs-admin/news/inthenews/archives/2005/12/061206AZrepublic.cfm (accessed 17 May 2007).

Hayter, T. (2004) *Open Borders: The Case Against Immigration Controls*, second edition, London: Pluto Press.

Hazbun, W. (2008) *Beaches, Ruins, Resorts: The Politics of Tourism in the Arab World*, Minneapolis and London: University of Minnesota Press.

Heater, D. (2002) *World Citizenship: Cosmopolitan Thinking and its Opponents*, London and New York: Continuum.

Held, D. (1995) *Democracy and the Global Order: From the Modern State to Cosmopolitan Governance*, Cambridge: Polity.

Henderson, H. (1968) 'Should business tackle society's problems?', *Harvard Business Review*, July/August, 46(4): 77–85.

Henderson, J. (2003) 'The politics of tourism in Myanmar', *Current Issues in Tourism*, 6(2): 97–118.

Henley and Partners Visa Restriction Index (2012) *Global Rankings 2012*. Available at https://www.henleyglobal.com/fileadmin/pdfs/visarestrictions/Global%20Ranking%20-%20Visa%20Restriction%20Index%202012–06.pdf (accessed 4 January 2012).

Henry, L.-A. and L. Smythe (2009) 'Shameful scenes as Romanians flee homes', *Belfast Telegraph*, 18 June. Available at http://www.belfasttelegraph.co.uk/news/local-national/shameful-scenes-as-romanians-flee-homes-14342491.html (accessed 22 July 2009).

Hernández Navarro, L. (2006) 'Repression and resistance in Oaxaca', *Counterpunch*, 21 November. Available at http://www.counterpunch.org/navarro11212006.html (accessed 12 October 2007).

Higgins-Desbiolles, F. (2006a) 'More than an "industry": the forgotten power of tourism as a social force', *Tourism Management*, 27(6): 1192–1208.

Higgins-Desbiolles, F. (2006b) 'Reconciliation tourism: healing divided societies', *IIPT Occasional Paper*, March, No. 7, pp. 1–17.

Higgins-Desbiolles, F. (2007) 'Hostile meeting grounds: encounters between the wretched of the earth and the tourist through tourism and terrorism in the 21st century', in P. Burns and M. Novelli (eds) *Tourism and Politics: Global Frameworks and Local Realities*, Oxford: Elsevier, pp. 309–332.

Higgins-Desbiolles, F. (2008) 'Justice tourism and globalisation', *Journal of Sustainable Tourism*, 16(3): 345–364.

Higgins-Desbiolles, F. (2012) 'The Hotel Bauen's challenge to cannibalizing capitalism', *Annals of Tourism Research*, 39(2): 620–640.

Hills, T. L. and J. Lundgren (1977) 'The impact of tourism in the Caribbean', *Annals of Tourism Research*, 4(5): 248–267.

Hindness, B. (1994) 'Citizenship in the modern West', in B. S. Turner (ed.) *Citizenship and Social Theory*, London: Sage, pp. 19–35.

Hipwell, W. T. (2007) 'Taiwan aboriginal ecotourism: Tanayiku National Ecology Park', *Annals of Tourism Research*, 34(4): 876–897.

Hirst, P. and G. Thompson (1999) *Globalization in Question*, second edition, Cambridge: Polity.

Hitchcock, M. (1998) 'Tourism, Taman Mini, and national identity', *Indonesia and the Malay World*, 26(75): 124–135.

Hitchcock, M. (1999) 'A special island', *The Guardian*, 16 October. Available at http://www.guardian.co.uk/travel/1999/oct/16/7 (accessed 28 March 2013).

Hitchcock, M. and I. Nyoman Darma Putra (2005) 'The Bali bombings: tourism crisis management and conflict avoidance', *Current Issues in Tourism*, 8(1): 62–76.

Hitchcock, M. and I. Nyoman Darma Putra (2010) 'Cultural perspectives on tourism and terrorism', in D. V. L. Macleod and J. G. Carrier (eds) *Tourism, Power and Culture: Anthropological Insights*, Bristol: Channel View Publications.

Hochuli, M. and C. Plüss (2005) *The WTO General Agreement on Trade in Services (GATS) and Sustainable Tourism in Developing Countries – in Contradiction?* Switzerland: Position Paper by Berne Declaration and the Working Group on Tourism and Development, pp. 1–16.

Hodal, K. (2013) 'Boracay islanders fear for their lives in battle with Philippine tourist trade', *The Guardian*, 2 June. Available at http://www.guardian.co.uk/world/2013/jun/02/boracay-islanders-philippine-tourist-trade (accessed 3 June 2013).

Holmes, J. T. (2010) 'Tourism and the making of ethnic citizenship in Belize', in D. V. L. Macleod and J. G. Carrier (eds) *Tourism, Power and Culture: Anthropological Insights*, Bristol: Channel View Publications, pp. 153–173.

Holzapfel, H. (2010) 'Everywhere and nowhere', *Le Monde Diplomatique*, May, pp. 14–15.

Honey, M. (n.d.) 'Tourism: preventing conflict, promoting peace', Washington, DC, and Stanford University: Center for Responsible Travel. Available at http://www.responsibletravel.org/resources/documents/reports/MHoney_Overview_Essay.pdf (accessed 9 December 2011).

Honey, M. (2008) *Ecotourism and Sustainable Development: Who Owns Paradise?* second edition, Washington, DC: Island Press.

Hongo, J. (2007) 'Will entry checks cross the line? Fingerprinting foreigners won't stop terrorists, critics say', *Japan Times*, 8 November. Available at http://www.japantimes. co.jp/news/2007/11/08/news/will-entry-checks-cross-the-line/#.UZN45Upv9EM (accessed 15 May 2013).

Hooks, B. (1992) *Black Looks: Race and Representation*, Boston, MA: South End Press.

Horáková, H. (2010) 'Post-Communist transformation of tourism in Czech rural areas: new dilemmas', *Anthropological Notebooks*, 16(1): 63–81.

Horne, D. (1984) *The Great Museum: The Re-Presentation of History*, London: Pluto Press.

Hotel, Travel and Hospitality News (2013) 'Chinese millionaires stay hungry for French luxury goods', 17 January. Available at http://www.4hoteliers.com/news/story/10872 (accessed 20 March 2013).

Hughes, H. (1991) 'Holidays and the economically disadvantaged', *Tourism Management*, 12(3): 193–196.

Hultsman, J. (1995) 'Just tourism: an ethical framework', *Annals of Tourism Research*, 22(3): 553–567.

Human Rights Watch (2011) 'France's compliance with the European free movement directive and the removal of ethnic Roma EU citizens', a Briefing Paper submitted to the European Commission, July. Available at http://www.hrw.org/news/2011/09/28/france-s-compliance-european-free-movement-directive-and-removal-ethnic-roma-euciti (accessed 19 May 2013).

Hutnyk, J. (2011) 'Tourism: trinketization and the manufacture of the exotic', *Anthropologies*, 15 April. Available at http://www.anthropologiesproject.org/2011/04/tourism-trinketization-and-manufacture.html (accessed 20 June 2012).

ICAO (1944) Convention on International Civil Aviation Done at Chicago on the 7th Day of December 1944, International Civil Aviation Organization. Available at http://www.icao.int/publications/Documents/7300_orig.pdf (accessed 17 May 2013).

Ignatieff, M. (1995) *Blood and Belonging: Journeys into the New Nationalism*, New York: Farrar, Straus and Giroux.

ILO (1970) *C-132 Holidays with Pay Convention (Revised)*, Geneva: International Labour Office. Available at http://www.ilo.org/dyn/normlex/en/f?p=1000:12100:0::NO::P12100_INSTRUMENT_ID:312277 (accessed 21 May 2013).

ILO (2010) *Developments and Challenges in the Hospitality and Tourism Sector, Issues Paper for Discussion at the Global Dialogue Forum for the Hotels, Catering and Tourism Sector*, Geneva: International Labour Office.

ILO (2013) *Global Employment Trends 2013: Recovering from Second Jobs Dip*, Geneva: International Labour Office. Available at http://www.ilo.org/global/research/global-reports/global-employment-trends/2013/lang--en/index.htm (accessed 3 May 2013).

IMSERSO (2013) *Programa de Vacaciones para Mayores (Turismo Social) 2012–2013*, Ministerio de Sanidad, Servicios Sociales e Igualdad, Instituto de Mayores y Servicios Sociales. Available at http://www.imserso.es/imserso_01/envejecimiento_activo/vacaciones/index.htm (accessed 21 May 2013).

Inayatullah, S. (1995) 'Rethinking tourism: unfamiliar histories and alternative futures', *Tourism Management*, 16(6): 411–415.

India Times (2011) 'Top 5 Global Travel Trend Forecasts for 2012', 25 December. Available at http://www.indiatimes.com/travel/top-5-travel-trend-forecasts-for-2012_-8567.html (accessed 25 January 2013).

Info Birmanie (2013) 'Rapport sur le tourisme en Birmanie', *Info Birmanie*. Available at http://www.info-birmanie.org (accessed 23 March 2013).

Inglis, F. (2000) *The Delicious History of the Holiday*, London: Routledge.

Inkson, C. and L. Minnaert (2012) *Tourism Management: An Introduction*, London: Sage.

International Bureau of Social Tourism (1996) 'Montreal Declaration'. Available at http://www.bits-int.org/files/1177334236_doc_Montreal%20Declaration.pdf (accessed 23 July 2008).

iRealty Times (2012) 'Thailand's luxury resort – aka "James Bond Island" – targeting Chinese buyers', *iRealty Times*, 19 September. Available at http://www.irealtytimes.com/articles/2786/20120919/thailand-s-luxury-resort-aka-james-bond.htm (accessed 9 October 2012).

Irish Times (2013) 'A middle class world', 16 March. Available at http://www.irishtimes.com/news/world/a-middle-class-world-1.1327741 (accessed 25 May 2013).

Isaac, R. K. (2009) 'Alternative tourism: can the segregation wall in Bethlehem be a tourist attraction?' *Tourism and Hospitality Planning and Development*, 6(3): 247–254.

Isaac, R. K. (2010) 'Alternative tourism: new forms of tourism in Bethlehem for the Palestinian tourism industry', *Current Issues in Tourism*, 13(1): 21–36.

Isin, E. F. and B. S. Turner (2007) 'Investigating citizenship: an agenda for citizenship studies', *Citizenship Studies*, 11(1): 5–17.

Isin, E. F. and P. K. Wood (1999) *Citizenship and Identity*, London: Sage.

Jack, I. (2008) 'Mumbai will never be the same again', *The Guardian*, 29 November. Available at http://www.guardian.co.uk/commentisfree/2008/nov/29/mumbai-india-travel-ian-jack (accessed 30 November 2008).

Jacques, M. (2012) *When China Rules the World*, London: Penguin Books.

Jenkins, C. L. and Z.-H. Liu (1997) 'China: economic liberalization and tourism development – the case of the People's Republic of China', in F. Go and C. L. Jenkins (eds) *Tourism and Economic Development in Asia and Australasia*, New York: Continuum, pp. 104–122.

Jenkins, R. (1987) 'Countering racial prejudice: anthropological and otherwise', *Anthropology Today*, 3(2): 3–4.

Jenkins, S. (2009) 'Don't blame the system for winter travel chaos. Stay put', *The Guardian*, 22 December. Available at http://www.guardian.co.uk/commentisfree/2009/dec/22/blame-for-winter-travel-chaos (accessed 22 December 2009).

Jeon, Y. S. (2011) 'Diagnosis and assessment of North Korea's sociocultural sector in 2012', *International Journal of Korean Unification Studies*, 20(2): 91–120.

Jones, R. (2008) 'How America blockades your credit card in Cuba', *The Guardian* (Money supplement), 13 September, p. 5.

Jones, S. (2006) 'A political ecology of wildlife conservation in Africa', *Review of African Political Economy*, 109: 483–495.

Joppke, C. (2004) 'The retreat of multiculturalism in the liberal state: theory and policy', *The British Journal of Sociology*, 55(2): 237–257.

Joseph, M. (1999) *Nomadic Identities: The Performance of Citizenship*, Minneapolis: University of Minnesota Press.

Josephides, N. (1994) 'Tour operators and the myth of self-regulation', *Tourism in Focus*, Winter, 14: 10–11.

Kalisch, A. (2002) 'Getting consumers on board', *Tourism in Focus*, Autumn, 44: 4.

Kamat, S. (2004) 'The privatization of public interest: theorizing NGO discourse in a neo-liberal era', *Review of International Political Economy*, 11(1): 155–176.

Kaplan, C. (1996) *Questions of Travel: Postmodern Discourses of Displacement*, Durham, NC, and London: Duke University Press.

Kaspar, J. (1981) 'Leisure, recreational and tourism in socialist countries', *International Journal of Tourism Management*, 1(4): 224–232.

Kassis, R. (2005) 'The Palestinians and justice tourism', in R. Solomon (ed.) *Pilgrimages for Transformation*, Proceedings of a Study Workshop on Interfaith Cooperation for Justice in the Occupied Territories – Human encounters for peace and reconciliation through Tourism, 21–24 October, Alexandria: Egypt, pp. 31–36.

Kassis, R. (2013) 'Personal communication', 30 March.

Kaur, R. and J. Hutnyk (1999) 'Introduction', in R. Kaur and J. Hutnyk (eds) *Travel Worlds: Journeys in Contemporary Cultural Politics*, London: Zed Books, pp. 1–13.

Keefe, J. and S. Wheat (1998) *Tourism and Human Rights*, London: Tourism Concern.

Keith, M. (1995) 'Making the street visible: placing racial violence in context', *New Community*, 21(4): 551–565.

Kellerman, A. (2008) 'International airports: passengers in an environment of "authorities"', *Mobilities*, 3(1): 161–178.

Kelsey, J. (2008) *Serving Whose Interests? The Political Economy of Trade in Services Agreements*, Abingdon and New York: Routledge-Cavendish.

Kennedy, H. (2004) 'Are human rights universal?' in R. Belcher (ed.) *Do Human Rights Travel?*, British Council 70th anniversary essays on cultural relations, London: British Council, pp. 8–24.

Kent, N. (1977) 'A new kind of sugar', in B. R. Finney and K. A. Watson (eds) *A New Kind of Sugar*, Honolulu: East-West Center, pp. 169–198.

Khair, T., M. Leer, J. D. Edwards, and H. Ziadeh (eds) (2005) *Other Routes: 1500 Years of African and Asian Travel Writing*, Bloomington: Indiana University Press.

Khid-arn, P. (2005) 'Justice tourism: challenges for global ecumenism', in R. Solomon (ed.) *Pilgrimages for Transformation*, Proceedings of a Study Workshop on Interfaith Cooperation for Justice in the Occupied Territories – Human encounters for peace and reconciliation through Tourism, 21–24 October, Alexandria: Egypt, pp. 11-13.

Kim, S. S. and B. Prideaux (2003) 'Tourism, peace, politics and ideology: impacts of the Mt. Gumgang tour project in the Korean peninsula', *Tourism Management*, 24: 675–685.

King, N. (2013) 'French man ripped veil from Muslim woman's face', *Arabian Business.com*, 14 March. Available at http://www.arabianbusiness.com/french-man-ripped-veil-from-muslim-woman-s-face-493031.html (accessed 15 March 2013).

King, R. (2012a) 'Biometric research note: US government driving biometrics', *BiometricUpdate.com*, 9 August. Available at http://www.biometricupdate.com/201208/biometric-research-note-u-s-government-driving-biometrics/ (accessed 25 April 2013).

King, R. (2012b) 'Biometric research note: commercial applications for biometrics growing', *BiometricUpdate.com*, 7 August. Available at http://www.biometricupdate.com/201208/biometric-research-note-commercial-applications-for-biometrics-growing/ (accessed 25 April 2013)

Kingsnorth, P. (2003) 'The citizens of nowhere', *New Statesman*, 1 September, pp. 22–23.

Kingsnorth, P. (2004) *One No, Many Yeses: A Journey to the Heart of the Global Resistance Movement*, London: The Free Press.

Kington, T. (2008) '68% of Italians want Roma expelled – poll', *The Guardian*, 17 May. Available at http://www.guardian.co.uk/world/2008/may/17/italy (accessed 18 September 2012).

Klein, N. (2001) 'Reclaiming the commons', *New Left Review*, II, 9: 81–89.

Klein, N. (2007) *The Shock Doctrine: The Rise of Disaster Capitalism*, London: Allen Lane.

Kousis, M. (2000) 'Tourism and the environment: a social movements perspective', *Annals of Tourism Research*, 27(2): 468–489.

Kozinn, A. (2013) 'Questions over Cuba trip of Beyoncé and Jay-Z', *New York Times*, 7 April. Available at http://www.nytimes.com/2013/04/08/arts/music/questions-over-cuba-trip-of-beyonce-and-jay-z.html (accessed 18 April 2013).

KPMG (2011) *Issues Monitor: Sharing Knowledge on Topical Issues in the Healthcare Sector*, May, Volume 7. Available at http://www.kpmg.com/CH/en/Library/Articles-Publications/Documents/Sectors/pub-20120207-issues-monitor-healthcare-medical-tourism-en.pdf (accessed 19 November 2011).

Kraul, C. (2003) 'Streets of Cancun paved with gold, inequity', *Los Angeles Times*, 14 September. Available at http://www.latimes.com (accessed 16 September 2003).

Krippendorf, J. (1993) 'Interview', *Journal of Sustainable Tourism*, 1(1): 55–60.

Kuoni (2011) *The Kuoni Code of Conduct: Ethical Behaviour Guidelines for the Kuoni Group*. Available at http://www.kuoni.com/docs/kodex_en_2_0.pdf (accessed 12 March 2013).

Kymlicka, W. (1989) *Liberalism, Community and Culture*, Oxford: Oxford University Press.

Kymlicka, W. (1995) *Multicultural Citizenship: A Liberal Theory of Minority Rights*, Oxford: Clarendon Press.

Kymlicka, W. (2001) *Politics in the Vernacular: Nationalism, Multiculturalism and Citizenship*, Oxford: Oxford University Press.

Laguerre, M. S. (1998) *Diasporic Citizens: Haitian Americans in Transnational America*, New York: St. Martin's Press.

Lapavitsas, C., A. Kaltenbrunner, G. Labrindis, D. Lindo, J. Meadway, J. Michell, J. P. Painceira, E. Pires, J. Powell, A. Stenfors, N. Teles and L. Vatikiotis (2012) *Crisis in the Eurozone*, London: Verso.

La Provincia (2009) 'El parque, la pensión de la ciudad', *La Provincia Diario de Las Palmas*, 9 May. Available at http://www.laprovincia.es/secciones/noticia.jsp?pRef=2009050900_4_228897__Las-Palmas-GC-parque-pension-ciudad (accessed 23 July 2009).

Lea, J. P. (1993) 'Tourism development ethics in the Third World', *Annals of Tourism Research*, 20: 701–715.

Lee, S. (2006) *When the Levees Broke: A Requiem in Four Acts*, Brooklyn, NY: 40 Acres and a Mule Filmworks.

Leed, E. J. (1991) *The Mind of the Traveller: From Gilgamesh to Global Tourism*, New York: Basic Books.

Legrand, C. (2013) 'Easter Island issues Chile with independence threat', *The Guardian*, 15 January. Available at http://m.guardian.co.uk/world/2013/jan/15/easter-island-independence-threat-chile (accessed 16 June 2013).

Leng, C. H. (2010) 'Medical tourism and the state in Malaysia and Singapore', *Global Social Policy*, 10(3): 336–357.

Leng, C. H. and A. Whittaker (2010) 'Guest editors' introduction to the special issue: why is medical travel of concern to global social policy', *Global Social Policy*, 10(3): 287–291.

Leong, W.-T. (1989) 'Culture and the state: manufacturing traditions for tourism', *Critical Studies in Mass Communication*, 6: 355–375.

Lewallen, A.-E. (2011) 'Performing identity, saving land: Ainu indigenous ecotourism as a stage for restitution of rights in Japan', Report of the International Symposium *Exploring Ethnicity and the State through Tourism in East Asia*. In Kanazawa University Japan-China Intangible Cultural Heritage Project Report Vol. 13. Kanazawa University College of Human and Social Sciences Conference Report, pp. 112–123.

Lewis, P. and M. Taylor (2010) 'Deportee asked for help on flight before dying, witness says', *The Guardian*, 15 October. Available at http://www.guardian.co.uk/uk/2010/oct/15/deportee-help-flight-dying-witness (accessed 8 January 2013).

Lichfield, J. (2006) 'France's nuclear tests in Pacific "gave islanders cancer"', *The Independent*, 4 August. Available at http://www.independent.co.uk/news/world/europe/frances-nuclear-tests-in-pacific-gave-islanders-cancer-410474.html (accessed 13 November 2012).

Lickorish, L. (1991) 'Developing a single European tourism policy', *Tourism Management*, 12(3): 178–184.

Lim, C. and Y. Wang (2008) 'China's post-1978 experience in outbound tourism', *Mathematics and Computers in Simulation*, 78: 450–458.

Lisle, D. (2007) 'Defending voyeurism: dark tourism and the problem of global security', in P. M. Burns and M. Novelli (eds) *Tourism and Politics: Global Frameworks and Local Realities*, Oxford: Elsevier, pp. 333–345.

Listner, R. (2012) 'Citizenship and gender', in E. Amenta, K. Nash and A. Scott (eds) *The Wiley-Blackwell Companion to Political Sociology*, Oxford: Wiley Blackwell, pp. 372–382.

Little, J., R. Panelli and A. Kraack (2005) 'Women's fear of crime: a rural perspective', *Journal of Rural Studies*, 21: 151–163.

Litvin, S. W. (1998) 'Tourism: the world's peace industry?', *Journal of Travel Research*, 37(1): 63–66.

Loader, I. (1999) 'Consumer culture and the commodification of policing and security', *Sociology*, 33(2): 373–392.

Loffell, B. (2008) 'Why are there so many plane crashes in Iran?', *ETN Global Travel Industry News*, 30 June. Available at http://www.eturbonews.com/3446/why-are-there-so-many-plane-crashes-iran (accessed 20 March 2013).

Löfgren, O. (2002) *On Holiday: A History of Vacationing*, Berkeley: University of California Press.

Lofstedt, R. E. and O. Renn (1997) 'Perspectives: the Brent Spar controversy – an example of risk communication gone wrong', *Risk Analysis*, 17(2): 131–136.

Lovelock, B. (2008) 'Ethical travel decisions: travel agents and human rights', *Annals of Tourism Research*, 35(2): 338–358.

Lowenthal, D. (1998) *The Heritage Crusade and the Spoils of History*, Cambridge: Cambridge University Press.

Lowles, N. (2011) 'What Britons really think about immigration', *The Guardian*, 26 February. Available at http://www.guardian.co.uk/uk/2011/feb/26/britons-immigration-multi-culturalism-study (accessed 29 April 2013).

Lunt, N., R. Smith, M. Exworthy, S. T. Green, D. Horsfall and R. Mannion (2011) *Medical Tourism: Treatments, Markets and Health System Implications: A Scoping Review*, Paris: Organisation for Economic Co-operation and Development.

Luxury Travel Advisor (2012) 'Alila Jabal Akhdar: Oman's latest luxury addition', 24 July. Available at http://www.luxurytraveladvisor.com/oman/alila-jabal-akhdar-omans-latest-luxury-addition-8422 (accessed 9 August 2012).

Luxury Travel News (2007) 'The "new jetrosexual" generation', *Luxury Travel News*, 1(7): 70–71.

Lyon, D. (2003) *Surveillance after September 11*, Cambridge: Polity.

Lyon, D. (2004) 'Technology vs. "terrorism": circuits of city surveillance since September 11, 2001', in S. Graham (ed.) *Cities, War, and Terrorism: Towards an Urban Geopolitics*, Oxford: Blackwell Publishing, pp. 297–311.

Lyon, D. (2008a) 'Filtering flows, friends and foes: global surveillance', in M. B. Salter (ed.) *Politics at the Airport*, Minneapolis: University of Minnesota Press, pp. 29–49.

Lyon, D. (2008b) 'The global airport: managing space, speed and security', in M. B. Salter (ed.) *Politics at the Airport*, Minneapolis: University of Minnesota Press, pp. 1–28.

Lyons, K., J. Hanley, S. Wearing and J. Neil (2012) 'Gap year volunteer tourism: myths of global citizenship?', *Annals of Tourism Research*, 39(1): 361–378.

Lyth, P. J. (2009) 'Flying visits: the growth of British air package tours 1945–1975', in L. Segreto, C. Manera and M. Pohl (eds) *Europe at the Seaside: The Economic History of Mass Tourism in the Mediterranean*, Oxford: Berghahn, pp. 11–30.

MacAskill, E. (2011) 'Obama acts to ease US embargo on Cuba', *The Guardian*, 15 January. Available at http://www.guardian.co.uk/world/2011/jan/15/barack-obama-us-embargo-cuba (accessed 17 May 2013).

McCabe, S. (2009) 'Who needs a holiday? Evaluating social tourism', *Annals of Tourism Research*, 36(4): 667–688.

MacCannell, D. (1992) *Empty Meeting Grounds: The Tourist Papers*, Routledge: London.

MacCannell, D. (1999) *The Tourist: A New Theory of the Leisure Class*, Berkeley: University of California Press (first published in 1976 by Schocken Books Inc.).

McCrystal, C. (1994) 'The gospel of Bryn Melyn: holidays for hooligans or ground-breaking treatment? Brendan McNutt's Centre has drawn fire over controversial methods', *The Independent*, 2 January. Available at http://www.independent.co.uk/news/uk/the-gospel-of-bryn-melyn-holidays-for-hooligans-or-groundbreaking-treatment-brendan-mcnutts-centre-has-drawn-fire-over-its-controversial-methods-1404355.html (accessed 15 July 2010).

McGehee, N. G. (2002) 'Alternative tourism and social movements', *Annals of Tourism Research*, 29(1): 124–143.

McGehee, N. G. (2012) 'Oppression, emancipation, and volunteer tourism: research propositions', *Annals of Tourism Research*, 39(1): 84–107.

McGirk, J. (2005) 'Lawsuit blocks Thai findings on tsunami', *The Independent*, 10 March. Available at http://www.independent.co.uk/news/world/asia/lawsuit-blocks-thai-findings-on-tsunami-6150670.html (accessed 7 January 2013).

McGrath, G. (2004) 'Is consumer demand the only hope for sustainable tourism?', *Travel Mole*, 13 May. Available at http://www.travelmole.com/mobi_news_feature.php?id=100482 (accessed 30 May 2013).

McGrath, M. (2000) 'On the road again', *The Guardian Weekend*, 10 June, pp. 9–14.

Mack, A. (ed.) (2005) *Human Security Report*, Vancouver: University of British Columbia.

Mackenzie, J. (2005) 'Empires of travel: British guide books and cultural imperialism in the 19th and 20th centuries', in J. K. Walton (ed.) *Histories of Tourism: Representation, Identity and Conflict*, Clevedon: Channel View Publications, pp. 19–38.

McLain, S. and J. Taylor (2013) 'British woman who "jumped from India hotel to escape sexual assault" returns to UK', *The Independent*, 20 March. Available at http://www.independent.co.uk/news/world/asia/british-woman-who-jumped-from-india-hotel-to-escape-sexual-assault-returns-to-uk-8540271.html (accessed 14 June 2103).

Macleod, D. V. L. (2004) *Tourism, Globalisation and Cultural Change: An Island Community Perspective*, Clevedon: Channel View Publications.

McMillan, M. (2004) 'Are you a bad tourist or a good traveller?', Editorial: Responsible Tourism?', *Just Change: The Tourism Issue*, Wellington, NZ: Dev-Change.

Magrath, B. (2001) 'Cernium's intelligent video surveillance installed at airports', *St. Louis Front Page*, 18 December. Available at http://www.slfp.com/121801BIZp.htm (accessed 18 May 2013).

Mann, M. (1987) 'Ruling strategies and citizenship', *Sociology*, 21(3): 339–354.

Marchand, M. H. (2005) 'Contesting the Free Trade Area of the Americas: invoking a Bolivarian geopolitical imagination to construct an alternative regional identity', in C. Eschle and B. Maiguaschca (eds) *Critical Theories, International Relations and the 'Anti-Globalisation Movement': The Politics of Global Resistance*, London: Routledge, pp. 103–116.

Mark, M. (2012) 'Full speed ahead for Africa's super-rich', *The Guardian*, 24 March, p. 25.

Marks, A. (2006/7) 'UK tour operators campaign against tourism development', *Tourism in Focus*, Winter: 6.

Martin, D. (2008) 'Ecotourism in Ethiopia', *Le Monde Diplomatique*, August, pp. 8–9.

Marshall, P. (1987) *Cuba Libre: Breaking the Chains*, London: Victor Gollancz Ltd.

Marshall, T. H. (1963) *Sociology at the Crossroads and Other Essays*, London: Heinemann.

Marshall, T. H. (1964) *Class, Citizenship and Social Development: Essays by T. H. Marshall*, New York: Doubleday and Co.

Marshall, T. H. (1992) 'Citizenship and social class', in T. H. Marshall and T. Bottomore (eds) *Citizenship and Social Class*, London: Pluto Press, pp. 3–51.

Marx, K. (1977) 'On the Jewish Question', in D. McLellan (ed.) *Karl Marx: Selected Writings*, Oxford: Oxford University Press, pp. 39–62.

Marx, K. and F. Engels (1985 [1888]) *The Manifesto of the Communist Party*, Harmondsworth: Penguin.

Mason, T. W. (1993) *Social Policy in the Third Reich: The Working Class and the National Community*, Oxford: Berg.

Mathers, K. and L. Landau (2007) 'Natives, tourists, and makwerekwere: ethical concerns with "Proudly South African" tourism', *Development Southern Africa*, 24(3): 523–537.

Matthews, H. G. (1978) *International Tourism: A Political and Social Analysis*, Cambridge, MA: Schenkman.

Mayo, M. (2006) *Global Citizens: Social Movements and the Challenge of Globalization*, London: Zed Books.

Mbogo, S. (2003) 'US, Britain set stringent conditions before they will lift the travel warnings', *Travel Wire News*, 20 June. Available at http://travelwirenews.com (accessed 24 June 2003).

Medical News Today (2012) '26% of working age adults in USA lack health insurance', 19 April. Available at http://www.medicalnewstoday.com/articles/244345.php (accessed 12 January 2013).

Mehta, S. (2008) 'The terrorists attacked my city because of its wealth', *The Guardian*, 28 November, p. 7.

Melzer, B. (2000) 'The business view', Burma: Your Views (Letters page), *Telegraph Travel (The Telegraph)*, 8 July, p. 13.

Mepham, D. (2013) 'Burma: the EU has been too quick to lift sanctions', *The Guardian*, 23 April. Available at http://m.guardian.co.uk/commentisfree/2013/apr/23/burma-eu-too-quick-lift-sanctions (accessed 16 June 2013).

Miles, A. (2011) 'The SAS rescue of British citizens? More like corporate citizens?', *New Statesman*, 7 March, p. 21.

Miles, R. (1994) 'Explaining racism in contemporary Europe', in A. Rattansi and A. Westwood (eds) *Racism, Modernity and Identity: On the Western Front*, Cambridge: Polity Press, pp. 189–221.

Miller, D. (1995) 'Citizenship and pluralism', *Political Studies*, 43(3): 432–450.

Milmo, D. (2010) 'BA must start again or fly into the sunset', *The Observer*, Business & Media, 31 January, pp. 4–5.

Milne, S. (2013) 'NSA and GCHQ: mass surveillance is about power as much as privacy', *The Guardian*, 11 June. Available at http://www.guardian.co.uk/commentisfree/2013/jun/11/surveilllance-about-power-as-much-as-privacy (accessed 13 June 2013).

Minh-ha, T. T. (1994) 'Other than myself/my other self', in G. Robertson, M. Marsh, L. Tickner, J. Bird, B. Curtis and T. Putnam (eds) *Travellers' Tales: Narratives of Home and Displacement*, London: Routledge, pp. 9–26.

Minnaert, L., A. Diekmann and S. McCabe (2011) 'Defining social tourism and its historical context', in S. McCabe, L. Minnaert and A Diekmann (eds) *Social Tourism in Europe: Theory and Practice*, Clevedon: Channel View Publications, pp. 18–30.

Minnaert, L., R. Maitland and G. Miller (2007) 'Social tourism and its ethical foundations', *Tourism Culture and Communication*, 7: 7–17.

Misra, M. (2008) 'The places I love lie in ruins. I am scared and very angry', *The Observer*, 30 November. Available at http://www.guardian.co.uk/commentisfree/2008/nov/30/mumbai-terror-attacks-india (accessed 1 December 2008).

Mitchell, D. (2009) 'Expensive air travel? It's just not cricket', *The Observer*, 19 July, p. 32.

Moișă, C. (2008) 'Some aspects regarding tourism and youth's mobility', *Tourism and Hospitality Management*, 14(1): 153–169.

Montefinise, A. (2009) 'Bomber was on a US watch list', *New York Post*, 27 December. Available at http://www.nypost.com/p/news/national/bomber_was_on_TpvPCXYKXcMNxiGrVfsFeM (accessed 4 June 2013).

Moore, P. V. (2012) 'Where is decent work in DfID policy? Marketisation and securitisation of UK international aid', *Global Labour Column*. Available at http://column.global-labour-university.org/2013/01/where-is-decent-work-in-dfid-policy.html (accessed 7 January 2013).

Morell, M. (2001) *The Eco-tax in the Balearics: A Case Study Where Politics and Environment Meet Tourism*, unpublished MA dissertation, University of North London.

Moreton, C. (2003) 'Is anywhere in the world safe?', *The Independent on Sunday*, 18 May, p. 17.

Morozov, E. (2011) *The Net Delusion: The Dark Side of Internet Freedom*, London: Allen Lane.

Morozov, E. (2013) 'How Facebook could get you arrested', *The Observer*, 9 March. Available at http://www.guardian.co.uk/technology/2013/mar/09/facebook-arrested-evgeny-morozov-extract (accessed 9 March 2013).

Morris-Suzuki, T. (2000) 'For and against NGOs: the politics of the lived world', *New Left Review*, II, 2: 63–84.

Moufakkir, O. and I. Kelly (eds) (2010) *Tourism, Progress and Peace*, Wallingford: CABI.

Mowforth, M. and I. Munt (1998) *Tourism and Sustainability: New Tourism in the Third World*, London: Routledge.

Mowforth, M. and I. Munt (2009) *Tourism and Sustainability: Development, Globalisation and New Tourism in the Third World*, third edition, London: Routledge.

MPR News (2008) 'Muslim cab drivers lose round in court', 9 September, *Minnesota Public Radio*. Available at http://minnesota.publicradio.org/display/web/2008/09/09/muslim_cabs_court (accessed 18 March 2013).

Munar, A.-M. (2007) 'Rethinking globalization theory in tourism', in P. Burns and M. Novelli (eds) *Tourism and Politics: Global Frameworks and Local Realities*, Oxford: Elsevier, pp. 347–367.

Muqbil, I. (2012) 'Anti-Arab/Muslim image will impact summer travel to Europe: UNWTO-ETC study'. Available at http://www.travel-impact-newswire.com/2012/05/anti-arabmuslim-image-will-impact-summer-travel-to-europe-unwto-etc-study/#axzz1v7hrQxip (accessed 21 June 2012).

Murià, M. and S. Chávez (2011) 'Shopping and working in the borderlands: enforcement, surveillance and marketing in Tijuana, Mexico', *Surveillance and Society*, 8(3): 355–373.

Murphy, S. (2010) 'Mad as hell: airport security screening protests mount', *Tech News Daily*, 16 November. Available at http://www.technewsdaily.com/1551-airport-security-screeners-causing-uproar.html (accessed 5 June 2013).

Murray, M. and B. Graham (1997) 'Exploring the dialectics of route-based tourism: the Camino de Santiago', *Tourism Management*, 18: 513–524.

Muse, T. (2011) 'Amazon town bans tourists', *The Guardian*, 25 March. Available at http://www.guardian.co.uk/world/2011/mar/25/indigenous-peoples-amazon-tourism-pressures (accessed 18 March 2013).

Mustonen, P. (2005) 'Volunteer tourism: postmodern pilgrimage?', *Journal of Tourism and Cultural Change*, 3(3): 160–177.

Nahdi, F. (2002) 'A cocktail of grievances in paradise', *The Guardian*, 29 November. Available at http://www.guardian.co.uk/world/2002/nov/29/kenya.terrorismandtravel1 (accessed 11 January 2013).

Nash, K. (2000) *Contemporary Political Sociology: Globalization, Politics, and Power*, Oxford: Blackwell.

National League for Democracy (2011) 'NLD statement on tourism', 20 May 2011. Available at http://www.burmacampaign.org.uk/index.php/burma/about-burma/about-burma/tourism-campaign (accessed 23 March 2013).

Neal, S. (2002) 'Rural landscapes, representations and racism: examining multicultural citizenship and policy making in the countryside', *Ethnic and Racial Studies*, 25(3): 442–461.

Noronha, F. (1999) 'Ten years later, Goa still uneasy over the impact of tourism', *International Journal of Contemporary Hospitality Management*, 11(2/3): 100–106.

Noronha, R. (1979) *Social and Cultural Dimensions of Tourism*, World Bank Staff Working Paper No. 326, Washington, DC: World Bank.

Nyaupane, G. P., V. Teye and C. Paris (2008) 'Innocents abroad: attitude change toward hosts', *Annals of Tourism Research*, 35(3): 650–667.

Oakley, L. (2012) 'SPA: Inside the MidEast's first Sea and Spa', *Hotelier Middle East*, 19 July. Available at http://www.hoteliermiddleeast.com/14768-spa-inside-the-mideasts-first-thalassa-sea-spa/ (accessed 12 November 2012).

Oberman, R., R. Dobbs, A. Budiman, F. Thompson and M. Rossé (2012) *The Archipelago Economy: Unleashing Indonesia's Potential*, McKinsey Global Institute. Available at http://www.mckinsey.com/insights/mgi/research/asia/the_archipelago_economy (accessed 19 December 2012).

Observer (2006) 'Luxury without the guilt', *The Observer*, 14 May. Available at http://www.guardian.co.uk/travel/2006/may/14/ecotourism.observerescapesection (accessed 30 April 2013).

O'Byrne, D. J. (2001) 'On passports and border controls', *Annals of Tourism Research*, 28(2): 399–416.

OECD (2011) *An Overview of Growing Income Inequalities in OECD Countries: Main Findings*, Paris: Organisation for Economic Co-operation and Development. Available at http://www.oecd.org/els/socialpoliciesanddata/49499779.pdf (accessed 19 December 2012).

O'Grady, A. (1990) *The Challenge of Tourism*, Bangkok: Ecumenical Coalition on Third World Tourism.

Ohmae, K. (1990) *The Borderless World*, London: Collins.

Ohmae, K. (1995) *The End of the Nation-State*, New York: Free Press.

O'Neil, C. (2005) 'The most magical corner of England: tourism, preservation and the development of the Lake District, 1919–39', in J. K. Walton (ed.) *Histories of Tourism: Representation, Identity and Conflict*, Clevedon: Channel View Publications, pp. 228–244.

Ong, A. (1999) *Flexible Citizenship: The Cultural Logics of Transnationality*, Durham, NC: Duke University Press.

Oommen, T. K. (1997) 'Introduction: conceptualizing the linkage between citizenship and national identity', in K. Oommen (ed.) *Citizenship, Nationality and Identity: From Colonialism to Globalism*, London: Blackwell, pp. 13–51.

O'Reilly, K. (2000) *The British on the Costa del Sol: Transnational Identities and Local Communities*, London: Routledge.

Organization for Security and Cooperation in Europe (1975) *Helsinki Final Act*. Available at http://www.osce.org/mc/39501 (accessed 27 May 2013).

Organization for Security and Cooperation in Europe (2013) *Helsinki Accords*. Available at http://chnm.gmu.edu/1989/archive/files/helsinki-accords_f9de6be034.pdf (accessed 12 September 2013).

Ormond, M. (2011a) 'Medical tourism, medical exile: responding to the cross-border pursuit of healthcare in Malaysia', in C. Minca and T. Oakes (eds) *Real Tourism: Practice, Care and Politics in Contemporary Travel*, London: Routledge.

Ormond, M. (2011b) 'Shifting subjects of health-care: placing "medical tourism" in the context of Malaysian domestic health-care reform', *Asia Pacific Viewpoint*, 52(3): 247–259.

Ormond, M. (2013) *Neoliberal Governance and International Medical Travel*, London: Routledge.

O'Rourke, D. (1988) *Cannibal Tours*, a film directed and produced by Dennis O'Rourke, Cairns (Australia): Camerawork Pty Ltd.

Ortíz, I. and M. Cummins (2011) *Global Inequality: Beyond the Bottom Billion. A Rapid Review of Income Distribution in 141 Countries*, New York: UNICEF. Available at http://www.unicef.org/socialpolicy/files/Global_Inequality.pdf (accessed 18 September 2012).

Pakulski, J. (1997) 'Cultural citizenship', *Citizenship Studies*, 1(1): 73–86.

Palmer, N. (2007) 'Ethnic equality, national identity and selective cultural representation in tourism promotion: Kyrgyzstan, Central Asia', *Journal of Sustainable Tourism*, 15(6): 645–662.

Palmer, T. and A. Riera (2003) 'Tourism and environmental taxes with special reference to the Balearic ecotax', *Tourism Management*, 24(6): 665–674.

Park, A., X. Song, J. Zhang and Y. Zhao (2003) 'The growth of wage inequality in urban China, 1988 to 1999', World Bank Working Paper. Available at http://siteresources.worldbank.org/INTPGI/Resources/13933_inequality_Yaohui_Zhao.pdf (accessed 23 December 2011).

Park, H. Y. (2009) 'Heritage, tourism and national identity: an ethnographic study of Changdeok Palace, Korea', *Korea Journal*, 49(4): 163–186.

Park, H.Y. (2010) 'Heritage tourism: emotional journeys into nationhood', *Annals of Tourism Research*, 37(1): 116–135.

Park, H. Y. and M. L. Stephenson (2007) 'A critical analysis of the symbolic significance of heritage tourism', *International Journal of Excellence in Tourism, Hospitality and Catering*, 1(2): 1–26.

Pascouau, Y. (2013) 'Strong attack against the freedom of movement of EU citizens: turning back the clock', *European Policy Centre*, 20 April. Available at http://www.epc.eu/pub_details.php?cat_id=4&pub_id=3491 (accessed 19 May 2013).

Patomaki, H. and T. Teivainen (2004) 'The World Social Forum: an open space or movement of movements?', *Theory, Culture and Society*, 21(6): 145–154.

Pattullo, P. (1996) *Last Resorts: The Cost of Tourism in the Caribbean*, London: Cassell.

Pattullo, P. (2006) *The Ethical Travel Guide: Your Passport to Exciting Alternative Holidays*, London: Earthscan.

Peace Corps (2013) *A Proud History*. Available at http://www.peacecorps.gov/about/history/ (accessed 5 September 2013).

Pearlman, M. (1981) 'Conflicts and constraints in Bulgaria's tourism sector', *Annals of Tourism Research*, 17(1): 103–122.

Peers, S. (2004) 'The legality of the regulation on EU citizens' passports', *Statewatch Analysis*, 26 November. Available at http://www.statewatch.org/news/2004/nov/11biometric-legal-analysis-htm.htm (accessed 17 May 2013).

Pérez, L. A. (1980) 'How tourism underdevelops tropical islands', in I. Vogeler and A. de Souza (eds) *Dialectics of Third World Development*, New Jersey: Allanheld, Osmun & Co., pp. 249–255.

Phillips, D. (2005) 'Iran sanctions' risk to air safety is cited in report', *New York Times*, 13 December. Available at http://boardingarea.com/blogs/flyingwithfish/2011/08/20/iran-seeks-to-privatize-iran-air-to-skirt-u-s-sanctions/ (accessed 20 March 2013).

Phipps, P. (1999) 'Tourists, terrorists, death and value', in R. Kaur and J. Hutnyk (eds) *Travel Words: Journeys in Contemporary Cultural Politics*, London: Zed Books, pp. 74–93.

Pignal, S. (2011) 'Bulgaria and Romania excluded from Schengen', *Financial Times*, 22 September. Available at http://www.ft.com/cms/s/0/dd7dfaea-e51f-11e0-9aa8-00144feabdc0.html#axzz1dJtID7Ol (accessed 10 November 2011).

Pilkington, E. (2009) 'Shell pays out $15.5m over Saro-Wiwa killing', *The Guardian*, 9 June. Available at http://www.guardian.co.uk/world/2009/jun/08/nigeria-usa (accessed 28 May 2013).

Pinder, J. (2001) *The European Union: A Very Short Introduction*, Oxford: Oxford University Press.

Pizam, A. (1996) 'Does tourism promote peace and understanding between unfriendly nations?', in A. Pizam and Y. Mansfeld (eds) *Tourism, Crime and International Security Issues*, Chichester: John Wiley, pp. 203–213.

Pollin, R. (2005) *Contours of Descent: US Economic Fractures and the Landscape of Global Austerity*, London and New York: Verso.

Popham, P. (2007) 'Outcasts: Italy, engulfed by moral panic turns on its immigrants in the wake of a murder', *The Independent* (cover story), 3 November, pp. 1–2.

Popham, P. (2008) 'The picture that shames Italy', *The Independent*, 22 July. Available at http://www.independent.co.uk/news/world/europe/article873743.ece?startindex=-1 (accessed 30 July 2008).

Poynting, S., G. Noble, P. Tabar and J. Collins (2004) *Bin Laden in the Suburbs: Criminalising the Arab Other*, Sydney: Federation Press.

Pratt, G. and B. Yeoh (2003) 'Transnational (counter) topographies', *Gender, Place and Culture*, 10(2): 159–166.

Pratt, M. L. (2008) *Imperial Eyes: Travel Writing and Transculturation*, second edition, London and New York: Routledge.

Prideaux, J. (2004) 'The new global elite', *New Statesman*, 5 April. Available at http://www.newstatesman.com/node/147642 (accessed 20 December 2012).

Przeclawski, K. (1988) 'Tourism and values', *Problems of Tourism*, 4(42): 3–11.

Putnam, R. D. (2000) *Bowling Alone: The Collapse and Revival of American Community*, New York: Simon and Schuster.

Raheb, M. (2004) *Bethlehem Besieged: Stories of Hope in Times of Trouble*, Minneapolis: Fortress Press.

Rahman, M. (2009) 'Dumped at sea: migrants accuse Thai army', *The Guardian*, 23 January, p. 25.

Rajendra, C. (1999) 'Contribution to debate – tourism on trial', *Tourism in Focus*, Autumn, 33: 6–9.

Ramrayka, L. (2005) 'Government urged to back "social tourism"', *The Guardian*, 8 February. Available at http://www.guardian.co.uk/society/2005/feb/08/socialexclusion.politics (accessed 26 April 2013).

Ratha, D. and A. Silwal (2012) 'Remittance flows in 2011: an update', *Migration and Development Brief*, No. 18, 23 April, Migration and Remittances Unit, World Bank. Available at http://siteresources.worldbank.org/INTPROSPECTS/Resources/334934-1110315015165/MigrationandDevelopmentBrief18.pdf (accessed 29 April 2013).

Reid, D. (2003) *Tourism, Globalization and Development: Responsible Tourism Planning*, London: Pluto Press.

Rekacewicz, P. (2008) 'The world on the move', *Le Monde Diplomatique*, April, pp. 8–9.

Rekacewicz, P. (2013) 'The airport malls', *Le Monde Diplomatique*, March, pp. 8–9.

Restakis, J. (2010) *Humanizing the Economy: Cooperatives in the Age of Capital*, British Columbia Canada: New Society Publishers.

Rice, A. (1991) 'Crisis on the crumbling costas', *The Observer*, 4 February, pp. 25–26.

Rice, A. (2005) *Post-tsunami Reconstruction and Tourism: A Second Disaster?*, London: Tourism Concern.

Rice, X. (2008) 'Sun, sea and miles of empty beach: the paradise that faces disaster', *The Guardian*, 8 February. Available at http://www.guardian.co.uk/world/2008/feb/08/kenya.travelnews (accessed 4 March 2013).

Richards, G. (1992) 'European social tourism: welfare or investment', *Tourism in Europe: The 1992 Conference*, 8–10 July, Durham, UK.

Richards, G. (1998) 'Time for a holiday? Social rights and international tourism consumption', *Time and Society*, 7(1): 145–160.

Richter, L. and W. L. Waugh Jr. (1986) 'Terrorism and tourism as logical companions', *Tourism Management*, 7, December: 230–238.

Richter, L. K. (1994) 'The political fragility of tourism in developing nations', *Teoros*, 13(2): 12–15.

Richter, L. K. (1995) 'Tourism politics – what has changed?', *Contours*, 7(4), December: 20–27.

Richter, L. K. (2000) *The Politics of Tourism in Asia*, India: Manohar (first published in 1989 by University of Hawaii Press, Honolulu).

Riddell, M. and T. Whitehead (2011) 'Immigration should be frozen, says Miliband advisor', *The Telegraph*, 22 July. Available at http://www.telegraph.co.uk/news/uknews/immigration/8643584/Immigration-should-be-frozen-says-Miliband-adviser.html (accessed 22 July 2011).

Rifkin, J. (2000) *The Age of Access: How the Shift from Ownership to Access is Transforming Modern Life*, London: Penguin.

Roberts, K. (2004) 'Leisure inequalities, class divisions and social exclusion in present day Britain', *Cultural Trends*, 13(5): 57–71.

Robinson, J. (2003) *Work to Live*, New York: The Berkley Publishing Group.

Roche, M. (2001) 'Citizenship, popular culture and Europe', in N. Stevenson (ed.) *Culture and Citizenship*, London: Sage, pp. 74–98.

Rodríguez, K. (2012) 'Highest court in the European Union to rule on biometrics privacy', *Electronic Frontier Foundation*, 15 October. Available at https://www.eff.org/deeplinks/2012/10/highest-court-european-union-rule-biometrics-privacy?utm_source=twitterfeed&utm_medium=twitter (accessed 24 December 2012).

Rogers, P. (2002) *Losing Control: Global Security in the Twenty-First Century*, London: Pluto Press.

Rojek, C. (1998) 'Tourism and citizenship', *International Journal of Cultural Policy*, 4(2): 291–310.

Romain, P. (2012) 'Une année d'enquête dans les entrailles de Roissy', *Le Figaro*, 23 October. Available at http://www.lefigaro.fr/actualite-france/2012/10/23/01016-20121023ARTFIG00624-une-annee-d-enquete-dans-les-entrailles-de-roissy.php (accessed 24 December 2012).

Rosenbloom, S. (2012) 'Speedy airport security: should you apply?', *New York Times*, 3 October. Available at http://www.nytimes.com/2012/10/07/travel/speedy-airport-security-should-you-apply.html?_r=0 (accessed 15 May 2013).

Routledge, P. (2001) '"Selling the rain": resisting the sale: resistant identities and the conflict over tourism in Goa', *Social and Cultural Geography*, 2(2): 221–240.

Royal Phuket Marina (2012) 'Gulu Lalvani', *Marina News superyachts.com*, 8 October. Available at http://www.royalphuketmarina.com/events/GULU-LALVANI-Marina-News-superyachts-com-.php (accessed 9 October 2012).

Rudner, M. (2008) 'Misuse of passports: identity fraud, the propensity to travel, and international terrorism', *Studies in Conflict and Terrorism*, 31: 95–110.

Rumford, C. (2006) 'Theorizing borders', *European Journal of Social Theory*, 9(2): 155–169.

Rumford, C. (2007) 'Does Europe have cosmopolitan borders?', *Globalizations*, 4(3): 327–339.

Ryan, C. (2002) 'Equity, management and power sharing and sustainability – issues of "new tourism"', *Tourism Management*, 23(1): 17–26.

Saarinen, J. (1999) 'Representations of "indigeneity": Sami culture in the discourses of tourism', in J. N. Brown and P. M. Sant (eds) *Indigeneity: Construction and Re/Presentation*, New York: Nova Science Publishers, Inc., pp. 231–249.

Sabaté Bel, F. (2001) 'Yendo pa' la mar, a por lapas y burgaos', *Cuadernos del Sureste*, No. 9 (March): 136–145.

Sabine, G. H. and T. L. Thorson (1973) *A History of Political Theory*, Hinsdale, IL: Dryden Press.

Sader, E. (2002) 'Beyond civil society', *New Left Review*, II, 17: 87–99.

Said, E. (1978) *Orientalism: Western Conceptions of the Orient*, London: Penguin.

Said, E. (2005) *From Oslo to Iraq and the Roadmap*, London: Bloomsbury.

Salas, A. (2011) 'Los hoteleros temen cierres por el recorte a los viajes para mayores', *La Verdad*. Available at http://www.laverdad.es/murcia/v/20110926/region/hoteleros-temen-cierres-recorte-20110926.html (accessed 5 October 2012).

Salazar, N. (2006) 'Building a "culture of peace" through tourism: reflexive and analytical notes and queries', *Universitas Humanistica*, July–December, 62: 319–333.

Salter, M. B. (2004) 'Passports, mobility, and security: how smart can the border be?', *International Studies Perspectives*, 5(1): 71–91.

Salter, M. B. (2006) 'The global visa regime and the political technologies of the international self: borders, bodies, biopolitics', *Alternatives: Global, Local, Political*, 31(2): 167–189.

Salter, M. B. (2008a) 'Introduction: airport assemblage', in M. B. Salter (ed.) *Politics at the Airport*, Minneapolis: University of Minnesota Press, pp. ix–xix.

Salter, M. B. (2008b) 'The global airport: managing space, speed, and security', in M. B. Salter (ed.) *Politics at the Airport*, Minneapolis: University of Minnesota Press, pp. 1–28.

Samatas, M. (2003) 'Greece in "Schengenland": blessing or anathema for citizens' and foreigners' rights', *Journal of Ethnic and Migration Studies*, 29(1): 141–156.

Sánchez, P. M. and K. M. Adams (2008) 'The janus-faced character of tourism in Cuba', *Annals of Tourism Research*, 35(1): 27–46.

Santana, G. (2001) 'Globalisation, safety and national security', in S. Wahab and C. Cooper (eds) *Tourism in the Age of Globalisation*, London: Routledge, pp. 213–241.

Scheper-Hughes, N. (2004) 'Parts unknown: undercover ethnography of the organs-trafficking underworld', *Ethnography*, 5(1): 29–73.

Scheper-Hughes, N. (2005) 'Katrina: the disaster and its doubles', *Anthropology Today*, 21(6): 2–4.

Scheyvens, R. (2002) *Tourism for Development: Empowering Communities*, Harlow: Prentice-Hall.

Scholte, J. A. (2005) *Globalization: A Critical Introduction*, second edition, London: Palgrave Macmillan.

Schwartz, R. D. (1991) 'Travellers under fire: tourists in the Tibetan uprising', *Annals of Tourism Research*, 18(4): 588–604.

Science Daily (2011) 'Insured and still at risk: number of underinsured in US increased 80 percent between 2003–2010', *Sciencedaily.com*, 8 September. Available at http://www.sciencedaily.com/releases/2011/09/110908081303.htm (accessed 21 May 2013).

Scott, A. (1990) *Ideology and the New Social Movements*, London: Unwin Hyman.

Scott, D. and S. Becken (2010) 'Adapting to climate change and climate policy: progress, problems and potentials', *Journal of Sustainable Tourism*, 18(3): 283–295.

Scott, J. (2012) 'Tourism, civil society and peace in Cyprus', *Annals of Tourism Research*, 39(4): 2114–2132.

Scott, J. E. (2005) 'Imagining the Mediterranean', *Journal of Mediterranean Studies*, 15(2): 219–244.

Scott, J. E. (2007) 'Place-making in Cyprus as theory and praxis', paper presented to the Annual Conference of the Association of Social Anthropologists, Thinking through Tourism, London Metropolitan University, 10–13 April.

Scott, J. E. (2008) 'The Mediterranean and the cosmopolitan imagination', keynote paper, International Symposium on Interculturality in the Mediterranean, Universitas Miguel Hernandez, Elche, Spain, 23–25 April.

Scratton, S. and B. Watson (1998) 'Gender cities; women and public leisure space in the "postmodern city"', *Leisure Studies*, 17: 123–137.

Scruton, R. (2000) *England: An Elegy*, London: Chatto and Windus.

Seekings, J. and N. Nattrass (2005) *Class, Race and Inequality in South Africa*, New Haven, CT: Yale University Press.

Selwyn, T. (2004) 'Privatising the Mediterranean coastline', in J. Boissevain and T. Selwyn (eds) *Contesting the Foreshore: Tourism, Society and Politics on the Coast*, Amsterdam: Amsterdam University Press, pp. 35–60.

Selwyn, T. (2009) 'Ghettoizing a matriarch and a city: an everyday story from the Palestinian/ Israeli borderlands', *Journal of Borderland Studies*, 24(3): 39–55.

Sengupta, S. (2008) 'Mumbai attacks politicize long-isolated elite', *New York Times*, 6 December. Available at http://www.nytimes.com/2008/12/07/world/asia/07india. html?pagewanted=all&_r=0 (accessed 10 December 2008).

Sennett, R. (2006) *The Culture of the New Capitalism*, New Haven, CT: Yale University Press.

Shanks, C. (2009) 'The global compact: the conservative politics of international tourism', *Futures*, 41: 360–366.

Sharpley, R., J. Sharpley and J. Adams (1996) 'Travel advice or trade embargo? The impacts and implications of official travel advice', *Tourism Management*, 17(1): 1–7.

Shear, M. D. (2009) 'Obama lifts some restrictions on Cuba', *The Washington Post*, 14 April. Available at http://voices.washingtonpost.com/44/2009/04/13/obama_to_lift_cuba_travel_rest.html (accessed 13 August 2009).

Sheller, M. (2009) 'The new Caribbean complexity: mobility systems, tourism and spatial rescaling', *Singapore Journal of Tropical Geography*, 30: 189–203.

Sherif, I. (2012) 'Gulf states ask citizens to avoid Lebanon travel', *Gulf News*, 20 May. Available at http://gulfnews.com/news/gulf/uae/government/gulf-states-ask-citizens-to-avoid-lebanon-travel-1.1025084 (accessed 1 June 2012).

Sherwood, H. (2012) 'Israeli separation wall threatens Battir's ancient terraces', *The Guardian*, 11 December. Available at http://www.guardian.co.uk/world/2012/dec/11/israel-palestinians-battir-separation-wall (accessed 27 March 2013).

Shipman, T. (2013) 'We won't be a soft touch for welfare tourists vows PM: Cameron says those from outside the EU should pay when they use British hospitals', *Mail Online*, 15 February. Available at http://www.dailymail.co.uk/news/article-2278887/We-wont-soft-touch-welfare-tourists-vows-PM-Cameron-says-outside-EU-pay-use-British-hospitals.html (accessed 29 April 2013).

Shivji, I. (1973) *Tourism and Socialist Development*, Dar es Salaam: Tanzania Publishing House.

Shore, C. (2000) *Building Europe: The Cultural Politics of European Integration*, London: Routledge.

Shore, C. and M. Abélès (2004) 'Debating the European Union', *Anthropology Today*, 20(2): 10–14.

Sigona, N. and N. Trehan (2009) 'Introduction: Romani politics in neoliberal Europe', in N. Sigona and N. Trehan (eds) *Romani Politics in Contemporary Europe: Poverty, Ethnic Mobilization and the Neoliberal Order*, London: Palgrave Macmillan, pp. 1–20.

Silverman, M. (1992) 'The revenge of civil society: state, nation and society in France', in D. Cesarani and M. Fulbrook (eds) *Citizenship, Nationality and Migration in Europe*, London: Routledge, pp. 146–158.

Simmons, B. A. (2004) 'Tourism and postcolonialism: contested discourses, identities and representations', in C. M. Hall and H. Tucker (eds) *Tourism and Postcolonialism: Contested Discourses, Identities and Representations*, London: Routledge, pp. 43–56.

Simpson, K. (2004) '"Doing development": the Gap Year, volunteer tourists and a popular practice of development', *Journal of International Development*, 16: 681–692.

Sindiga, I. (1996) 'International tourism in Kenya and the marginalisation of the Waswahili', *Tourism Management*, 17: 425–432.

Sivanandan, A. (1990) *Communities of Resistance: Writing on Black Struggles for Socialism*, London: Verso.

Sklair, L. (2001) *The Transnational Capitalist Class*, Oxford: Blackwell.

Smith, A. and C. Mar-Molinero (1996) 'The myths and realities of nation-building in the Iberian peninsula', in C. Mar-Molinero and A. Smith (eds) *Nationalism and the Nation in the Iberian Peninsula*, Oxford: Berg, pp. 1–30.

Smith, H. (2002) 'The politics of "regulated liberalism": a historical materialist approach to European integration', in M. Rupert and H. Smith (eds) *Historical Materialism and Globalization*, London: Routledge, pp. 257–283.

Smith, H. (2007) 'An idyllic Greek island becomes the new frontier for African migrants', *The Guardian*, 3 December, p. 23.

Smith, H. (2010) 'Greece pledges help for stranded tourists as strike paralyses nation', *The Guardian*, 9 July, p. 18.

Smith, H. (2013) 'Qatari emir buys six Greek islands for a song', *The Guardian*, 4 March. Available at http://www.guardian.co.uk/world/2013/mar/04/qatar-emir-buys-six-greek-islands (accessed 18 March 2013).

Smith, K. (2012) 'The problematization of medical tourism: a critique of neoliberalism', *Developing World Bioethics*, 12(1): 1–8.

Smith, M. and R. Duffy (2003) *The Ethics of Tourism Development*, London: Routledge.

Smith, M. K. (2003a) 'Holistic holidays: tourism and the reconciliation of the body, mind, spirit', *Tourism Recreation Research*, 28(1): 103–108.

Smith, M. K. (2003b) *Issues in Cultural Tourism Studies*, London: Routledge.

Smith, V. and H. Hughes (1999) 'Disadvantaged families and the meaning of a holiday', *International Journal of Tourism Research*, 1(2): 123–133.

Soames, N. and F. Field (2013) 'Britain can't afford this level of immigration', *The Telegraph*, 28 March. Available at http://www.telegraph.co.uk/news/uknews/immigration/9959813/Britain-cant-afford-this-level-of-immigration.html (accessed 14 May 2013).

Sofia Echo (2010) 'Albania, Bosnia to get Schengen visa-free access in mid-December 2010', *Sofiaecho.com*, 8 November. Available at http://sofiaecho.com/2010/11/08/989854_albania-bosnia-to-get-schengen-visa-free-access-in-mid-december-2010 (accessed 20 May 2013).

Sofield, T. H. B. (2006) 'Border tourism and border communities: an overview', *Tourism Geographies*, 8(2): 102–121.

Solnit, R. (2002) *Wanderlust: A History of Walking*, London: Verso.

Somers, M. R. (2008) *Genealogies of Citizenship: Markets, Statelessness, and the Right to Have Rights*, Cambridge: Cambridge University Press.

Song, S. (2005) 'Majority norms, multiculturalism, and gender equality', *American Political Science Review*, 99(4): 237–256.

Sönmez, S. (1998) 'Tourism, terrorism and political instability', *Annals of Tourism Research*, 25(2): 416–456.

Soysal, Y. N. (1994) *Limits of Citizenship: Migrants and Postnational Membership in Europe*, Chicago: Chicago University Press.

Soysal, Y. N. (1997) 'Changing parameters of citizenship and claims-making: organised Islam in European public spheres', *Theory and Society*, 26(4): 509–527.

Srisang, K. (1992) 'Third world tourism – the new colonialism', *Tourism in Focus*, Summer, 4: 2–3.

St. Clair, J. (1999) 'Seattle diary: it's a gas, gas, gas', *New Left Review*, II, 238: 81–96.

Stancliffe, A. and T. Barnett (2010) 'Laying the foundations', *Tourism in Focus*, Autumn/Winter: 6–7.

Stebner, B. (2013) 'Jay-Z needs to get informed: Florida Sen. Marco Rubio slams rapper's "hypocritical" visit to Cuba with wife Beyoncé', *Mail Online*, 14 April. Available at http://www.dailymail.co.uk/news/article-2309072/Jay-Zs-Cuba-rap-Open-Letter-Marco-Rubio-slams-rappers-hypocritical-trip-Beyonce.html (accessed 20 April 2013).

Stein, R. (2001) '"First contact" and other Israeli fictions: tourism, globalization, and the Middle East Peace Process', *Public Culture*, 14(3): 515–543.

Stein, N. (2012) 'Is 2012 the year of the volunteer tourist?', *Travelmole.com*, 17 January. Available at http://www.travelmole.com/news_feature.php?news_id=1151074 (accessed 23 January 2012).

Steiner, C. (2007) 'Political instability, transnational tourist companies and destination recovery in the Middle East after 9/11', *Tourism and Hospitality Planning & Development*, 4(3): 169–190.

Steinmetz, T. (2007) 'Dr Pradhanang expressed deep sorrow on beating tourists', *eTurboNews, Global Travel Industry News*, 12 December 2007. Available at http://www.eturbonews.com/365/dr-pradhanang-expressed-deep-sorrow-beating-tourists (accessed 19 December 2007).

Steinmetz, T. (2009a) 'Hilton on Margarita Island seized by Venezuelan government', *eTurboNews, Global Travel Industry News*, 15 October. Available at http://www.eturbonews.com/12280/hilton-margarita-island-seized-venezuelan-government (accessed 8 January 2010).

Steinmetz, T. (2009b) 'Sol Meliá to gain from US repeal of Cuba travel ban', *eTurboNews, Global Travel Industry News*, 18 November. Available at http://www.eturbonews.com/print/12832 (accessed 18 November 2009).

Stephenson, M. L. (1994) 'White of the eye: perceiving Manchester's heritage', *Tourism in Focus*, 12: 14–15.

Stephenson, M. L. (2002) 'Travelling to the ancestral homelands: the aspirations and experiences of a UK Caribbean community', *Current Issues in Tourism*, 5(5): 378–425.

Stephenson, M. L. (2004) 'Tourism, racism and the UK Afro-Caribbean diaspora', in T. Coles and D. J. Timothy (eds) *Tourism, Diasporas and Space*, London: Routledge, pp. 62–77.

Stephenson, M. L. (2006) 'Travel and the freedom of movement: racialised encounters and experiences amongst ethnic minority tourists in the EU', *Mobilities*, 1(2): 285–306.

Stephenson, M. L. (2007) 'The socio-political implications of rural racism and tourism experiences', in J. Tribe and D. Airey (eds) *Developments in Tourism Research: New Directions, Challenges and Applications*, Oxford: Elsevier, pp. 171–184.

Stephenson, M. L. (in press, 2014a) 'Deciphering "Islamic hospitality": developments, challenges and opportunities', *Tourism Management*, 40: 155–164.

Stephenson, M. L. (in press, 2014b) 'Tourism, development and "destination Dubai": cultural dilemmas and future challenges', *Current Issues in Tourism*.

Stephenson, M. L. and J. Ali-Knight (2010) 'Dubai's tourism industry and its societal impact: social implications and sustainable challenges', *Journal of Tourism and Cultural Change* (The Middle East and North Africa Special Issue), 8(4): 278–292.

Stephenson, M. L. and H. L. Hughes (1995) 'Holidays and the UK Afro-Caribbean community', *Tourism Management*, 16(6): 429–435.

Stephenson, M. L. and H. L. Hughes (2005) 'Racialised boundaries in tourism and travel: a case study of the UK Black Caribbean community', *Leisure Studies*, 24(2): 137–160.

Stephenson, M. L., K. A. Russell and D. Edgar (2010) 'Islamic hospitality in the UAE: indigenization of products and human capital', *Journal of Islamic Marketing*, 1(1): 9–24.

Steves, R. (2009) *Travel as a Political Act*, New York: Nation Books.

Steward, F. (1991) 'Citizens of planet earth', in G. Andrews (ed.) *Citizenship*, London: Lawrence and Wishart, pp. 65–75.

Steward, J. (2005) '"How and where to go": the role of travel journalism in Britain and evolution of foreign tourism, 1840–1914', in J. K. Walton (ed.) *Histories of Tourism: Representation, Identity and Conflict*, Clevedon: Channel View Publications, pp. 39–54.

Strack, H. (1978) *Sanctions: The Case of Rhodesia*, Syracuse, NY: Syracuse University Press.

Strange, S. (1994) *States and Markets*, London and Washington: Pinter.

Streeck, W. (2012) 'Citizens as consumers: considerations on the new politics of consumption', *New Left Review*, II, 76: 27–47.

Susser, I. (2006) 'Global visions and grassroots movements: an anthropological perspective', *International Journal of Urban and Regional Research*, 30(1): 212–218.

Swain, M. B. (2009) 'The cosmopolitan hope of tourism: critical action and worldmaking vistas', *Tourism Geographies*, 11(4): 505–525.

Swain, M. B. and D. R. Hall (2007) 'Gender analysis in tourism: personal and global dialectics', in I. Ateljevic, A. Pritchard and N. Morgan (eds) *The Critical Turn in Tourism Studies: Innovative Research Methodologies*, Amsterdam: Elsevier, pp. 91–104.

Swiss Confederation (2013) 'Embassy of Switzerland – Foreign Interests Section', Federal Department of Foreign Affairs. Available at http://www.eda.admin.ch/eda/en/home/reps/asia/virn/fosteh.html (accessed 29 May 2013).

Tambini, D. (2001) 'Post-national citizenship', *Ethnic and Racial Studies*, 24(2): 195–217.

Tarlow, P. E. (2006) 'Tourism and terrorism', in J. Wilks, D. Pendergast and P. Leggatt (eds) *Tourism in Turbulent Times: Towards Safe Experiences for Visitors*, Oxford: Elsevier, pp. 79–92.

Tarrow, S. (2005) *The New Transnational Activism*, Cambridge: Cambridge University Press.

Tarrow, S. G. (2011) *Power in Movement: Social Movements and Contentious Politics*, third edition, Cambridge: Cambridge University Press.

Tax Reporting Team (2009) 'Firms' secret tax avoidance schemes cost UK billions', *The Guardian*, 2 February. Available at http://www.guardian.co.uk/business/2009/feb/02/tax-gap-avoidance (accessed 2 April 2013).

Taylor, E. P. (2012) 'Museums narrating the nation: case studies from Greece and Bosnia-Herzegovina', *Totem: The University of Western Ontario Journal of Anthropology*, 20(1), Article 4. Available at http://ir.lib.uwo.ca/cgi/viewcontent.cgi?article=1231&context=totem (accessed 29 April 2013).

Taylor, I. (2013) 'Abta urges Balearics to reconsider car hire tax', *Travel Weekly*, 21 February. Available at http://www.travelweekly.co.uk/articles/2013/02/21/43242/abta+urges+balearics+to+reconsider+car+hire+tax.html (accessed 16 June 2013).

Taylor, J. (2013) 'The truth about Romania's gypsies: not coming over here, not stealing our jobs', *The Independent*, 11 February. Available at http://www.independent.co.uk/news/world/europe/the-truth-about-romanias-gypsies-not-coming-over-here-not-stealing-our-jobs-8489097.html (accessed 19 May 2013).

Tax Reporting Team (2009) 'Firms' secret tax avoidance schemes cost UK billions', *The Guardian*, 2 February. Available at http://www.guardian.co.uk/business/2009/feb/02/tax-gap-avoidance (accessed 2 April 2013).

Telegraph (2011) 'Nicolas Sarkozy tells under fire ministers to holiday in France', *The Telegraph*, 9 February. Available at http://www.telegraph.co.uk/news/worldnews/europe/france/8313179/Nicolas-Sarkozy-tells-under-fire-ministers-to-holiday-in-France.html (accessed 10 February 2011).

TEN (1984) *Declaration of the Third World European Tourism Network*. Available at http://www.ten-tourism.org/declaration.html (accessed 17 March 2013).

Tesfahuney, M. (1998) 'Mobility, racism, geopolitics', *Political Geography*, 17(5): 499–515.

Teuscher, H. (1983) 'Social tourism for all: the Swiss Travel Fund', *Tourism Management*, 4(3): 216–219.

Tezcan, E. (2010) 'Yes to Serbia, Montenegro and Macedonia, but what about Turkey?', *Turkish Weekly*, 19 January. Available at http://www.turkishweekly.net/print.asp?type=4&id=3275 (accessed 25 June 2010).

Theodossopoulos, D. (2010) 'Tourists and indigenous culture as resources: lessons from Embera cultural tourism in Panama', in D.V. L. Macleod and J. G. Carrier (eds) *Tourism, Power and Culture: Anthropological Insights*, Clevedon: Channel View Publications, pp. 115–131.

Theodoulou, M. (2010) 'Iranian students feel the sanctions heat', *The National*, 26 July. Available at http://www.thenational.ae/news/world/middle-east/iranian-students-feel-the-sanctions-heat#page1 (accessed 20 March 2013).

Thomas, C. (1987) *In Search of Security: The Third World in International Relations*, Boulder, CO: Lynne Rienner Publishing Inc.

Till, K. E. (2005) *The New Berlin: Memory, Politics, Place*, Minneapolis: University of Minnesota Press.

Tilly, C. (1999) 'Where do rights come from?', in T. Skoepol (ed.) *Democracy, Revolution and History*, Ithaca, NY: Cornell University Press, pp. 55–72.

Tomazos, K. and W. Cooper (2012) 'Volunteer tourism: at the crossroads of commercialization and service?', *Current Issues in Tourism*, 15(5): 405–423.

Toolis, K. (2004) 'Rise of the terrorist professors', *New Statesman*, 14 June, pp. 26–27.

Topham, G. (2012) 'Fastjet takes EasyJet low-cost model into African airspace', *The Observer*, 18 November. Available at http://www.guardian.co.uk/business/2012/nov/18/fastjet-low-cost-african-airspace (accessed 15 April 2013).

Torpey, J. (1998) 'Coming and going: on the state monopolization of the legitimate means of movement', *Sociological Theory*, 16(3): 239–259.

Torpey, J. (2000) *The Invention of the Passport: Surveillance, Citizenship and the State*, Cambridge: Cambridge University Press.

Tourism Concern (1995) 'Forced labour and relocations in Burma', *Tourism in Focus*, Spring, 15: 6–7.

Tourism Concern (2000) 'Boycott Lonely Planet', press release, 26 May.

Tourism Concern (2003) *FCO Travel Advisories: The Case for Transparency and Balance*, London: Tourism Concern.

Tourism Concern (2005) *Post-tsunami Reconstruction and Tourism: A Second Disaster?* London: Tourism Concern.

Tourism Concern (2008) 'How UK tour operators are supporting Burma's military regime through tourism', press briefing, London: Tourism Concern.

Tourism Concern (2009) 'World Social Forum calls for truly sustainable tourism', 1 February. Available at http://www.tourismconcern.org.uk/index.php/news/105/154/World-Social-Forum-calls-for-truly-sustainable-tourism.html (accessed 14 June 2013).

Tourism Concern (2012) 'All-inclusive holidays – excluding local people in tourist destinations'. Available at http://www.tourismconcern.org.uk/all-inclusive-holidays-excluding-local-people.html (accessed 18 July 2012).

Tourism Review (2010) 'New EU initiative: the right to travel', *Tourism Review.com*, 15 June. Available at http://www.tourism-review.com/new-eu-initiative-the-right-to-travel-news2236 (accessed 22 August 2010).

Tourism Review (2012) 'Russia is already the 6th largest tourism source market', *Tourism Review.com*, 30 April. Available at http://www.tourism-review.com/russia-6th-largest-tourism-source-market-news3225 (accessed 1 May 2012).

Tran, M. (2009) 'Hitler's plans to turn Blackpool into Nazi resort come to light', *The Guardian*, 23 February. Available at http://www.guardian.co.uk/uk/2009/feb/23/hitler-blackpool-resort-plans (accessed 24 February 2009).

Travel Mail Reporter (2013) 'Going up: flight prices increase from today as Air Passenger Duty levy kicks in', *Mail Online*, 1 April. Available at http://www.dailymail.co.uk/travel/article-2302279/APD-hike-Flight-prices-increase-today-Air-Passenger-Duty-levy-kicks-in.html (accessed 29 April 2013).

Travelmole (2003a) 'Kuoni to drop Burma', *Travelmole.com*, 1 May. Available at http://www.travelmole.com/cgi-bin/item.cgi?id=97693&d=339&h=341&f=340 (accessed 1 May 2003).

Travelmole (2003b) 'A&K to stop promoting Burma', *Travelmole.com*, 29 July. Available at http://www.travelmole.com/cgi-bin/item.cgi?id=98252&d=339&h=341&f=340 (accessed 1 October 2003).

Traynor, I. (2008a) 'Government wants personal details of every traveller', *The Guardian*, 23 February. Available at http://www.guardian.co.uk/uk/2008/feb/23/uksecurity.terrorismandtravel (accessed 19 September 2008).

Traynor, I. (2008b) 'New pact would give EU citizens' data to US', *The Guardian*, 30 June. Available at http://www.guardian.co.uk/world/2008/jun/30/eu.privacy (accessed 19 September 2008).

Traynor, I. (2010a) 'Gaddafi bans most Europeans from travelling to Libya', *The Guardian*, 15 February. Available at http://m.guardian.co.uk/world/2010/feb/15/libya-gaddafi-schengen-travel-ban (accessed 20 April 2013).

Traynor, I. (2010b) 'Roma deportations by France a disgrace, says EU', *The Guardian*, 14 September. Available at http://www.guardian.co.uk/world/2010/sep/14/roma-deportations-france-eu-disgrace (accessed 10 October 2011).

Traynor, I. (2011) 'Europe moves to end passport-free travel in migrant row', *The Guardian*, 12 May. Available at http://www.guardian.co.uk/world/2011/may/12/europe-to-end-passport-free-travel?INTCMP=SRCH) (accessed 21 July 2011).

Tremlett, G. (2007) 'Wayne Rooney shirts and a pint of bitter – a big role for little Britain in Spain's local elections', *The Guardian*, 22 May, p. 23.

TUI Travel (2012) *Sustainable Holidays. Spreading Smiles: Sustainable Holidays Plan 2012–2014*. Available at http://www.tuitravelplc.com/sites/default/files/attachments/TUITravelSustainableHolidaysPlan2012–2014_2.pdf (accessed 12 March 2013).

Turgut, P. (2008) 'Constantinople's gypsies not welcome in Istanbul', *Time* online, 9 June. Available at http://www.time.com/time/world/article/0,8599,1812905,00.html (accessed 16 June 2010).

Turner, B. S. (1986) *Citizenship and Capitalism*, London: Allen and Unwin.

Turner, B. S. (1994a) 'Contemporary problems in the theory of citizenship', in B. S. Turner (ed.) *Citizenship and Social Theory*, London: Sage, pp. 1–18.

Turner, B. S. (1994b) 'Preface', in B. S. Turner (ed.) *Citizenship and Social Theory*, London: Sage, pp. vii–xii.

Turner, B. S. (1994c) 'Postmodern culture / modern citizens', in B. van Steenbergen (ed.) *The Condition of Citizenship*, London: Sage, pp. 155–168.

Turner, B. S. (1997) 'Citizenship studies: a general theory', *Citizenship Studies*, 1(1): 5–18.

Turner, B. S. (2001) 'The erosion of citizenship', *British Journal of Sociology*, 52(2): 189–209.

Turner, B. S. (2009) 'Thinking Citizenship Series: T. H. Marshall, social rights and English national identity', *Citizenship Studies*, 13(1): 65–73.

Turner, L. and J. Ash (1975) *The Golden Hordes: International Tourism and the Pleasure Periphery*, London: Constable.

Turton, D. (1987) 'The Mursi and National Park development in the Lower Omo Valley', in D. Anderson and R. Grove (eds) *Conservation in Africa: People, Policies and Practice*, Cambridge: Cambridge University Press, pp. 169–186.

Tutu, D. (1999) *No Future Without Forgiveness*, London: Rider.

Twain, M. (1869) *The Innocents Abroad, or The New Pilgrims' Progress*, Hartford, CT: American Publishing Company.

UK Visa Bureau (2012) 'Minister plans UK visa simplification for Chinese tourists', UK Visa Bureau, 7 November. Available at http://www.visabureau.com/uk/news/07–11–2012/minister-plans-uk-visa-simplification-for-chinese-tourists.aspx (accessed 27 December 2012).

United Nations (1948) *Universal Declaration of Human Rights*, New York: United Nations. Available at http://www.un.org/Overview/rights.html (accessed 19 December 2007).

United Nations (1986) Declaration on the Right to Development, UN General Assembly. Available at http://www.un.org/documents/ga/res/41/a41r128.htm (accessed 30 April 2013).

UNCTAD (United Nations Conference on Trade and Development) (1973) *Elements of Tourism Policy in Developing Countries*, New York: United Nations Publications TD/B/C.3/89/Rev. 1.

UNCTAD (United Nations Conference on Trade and Development) (2012) *Trade and Development Report: Policies for Inclusive and Balanced Growth*, New York and Geneva: United Nations. Available at http://unctad.org/en/pages/PublicationWebflyer.aspx?publicationid=210 (accessed 4 March 2013).

UNDP (United Nations Development Programme) (2011) *Human Development Report: Sustainability and Equity: A Better Future for All*, New York: Oxford University Press. Available at http://hdr.undp.org/en/media/HDR_2011_EN_Tables.pdf (accessed 12 November 2012).

UNDP (United Nations Development Programme) (2013) *Human Development Report: The Rise of the South: Human Progress in a Diverse World*, New York: Oxford University Press. Available at http://hdr.undp.org/en/media/HDR_2013_EN_complete.pdf (accessed 15 April 2013).

UNESCO (n.d.) *Introducing UNESCO: What We Are*. Available at http://www.unesco.org/new/en/unesco/about-us/who-we-are/introducing-unesco/ (accessed 21 September 2010).

UNESCO (n.d.) *World Heritage*. Available at http://whc.unesco.org/en/about/ (accessed 21 September 2010).

UNHCR (2012) 'UNHCR: Report – 800,000 people forced to flee in 2011', *Refugees Daily*. Available at http://www.unhcr.org/cgi-bin/texis/vtx/refdaily?pass=463ef21123&id=4fded41d5 (accessed 17 June 2012).

UNWTO (United Nations World Tourism Organization) (1999) *Global Code of Ethics for Tourism*, Madrid: UNWTO. Available at http://www.unwto.org/ethics/full_text/en/pdf/Codigo_Etico_Ing.pdf (accessed 29 December 2012).

UNWTO (United Nations World Tourism Organization) (2009) 'Ethical challenges posed by the economic crisis are cause of deep concern', press release, 24 June, San José, Costa Rica. Madrid: UNWTO. Available at http://www.unwto.org/media/news/en/press_det.php?id=4391&idioma=E (accessed 22 July 2009).

UNWTO (United Nations World Tourism Organization) (2010) *China – The World's Fastest Growing Outbound Market and the Largest Source Market in Asia*, Madrid: UNWTO. Available at http://www.unwto.org/asia/news/en/news_det.php?id=6301 (accessed 18 July 2010).

UNWTO (United Nations World Tourism Organization) (2011) *Annual Report*, Madrid: UNWTO. Available at http://dtxtq4w60xqpw.cloudfront.net/sites/all/files/pdf/annual_report_2011.pdf (accessed 13 July 2012).

UNWTO (United Nations World Tourism Organization) (2012) *Tourism Highlights*, Madrid: UNWTO. Available at http://dtxtq4w60xqpw.cloudfront.net/sites/all/files/docpdf/unwtohighlights12enhr_1.pdf (accessed 28 March 2013).

UNWTO (United Nations World Tourism Organization) (2013) *World Tourism Barometer*, Vol. 11, January. Available at http://mkt.unwto.org/en/barometer/january-2013-volume-11 (accessed 30 April 2013).

United States–Mexico Chamber of Commerce (2011) 'Tourism development, medical tourism, and safe and secure tourism in Mexico', *Issues Paper* 3, Washington, DC, pp. 1–6.

University of Oxford (2012) 'Vice-chancellor announces £3b funding target', University of Oxford Press Office, 2 October. Available at http://www.ox.ac.uk/media/news_stories/2012/121002.html (accessed 8 October 2012).

Urry, J. (1990) *The Tourist Gaze: Leisure and Travel in Contemporary Societies*, London: Sage.

Urry, J. (1995) *Consuming Places*, London: Routledge.

Urry, J. (2000) *Sociology Beyond Societies: Mobilities for the Twenty-First Century*, London: Routledge.

Urry, J. (2002) *The Tourist Gaze: Leisure and Travel in Contemporary Societies*, second edition, London: Sage.

Urry, J. (2013) *Societies Beyond Oil: Oil Dregs and Social Futures*, London: Zed Books.

US Department of State (2013a) 'Passport statistics', *Travel.State.Gov.*, Bureau of Consular Affairs. Available at http://travel.state.gov/passport/ppi/stats/stats_890.html (accessed 23 April 2013).

US Department of State (2013b) 'Libya: travel warning', *Travel.State.Gov.*, Bureau of Consular Affairs, 9 May. Available at http://travel.state.gov/travel/cis_pa_tw/tw/tw_5853.html (accessed 10 May 2013).

US Department of State (2013c) 'Iran country specific information', *Travel.State.Gov.*, Bureau of Consular Affairs. Available at http://travel.state.gov/travel/cis_pa_tw/cis/cis_1142.html (accessed 29 May 2013).

Valdivielso, J. (2001) 'Poder y hegemonía el la batalla de la ecotaxa', in J. Valdivielso (ed.) *¿A qué llamamos ecotasa?* Palma: Monograma, pp. 9–40..

Valencia Sáiz, A. (2005) 'Globalisation, cosmopolitanism and ecological citizenship', *Environmental Politics*, 14(2): 163–178.

Valentine, G. (1989) 'The geography of women's fear', *Area*, 21(4): 385–390.

van Steenbergen, B. (1994) 'Towards a global ecological citizen', in B. van Steenbergen (ed.) *The Condition of Citizenship*, London: Sage, pp. 141–152.

Var, T., J. Ap and C. Van Doren (1994) 'Tourism and world peace', in W. Theobald (ed.) *Global Tourism: The Next Decade*, Oxford: Butterworth-Heinemann, pp. 27–39.

Verkaik, R. (2007) 'Major airline refuses to help with forcible removal of immigrants', *The Independent*, 8 October. Available at http://www.independent.co.uk/news/uk/crime/major-airline-refuses-to-help-with-forcible-removal-of-immigrants-394451.html (accessed 24 October 2011).

Verstraete, G. (2010) *Tracking Europe: Mobility, Diaspora and the Politics of Location*, London: Duke University Press.

Vertovec, S. and R. Cohen (2002) 'Introduction: conceiving cosmopolitanism', in S.Vertovec and R. Cohen (eds) *Conceiving Cosmopolitanism*, Oxford: Oxford University Press, pp. 1–22.

Vicent, M. (2008) 'Raúl Castro autoriza el libre acceso de los cubanos a los hoteles', *El País*, 31 March. Available at http://www.elpais.com/articulo/internacional/Raul/Castro/autoriza/libre/acceso/cubanos/hoteles/elpepuint/20080331elpepuint_10/Tes (accessed 25 June 2010).

Villarreal, R. (2012) 'A tale of two tropical paradises: Venezuela fails at tourism, while Colombia goes mainstream', *International Business Times*, 15 September. Available at http://www.ibtimes.com/tale-two-tropical-paradises-venezuela-fails-tourism-while-colombia-goes-mainstream-790180 (accessed 26 April 2013).

Wade, R. (2004) *Governing the Market*, Berkeley: University of California Press.

Waldren, J. (1996) *Insiders and Outsiders: Paradise and Reality in Mallorca*, Oxford: Berghahn.

Walton, J. K. (2005) 'Paradise lost and found: tourists and expatriates in El Terreno, Palma de Mallorca, from the 1920s to the 1950s', in J. K. Walton (ed.) *Histories of Tourism: Representation, Identity and Conflict*, Clevedon: ChannelView Publications, pp. 179–194.

Ward, C. (1999) *Canaries on the Rim*, London: Verso.

Ward, S.V. (1998) *Selling Places: The Marketing and Promotion of Towns and Cities 1850–2000*, Abingdon: Spon Press.

Watson, W. (2013) 'Personal communication', Director of Tourism Concern.

Watt, N. (2013) 'George Osborne opens doors to rich Chinese with new visa system', *The Guardian*, 13 October. Available at http://www.theguardian.com/politics/2013/oct/14/george-osborne-china-visa (accessed 4 November 2013).

Watts, J. (2007) 'Going under', *The Guardian*, 20 June. Available at http://www.guardian.co.uk/uk/2007/jun/20/ukcrime.humanrights (accessed 23 March 2003).

Wazir, B. (2001) 'British Muslims fly into a hostile climate', *The Observer*, 21 October, p. 4.

WCED (The World Commission on Environment and Development) (1987) *Our Common Future*, Oxford: Oxford University Press.

WDM (World Development Movement) (2013) *Campaign Update: Aid. Think Global*, January. London: WDM.

Wearing, B. and S.Wearing (1996) 'Refocussing the tourist experience: the flâneur and the choraster', *Leisure Studies*, 15(4): 229–243.

Wearing, S. (2001) *Volunteer Tourism: Experiences that Make a Difference*, Oxford: CABI.

Weaver, A. (2008) 'When tourists become data: consumption surveillance and commerce', *Current Issues in Tourism*, 11(1): 1–23.

Weber, M. (1958) *The City*, New York: Free Press.

Webster, C. and D. J.Timothy (2006) 'Travelling to the "other side": the occupied zone and Greek Cypriot views of crossing the Green Line', *Tourism Geographies*, 8(2): 162–181.

Weinglass, L. (2006) 'Cuba's war against terrorism', *Le Monde Diplomatique*, February, p. 10.

Werbner, P. (2002) 'The place which is diaspora: citizenship, religion and gender in the making of chaordic transnationalism', *Journal of Ethnic and Migration Studies*, 28(1): 119–133.

Wheeler, B. (1993) 'Sustaining the ego', *Journal of Sustainable Tourism*, 1(2): 21–29.

Whitaker, B. E. (2007) 'Exporting the Patriot Act? Democracy and the "war on terror" in the Third World', *Third World Quarterly*, 28(5): 1017–1032.

White, J. H. (2011) 'Hudson river steamboats', *Invention and Technology*, 25(4): 20–39.

Whitelegg, D. (2003) 'Touching down: globalisation, labour and the airline industry', *Antipode*, 3(2): 244–263.

Wilkin, P. (2002) 'Global poverty and orthodox security', *Third World Quarterly*, 23(4): 633–645.

Wilks, J., D. Pendergast and P. Leggat (eds) (2006) *Tourism in Turbulent Times: Towards Safe Experiences for Visitors*, Oxford: Elsevier.

Williams, A. M., R. King and T. Warnes (1997) 'A place in the sun: international retirement migration from Northern to Southern Europe', *European Urban and Regional Studies*, 4(2): 115–134.

Williams, A. M and V. Balaz (2001) 'From collective provision to commodification of tourism?', *Annals of Tourism Research*, 28(1): 27–49.

Wilson, D. and L. Weber (2008) 'Surveillance, risk and preemption on the Australian border', *Surveillance and Society*, 5(2): 124–141.

Wilson, E. and D. E. Little (2008) 'The solo female travel experience: exploring the "geography of women's fear"', *Current Issues in Tourism*, 11(2): 167–186.

Wilson, J. (2005) 'Air marshals knew man was mentally ill before opening fire', *The Guardian*, 9 December. Available at http://www.guardian.co.uk/world/2005/dec/09/usa.jamiewilson (accessed 18 May 2013).

Wilson, K. (2010) 'Manila might lift donation ban', *The National*, 8 August, p. 9.

Winnett, R. and H. Watt (2006) 'Britain, world's first onshore tax haven: billionaires pay out tiny fraction of wealth', *The Sunday Times*, 3 December. Available at http://www.timesonline.co.uk/tol/news/uk/article658376.ece (accessed 16 June 2009).

Witte, R. (1995) 'Racial violence in Western Europe', *New Community*, 21(4): 489–500.

Wolf, E. (1982) *Europe and the People Without History*, Berkeley: University of California Press.

Wolff, J. (1993) 'On the road again: metaphors of travel in cultural criticism', *Cultural Studies*, 7(2): 224–239.

Woo, S. (2011) 'Indonesian women splash out at Islamic spas', *Jakarta Globe*, 15 February. Available at http://www.thejakartaglobe.com/bisindonesia/indonesian-women-splash-out-at-islamic-spas/422760#Scene_1 (accessed 26 April 2013).

Wood, R. E. (1979) 'Tourism and underdevelopment in Southeast Asia', *Journal of Contemporary Asia*, 9: 274–287.

World Travel Guide (2013) 'Iran Travel Advice, Embassies & Tourist Offices'. Available at http://www.worldtravelguide.net/iran/travel-advice (accessed 15 January 2012).

WTO (World Tourism Organization) (1980) *Manila Declaration on World Tourism*, Madrid: WTO. Available at http://www.world-tourism.org (accessed 27 April 2007).

WTO (World Tourism Organization) (1999) *Global Code of Ethics for Tourism*, Madrid: WTO. Available at http://www.unwto.org/ethics/index.php (accessed 13 July 2012).

WTO (World Tourism Organization) (2006) *Tourism Market Trends*, Madrid: WTO.

WTTC (World Travel and Tourism Council) (2003) *Travel and Tourism Security Action Plan*, London: WTTC.

Wright, E. O. (2009) 'Understanding class: towards an integrated analytical approach', *New Left Review*, II, 60: 101–116.

Yale, P. (1997) 'Is this conservation?', *Tourism In Focus*, Spring, 23: 8–9.

Year Out Group (n.d.) 'What employers say'. Available at http://www.yearoutgroup.org/benefits-of-gapping/what-employers-say/ (accessed 21 February 2013).

Yeoh, B. S. A. and K. Willis (2005) 'Singaporeans in China: transnational women elites and the negotiation of gendered identities', *Geoforum*, 36(2): 211–222.

Yeoh, B. S. A., H. Shirlena and K. Willis (2000) 'Global cities, transnational flows and gender dimensions: the view from Singapore', *Tijdschrift Voor Economische en Social Geografie (Journal of Economic and Social Geography)*, 2: 147–158.

Yeoman, I. (2008) *Tomorrow's Tourist: Scenarios and Trends*, Oxford: Butterworth and Heinemann.

Yeoman, I. (2012) *2050 – Tomorrow's Tourism*, Bristol: Channel View Publications.

Yingying, S. (2010) 'ROK police halt suspected people smuggle', *China Daily*, 22 October. Available at http://www.chinadaily.com.cn/china/2010–10/22/content_11442746.htm (accessed 25 October 2010).

Young, G. (1973) *Tourism: Blessing or Blight?* Harmondsworth: Penguin.

Younge, G. (2000) *No Place Like Home: A Black Briton's Journey Through the American South*, London: Picador.

Zagaria, C. (2008) 'Bimbe rom annegate, lo sdegno sul web', *La Reppublica Napoli*, 20 July. Available at http://napoli.repubblica.it/dettaglio/Bimbe-rom-annegate:-Uccise-dallindifferenza/1490675 (accessed 18 September 2012).

Zinn, H. (2003) *A People's History of the United States: 1492–Present*, third edition, London: Pearson Longman.

Žižek, S. (2009) *Violence*, London: Profile Books.

INDEX

Locators shown in *italics* refer to tables and plates.